An Introduction to Poetry

An Introduction to Poetry

FOURTH EDITION

X. J. KENNEDY

Tufts University

LITTLE, BROWN AND COMPANY

Boston • Toronto

Library of Congress Catalog Card No. 77–88044

ISBN 0-316-488690

10   9   8   7   6   5

MU

Published simultaneously in Canada
by Little, Brown & Company (Canada) Limited

Printed in the United States of America

Acknowledgments

The paintings by Pieter Breughel on page 175 (*The Kermess*, collection of Kunsthistoriches Museum, Vienna) and page 312 (*Landscape with Fall of Icarus*, collection of Museum der Schone Kunste, Brussels) are reproduced courtesy of Marburg Art Reference Bureau.

James Agee. "Sunday: Outskirts of Knoxville, Tennessee" from *The Collected Poems of James Agee*. Copyright © 1962, 1968 by the James Agee Trust. Reprinted by permission of Houghton Mifflin Company.
Edward Hathaway Allen. "The Best Line Yet," © 1972 by Edward H. Allen. First appeared in *Counter/Measures*. Reprinted by permission of the poet.
A. R. Ammons. "Auto Mobile" and "Spring Coming" from *Collected Poems, 1951-1971* by A. R. Ammons. Copyright © 1972 by A. R. Ammons. Reprinted by permission of W. W. Norton & Company, Inc.
Maya Angelou. "Harlem Hopscotch" from *Just Give Me a Cool Drink of Water 'Fore I Die* by Maya Angelou. Copyright © 1971 by Maya Angelou. Reprinted by permission of Random House, Inc.
John Ashbery. "City Afternoon" from *Self-Portrait in a Convex Mirror* by John Ashbery. Copyright © 1974 by John Ashbery. Reprinted by permission of The Viking Press.
W. H. Auden. "As I Walked Out One Evening," "Musée des Beaux Arts," and "The Unknown Citizen" from *Collected Poems* by W. H. Auden. Copyright 1940, renewed 1968 by W. H. Auden. Reprinted by permission of Random House, Inc., and Faber and Faber Ltd. "James Watt" from *Academic Graffiti* by W. H. Auden. Copyright © 1960 by W. H. Auden. Reprinted by permission of Random House, Inc.
David B. Axelrod. "Once in a While a Protest Poem" from *A Dream of Feet* by David B. Axelrod. Copyright © 1976 by David B. Axelrod. Reprinted by permission of the poet and Cross-Cultural Communications.
Max Beerbohm. "On the imprint of the first English edition of *The Works of Max Beerbohm*." Reprinted by permission of Sir Geoffrey Keynes.
Hilaire Belloc. "The Hippopotamus" from *Cautionary Verses* by Hilaire Belloc. Published in 1940 by Gerald Duckworth & Co. Ltd., 1941 by Alfred A. Knopf, Inc. Reprinted by permission of the publishers.
Edmund Clerihew Bentley. "Sir Christopher Wren" from *Clerihews Complete* by E. C. Bentley. Reprinted by permission of Nicholas Bentley.
John Berryman. "Life, friends, is boring . . ." from *77 Dream Songs* by John Berryman. Copyright © 1959, 1962, 1963, 1964 by John Berryman. Reprinted by permission of Farrar, Straus & Giroux, Inc.
John Betjeman. "In Westminster Abbey" from *Collected Poems* by John Betjeman. (Houghton Mifflin Company, 1959). Reprinted by permission of John Murray Publishers Ltd.
Elizabeth Bishop. "The Fish," "Late Air," "The Filling Station," and lines from "Little Exercise" from *The Complete Poems* by Elizabeth Bishop. Copyright 1940, 1946, 1949, © 1955 by Elizabeth Bishop, renewed © 1973 by Elizabeth Bishop. "Five Flights Up" from *Geography III* by Elizabeth Bishop. Copyright © 1974 by Elizabeth Bishop. "The Filling Station" and "Five Flights Up" appeared originally in *The New Yorker*. Reprinted by permission of Farrar, Straus & Giroux, Inc.
Robert Bly. "Driving to Town Late to Mail a Letter" from *Silence in the Snowy Field* by Robert Bly (Wesleyan University Press, 1962) and "Inward Conversation." Reprinted by permission of the poet.
Richard Brautigan. "Haiku Ambulance" excerpted from *The Pill Versus the Springhill Mine Disaster* by Richard Brautigan. Copyright © 1968 by Richard Brautigan. Reprinted by permission of Delacorte Press/Seymour Lawrence.
Gwendolyn Brooks. "The Bean Eaters" and "We Real Cool" from *The World of Gwendolyn Brooks*. Copyright © 1959 by Gwendolyn Brooks. Reprinted by permission of Harper & Row, Publishers.
Taniguchi Buson. "The Sudden Chilliness" from *An Introduction to Haiku* by Harold G. Henderson. Copyright © 1958 by Harold G. Henderson. Reprinted by permission of Doubleday & Company, Inc.
James Camp. "At the First Avenue Redemption Center" from *Carnal Refreshment*. Copyright © 1975. Reprinted by permission of the poet.
Roy Campbell. "On Some South African Novelists" from *Adamastor* by Roy Campbell. Reprinted by permission of Curtis Brown Ltd. on behalf of the Estate of Roy Campbell.
Bliss Carman. Lines from "A Vagabond Song" from *Bliss Carman's Poems*. Reprinted by permission of Dodd, Mead & Company and McClelland & Stewart Ltd.
Fred Chappell. "Skin Flick" from *The World Between the Eyes* by Fred Chappell. Copyright © 1971. Reprinted by permission of Louisiana State University Press.
Geoffrey Chaucer. Lines from Part I. "Merciles Beaute" from *The Works of Geoffrey Chaucer*. Second Edition, edited by F. N. Robinson (1957). Reprinted by permission of Houghton Mifflin Company.
G. K. Chesterton. "The Donkey" from *The Wild Knight and Other Poems* by G. K. Chesterton. Reprinted by permission of J. M. Dent & Sons Ltd.

(continued on page 435)

PREFACE

What is poetry? Pressed for an answer, Robert Frost made a classic reply: "Poetry is the kind of thing poets write." In all likelihood, Frost was not trying merely to evade the question but to chide his questioner into thinking for himself. A trouble with definitions is that they may stop thought. If Frost had said, "Poetry is a rhythmical composition of words expressing an attitude, designed to surprise and delight, and to arouse an emotional response," the questioner might have settled back in his chair, content to have learned the truth about poetry. He would have learned nothing, or not so much as he might learn by continuing to wonder.

The nature of poetry eludes simple definitions. (In this respect it is rather like jazz. Asked after one of his concerts, "What is jazz?" Louis Armstrong replied, "Man, if you gotta ask, you'll never know.") Definitions will be of little help at first, if we are to know poetry and respond to it. We have to go to it willing to see and hear. For this reason, you are asked in reading this book not to be in any hurry to decide what poetry is, but instead to study poems and to let them grow in your mind. At the end of the book, the problem of definition will be taken up again (for those who may wish to pursue it).

Confronted with *An Introduction to Poetry,* you may be wondering "Who needs it?" and you may well be right. You hardly can have avoided meeting poetry before; and perhaps you already have a friendship, or at least a fair acquaintance, with some of the great English-speaking poets of all time. What this book provides is an introduction to the *study* of poetry. It tries to help you look at a poem closely, to offer you a wider and more accurate vocabulary with which to express what poems say to you. It will suggest ways to judge for yourself the poems you read. It may set forth some poems new to you.

A frequent objection to a book such as this is that poetry ought not to be studied at all. In this view, a poem is either a series of gorgeous noises to be funneled through one ear and out the other without being allowed to trouble the mind or an experience so holy that to analyze it in a classroom is as cruel and mechanical as dissecting a hummingbird. To the first view, it might be countered that a good poem has something to say that perhaps is worth listening to. To the second view, it might be argued that poems are much less perishable than hummingbirds, and luckily, we can study them in flight. The risk of a poem's dying from observation is not nearly so great as the risk of not really seeing it at all. It is doubtful that any excellent poem has ever vanished from human memory because people have read it too closely. More likely, poems that vanish are poems that no one reads closely, for no one cares.

Good poetry is something to care about. In fact, an ancient persuasion of mankind is that the hearing of a poem, as well as the making of a poem, can be a religious act. Poetry, in speech and song, was part of classic Greek drama, which for playwright, actor, and spectator alike was a holy-day ceremony. The Greeks' belief that a poet writes a poem only by supernatural assistance is clear from the invocations to the Muse that begin the *Iliad* and the *Odyssey* and from the opinion of Socrates (in Plato's *Ion*) that a poet has no powers of invention until divinely inspired. Among the ancient Celts, poets were regarded as magicians and priests, and whoever insulted one of them might expect to receive a curse in rime potent enough to afflict him with boils and to curdle the milk of his cows. Such identifications between the poet and the magician are less common these days, although we know that poetry is involved in the primitive white-magic of children, who bring themselves good luck in a game with the charm "Roll, roll, Tootsie-roll!/ Roll the marble in the hole!" and who warn against a hex while jumping a sidewalk: "Step on a crack, / Break your mother's back." But in this age when men pride themselves that a computer may solve the riddle of all creation as soon as it is programmed, magic seems to some people of small importance and so does poetry. It is dangerous, however, to dismiss what we do not logically understand. To read a poem at all, we have to be willing to offer it responses *besides* a logical understanding. Whether we attribute the effect of a poem to a divine spirit or to the reactions of our glands and cortexes, we have to take the reading of poetry seriously (not solemnly), if only because — as some of the poems in this book may demonstrate — few other efforts can repay us so generously, both in wisdom and in joy.

If, as I hope you will do, you sometimes browse in the book for fun, you may be annoyed to see so many questions following the poems. Should you feel this way, try reading with a slip of paper to cover up the questions. You will then — if the Muse should inspire you — have paper in hand to write a poem.

A Note on Texts and Dates

In this edition, poems are dated. To the right of each poem title is the date of its first known publication in book form. A date in parenthesis is a date of composition — given when it is known that a poem was composed much earlier than it was first printed (as in the case of the poems of Emily Dickinson). No attempt has been made to date traditional English and Scottish popular ballads such as "Bonny Barbara Allan," because such an attempt would be merely wild guesswork. Spelling has been modernized (*rose-lipped* for *ros-lip'd*) and made American, unless the sound of a word would be altered. But I have left the *y* in Blake's strange "Tyger" and let Walt Whitman keep his *bloom'd* on the conviction that *bloomed* would no more resemble Whitman than a portrait of him in a starched collar. Untitled poems are identified by their first lines, except for those given titles by custom ("The Twa Corbies," "Western Wind").

Further Changes

A lengthy discussion of the changes in organization and content can be found in the preface to the *Instructor's Manual to Accompany An Introduction to Poetry*, 4th Edition.

Acknowledgments

Besides all the debts this book has contracted in the past, it now owes much to many who made fresh contributions. Kevin Hayter suggested teachable poems; so did these anthologists: Richard Abcarian, John Ciardi and Miller Williams, William Cole, Myra Cohn Livingston, David McCord, John T. Shawcross and Frederick R. Lapides, and Henry Taylor. Michael Fixler gave of his wisdom about poetry and how to teach it. Other users of the last edition who made specific suggestions and corrections, either by mail or in person, include David Anderson, Dennis Berthiaume, Michael D. Bliss, Hale Chatfield, William L. Edgerton, Gerard L. Evans, Charles Fanning, Albert Furtwangler, Madeleine Hamermesh, Neva N. Harden, Iris Jennings, Lucille Johnsen, C. W. Kaltenbach, Stanley J. Kozikowski, Ralph Latham, Elsie Leach, Patrick Lesley, David H. Lindstrom, J. M. Linebarger, Gary Litt, James Lynch, James Martin, Sister Miriam J. Murphy, M. A. Nelson, James W. Newcomb, Jim Perkins, Thom Pigaga, G. E. Pittenger, M. Evelyn Poe, Joseph Raboy (who wanted all the poems dated), Robert Reiter, Martin J. Rosenblum, Mary Savage, Mariette T. Sawchuk, William D. Shanebeck, John L. Simons, Keith Slocum, Robert L. Vales, Steve A. Ward, Michelle Werner (while a student at Kenyon College), and Clemewell Young. On the publisher's staff, Dale Anderson, Jan Beatty, Katie Carlone, S. Woodworth Chittick, Charles H. Christensen, Kathleen Field, Elizabeth Philipps, and Andrea Pozgay were just some of those who made the book a mutual cause, not just a mutual product. Sylvan Barnet has continued to be like a father to me and my manuscript. I am still grateful to students at Tufts, Wellesley, Michigan, North Carolina (Greensboro), California (Irvine), and Leeds for helping me to see through some of the poems. Most of all I thank Dorothy M. Kennedy.

TOPICAL CONTENTS

1   **Entrances**   1

2   **Listening to a Voice**   9

    TONE   9
    THE PERSON IN THE POEM   13
    IRONY   18
    FOR REVIEW AND FURTHER STUDY   24

3   **Words**   30

    LITERAL MEANING: WHAT A POEM SAYS FIRST   30
    THE VALUE OF A DICTIONARY   37
    WORD CHOICE AND WORD ORDER   43

4   **Imagery**   54

    MORE ABOUT HAIKU   60
    FOR REVIEW AND FURTHER STUDY   61

5   **Saying and Suggesting**   66

6   **Figures of Speech**   77

    WHY SPEAK FIGURATIVELY?   77
    METAPHOR AND SIMILE   80
    OTHER FIGURES   85
    FOR REVIEW AND FURTHER STUDY   92

7 Song   99

SINGING AND SAYING   99
BALLADS   105
FOR REVIEW AND FURTHER STUDY   114

8 Sound   119

SOUND AS MEANING   119
ALLITERATION AND ASSONANCE   123
RIME   126
READING AND HEARING POEMS ALOUD   132

9 Rhythm   136

STRESSES AND PAUSES   136
METER   145

10 Closed Form, Open Form   156

CLOSED FORM: BLANK VERSE, STANZA, SONNET   157
OPEN FORM   169
FOR REVIEW AND FURTHER STUDY   179

11 Poems for the Eye   187

12 Symbol   197

13 Myth   210

14 Telling Good from Bad   230

15 Knowing Excellence   250

16 Alternatives   263

THE POET'S REVISIONS   263
TRANSLATIONS   268
PARODY   273

17 Writing about Poems 279

EXPLICATION 280
ANALYSIS 285
COMPARISON AND CONTRAST 287
HOW TO QUOTE A POEM 291
BEFORE YOU BEGIN 292
TOPICS FOR WRITING 294

18 What Is Poetry? 297

ANTHOLOGY 301

Appendix: Writing about Literature 421

SOME APPROACHES TO LITERATURE 423
FINDING A TOPIC 425
ORGANIZING YOUR THINKING 427
WRITING A DRAFT 429
REVISING 431
THE FORM OF YOUR FINISHED PAPER 432

INDEX OF FIRST LINES 439
INDEX OF AUTHORS AND TITLES 445
INDEX OF TERMS *inside back cover*

CONTENTS

1   **Entrances**   1

A. E. HOUSMAN, *Loveliest of trees, the cherry now*   3
ROBERT FRANCIS, *Catch*   6
EMILY DICKINSON, *I taste a liquor never brewed*   6
DONALD FINKEL, *Hands*   7
ROBINSON JEFFERS, *To the Stone-Cutters*   8
WILLIAM SHAKESPEARE, *Not marble nor the gilded monuments*   8

2   **Listening to a Voice**   9

TONE   9

THEODORE ROETHKE, *My Papa's Waltz*   9
COUNTEE CULLEN, *For a Lady I Know*   10
ANNE BRADSTREET, *The Author to Her Book*   11
WALT WHITMAN, *To a Locomotive in Winter*   12
EMILY DICKINSON, *I like to see it lap the Miles*   13

THE PERSON IN THE POEM   13

TRUMBULL STICKNEY, *Sir, say no more*   14
RANDALL JARRELL, *A Sick Child*   15
ALDEN NOWLAN, *The Loneliness of the Long Distance Runner*   16
WILLIAM WORDSWORTH, *I Wandered Lonely as a Cloud*   16
WILLIAM CARLOS WILLIAMS, *The Red Wheelbarrow*   18

IRONY   18

ROBERT CREELEY, *Oh No*   19
W. H. AUDEN, *The Unknown Citizen*   20
JOHN BETJEMAN, *In Westminster Abbey*   21
SARAH N. CLEGHORN, *The Golf Links*   23
THOMAS HARDY, *The Workbox*   23

FOR REVIEW AND FURTHER STUDY   24

Ted Hughes, *Secretary*   24
John Berryman, *Life, friends, is boring. We must not say so*   25
Richard Lovelace, *To Lucasta*   26
Wilfred Owen, *Dulce et Decorum Est*   26
James Stephens, *A Glass of Beer*   27
Jonathan Swift, *On Stella's Birthday*   28
William Blake, *The Chimney Sweeper*   28

3   Words   30

LITERAL MEANING: WHAT A POEM SAYS FIRST   30

William Carlos Williams, *This Is Just to Say*   31
Knute Skinner, *The Cold Irish Earth*   33
Henry Taylor, *Riding a One-Eyed Horse*   33
Robert Graves, *Down, Wanton, Down!*   34
Peter Davison, *The Last Word*   35
David B. Axelrod, *Once in a While a Protest Poem*   35
Miller Williams, *On the Symbolic Consideration of Hands and the Significance of Death*   36
John Donne, *Batter my heart, three-personed God, for You*   36

THE VALUE OF A DICTIONARY   37

Richard Wilbur, *In the Elegy Season*   38
Cid Corman, *The Tortoise*   40
J. V. Cunningham, *Friend, on this scaffold Thomas More lies dead*   40
Herman Melville, *The Portent*   40
John Clare, *Mouse's Nest*   41
Lewis Carroll, *Jabberwocky*   41
Wallace Stevens, *Metamorphosis*   42
J. V. Cunningham, *Motto for a Sun Dial*   43

WORD CHOICE AND WORD ORDER   43

Josephine Miles, *Reason*   46
Hugh MacDiarmid, *Wheesht, Wheesht*   47
Reed Whittemore, *The Fall of the House of Usher*   49
E. E. Cummings, *anyone lived in a pretty how town*   49
Richard Eberhart, *The Fury of Aerial Bombardment*   50
Anonymous, *As I was laying on the green*   51
A. R. Ammons, *Spring Coming*   51
William Wordsworth, *My heart leaps up when I behold*   52
William Wordsworth, *Mutability*   52
Anonymous, *Scottsboro*   53

4 Imagery 54

Ezra Pound, *In a Station of the Metro* 54
Taniguchi Buson, *The piercing chill I feel* 54
Wallace Stevens, *Study of Two Pears* 56
Theodore Roethke, *Root Cellar* 57
Elizabeth Bishop, *The Fish* 58

MORE ABOUT HAIKU 60

Richard Brautigan, *Haiku Ambulance* 61
Paul Goodman, Raymond Roseliep, Gary Snyder, A selection of haiku 61

FOR REVIEW AND FURTHER STUDY 61

Jean Toomer, *Reapers* 61
Gerard Manley Hopkins, *Pied Beauty* 62
John Keats, *Bright star! would I were steadfast as thou art* 63
Carl Sandburg, *Fog* 63
Walt Whitman, *The Runner* 64
T. E. Hulme, *Image* 64
William Carlos Williams, *The Great Figure* 64
Robert Bly, *Driving to Town Late to Mail a Letter* 64
H. D., *Heat* 65

5 Saying and Suggesting 66

John Masefield, *Cargoes* 67
William Blake, *London* 68
Wallace Stevens, *Disillusionment of Ten O'Clock* 70
Guy Owen, *The White Stallion* 71
Samuel Johnson, *A Short Song of Congratulation* 71
Denise Levertov, *Sunday Afternoon* 72
James Camp, *At the First Avenue Redemption Center* 73
Richard Snyder, *A Mongoloid Child Handling Shells on the Beach* 73
Elizabeth Bishop, *Late Air* 74
W. S. Merwin, *Dead Hand* 75
Geoffrey Hill, *Merlin* 75
Wallace Stevens, *The Emperor of Ice-Cream* 76
Robert Frost, *Fire and Ice* 76

6 Figures of Speech 77

WHY SPEAK FIGURATIVELY? 77

Alfred, Lord Tennyson, *The Eagle* 78
William Shakespeare, *Shall I compare thee to a summer's day?* 78
Howard Moss, *Shall I compare thee to a summer's day?* 79

METAPHOR AND SIMILE   80

RICHARD WILBUR, *A Simile for Her Smile*   81
ALFRED, LORD TENNYSON, *Flower in the Crannied Wall*   81
WILLIAM BLAKE, *To see a world in a grain of sand*   82
SYLVIA PLATH, *Metaphors*   82
EMILY DICKINSON, *It dropped so low—in my Regard*   83
ANONYMOUS, *There was a man of double deed*   83
RUTH WHITMAN, *Castoff Skin*   84
DENISE LEVERTOV, *Leaving Forever*   84

OTHER FIGURES   85

JAMES STEPHENS, *The Wind*   85
CHIDIOCK TICHBORNE, *Elegy, Written with His Own Hand*   88
GEORGE HERBERT, *The Pulley*   89
EDMUND WALLER, *On a Girdle*   90
JOHN DONNE, *A Hymn to God the Father*   90
THEODORE ROETHKE, *I Knew a Woman*   91

FOR REVIEW AND FURTHER STUDY   92

ROBERT FROST, *Tree at My Window*   92
JAMES C. KILGORE, *The White Man Pressed the Locks*   93
ELIZABETH JENNINGS, *Delay*   93
RICHARD WILBUR, *Sleepless at Crown Point*   94
ANONYMOUS, *The fortunes of war, I tell you plain*   94
A. E. HOUSMAN, *From the wash the laundress sends*   94
ROBERT FROST, *The Secret Sits*   94
CHARLES SIMIC, *Fork*   95
ISHMAEL REED, *.05*   95
A. R. AMMONS, *Auto Mobile*   95
W. S. MERWIN, *Song of Man Chipping an Arrowhead*   96
ROBERT BURNS, *Oh, my love is like a red, red rose*   96
OGDEN NASH, *Very Like a Whale*   96

7   **Song**   99

SINGING AND SAYING   99

BEN JONSON, *To Celia*   100
ANONYMOUS, *The Cruel Mother*   101
EDWIN ARLINGTON ROBINSON, *Richard Cory*   104
PAUL SIMON, *Richard Cory*   104

BALLADS   105

ANONYMOUS, *Bonny Barbara Allan*   106
ANONYMOUS, *Still Growing*   109

Woody Guthrie, *Plane Wreck at Los Gatos (Deportee)*   111
Anonymous, *Frankie and Johnny*   112

FOR REVIEW AND FURTHER STUDY   114

Anonymous, *Fa, mi, fa, re, la, mi*   115
Anonymous, *The silver swan, who living had no note*   115
Ern Alpaugh and Dewey G. Pell, *Swinging Chick*   115
John Lennon and Paul McCartney, *Eleanor Rigby*   116
Joni Mitchell, *Black Crow*   117
Anonymous, *Good Mornin', Blues*   118

8   Sound   119

SOUND AS MEANING   119

William Butler Yeats, *Who Goes with Fergus?*   121
John Updike, *Winter Ocean*   122
Frances Cornford, *The Watch*   122
William Wordsworth, *A Slumber Did My Spirit Seal*   123
Emanuel diPasquale, *Rain*   123

ALLITERATION AND ASSONANCE   123

A. E. Housman, *Eight O'Clock*   125
Alexander Pope, *Epitaph, Intended for Sir Isaac Newton in Westminster Abbey*   125
J. C. Squire, *It did not last*   125
Alfred, Lord Tennyson, *The splendor falls on castle walls*   126

RIME   126

Anonymous, *Julius Caesar*   127
William Blake, *The Angel that presided o'er my birth*   128
John Frederick Nims, *Perfect Rhyme*   128
Hilaire Belloc, *The Hippopotamus*   130
William Butler Yeats, *Leda and the Swan*   130
Allen Ginsberg, *Postcard to D----*   131
Gerard Manley Hopkins, *God's Grandeur*   131

READING AND HEARING POEMS ALOUD   132

James Wright, *Saying Dante Aloud*   134
A. E. Housman, *With rue my heart is laden*   134
T. S. Eliot, *Virginia*   134

9   Rhythm   136

STRESSES AND PAUSES   136

Gwendolyn Brooks, *We Real Cool*   141

ROBERT FROST, *Never Again Would Birds' Song Be the Same*   141
BEN JONSON, *Slow, slow, fresh fount, keep time with my salt tears*   142
ROBERT LOWELL, *At the Altar*   142
ALEXANDER POPE, *Atticus*   143
SIR THOMAS WYATT, *With serving still*   144
DOROTHY PARKER, *Résumé*   145

METER   145

MAX BEERBOHM, *On the imprint of the first English edition of "The Works
    of Max Beerbohm"*   146
THOMAS CAMPION, *Rose-cheeked Laura, come*   150
WALTER SAVAGE LANDOR, *On Seeing a Hair of Lucretia Borgia*   151
GEORGE GORDON, LORD BYRON, *The Destruction of Sennacherib*   152
EDNA ST. VINCENT MILLAY, *Counting-out Rhyme*   153
A. E. HOUSMAN, *When I was one-and-twenty*   153
WILLIAM CARLOS WILLIAMS, *The Descent of Winter* (Section 10/30)   154
WALT WHITMAN, *Beat! Beat! Drums!*   154

10   Closed Form, Open Form   156

CLOSED FORM: BLANK VERSE, STANZA, SONNET   157

JOHN KEATS, *This living hand, now warm and capable*   158
JOHN DONNE, *Song ("Go and catch a falling star")*   160
ROY CAMPBELL, *On Some South African Novelists*   162
RONALD GROSS, *Yield*   162
MICHAEL DRAYTON, *Since there's no help, come let us kiss and part*   164
ELIZABETH BARRETT BROWNING, *Grief*   165
ALEXANDER POPE, MARTIAL, SIR JOHN HARRINGTON, WILLIAM BLAKE,
    E. E. CUMMINGS, J. V. CUNNINGHAM, KEITH WALDROP, A selection of
    epigrams   166
DYLAN THOMAS, *Do not go gentle into that good night*   169

OPEN FORM   169

DENISE LEVERTOV, *Six Variations* (part iii)   170
E. E. CUMMINGS, *Buffalo Bill's*   174
EMILY DICKINSON, *Victory comes late*   174
WILLIAM CARLOS WILLIAMS, *The Dance*   175
ROBERT HERRICK, *Upon a Child That Died*   176
SAINT GERAUD, *Poem ("The only response")*   176
STEPHEN CRANE, *The Heart*   176
WALT WHITMAN, *Cavalry Crossing a Ford*   177
GARY GILDNER, *First Practice*   177

FOR REVIEW AND FURTHER STUDY   179

LEIGH HUNT, *Rondeau*   179

FRANK SIDGWICK, *The Aeronaut to His Lady*   179

STEVIE SMITH, *I Remember*   180

THOMAS HARDY, *At a Hasty Wedding*   181

GEOFFREY CHAUCER, *Your yen two wol slee me sodenly*   181

WALLACE STEVENS, *Thirteen Ways of Looking at a Blackbird*   182

E. E. CUMMINGS, *in Just-*   184

MYRA COHN LIVINGSTON, *Driving*   185

DONALD FINKEL, *Gesture*   185

CHARLES OLSON, *La Chute*   186

11   Poems for the Eye   187

GEORGE HERBERT, *Easter Wings*   187

JOHN HOLLANDER, *Skeleton Key*   189

E. E. CUMMINGS, *r-p-o-p-h-e-s-s-a-g-r*   190

MAY SWENSON, *Stone Gullets*   191

WANG WEI, *Bird-Singing Stream*   192

REINHARD DÖHL, *a concrete poem*   193

IAN HAMILTON FINLAY, *The Horizon of Holland*   194

EDWIN MORGAN, *Siesta of a Hungarian Snake*   195

DORTHI CHARLES, *Concrete Cat*   196

12   Symbol   197

T. S. ELIOT, *The Boston Evening Transcript*   198

EMILY DICKINSON, *The Lightning is a yellow Fork*   199

EMILY DICKINSON, *I heard a Fly buzz—when I died*   201

THOMAS HARDY, *Neutral Tones*   202

MATTHEW 13:24–30, *The Parable of the Good Seed*   203

GEORGE HERBERT, *Redemption*   203

SIR PHILIP SIDNEY, *You that with allegory's curious frame*   204

MINA LOY, *Omen of Victory*   205

HART CRANE, *Black Tambourine*   205

WILLIAM CARLOS WILLIAMS, *Poem ("As the cat")*   206

THEODORE ROETHKE, *Night Crow*   206

JOHN DONNE, *A Burnt Ship*   207

WALLACE STEVENS, *Anecdote of the Jar*   207

T. S. ELIOT, *Rhapsody on a Windy Night*   207

13   Myth   210

D. H. LAWRENCE, *Bavarian Gentians*   212

THOMAS HARDY, *The Oxen*   213

WILLIAM WORDSWORTH, *The World Is Too Much with Us*   214

WILLIAM BUTLER YEATS, *The Second Coming*   215

John Heath-Stubbs, *A Charm Against the Toothache*   216
David Wagoner, *Muse*   218
Edward Allen, *The Best Line Yet*   219
Anonymous, *Thomas the Rimer*   219
John Keats, *La Belle Dame sans Merci*   222
John Milton, *Lycidas*   223

14   Telling Good from Bad   230

Anonymous, *O Moon, when I gaze on thy beautiful face*   233
Grace Treasone, *Life*   233
William Ernest Henley, *Madam Life's a piece in bloom*   233
Stephen Tropp, *My Wife Is My Shirt*   234
M. Krishnamurti, *The Spirit's Odyssey*   234
Robert Burns, *John Anderson my jo, John*   238
Exercise
    The Old Arm-Chair   238
    Piano   239
Rod McKuen, *Thoughts on Capital Punishment*   239
William Stafford, *Traveling Through the Dark*   240
Ralph Waldo Emerson, *Days*   241
Philip Larkin, *Days*   241
O. Emil Rauter, *Our Minted Days*   242
Abraham Lincoln, *My Childhood-Home I See Again*   243
Fred Emerson Brooks, *Pat's Opinion of Flags*   246
Anthony Hecht, *Japan*   247

15   Knowing Excellence   250

William Butler Yeats, *Sailing to Byzantium*   250
Arthur Guiterman, *On the Vanity of Earthly Greatness*   253
Percy Bysshe Shelley, *Ozymandias*   253
John Lyly, *Daphne*   254
William Shakespeare, *My mistress' eyes are nothing like the sun*   255
Thomas Campion, *There is a garden in her face*   255
Walt Whitman, *O Captain! My Captain!*   256
Matthew Arnold, *Below the surface-stream, shallow and light*   258
Thomas Gray, *Elegy Written in a Country Churchyard*   258

16   Alternatives   263

THE POET'S REVISIONS   263

William Butler Yeats, *The Old Pensioner*   264
William Butler Yeats, *The Lamentation of the Old Pensioner*   264

WALT WHITMAN, *A Noiseless Patient Spider*   266
WALT WHITMAN, *The Soul, reaching, throwing out for love*   267
DONALD HALL, *My Son, My Executioner*   267

TRANSLATIONS   268

WILLIAM CORY, *Heraclitus*   269
DUDLEY FITTS, *Elegy on Herakleitos*   269
FEDERICO GARCÍA LORCA, *La guitarra (Guitar)*   269
HORACE, *Odes I (38)*   270
CHARLES BAUDELAIRE, *Recueillement (Meditation)*   271

PARODY   273

T. E. BROWN, *My Garden*   273
J. A. LINDON, *My Garden*   273
HUGH KINGSMILL, *What, still alive at twenty-two*   274
KENNETH KOCH, *Mending Sump*   274
JOHN FREDERICK NIMS, *Old Bethinkings of a Day of "Showers Likely" at Beansey Ridge*   275
E. B. WHITE, *A Classic Waits for Me*   276

17 Writing about Poems   279

EXPLICATION   280
ROBERT FROST, *Design*   281
ANALYSIS   285
COMPARISON AND CONTRAST   287
ABBIE HUSTON EVANS, *Wing-Spread*   288
HOW TO QUOTE A POEM   291
BEFORE YOU BEGIN   292
TOPICS FOR WRITING   294

18 What Is Poetry?   297

ARCHIBALD MACLEISH, *Ars Poetica*   297

ANTHOLOGY   301

ANONYMOUS, *Edward*   303
ANONYMOUS, *Sir Patrick Spence*   304
ANONYMOUS, *The Three Ravens*   305
ANONYMOUS, *The Twa Corbies*   306
ANONYMOUS, *Western Wind*   307
JAMES AGEE, *Sunday: Outskirts of Knoxville, Tennessee*   307
MAYA ANGELOU, *Harlem Hopscotch*   308
MATTHEW ARNOLD, *Dover Beach*   308

John Ashbery, *City Afternoon*   309

W. H. Auden, *As I Walked Out One Evening*   310

W. H. Auden, *Musée des Beaux Arts*   311

Elizabeth Bishop, *Filling Station*   312

Elizabeth Bishop, *Five Flights Up*   313

William Blake, *Long John Brown and Little Mary Bell*   314

William Blake, *The Sick Rose*   315

William Blake, *The Tyger*   315

Gwendolyn Brooks, *The Bean Eaters*   316

Robert Browning, *My Last Duchess*   316

Robert Browning, *Soliloquy of the Spanish Cloister*   317

Fred Chappell, *Skin Flick*   319

G. K. Chesterton, *The Donkey*   320

Samuel Taylor Coleridge, *Kubla Khan*   320

Robert Creeley, *Naughty Boy*   322

Countee Cullen, *Saturday's Child*   322

E. E. Cummings, *All in green went my love riding*   323

Walter de la Mare, *The Listeners*   324

James Dickey, *Cherrylog Road*   325

Emily Dickinson, *Because I could not stop for Death*   327

Emily Dickinson, *I started Early–Took my Dog*   328

Emily Dickinson, *The Soul selects her own Society*   329

John Donne, *The Bait*   329

John Donne, *The Flea*   330

John Donne, *A Valediction: Forbidding Mourning*   331

John Dryden, *To the Memory of Mr. Oldham*   332

Alan Dugan, *Love Song: I and Thou*   332

Bob Dylan, *Subterranean Homesick Blues*   333

T. S. Eliot, *Journey of the Magi*   335

T. S. Eliot, *The Love Song of J. Alfred Prufrock*   336

Robert Frost, *Mending Wall*   340

Robert Frost, *Stopping by Woods on a Snowy Evening*   341

Robert Frost, *The Witch of Coös*   341

Donald Hall, *The Town of Hill*   345

Thomas Hardy, *Channel Firing*   345

Thomas Hardy, *The Convergence of the Twain*   347

Robert Hayden, *A Road in Kentucky*   348

Seamus Heaney, *Digging*   348

Anthony Hecht, *The Vow*   349

George Herbert, *Love*   350

Robert Herrick, *Delight in Disorder*   351

Robert Herrick, *To the Virgins, to Make Much of Time*   351

Gerard Manley Hopkins, *The Windhover*   352

A. E. Housman, *Terence, this is stupid stuff*   353

A. E. Housman, *To an Athlete Dying Young*   354

LANGSTON HUGHES, *Dream Deferred*   355

TED HUGHES, Three poems from *Crow*   356

DAVID IGNATOW, *Get the Gasworks*   357

RANDALL JARRELL, *The Death of the Ball Turret Gunner*   358

RANDALL JARRELL, *The Woman at the Washington Zoo*   358

JOHN KEATS, *Ode on a Grecian Urn*   359

JOHN KEATS, *On First Looking into Chapman's Homer*   361

JOHN KEATS, *To Autumn*   361

MAXINE KUMIN, *Woodchucks*   362

PHILIP LARKIN, *Vers de Société*   363

PHILIP LARKIN, *Wedding-Wind*   364

D. H. LAWRENCE, *A Youth Mowing*   365

IRVING LAYTON, *The Bull Calf*   365

DENISE LEVERTOV, *Ways of Conquest*   366

PHILIP LEVINE, *To a Child Trapped in a Barber Shop*   367

VACHEL LINDSAY, *Factory Windows Are Always Broken*   367

ROBERT LOWELL, *Skunk Hour*   368

ARCHIBALD MACLEISH, *The End of the World*   369

CHRISTOPHER MARLOWE, *The Passionate Shepherd to His Love*   370

ANDREW MARVELL, *To His Coy Mistress*   370

JAMES MERRILL, *Laboratory Poem*   372

W. S. MERWIN, *For the Anniversary of My Death*   372

JOHN MILTON, *When I consider how my light is spent*   373

MARIANNE MOORE, *The Mind is an Enchanting Thing*   373

SYLVIA PLATH, *Daddy*   374

SYLVIA PLATH, *Morning Song*   376

SYLVIA PLATH, *Poppies in October*   377

ALEXANDER POPE, *An Essay on Man (Epistle II, part I)*   378

EZRA POUND, *The River-Merchant's Wife: a letter*   379

EZRA POUND, *The Seafarer*   380

DUDLEY RANDALL, *Ballad of Birmingham*   382

JOHN CROWE RANSOM, *Janet Waking*   383

HENRY REED, *Naming of Parts*   384

ADRIENNE RICH, *Diving into the Wreck*   385

EDWIN ARLINGTON ROBINSON, *Mr. Flood's Party*   387

THEODORE ROETHKE, *Frau Bauman, Frau Schmidt, and Frau Schwartze*   388

THEODORE ROETHKE, *The Waking*   389

ANNE SEXTON, *The Fury of Overshoes*   390

ANNE SEXTON, *The Kiss*   391

WILLIAM SHAKESPEARE, *That time of year thou mayst in me behold*   392

WILLIAM SHAKESPEARE, *When, in disgrace with Fortune and men's eyes*   392

WILLIAM SHAKESPEARE, *When daisies pied and violets blue*   392

WILLIAM SHAKESPEARE, *When icicles hang by the wall*   393

KARL SHAPIRO, *The Dirty Word*   394

PERCY BYSSHE SHELLEY, *Ode to the West Wind*   394

CHRISTOPHER SMART, *For I will consider my Cat Jeoffry*   396

WILLIAM JAY SMITH, *American Primitive*   398

W. D. SNODGRASS, *The Operation*   399

GARY SNYDER, *Milton by Firelight*   400

WILLIAM STAFFORD, *At the Klamath Berry Festival*   401

WILLIAM STAFFORD, *Written on the Stub of the First Paycheck*   401

WALLACE STEVENS, *Peter Quince at the Clavier*   402

MARK STRAND, *Eating Poetry*   404

JAMES TATE, *Flight*   404

ALFRED, LORD TENNYSON, *Dark house, by which once more I stand*   405

ALFRED, LORD TENNYSON, *Ulysses*   405

DYLAN THOMAS, *Fern Hill*   407

DYLAN THOMAS, *Twenty-four years*   408

ROSMARIE WALDROP, *Confession to Settle a Curse*   409

WALT WHITMAN, *I Saw in Louisiana a Live-Oak Growing*   410

WALT WHITMAN, *When I Heard the Learn'd Astronomer*   410

RICHARD WILBUR, *Junk*   410

WILLIAM CARLOS WILIAMS, *Spring and All*   412

WILLIAM CARLOS WILLIAMS, *To Waken an Old Lady*   413

YVOR WINTERS, *At the San Francisco Airport*   413

WILLIAM WORDSWORTH, *Composed upon Westminster Bridge*   414

WILLIAM WORDSWORTH, *Stepping Westward*   415

JAMES WRIGHT, *A Blessing*   415

JAMES WRIGHT, *Autumn Begins in Martins Ferry, Ohio*   416

JUDITH WRIGHT, *Woman to Man*   416

JUDITH WRIGHT, *Woman to Child*   417

WILLIAM BUTLER YEATS, *Crazy Jane Talks with the Bishop*   418

WILLIAM BUTLER YEATS, *The Lake Isle of Innisfree*   418

WILLIAM BUTLER YEATS, *Lapis Lazuli*   419

WILLIAM BUTLER YEATS, *The Magi*   420

Appendix: Writing about Literature   421

SOME APPROACHES TO LITERATURE   423

FINDING A TOPIC   425

ORGANIZING YOUR THINKING   427

WRITING A DRAFT   429

REVISING   431

THE FORM OF YOUR FINISHED PAPER   432

INDEX OF FIRST LINES   439

INDEX OF AUTHORS AND TITLES   445

INDEX OF TERMS   *inside back cover*

TO THE MUSE

Give me leave, Muse, in plain view to array
Your shift and bodice by the light of day.
I would have brought an epic. Be not vexed
Instead to grace a niggling schoolroom text;
Let down your sanction, help me to oblige
Him who would lead fresh devots to your liege,
And at your altar, grant that in a flash
They, he and I know incense from dead ash.

X.J.K.

An Introduction to Poetry

1 Entrances

How do we read a poem? A literal-minded answer might be, "Just let your eye light on it"; but there is more to poetry than meets the eye. What Shakespeare called "the mind's eye" also plays a part. Many a reader who has no trouble understanding and enjoying prose finds poetry difficult. This is to be expected. At first glance, a poem usually will make some sense and give some pleasure, but it may not yield everything at once. Sometimes it only hints at meaning still to come if we will keep after it. Poetry is not to be galloped over like the daily news: a poem differs from most prose in that it is to be read slowly, carefully, and attentively. Not all poems are difficult, of course, and some can be understood and enjoyed on first seeing. But good poems yield more if read twice; and the best poems — after ten, twenty, or a hundred readings — still go on yielding.

Approaching a thing written in lines and surrounded with white space, we need not expect it to be a poem just because it is **verse.** (Any composition in lines of more or less regular rhythm, usually ending in rimes, is verse.) Here, for instance, is a specimen of verse that few will call poetry:

Thirty days hath September,
April, June, and November;
All the rest have thirty-one
Excepting February alone,
To which we twenty-eight assign
Till leap year makes it twenty-nine.

To a higher degree than that classic memory-tickler, poetry appeals to the mind and arouses feelings. Poetry may state facts, but, more important, it makes imaginative statements that we may value even if its facts are incorrect. Coleridge's error in placing a star within the horns of the crescent moon in "The Rime of the Ancient Mariner" does not stop the passage from being good poetry, though it is faulty astronomy. According to one poet, Gerard Manley Hopkins, poetry is "to be heard for its own sake and interest even over and above its interest of meaning."

There are other elements in a poem besides plain prose sense: sounds, images, rhythms, figures of speech. These may strike us and please us even before we ask, "But what does it all mean?"

This is a truth not readily grasped by anyone who regards a poem as a kind of puzzle written in secret code with a message slyly concealed. The effect of a poem (one's whole mental and emotional response to it) consists in much more than simply a message. By its musical qualities, by its suggestions, it can work on the reader's unconscious. T. S. Eliot put it well when he said in *The Use of Poetry and the Use of Criticism* that the prose sense of a poem is chiefly useful in keeping the reader's mind "diverted and quiet, while the poem does its work upon him." Eliot went on to liken the meaning of a poem to the bit of meat a burglar brings along to throw to the family dog. What is the work of a poem? To touch us, to stir us, to make us glad, and possibly even to tell us something.

How to set about reading a poem? Here are a few suggestions.

To begin with, read the poem once straight through, with no particular expectations; read open-mindedly. Let yourself experience whatever you find, without worrying just yet about the large general and important ideas the poem contains (if indeed it contains any). Don't dwell on a troublesome word or difficult passage — just push on. Some of the difficulties may seem smaller when you read the poem for a second time; at least, they will have become parts of a whole for you.

On second reading, read for the exact sense of all the words; if there are words you don't understand, look them up in a dictionary. Dwell on any difficult parts as long as you need to.

If you read the poem silently to yourself, sound its words in your mind. (This is a technique that will get you nowhere in a speed-reading course, but it may help the poem to do its work on you.) Better still, read the poem aloud, or hear someone else read it. You may discover meanings you didn't perceive in it before. Even if you are no actor, to decide how to speak a poem can be an excellent method of getting to understand it. Some poems, like bells, seem heavy till heard. Listen while reading the following lines from Alexander Pope's *Dunciad*. Attacking the minor poet James Ralph, who had sung the praises of a mistress named Cynthia, Pope makes the goddess of Dullness exclaim:

> "Silence, ye wolves! while Ralph to Cynthia howls,
> And makes night hideous — answer him, ye owls!"

When *ye owls* slide together and become *yowls*, poor Ralph's serenade is turned into the nightly outcry of a cat.

Try to **paraphrase** the poem as a whole, or perhaps just the more difficult lines. In paraphrasing, we put into our own words what we understand the poem to say, restating ideas that seem essential, coming out and stating what the poem may only suggest. This may sound like a heartless thing to do to a poem, but good poems can stand it. In fact, to compare a poem to its paraphrase is an excellent way to see the distance between poetry and prose.

A. E. Housman (1859–1936)
LOVELIEST OF TREES, THE CHERRY NOW   1896

Loveliest of trees, the cherry now
Is hung with bloom along the bough,
And stands about the woodland ride
Wearing white for Eastertide.

Now, of my threescore years and ten,   5
Twenty will not come again,
And take from seventy springs a score,
It only leaves me fifty more.

And since to look at things in bloom
Fifty springs are little room,   10
About the woodlands I will go
To see the cherry hung with snow.

Though simple, Housman's poem is far from simple-minded, and it contains at least one possible problem: what, in this instance, is a *ride*? If we guess, we won't be far wrong; but a dictionary helps: "a road or path through the woods, especially for horseback riding." A paraphrase of the poem might say something like this (in language easier to forget than the original): "Now it is Easter time, and the cherry tree in the woods by the path is in blossom. I'm twenty, my life is passing. I expect to live the average life-span of seventy. That means I'm going to see only fifty more springs, so I had better go out into the woods and start looking." And the paraphrase might add, to catch the deeper implication, "Life is brief and fleeting: I must enjoy beauty while I may."

These dull remarks, roughly faithful to what Housman is saying, are clearly as far from being poetry as a cherry pit is far from being a cherry. Still, they can help whoever makes the paraphrase to see the main argument of Housman's poem: its **theme** or central thought. Theme isn't the same thing as **subject,** the central topic. In "Loveliest of trees," the subject is cherry blossoms, or the need to look at them, but the theme is "Time flies: enjoy beauty now!" Not all poems clearly assert a proposition, but many do; some even declare their themes in their very first lines: "Gather ye rose-buds while ye may" — enjoy love before it's too late. The theme stated in that famous opening line (from Robert Herrick's "To the Virgins, to Make Much of Time," page 351) is so familiar that it has a name: **carpe diem** (Latin for "seize the day"), a favorite argument of poets from Horace to Housman.

A paraphrase, of course, never tells *all* that a poem contains; nor will every reader agree that a particular paraphrase is accurate. We all make our own interpretations; and sometimes the total meaning of a poem evades even the poet who wrote it. Asked to explain his difficult *Sordello,* Robert Browning replied that when he had written the poem only God and he knew what it meant; but "Now, only God knows." Still, to analyze a poem *as if* we could be certain of its meaning is, in general, more fruitful than to proceed as if no certainty could ever be had. The latter approach is likely to end in complete subjectivity: the attitude of the reader who says, "Housman's 'Loveliest of trees' is really about a walk in the snow; it is, because I think it is. How can you prove me wrong?"

All of us bring to our readings of poems certain personal associations, as Housman's "Loveliest of trees" might convey a particular pleasure to a reader who had climbed cherry trees when he was small. To some extent, these associations are inevitable, even to be welcomed. But we need to distinguish between irrelevant, tangential responses and those the poem calls for. The reader who can't stand "Loveliest of trees" because cherries remind him of blood, is reading a poem of his own, not Housman's.

Housman's poem is a **lyric:** a short poem expressing the thoughts and feelings of a single speaker. (As its Greek name suggests, a lyric originally was sung to the music of a lyre.) Often a lyric is written in the first person ("About the woodlands *I* will go"), but not always. It may be, for instance, a description of an object or an experience in which the poet isn't even mentioned. Housman's first stanza, printed by itself as a complete poem, would still be a lyric. Though a lyric may relate an incident, we tend to think of it as a reflective poem in which little physical action takes place — unlike a **narrative poem,** one whose main concern is to tell a story.

At the moment, it is a safe bet that, in English and other Western languages, lyrics are more plentiful than other kinds of poetry (novels having virtually replaced the long narrative poems esteemed from the time of Homer's *Odyssey* to the time of Tennyson's *Idylls of the King*). **Didactic poetry,** to mention one other kind, is poetry apparently written to teach or to state a message. In a lyric, the speaker may express sadness; in a didactic poem, he may explain that sadness is inherent in life. Poems that impart a body of knowledge, like Ovid's *Art of Love* and Lucretius's *On the Nature of Things,* are didactic. Such instructive poetry was favored especially by classical Latin poets and by English poets of the eighteenth century. In *The Fleece* (1757), John Dyer celebrated the British woolen industry and included practical advice on raising sheep:

> In cold stiff soils the bleaters oft complain
> Of gouty ails, by shepherds termed the halt:
> Those let the neighboring fold or ready crook
> Detain, and pour into their cloven feet

Corrosive drugs, deep-searching arsenic,
Dry alum, verdegris, or vitriol keen.

One might agree with Dr. Johnson's comment on Dyer's effort: "The subject, Sir, cannot be made poetical." But it may be argued that didactic poetry (to quote a recent view) "is not intrinsically any less poetic because of its subject-matter than lines about a rose fluttering in the breeze are intrinsically more poetic because of their subject-matter."[1] John Milton also described sick sheep in "Lycidas," a poem few readers have thought unpoetic:

The hungry sheep look up, and are not fed,
But, swoll'n with wind and the rank mist they draw,
Rot inwardly, and foul contagion spread . . .

What makes Milton's lines better poetry than Dyer's is, among other things, a difference in attitude. Sick sheep to Dyer mean the loss of a few shillings and pence; to Milton, whose sheep stand for English Christendom, they mean a moral catastrophe.

Now and again we meet a poem — perhaps startling and memorable — into which the method of paraphrase won't take us far. Some portion of any deep poem resists explanation, but certain poems resist it almost entirely. Many poems of religious mystics seem closer to dream than waking. So do poems that record hallucinations or drug experiences, such as Coleridge's "Kubla Khan" (page 320), as well as poems that embody some private system of beliefs, such as Blake's "The Sick Rose" (page 315), or the same poet's lines from *Jerusalem*,

For a Tear is an Intellectual thing,
And a Sigh is the Sword of an Angel King.

So do nonsense poems, translations of primitive folk songs, and surreal poems.[2] Such poetry may move us and give pleasure (although not, perhaps, the pleasure of mental understanding). We do it no harm by trying to paraphrase it, though we may fail. Whether logically clear or strangely opaque, good poems appeal to the intelligence and do not shrink from it.

So far, we have taken it for granted that poetry differs from prose; yet all our strategies for reading poetry — plowing straight on through and then going back, isolating difficulties, trying to paraphrase, reading aloud, using a dictionary — are no different from those we might employ

[1] Sylvan Barnet, Morton Berman, and William Burto, *A Dictionary of Literary, Dramatic, and Cinematic Terms*, 2nd ed. (Boston: Little, Brown, 1971).
[2] The French poet André Breton, founder of **surrealism,** a movement in art and writing, declared that a higher reality exists, which to mortal eyes looks absurd. To mirror that reality, surrealist poets are fond of bizarre and dreamlike objects such as soluble fish and white-haired revolvers.

in unraveling a complicated piece of prose. Poetry, after all, is similar to prose in most respects; at the very least, it is written in the same language. And like prose, poetry imparts knowledge. It tells us, for instance, something about the season and habitat of cherry trees and how one can feel toward them. Maybe a poet knows no more of cherry trees than a writer of seed-catalog descriptions, if as much. And yet Housman's perception of cherry blossoms as snow, with the implication that they too will soon melt and disappear, indicates a kind of knowledge that seed catalogs do not ordinarily reveal.

Robert Francis (b. 1901)

CATCH 1950

Two boys uncoached are tossing a poem together,
Overhand, underhand, backhand, sleight of hand, every hand,
Teasing with attitudes, latitudes, interludes, altitudes,
High, make him fly off the ground for it, low, make him stoop,
Make him scoop it up, make him as-almost-as-possible miss it, 5
Fast, let him sting from it, now, now fool him slowly,
Anything, everything tricky, risky, nonchalant,
Anything under the sun to outwit the prosy,
Over the tree and the long sweet cadence down,
Over his head, make him scramble to pick up the meaning, 10
And now, like a posy, a pretty one plump in his hands.

QUESTIONS

1. Who are the two boys in this poem?
2. Point out a few of the most important similarities in this extended comparison.
3. Consider especially line 8: *Anything under the sun to outwit the prosy.* What, in your own words, does Robert Francis mean?

Emily Dickinson (1830–1886)

I TASTE A LIQUOR NEVER BREWED (about 1860)

I taste a liquor never brewed–
From Tankards scooped in Pearl–
Not all the Frankfort Berries
Yield such an Alcohol!

Inebriate of Air–am I– 5
And Debauchee of Dew–
Reeling–thro endless summer days–
From inns of Molten Blue–

When "Landlords" turn the drunken Bee
Out of the Foxglove's door –
When Butterflies – renounce their "drams" –
I shall but drink the more!

Till Seraphs swing their snowy Hats –
And Saints – to windows run –
To see the little Tippler
From Manzanilla come!

I TASTE A LIQUOR NEVER BREWED. 3. *Frankfort Berries:* grapes of the many vineyards near Frankfort on the Main, Germany. In another version of this poem, the third line reads, "Not all the Vats upon the Rhine." 16. *Manzanilla:* Perhaps the poet was thinking of Manzanillo, a port city in Cuba from which rum was shipped; there is also a Spanish sherry called Manzanilla. In the poet's other version, the last line reads, "Leaning against the – Sun –."

QUESTIONS

1. Is this lyric, narrative, or didactic poetry?
2. Does Emily Dickinson say anything in particular in this poem, or is she just waxing ecstatic? Try to paraphrase her poem and state its theme.
3. After having made your paraphrase, go back to the poem and see what qualities or elements it has that your paraphrase (naturally) lacks. What does this comparison tell you about the differences between prose and poetry?

Donald Finkel (b. 1929)

HANDS   1966

The poem makes truth a little more disturbing,
like a good bra, lifts it and holds it out
in both hands. (In some of the flashier stores
there's a model with the hands stitched on, in red or black.)

Lately the world you wed, for want of such hands,
sags in the bed beside you like a tired wife.
For want of such hands, the face of the moon is bored;
the tree does not stretch and yearn, nor the groin tighten.

Devious or frank, in any case,
the poem is calculated to arouse.
Lean back and let its hands play freely on you:
there comes a moment, lifted and aroused,
when the two of you are equally beautiful.

QUESTIONS

1. At what moments in "Hands" do you sense that the poet is kidding?
2. Playful as this poem may be, what serious points does Finkel make about the nature of poetry? Explain how, in his view, "real life" relates to poetry (lines

1–3); how the world seems poorer without poetry (lines 5–9); how the reader can be *lifted and aroused* (line 12).

Robinson Jeffers (1887–1962)

TO THE STONE-CUTTERS   1925

Stone-cutters fighting time with marble, you foredefeated
Challengers of oblivion
Eat cynical earnings, knowing rock splits, records fall down,
The square-limbed Roman letters
Scale in the thaws, wear in the rain. The poet as well   5
Builds his monument mockingly;
For man will be blotted out, the blithe earth die, the brave sun
Die blind, his heart blackening:
Yet stones have stood for a thousand years, and pained thoughts found
The honey of peace in old poems.   10

William Shakespeare (1564–1616)

NOT MARBLE NOR THE GILDED MONUMENTS   1609

Not marble nor the gilded monuments
Of princes shall outlive this pow'rful rime;
But you shall shine more bright in these contènts
Than unswept stone, besmeared with sluttish time.
When wasteful war shall statues overturn,   5
And broils° root out the work of masonry,   *brawls, battles*
Nor Mars his sword nor war's quick fire shall burn
The living record of your memory.
'Gainst death and all oblivious enmity
Shall you pace forth; your praise shall still find room   10
Even in the eyes of all posterity
That wear this world out to the ending doom.
   So, till the Judgment that° yourself arise,   *when*
   You live in this, and dwell in lovers' eyes.

QUESTIONS

1. What subject do these two poems have in common?
2. State in your own words each poet's theme. How do the two appear to differ in their attitudes toward poetry?
3. Is Shakespeare making a wild boast, or does the statement in lines 1–8 seem at all borne out by events of the past four centuries?

2 Listening to a Voice

TONE

In late-show Westerns, when one hombre taunts another, it is customary for the second to drawl, "Smile when you say that, pardner" or "Mister, I don't like your tone of voice." Sometimes in reading a poem, although we neither can see a face nor hear a voice, we can infer the poet's attitude from other evidence.

Like tone of voice, **tone** in literature often conveys an attitude toward the person addressed. Like the manner of a person, the manner of a poem may be friendly or belligerent toward its reader, condescending or respectful. Again like tone of voice, the tone of a poem may tell us how the speaker feels about himself or herself: cocksure or humble, for example. But most of the time when we ask, "What is the tone of a poem?" we mean, "What attitude does the poet take toward a theme or a subject?" Is the poet being affectionate, hostile, earnest, playful, sarcastic, or what? We may never be able to know, of course, the poet's personal feelings. All we need know is how to feel when we read a poem.

Strictly speaking, tone isn't an attitude; it is whatever in the poem makes an attitude clear to us: the choice of certain words instead of others, the picking out of certain details. In Housman's "Loveliest of trees," for example, the poet communicates his admiration for a cherry tree's beauty by singling out for attention its white blossoms; had he wanted to show his dislike for the tree, he might have concentrated on its broken branches, birdlime, or snails. Rightly to perceive the tone of a poem, we need to read the poem carefully, paying attention to whatever suggestions we find in it.

Theodore Roethke (1908–1963)

MY PAPA'S WALTZ   1948

The whiskey on your breath
Could make a small boy dizzy;
But I hung on like death:
Such waltzing was not easy.

We romped until the pans   5
Slid from the kitchen shelf;
My mother's countenance
Could not unfrown itself.

The hand that held my wrist
Was battered on one knuckle;   10
At every step you missed
My right ear scraped a buckle.

You beat time on my head
With a palm caked hard by dirt,
Then waltzed me off to bed   15
Still clinging to your shirt.

What is the tone of this poem? Most readers find the speaker's attitude toward his father warmly affectionate, and take this recollection of
childhood to be a happy one. But at least one reader, concentrating on
certain details and ignoring others, once wrote: "Roethke expresses his
resentment for his father, a drunken brute with dirty hands and a
whiskey breath who carelessly hurt the child's ear and manhandled
him." Although this reader accurately noticed some of the events in the
poem, he completely missed the tone of the poem, and so misunder-
stood it altogether. Among other things, this reader didn't notice the
rollicking rhythms of the poem; the playfulness of a rime like *dizzy* and
easy; the joyful suggestions of the words *waltz, waltzing,* and *romped.*
Probably the reader didn't stop to visualize this scene in all its comedy,
with kitchen pans falling and the father happily using his son's head for
a drum. Nor did he stop to feel the suggestions in the last line, with the
boy *still clinging* with persistent love.

Such a poem, though it includes lifelike details that aren't pretty,
has a tone relatively easy to recognize. So does **satiric poetry,** a kind of
comic poetry that generally conveys a message. Usually its tone is one of
detached amusement, withering contempt, and implied superiority. In
a satiric poem, the poet ridicules some person or persons (or perhaps
some kind of human behavior), examining the victim by the light of
certain principles and implying that the reader, too, ought to feel contempt for the victim.

Countee Cullen (1903–1946)
For a Lady I Know   1925

She even thinks that up in heaven
  Her class lies late and snores,
While poor black cherubs rise at seven
  To do celestial chores.

1. What is Cullen's message?
2. How would you characterize the tone of this poem? Wrathful? Amused?

In some poems the poet's attitude may be plain enough; while in other poems attitudes may be so mingled that it is hard to describe them tersely without doing injustice to the poem. Does Andrew Marvell in "To His Coy Mistress" (page 370) take a serious or playful attitude toward the fact that he and his lady are destined to be food for worms? No one-word answer will suffice. And what of T. S. Eliot's "Love Song of J. Alfred Prufrock" (page 336)? In his attitude toward his redemption-seeking hero who wades with trousers rolled, Eliot is seriously funny. Such a mingled tone may be seen in the following poem by the wife of a governor of the Massachusetts Bay Colony and the earliest American poet of note. Anne Bradstreet's first book, *The Tenth Muse Lately Sprung Up in America* (1650), had been published in England without her consent. She wrote these lines to preface a second edition:

Anne Bradstreet (1612?–1672)
THE AUTHOR TO HER BOOK   1678

Thou ill-formed offspring of my feeble brain,
Who after birth did'st by my side remain,
Till snatched from thence by friends, less wise than true,
Who thee abroad exposed to public view;
Made thee in rags, halting, to the press to trudge,   5
Where errors were not lessened, all may judge.
At thy return my blushing was not small,
My rambling brat (in print) should mother call;
I cast thee by as one unfit for light,
Thy visage was so irksome in my sight;   10
Yet being mine own, at length affection would
Thy blemishes amend, if so I could:
I washed thy face, but more defects I saw,
And rubbing off a spot, still made a flaw.
I stretched thy joints to make thee even feet,   15
Yet still thou run'st more hobbling than is meet;
In better dress to trim thee was my mind,
But nought save homespun cloth in the house I find.
In this array, 'mongst vulgars may'st thou roam;
In critics' hands beware thou dost not come;   20
And take thy way where yet thou are not known.
If for thy Father asked, say thou had'st none;
And for thy Mother, she alas is poor,
Which caused her thus to send thee out of door.

In the author's comparison of her book to an illegitimate ragamuffin, we may be struck by the details of scrubbing and dressing a child: details that might well occur to a mother who had scrubbed and dressed many. As she might feel toward such a child, so she feels toward her book. She starts by deploring it but, as the poem goes on, cannot deny it her affection. Humor enters (as in the pun in line 15). She must dress the creature in *homespun cloth,* something both crude and serviceable. By the end of her poem, Mrs. Bradstreet seems to regard her book-child with tenderness, amusement, and a certain indulgent awareness of its faults. To read this poem is to sense its mingling of several attitudes. Simultaneously, a poet can be merry and in earnest.

Walt Whitman (1819–1892)

To a Locomotive in Winter   1881

Thee for my recitative,
Thee in the driving storm even as now, the snow, the winter-day
 declining,
Thee in thy panoply°, thy measur'd dual throbbing and thy   *suit of*
 beat convulsive,   *armor*
Thy black cylindric body, golden brass and silvery steel,
Thy ponderous side-bars, parallel and connecting rods, gyrating,
 shuttling at thy sides,   5
Thy metrical, now swelling pant and roar, now tapering in the distance,
Thy great protruding head-light fix'd in front,
Thy long, pale, floating vapor-pennants, tinged with delicate purple,
The dense and murky clouds out-belching from thy smoke-stack,
Thy knitted frame, thy springs and valves, the tremulous twinkle of
 thy wheels,   10
Thy train of cars behind, obedient, merrily following,
Through gale or calm, now swift, now slack, yet steadily careering;
Type of the modern—emblem of motion and power—pulse of the continent,
For once come serve the Muse and merge in verse, even as here I
 see thee,
With storm and buffeting gusts of wind and falling snow,   15
By day thy warning ringing bell to sound its notes,
By night thy silent signal lamps to swing.

Fierce-throated beauty!
Roll through my chant with all thy lawless music, thy swinging lamps
 at night,
Thy madly-whistled laughter, echoing, rumbling like an earthquake,
 rousing all,   20
Law of thyself complete, thine own track firmly holding,
(No sweetness debonair of tearful harp or glib piano thine,)
Thy trills of shrieks by rocks and hills return'd,
Launch'd o'er the prairies wide, across the lakes,
To the free skies unpent and glad and strong.   25

Emily Dickinson (1830–1886)

I LIKE TO SEE IT LAP THE MILES   (about 1862)

I like to see it lap the Miles–
And lick the Valleys up–
And stop to feed itself at Tanks–
And then–prodigious step

Around a Pile of Mountains–   5
And supercilious peer
In Shanties–by the sides of Roads–
And then a Quarry pare

To fit its Ribs
And crawl between   10
Complaining all the while
In horrid–hooting stanza–
Then chase itself down Hill–

And neigh like Boanerges–
Then–punctual as a Star   15
Stop–docile and omnipotent
At its own stable door–

QUESTIONS

1. What differences in tone do you find between Whitman's and Emily Dickinson's poems? Point out in each poem whatever contributes to these differences.
2. *Boanerges* in Emily Dickinson's last stanza means "sons of thunder," a name given by Christ to the disciples John and James (see Mark 3:17). How far should the reader work out the particulars of this comparison? Does it make the tone of the poem serious?
3. In Whitman's opening line, what is a *recitative*? What other specialized terms from the vocabulary of music and poetry does each poem contain? How do they help underscore Whitman's theme?
4. Poets and song-writers probably have regarded the locomotive with more affection than they have shown most other machines. Why do you suppose this to be? Can you think of any other poems or songs for example?
5. What do these two poems tell you about locomotives that you would not be likely to find in a technical book on railroading?
6. Are the subjects of the two poems identical? Discuss.

THE PERSON IN THE POEM

The tone of a poem, we said, is like tone of voice in that both communicate feelings. Still, this comparison raises a question: when we read a poem, whose "voice" speaks to us?

"The poet's" is one possible answer; and in the case of many a poem, that answer may be right. Reading Anne Bradstreet's "The Author to Her Book," we can be reasonably sure that the poet speaks of her very own book, and of her own experiences. In order to read a poem, we seldom need to read a poet's biography; but in truth there are certain poems whose full effect depends upon our knowing at least a fact or two of the poet's life. In this poem, surely the poet refers to himself:

Trumbull Stickney (1874–1904)
SIR, SAY NO MORE   1905

Sir, say no more,
Within me 'tis as if
The green and climbing eyesight of a cat
Crawled near my mind's poor birds.

The subject of Stickney's poem is not some nightmare or hallucination. The poem may mean more to you if you know that Stickney, who wrote it shortly before his death, had been afflicted by cancer of the brain. But the poem is not a prosaic entry in the diary of a dying man, nor is it a good poem because a dying man wrote it. Not only does it tell truth from experience, it speaks in memorable words.

Most of us can tell the difference between a person we meet in life and a person we meet in a work of art—unlike the moviegoer in the Philippines who, watching a villain in an exciting film, pulled out a revolver and peppered the screen. And yet, in reading poems, we are liable to temptation. When the poet says "I," we may want to assume that he, like Trumbull Stickney, is making a personal statement. But reflect: do all poems have to be personal? Here is a brief poem inscribed on the tombstone of an infant in Burial Hill cemetery, Plymouth, Massachusetts:

Since I have been so quickly done for,
I wonder what I was begun for.

We do not know who wrote those lines, but it is clear that the poet was not a short-lived infant writing from personal experience. In other poems, the speaker is obviously a fictitious character. As a grown man William Blake, a skilled professional engraver, wrote a poem in the voice of a boy, an illiterate chimney sweeper. (The poem appears on page 28.) No law decrees that the speaker in a poem even has to be human: good poems have been uttered by clouds, pebbles, and cats. A **dramatic monologue** is a poem written as a speech made at some decisive or revealing moment. It is usually addressed by the speaker to some other character (who remains silent). Robert Browning, who developed the form, liked to put words into the mouths of characters stupider, weaker, or nastier than he: for instance see "My Last Duchess" (page 316), in which the speaker is an arrogant Renaissance duke. Browning himself, from all reports, was neither domineering nor merciless.

Let's consider a poem spoken by a fictitious character—in this case, a child. To understand the poem, you need to pay attention not only to what the child says, but also to how the poet seems to feel about it.

Randall Jarrell (1914–1965)
A Sick Child   1951

The postman comes when I am still in bed.
"Postman, what do you have for me today?"
I say to him. (But really I'm in bed.)
Then he says—what shall I have him say?

"This letter says that you are president   5
Of—this word here; it's a republic."
Tell them I can't answer right away.
"It's your duty." No, I'd rather just be sick.

Then he tells me there are letters saying everything
That I can think of that I want for them to say.   10
I say, "Well, thank you very much. Good-bye."
He is ashamed, and turns and walks away.

If I can think of it, it isn't what I want.
I want . . . I want a ship from some near star
To land in the yard, and beings to come out   15
And think to me: "So this is where you are!

Come." Except that they won't do,
I thought of them. . . . And yet somewhere there must be
Something that's different from everything.
All that I've never thought of—think of me!

QUESTIONS

1. Would you call the speaker unfeeling or sensitive? Unimaginative or imaginative? How do you know?
2. Why is the postman *ashamed*?
3. Besides sickness, what is bothering the child? What does the child long for?
4. Do you think Jarrell sympathizes with the child's wishes and longings? By what means does he indicate his own attitude?

We tend to think of a poem as simply an expression of the feelings a poet had while writing it. And yet, as the following comic poem indicates, sometimes a poet in the process of writing a poem has feelings that the poem doesn't mention.

Alden Nowlan (b. 1933)

The Loneliness of the Long Distance Runner   1967

My wife bursts into the room
where I'm writing well
of my love for her

and because now
the poem is lost

I silently curse her.

Humorously, Nowlan suggests that loving his wife isn't the same as writing a poem about loving her. A good poem (if the poet can finish it) is a fixed and changeless thing; but evidently a living, changing poet with various emotions had to take a certain length of time in writing it.

In a famous definition, William Wordsworth calls poetry "the spontaneous overflow of powerful feelings . . . recollected in tranquillity." But in the case of the following poem, Wordsworth's feelings weren't all his; they didn't just overflow spontaneously; and the process of tranquil recollection had to go on for years.

William Wordsworth (1770–1850)

I Wandered Lonely as a Cloud

I wandered lonely as a cloud
  That floats on high o'er vales and hills,
When all at once I saw a crowd,
  A host, of golden daffodils,
Beside the lake, beneath the trees,   5
Fluttering and dancing in the breeze.

Continuous as the stars that shine
  And twinkle on the milky way,
They stretched in never-ending line
  Along the margin of a bay: 10
Ten thousand saw I at a glance,
Tossing their heads in sprightly dance.

The waves beside them danced; but they
  Out-did the sparkling waves in glee;
A poet could not but be gay,   15
  In such a jocund company;
I gazed — and gazed — but little thought
What wealth the show to me had brought:

For oft, when on my couch I lie
  In vacant or in pensive mood,20
They flash upon that inward eye
  Which is the bliss of solitude;
And then my heart with pleasure fills,
And dances with the daffodils.

Between the first printing of the poem in 1807 and the version of 1815 given here, Wordsworth made several deliberate improvements. He changed *dancing* to *golden* in line 4, *Along* to *Beside* in line 5, *Ten thousand* to *Fluttering and* in line 6, *laughing* to *jocund* in line 16, and he added a whole stanza (the second). In fact, the writing of the poem was unspontaneous enough for Wordsworth, at a loss for lines 21–22, to take them from his wife Mary. It is likely that the experience of daffodil-watching was not entirely his to begin with but was derived in part from the recollections his sister Dorothy Wordsworth had set down in her journal of April 15, 1802, two years before he first drafted his poem:

> When we were in the woods beyond Gowbarrow Park we saw a few daffodils close to the water-side. We fancied that the lake had floated the seeds ashore, and that the little colony had so sprung up. But as we went along there were more and yet more; and at last, under the boughs of the trees, we saw that there was a long belt of them along the shore, about the breadth of a country turnpike road. I never saw daffodils so beautiful. They grew among the mossy stones about and about them; some rested their heads upon these stones as on a pillow for weariness; and the rest tossed and reeled and danced, and seemed as if they verily laughed with the wind, that flew upon them over the Lake; they looked so gay, ever glancing, ever changing. This wind blew directly over the Lake to them. There was here and there a little knot, and a few stragglers a few yards higher up; but they were so few as not to disturb the simplicity, unity, and life of that one busy highway.

Notice that Wordsworth's poem echoes a few of his sister's observations. Weaving poetry out of their mutual memories, Wordsworth has offered the experience as if altogether his own, made himself lonely, and left Dorothy out. The point is not that Wordsworth is a liar or a plagiarist but that, like any other good poet, he has transformed ordinary life into art. A process of interpreting, shaping, and ordering had to intervene between the experience of looking at daffodils and the finished poem.

We need not deny that a poet's experience can contribute to a poem nor that the emotion in the poem can indeed be the poet's. Still, to write a good poem one has to do more than live and feel. It seems a pity that, as Randall Jarrell has said, a cardinal may write verses worse than his youngest choirboy's. But writing poetry takes skill and imagination — qualities that extensive travel and wide experience do not necessarily give. For much of her life, Emily Dickinson seldom strayed from her family's house and grounds in Amherst, Massachusetts; yet her rimed lifestudies of a snake, a bee, and a hummingbird contain more poetry than we find in any firsthand description (so far) of the surface of the moon.

EXPERIMENT: *Reading with and without Biography*

Read the following poem and state what you understand from it. Then consider the circumstances in which it probably came to be written. (Some information is offered in a note at the end of this chapter.) Does the meaning of the poem change? To what extent does an appreciation of the poem need the support of biography?

William Carlos Williams (1883–1963)
THE RED WHEELBARROW   1923

so much depends
upon

a red wheel
barrow

glazed with rain
water

beside the white
chickens.

IRONY

To see a distinction between the poet and the words of a fictitious character — between Randall Jarrell and "A Sick Child" — is to be aware of **irony:** a manner of speaking that implies a discrepancy. If the mask says one thing and we sense that the writer is in fact saying something else, the writer has adopted an **ironic point of view.** No finer illustration exists in English than Jonathan Swift's "A Modest Proposal," an essay in which Swift speaks as an earnest, humorless citizen who sets forth his reasonable plan to aid the Irish poor. The plan is so monstrous no sane reader can assent to it: the poor are to sell their children as meat for the tables of their landlords. From behind his falseface, Swift is actually recommending not cannibalism but love and Christian charity.

A poem is often made complicated and more interesting by another kind of irony. **Verbal irony** occurs whenever words say one thing but mean something else, usually the opposite. The word *love* means *hate* here: "I just *love* to stay home and do my hair on a Saturday night!" If the verbal irony is conspicuously bitter, heavy-handed, and mocking, it is **sarcasm:** "Oh, he's the biggest spender in the world, all right!" (The sarcasm, if that statement were spoken, would be underscored by the speaker's tone of voice.) A famous instance of sarcasm is Mark Antony's line in his oration over the body of slain Julius Caesar: "Brutus is an honorable man." Antony repeats this line until the enraged populace begins shouting exactly what he means to call Brutus and the other conspirators: traitors, villains, murderers. We had best be alert for irony on the printed page, for if we miss it, our interpretations of a poem may go wild.

Robert Creeley (b. 1926)

OH NO   1959

If you wander far enough
you will come to it
and when you get there
they will give you a place to sit

for yourself only, in a nice chair,
and all your friends will be there
with smiles on their faces
and they will likewise all have places.

This poem is rich in verbal irony. The title helps point out that between the speaker's words and attitude lie deep differences. In line 2, what is *it*? Old age? The wandering suggests a conventional metaphor: the journey of life. Is *it* literally a rest home for "senior citizens," or perhaps some naïve popular concept of heaven (such as we meet in comic strips: harps, angels with hoops for halos) in which the saved all sit around in a ring, smugly congratulating one another? We can't be sure, but the speaker's attitude toward this final sitting-place is definite. It is a place for the selfish, as we infer from the phrase *for yourself only*. And *smiles on their faces* may hint that the smiles are unchanging and forced. There is a difference between saying "They had smiles on their faces" and "They smiled": the latter suggests that the smiles came from within. The word *nice* is to be regarded with distrust. If we see through this speaker, as Creeley implies we can do, we realize that, while pretending to be sweet-talking us into a seat, actually he is revealing the horror of a little hell. And the title is the poet's reaction to it (or the speaker's unironic, straightforward one): "Oh no! Not *that!*"

Dramatic irony, like verbal irony, contains an element of contrast, but it usually refers to a situation in a play wherein a character, whose knowledge is limited, says, does, or encounters something of greater significance than he or she knows. We, the spectators, realize the meaning of this speech or action, for the playwright has afforded us superior knowledge. In Sophocles' *King Oedipus,* when Oedipus vows to punish whoever has brought down a plague upon the city of Thebes, we know — as he does not — that the man he would punish is himself. (Referring to such a situation that precedes the downfall of a hero in a tragedy, some critics speak of **tragic irony** instead of dramatic irony.) Superior knowledge can be enjoyed not only by spectators in a theater but by readers of poetry as well. In *Paradise Lost,* we know in advance that Adam will fall into temptation, and we recognize his overconfidence when he neglects a warning. The situation of Oedipus contains also **cosmic irony,** or **irony of fate:** some Fate with a grim sense of humor seems cruelly to trick a human being. Cosmic irony clearly exists in poems in which fate or the Fates are personified and seen as hostile, as in Thomas Hardy's "The Convergence of the Twain" (p. 347); and it may be said to occur too in a poem such as Robinson's "Richard Cory" (p. 104) and in MacLeish's "The End of the World" (p. 369). Evidently it is a twist of fate for the most envied man in town to kill himself and another twist of fate for spectators at a circus to find themselves suddenly beholding a greater and more horrific show than they had paid for: the end of the world.

To sum up: the effect of irony depends upon the reader's noticing some incongruity or discrepancy between two things. In *verbal irony,* there is a contrast between the speaker's words and meaning; in an *ironic point of view,* between the writer's attitude and what is spoken by a fictitious character; in *dramatic irony,* between the limited knowledge of a character and the fuller knowledge of the reader or spectator; in *cosmic irony,* between a character's aspiration and the treatment he or she receives at the hands of Fate. Although in the work of an inept poet irony can be crude and obvious sarcasm, it is invaluable to a poet of more complicated mind, who imagines more than one perspective.

W. H. Auden (1907–1973)

THE UNKNOWN CITIZEN   1940

(To JS/07/M/378
This Marble Monument
Is Erected by the State)

He was found by the Bureau of Statistics to be
One against whom there was no official complaint,
And all the reports on his conduct agree
That, in the modern sense of an old-fashioned word, he was a saint,
For in everything he did he served the Greater Community.   5
Except for the War till the day he retired
He worked in a factory and never got fired,
But satisfied his employers, Fudge Motors Inc.

Yet he wasn't a scab or odd in his views,
For his Union reports that he paid his dues, 10
(Our report on his Union shows it was sound)
And our Social Psychology workers found
That he was popular with his mates and liked a drink.
The Press are convinced that he bought a paper every day
And that his reactions to advertisements were normal in every way. 15
Policies taken out in his name prove that he was fully insured,
And his Health-card shows he was once in hospital but left it cured.
Both Producers Research and High-Grade Living declare
He was fully sensible to the advantages of the Installment Plan
And had everything necessary to the Modern Man, 20
A phonograph, a radio, a car and a frigidaire.
Our researchers into Public Opinion are content
That he held the proper opinions for the time of year;
When there was peace, he was for peace; when there was war, he went.
He was married and added five children to the population, 25
Which our Eugenist says was the right number for a parent of his
   generation,
And our teachers report that he never interfered with their education.
Was he free? Was he happy? The question is absurd:
Had anything been wrong, we should certainly have heard.

Questions

1. Read the three-line epitaph at the beginning of the poem as carefully as you read what follows. How does the epitaph help establish the voice by which the rest of the poem is spoken?
2. Who is speaking?
3. What ironic discrepancies do you find between the speaker's attitude toward the subject and that of the poet himself? By what is the poet's attitude made clear?
4. In the phrase "The Unknown Soldier" (of which "The Unknown Citizen" reminds us), what does the word *unknown* mean? What does it mean in the title of Auden's poem?
5. What tendencies in our civilization does Auden satirize?
6. How would you expect the speaker to define a Modern Man, if a phonograph, a radio, a car, and a refrigerator are "everything" a Modern Man needs?

John Betjeman (b. 1906)

In Westminster Abbey 1940

Let me take this other glove off
   As the *vox humana* swells,
And the beauteous fields of Eden
   Bask beneath the Abbey bells.
Here, where England's statesmen lie, 5
Listen to a lady's cry.

Gracious Lord, oh bomb the Germans.
  Spare their women for Thy Sake,
And if that is not too easy
   We will pardon Thy Mistake.   10
But, gracious Lord, whate'er shall be,
Don't let anyone bomb me.

Keep our Empire undismembered,
  Guide our Forces by Thy Hand,
Gallant blacks from far Jamaica,   15
  Honduras and Togoland;
Protect them Lord in all their fights,
And, even more, protect the whites.

Think of what our Nation stands for:
  Books from Boots' and country lanes,   20
Free speech, free passes, class distinction,
  Democracy and proper drains.
Lord, put beneath Thy special care
One-eighty-nine Cadogan Square.

Although dear Lord I am a sinner,   25
  I have done no major crime;
Now I'll come to Evening Service
  Whensoever I have the time.
So, Lord, reserve for me a crown,
And do not let my shares° go down.   *stocks* 30

I will labor for Thy Kingdom,
  Help our lads to win the war,
Send white feathers to the cowards,
  Join the Women's Army Corps,
Then wash the Steps around Thy Throne   35
In the Eternal Safety Zone.

Now I feel a little better,
  What a treat to hear Thy Word,
Where the bones of leading statesmen
  Have so often been interred.   40
And now, dear Lord, I cannot wait
Because I have a luncheon date.

IN WESTMINSTER ABBEY. First printed during World War II. 2. *vox humana:* an organ stop that makes tones similar to those of the human voice. 20. *Boots':* a cut-rate pharmacy.

QUESTIONS

1. Who is the speaker? What do we know about her life style? About her prejudices?
2. Point out some of the places in which she contradicts herself.

3. How would you describe the speaker's attitude toward religion?
4. Through the medium of irony, what positive points do you believe Betjeman makes?

Sarah N. Cleghorn (1876–1959)

THE GOLF LINKS   1917

The golf links lie so near the mill
   That almost every day
The laboring children can look out
   And see the men at play.

QUESTIONS

1. Is this brief poem satiric? Does it contain any verbal irony? Is the poet making a matter-of-fact statement in words that mean just what they say?
2. What other kind of irony is present in the poem?
3. Sarah N. Cleghorn's poem dates from before the enactment of legislation against child labor. Is it still a good poem, or is it hopelessly outdated?
4. How would you state its theme?

EXERCISE: *Detecting Irony*

Point out the kinds of irony that occur in the following poem.

Thomas Hardy (1840–1928)

THE WORKBOX   1914

"See, here's the workbox, little wife,
   That I made of polished oak."
He was a joiner°, of village life;   *carpenter*
   She came of borough folk.

He holds the present up to her   5
   As with a smile she nears
And answers to the profferer,
   " 'Twill last all my sewing years!"

"I warrant it will. And longer too.
   'Tis a scantling that I got   10
Off poor John Wayward's coffin, who
   Died of they knew not what.

"The shingled pattern that seems to cease
   Against your box's rim
Continues right on in the piece   15
   That's underground with him.

"And while I worked it made me think
    Of timber's varied doom:
One inch where people eat and drink,
    The next inch in a tomb.   20

"But why do you look so white, my dear,
    And turn aside your face?
You knew not that good lad, I fear,
    Though he came from your native place?"

"How could I know that good young man,   25
    Though he came from my native town,
When he must have left far earlier than
    I was a woman grown?"

"Ah, no. I should have understood!
    It shocked you that I gave   30
To you one end of a piece of wood
    Whose other is in a grave?"

"Don't, dear, despise my intellect,
    Mere accidental things
Of that sort never have effect   35
    On my imaginings."

Yet still her lips were limp and wan,
    Her face still held aside,
As if she had known not only John,
    But known of what he died.   40

FOR REVIEW AND FURTHER STUDY

Ted Hughes (b. 1930)

SECRETARY   1957

If I should touch her she would shriek and weeping
Crawl off to nurse the terrible wound: all
Day like a starling under the bellies of bulls
She hurries among men, ducking, peeping,

Off in a whirl at the first move of a horn.   5
At dusk she scuttles down the gauntlet of lust
Like a clockwork mouse. Safe home at last
She mends her socks with holes, shirts that are torn

For father and brother, and a delicate supper cooks:
Goes to bed early, shuts out with the light   10
Her thirty years, and lies with buttocks tight,
Hiding her lovely eyes until day break.

1. Comment on the phrase in line 2, *the terrible wound.* Would the speaker himself regard the offense as "terrible"?
2. What traits has the secretary in common with *a starling* (line 3) and *a clockwork mouse* (line 7)?
3. Does the poet express one attitude toward his subject or is the tone of his poem a mingling of more than one ? Explain, referring to particulars in the poem.

John Berryman (1914–1972)

LIFE, FRIENDS, IS BORING. WE MUST NOT SAY SO   1964

Life, friends, is boring. We must not say so.
After all, the sky flashes, the great sea yearns,
we ourselves flash and yearn,
and moreover my mother told me as a boy
(repeatingly) "Ever to confess you're bored   5
means you have no

Inner Resources." I conclude now I have no
inner resources, because I am heavy bored.
Peoples bore me,
literature bores me, especially great literature,   10
Henry bores me, with his plights & gripes
as bad as achilles,

who loves people and valiant art, which bores me.
And the tranquil hills, & gin, look like a drag
and somehow a dog   15
has taken itself & its tail considerably away
into mountains or sea or sky, leaving
behind: me, wag.

QUESTIONS

1. Henry (line 11) is the central figure of Berryman's *77 Dream Songs.* Achilles (line 12), Greek hero of the Trojan war, was portrayed by Shakespeare as a sulking malcontent. Is a comparison of Henry, a rather ordinary American citizen, to Achilles likely to result in a heightening of Henry's importance or in a sense of ironic discrepancy? Discuss.
2. What is confused or self-contradictory in the precept "Ever to confess you're bored means you have no Inner Resources"?
3. What could the poet be trying to indicate by capitalizing *Inner Resources* in line 7 but not in line 8? By writing *achilles* with a small letter?
4. In line 14, what discrepancy do you find between the phrases *the tranquil hills* and *a drag*?
5. In the last line, what double meaning is there in the word *wag*?
6. True or false? "In comparing 'ourselves' to the sky and to the 'great sea,' the

speaker takes the attitude that he and his readers have dignity and grandeur, their emotions being as powerful as lightningbolts and tides." Do you find this paraphrase consistent or inconsistent with the tone of the poem? Why?

EXERCISE: *Telling Tone*

Here are two radically different poems on a similar subject. Try stating the theme of each poem in your own words. How is tone (the speaker's attitude) different in the two poems?

Richard Lovelace (1618–1658)

To Lucasta   1649

On Going to the Wars

Tell me not, Sweet, I am unkind
   That from the nunnery
Of thy chaste breast and quiet mind,
   To war and arms I fly.

True, a new mistress now I chase,   5
   The first foe in the field;
And with a stronger faith embrace
   A sword, a horse, a shield.

Yet this inconstancy is such
   As you too shall adore;   10
I could not love thee, Dear, so much,
   Loved I not Honor more.

Wilfred Owen (1893–1918)

Dulce et Decorum Est   1920

Bent double, like old beggars under sacks,
Knock-kneed, coughing like hags, we cursed through sludge,
Till on the haunting flares we turned our backs
And towards our distant rest began to trudge.
Men marched asleep. Many had lost their boots   5
But limped on, blood-shod. All went lame; all blind;
Drunk with fatigue; deaf even to the hoots
Of tired, outstripped Five-Nines° that dropped behind.   *gas-shells*

Gas! Gas! Quick, boys! — An ecstasy of fumbling,
Fitting the clumsy helmets just in time;   10
But someone still was yelling out and stumbling
And flound'ring like a man in fire or lime . . .

Dim, through the misty panes and thick green light,
As under a green sea, I saw him drowning.
In all my dreams, before my helpless sight,   15
He plunges at me, guttering, choking, drowning.

If in some smothering dreams you too could pace
Behind the wagon that we flung him in,
And watch the white eyes writhing in his face,
His hanging face, like a devil's sick of sin;   20
If you could hear, at every jolt, the blood
Come gargling from the froth-corrupted lungs,
Obscene as cancer, bitter as the cud
Of vile, incurable sores on innocent tongues, —
My friend, you would not tell with such high zest   25
To children ardent for some desperate glory,
The old Lie: Dulce et decorum est
Pro patria mori.

DULCE ET DECORUM EST. A British infantry officer in World War I, Owen was killed in action. 17. *you too:* Some manuscript versions of this poem carry the dedication "To Jessie
Pope" (a writer of patriotic verse) or "To a certain Poetess." 27–28. *Dulce et . . . mori:* a quotation from the Latin poet Horace, "It is sweet and fitting to die for one's country."

James Stephens (1882–1950)

A GLASS OF BEER   1918

The lanky hank of a she in the inn over there
Nearly killed me for asking the loan of a glass of beer;
May the devil grip the whey-faced slut by the hair,
And beat bad manners out of her skin for a year.

That parboiled ape, with the toughest jaw you will see   5
On virtue's path, and a voice that would rasp the dead,
Came roaring and raging the minute she looked at me,
And threw me out of the house on the back of my head!

If I asked her master he'd give me a cask a day;
But she, with the beer at hand, not a gill° would arrange!   *quarter-pint* 10
May she marry a ghost and bear him a kitten, and may
The High King of Glory permit her to get the mange.

QUESTIONS

1. Who do you take to be the speaker? Is it the poet? The speaker may be angry,
   but what is the tone of this poem?
2. Would you agree with a commentator who said, "To berate anyone in truly
   memorable language is practically a lost art in America"? How well does the
   speaker (an Irishman) succeed? Which of his epithets and curses strike you
   as particularly imaginative?

Jonathan Swift (1667–1745)

On Stella's Birthday

(1718–1719)

Stella this day is thirty-four
(We shan't dispute a year or more) —
However, Stella, be not troubled,
Although thy size and years are doubled,
Since first I saw thee at sixteen, 5
The brightest virgin on the green,
So little is thy form declined,
Made up so largely in thy mind.
Oh, would it please the gods, to split
Thy beauty, size, and years, and wit, 10
No age could furnish out a pair
Of nymphs so graceful, wise, and fair,
With half the luster of your eyes,
With half your wit, your years, and size.
And then, before it grew too late, 15
How should I beg of gentle Fate
(That either nymph might have her swain)
To split my worship too in twain.

On Stella's Birthday. For many years Swift made an annual birthday gift of a poem to his close friend Mrs. Esther Johnson, the degree of whose nearness to the proud and lonely Swift remains an enigma to biographers. 18. *my worship:* as Dean of St. Patrick's in Dublin, Swift was addressed as "Your Worship."

Questions

1. If you were Stella, would you be amused or insulted by the poet's references to your *size?*
2. According to Swift in lines 7–8, what has compensated Stella for what the years have taken away?
3. Comment on the last four lines. Does Swift exempt himself from growing old?
4. How would you describe the tone of this poem? Offensive (like the speaker's complaints in "A Glass of Beer")? Playfully tender? Sad over Stella's growing fat and old?

William Blake (1757–1827)

The Chimney Sweeper

1789

When my mother died I was very young,
And my father sold me while yet my tongue
Could scarcely cry " 'weep! 'weep! 'weep! 'weep!"
So your chimneys I sweep, and in soot I sleep.

There's little Tom Dacre, who cried when his head,   5
That curled like a lamb's back, was shaved: so I said
"Hush, Tom! never mind it, for when your head's bare
You know that the soot cannot spoil your white hair."

And so he was quiet, and that very night,
As Tom was a-sleeping, he had such a sight!   10
That thousands of sweepers, Dick, Joe, Ned, and Jack,
Were all of them locked up in coffins of black.

And by came an Angel who had a bright key,
And he opened the coffins and set them all free;
Then down a green plain leaping, laughing, they run,   15
And wash in a river, and shine in the sun.

Then naked and white, all their bags left behind,
They rise upon clouds and sport in the wind;
And the Angel told Tom, if he'd be a good boy,
He'd have God for his father, and never want joy.   20

And so Tom awoke; and we rose in the dark,
And got with our bags and our brushes to work.
Though the morning was cold, Tom was happy and warm;
So if all do their duty they need not fear harm.

QUESTIONS

1. What does Blake's poem reveal about conditions of life in the London of his day?
2. What does this poem have in common with "The Golf Links" (page 23)?
3. How does "The Chimney Sweeper" resemble "A Sick Child" (page 15)? In what ways does Blake's poem seem much different?
4. Sum up your impressions of the speaker's character. What does he say and do that displays it to us?
5. What pun do you find in line 3? Is its effect comic or serious?
6. In Tom Dacre's dream (lines 11–20), what wishes come true? Do you understand them to be the wishes of the chimney sweepers, of the poet, or of both?
7. In the last line, what is ironic in the speaker's assurance that the dutiful *need not fear harm*? What irony is there in his urging all to *do their duty*? (Who have failed in their duty to *him*?)
8. What is the tone of Blake's poem? Angry? Hopeful? Sorrowful? Compassionate? (Don't feel obliged to sum it up in a single word.)

INFORMATION FOR EXPERIMENT: *Reading with and without Biography*

THE RED WHEELBARROW (p. 18). Dr. Williams's poem reportedly contains a personal experience: he was gazing from the window of the house where one of his patients, a small girl, lay suspended between life and death. (This account, from the director of the public library in Williams's native Rutherford, N.J., is given by Geri M. Rhodes in "The Paterson Metaphor in William Carlos Williams' *Paterson*," master's essay, Tufts University, June 1965.)

3 Words

LITERAL MEANING:
WHAT A POEM SAYS FIRST

Although successful as a painter, Edgar Degas struggled to produce sonnets, and found poetry discouragingly hard to write. To his friend, the poet Stéphane Mallarmé, he complained, "What a business! My whole day gone on a blasted sonnet, without getting an inch further . . . and it isn't ideas I'm short of . . . I'm full of them, I've got too many . . ."

"But Degas," said Mallarmé, "you can't make a poem with ideas — you make it with *words!*"[1]

Like the celebrated painter, some people assume that all it takes to make a poem is a bright idea. Poems state ideas, to be sure, and sometimes the ideas are invaluable; and yet the most impressive idea in the world will not make a poem unless its words are selected and arranged with loving art. Some poets take great pains to find the right word. Unable to fill a two-syllable gap in an unfinished line that went, "The seal's wide — — gaze toward Paradise," Hart Crane paged through an unabridged dictionary. When he reached *S*, he found the object of his quest in *spindrift:* "spray skimmed from the sea by a strong wind." The word is exact and memorable. Any word can be the right word, however, if artfully chosen and placed. It may be a word as ordinary as *from.* Consider the difference between "The sedge is withered *on* the lake" (a misquotation of a line by Keats) and "The sedge is withered *from* the lake" (what Keats in fact wrote). Keats's original line suggests, as the altered line doesn't, that because the sedge (a growth of grasslike plants) has withered *from* the lake, it has withdrawn mysteriously.

In reading a poem, some people assume that its words can be skipped over rapidly, and they try to leap at once to the poem's general theme. It is as if they fear being thought clods unless they can find huge ideas in the poem (whether or not there are any). Such readers often ig-

---

[1] Paul Valéry, *Degas . . . Manet . . . Morisot,* translated by David Paul (New York: Pantheon, 1960), page 62.

nore the literal meanings of words: the ordinary, matter-of-fact sense to be found in a dictionary. (As you will see in Chapter Five, "Saying and Suggesting," words possess not only dictionary meanings — **denotations** — but also many associations and suggestions — **connotations**.) Consider the following poem and see what you make of it.

William Carlos Williams (1883–1963)
THIS IS JUST TO SAY   1934

I have eaten
the plums
that were in
the icebox
and which   5
you were probably
saving
for breakfast

Forgive me
they were delicious   10
so sweet
and so cold

Some readers distrust a poem so simple and candid. They think, "What's wrong with me? There has to be more to it than this!" But poems seldom are puzzles in need of solutions. We can begin by accepting the poet's statements, without suspecting him of trying to hoodwink us. On later reflection, of course, we might possibly decide that the poet is playfully teasing or being ironic; but Williams gives us no reason to think that. There seems no need to look beyond the literal sense of his words, no profit in speculating that the plums symbolize worldly joys and that the icebox stands for the universe. Clearly, a reader who held such a grand theory would have overlooked (in eagerness to find a significant idea) the plain truth that the poet makes clear to us: that ice-cold plums are a joy to taste, especially if one knows they'll be missed the next morning.

To be sure, Williams's small poem is simpler than most poems are; and yet in reading any poem, no matter how complicated, you will do well to reach slowly and reluctantly for generalizations. An adept reader of poetry reads with open mind — with (in Richard L. McGuire's phrase) "as much innocence as he can muster." For in order to experience a poem, you first have to pay attention to its words; and only if you see what the words are saying are you likely to come to the poem's true theme. Recall Housman's "Loveliest of trees" (page 3): a poem that contains a message (how rapidly life passes, how vital it is to make the most of every spring). Yet before you can realize that theme, you have to notice the color, the quantity, and the weight (*hung with bloom*) of Housman's imagined cherry blossoms.

Poets often strive for words that point to physical details and solid objects. They may do so even when speaking of an abstract idea:

> Beauty is but a flower
> Which wrinkles will devour;
> Brightness falls from the air,
> Queens have died young and fair,
> Dust hath closed Helen's eye.
> I am sick, I must die:
>> Lord, have mercy on us!

In these lines by Thomas Nashe, the abstraction *beauty* has grown petals that shrivel. Brightness may be a general name for light, but Nashe succeeds in giving it the weight of a falling body.

If a poem reads *daffodils* instead of *vegetation, diaper years* instead of *infancy,* and *eighty-four* instead of *numerous,* we call its **diction** — its choice of words — particular and concrete, rather than general and abstract. In an apt criticism, William Butler Yeats once took to task the poems of W. E. Henley for being "abstract, as even an actor's movement can be when the thought of doing is plainer to his mind than the doing itself: the straight line from cup to lip, let us say, more plain than the hand's own sensation weighed down by that heavy spillable cup."[2] To convey the sense of that heavy spillable cup was to Yeats a goal, one that surely he attained in "Among School Children" by describing a woman's stark face: "Hollow of cheek as though it drank the wind / And took a mess of shadows for its meat." A more abstract-minded poet might have written "Her hollow cheek and wasted, hungry look." Ezra Pound gave a famous piece of advice to his fellow poets: "Go in fear of abstractions." This is not to say that a poet cannot employ abstract words, nor that all poems have to be about physical things. Much of T. S. Eliot's *Four Quartets* is concerned with time, eternity, history, language, reality, and other things that cannot be handled. But Eliot, however high he may soar for a general view, keeps returning to earth. He makes us aware of *things,* as Thomas Carlyle said a good writer has to do: "Wonderful it is with what cutting words, now and then, he severs asunder the confusion; shears it down, were it furlongs deep, into the true center of the matter; and there not only hits the nail on the head, but with crushing force smites it home, and buries it." Like other good

---

[2] *The Trembling of the Veil* (1922), reprinted in *The Autobiography of William Butler Yeats* (New York: Macmillan, 1953), p. 177.

writers, good poets remind us of that smitten nail and that spillable cup. "Perhaps indeed," wrote Walt Whitman in *Specimen Days*, "the efforts of the true poets, founders, religions, literatures, all ages, have been, and ever will be, our time and times to come, essentially the same — to bring people back from their persistent strayings and sickly abstractions, to the costless, average, divine, original concrete."

Knute Skinner (b. 1929)

THE COLD IRISH EARTH   1968

I shudder thinking
of the cold Irish earth.
The firelighter flares
in the kitchen range,
but a cold rain falls   5
all around Liscannor.
It scours the Hag's face
on the Cliffs of Moher.
It runs through the bog
and seeps up into mounds   10
of abandoned turf.
My neighbor's fields are chopped
by the feet of cattle
sinking down to the roots
of winter grass.   15
That coat hangs drying now
by the kitchen range,
but down at Healy's cross
the Killaspuglonane graveyard
is wet to the bone.   20

QUESTIONS

1. To what familiar phrase does Skinner's poem lend fresh meaning? What is its usual meaning?
2. What details in the poem show us that, in using the old phrase, Skinner literally means what he says?

Henry Taylor (b. 1942)

RIDING A ONE-EYED HORSE   1975

One side of his world is always missing.
You may give it a casual wave of the hand
or rub it with your shoulder as you pass,
but nothing on his blind side ever happens.

Hundreds of trees slip past him into darkness,   5
drifting into a hollow hemisphere
whose sounds you will have to try to explain.
Your legs will tell him not to be afraid

if you learn never to lie. Do not forget
to turn his head and let what comes come seen: 10
he will jump the fences he has to if you swing
toward them from the side that he can see

and hold his good eye straight. The heavy dark
will stay beside you always; let him learn
to lean against it. It will steady him   15
and see you safely through diminished fields.

QUESTION

Do you read this poem as a fable in which the horse stands for something, or as
a set of instructions for riding a one-eyed horse?

Robert Graves (b. 1895)

DOWN, WANTON, DOWN!   1933

Down, wanton, down! Have you no shame
That at the whisper of Love's name,
Or Beauty's, presto! up you raise
Your angry head and stand at gaze?

Poor bombard-captain, sworn to reach   5
The ravelin and effect a breach —
Indifferent what you storm or why,
So be that in the breach you die!

Love may be blind, but Love at least
Knows what is man and what mere beast;   10
Or Beauty wayward, but requires
More delicacy from her squires.

Tell me, my witless, whose one boast
Could be your staunchness at the post,
When were you made a man of parts   15
To think fine and profess the arts?

Will many-gifted Beauty come
Bowing to your bald rule of thumb,
Or Love swear loyalty to your crown?
Be gone, have done! Down, wanton, down!   20

DOWN, WANTON, DOWN! 5. *bombard-captain:* officer in charge of a bombard, an early type of
cannon that hurled stones. 6. *ravelin:* fortification with two faces that meet in a protruding
angle. *effect a breach:* break an opening through (a fortification). 15. *man of parts:* man of
talent or ability.

1. How do you define a wanton?
2. What wanton does the poet address?
3. Explain the comparison drawn in the second stanza.
4. In line 14, how many meanings do you find in *staunchness at the post*?
5. Explain any other puns you find in lines 15-19.
6. Do you take this to be a cynical poem making fun of Love and Beauty, or is Graves making fun of stupid, animal lust?

Peter Davison (b. 1928)

THE LAST WORD   1970

When I saw your head bow, I knew I had beaten you.
You shed no tears — not near me — but held your neck
Bare for the blow I had been too frightened
Ever to deliver, even in words. And now,
In spite of me, plummeting it came.   5
Frozen we both waited for its fall.

Most of what you gave me I have forgotten
With my mind but taken into my body,
But this I remember well: the bones of your neck
And the strain in my shoulders as I heaved up that huge   10
Double blade and snapped my wrists to swing
The handle down and hear the axe's edge
Nick through your flesh and creak into the block.

QUESTIONS

1. "The Last Word" stands fourth in a series titled "Four Love Poems." Sum up what happens in this poem. Do you take this to be *merely* a literal account of an execution? Explain the comparison.
2. Which words embody concrete things and show us physical actions? Which words have sounds that especially contribute to the poem's effectiveness?

David B. Axelrod (b. 1943)

ONCE IN A WHILE A PROTEST POEM   1976

Over and over again the papers print
the dried-out tit of an African woman
holding her starving child. Over
and over, cropping it each time to one
prominent, withered tit, the feeble   5
infant face. Over and over to toughen
us, teach us to ignore the foam turned
dusty powder on the infant's lips,
the mother's sunken face (is cropped)
and filthy dress. The tit remains;   10

the tit held out for everyone to see,
reminding us only that we are not so hungry
ogling the tit, admiring it and in our
living rooms, making it a symbol of starving
millions; our sympathy as real as silicone.   15

QUESTIONS

1. Why is the last word in this poem especially meaningful?
2. What does the poet protest?

Miller Williams (b. 1930)

ON THE SYMBOLIC CONSIDERATION OF HANDS
AND THE SIGNIFICANCE OF DEATH   1973

Watch people stop by bodies in funeral homes.
You know their eyes will fix on the hands and they do.
Because a hand that has no desire to make
a fist again or cut bread or lay stones
is among those things most difficult to believe.
It is believed for a fact by a very few
old nuns in France who carve beads out of knuckle bones.

QUESTIONS

1. Why, according to the poet, is it hard for us to believe in the literal fact of death? Why isn't such belief a problem for the nuns?
2. From just the title of the poem, would you expect the poem to be written in plain, simple language, or in very abstract, general language? In what kind of language *is* it written?
3. What possible reason could the poet have for choosing such a title? (Besides being a poet, Miller Williams is a critic and teacher of poetry. He probably knows many readers and students of poetry who expect poems *necessarily* to deal in symbolic considerations and large significances.)

John Donne (1572–1631)

BATTER MY HEART, THREE-PERSONED GOD, FOR YOU   1633

Batter my heart, three-personed God, for You
As yet but knock, breathe, shine, and seek to mend.
That I may rise and stand, o'erthrow me, and bend
Your force to break, blow, burn, and make me new.
I, like an usurped town to another due,   5
Labor to admit You, but Oh! to no end.
Reason, Your viceroy in me, me should defend,
But is captived, and proves weak or untrue.

Yet dearly I love You, and would be lovèd fain,
But am betrothed unto Your enemy;   10
Divorce me, untie or break that knot again;
Take me to You, imprison me, for I,
Except You enthrall me, never shall be free,
Nor ever chaste, except You ravish me.

QUESTIONS

1. In the last line of this sonnet, to what does Donne compare the onslaught of God's love? Do you think the poem weakened by the poet's comparing a spiritual experience to something so grossly carnal? Discuss.
2. Explain the seeming contradiction in the last line: in what sense can a ravished person be *chaste*? Explain the seeming contradictions in lines 3–4 and 12–13: how can a person thrown down and destroyed be enabled to *rise and stand*; an imprisoned person be *free*?
3. In lines 5–6 the speaker compares himself to a *usurped town* trying to throw off its conqueror by admitting an army of liberation. Who is the "usurper" in this comparison?
4. Explain the comparison of *Reason* to a *viceroy* (lines 7–8).
5. Sum up in your own words the message of Donne's poem. In stating its theme, did you have to read the poem for literal meanings, figurative comparisons, or both?

THE VALUE OF A DICTIONARY

If a poet troubles to seek out the best words available, the least we can do is to find out what the words mean. The dictionary is a firm ally in reading poems; if the poems are more than a century old, it is indispensable. Meanings change. When the Elizabethan poet George Gascoigne wrote, "O Abraham's brats, O brood of blessed seed," the word *brats* implied neither irritation nor contempt. When in the seventeenth century Andrew Marvell imagined two lovers' "vegetable love," he referred to a vegetative or growing love, not one resembling a lettuce. And when King George III called a building an "awful artificial spectacle," he was not condemning it but praising it as an awe-inspiring work of art.

In reading poetry, there is nothing to be done about this inevitable tendency of language except to watch out for it. If you suspect that a word has shifted in meaning over the years, most standard desk dictionaries will be helpful, an unabridged dictionary more helpful yet, and most helpful of all the *Oxford English Dictionary (OED)*, which gives, for each definition, successive examples of the word's written use down through the past thousand years. You need not feel a grim obligation to keep interrupting a poem in order to rummage the dictionary; but if the poem is worth reading very closely, you may wish any aid you can find.

One of the valuable services of poetry is to recall for us the concrete, physical sense that certain words once had, but since have lost. As the English critic H. Coombes has remarked in *Literature and Criticism,*

> We use a word like *powerful* without feeling that it is really "power-full." We do not seem today to taste the full flavor of words as we feel that Falstaff (and Shakespeare, and probably his audience) tasted them when he was applauding the virtues of "good sherris-sack," which makes the brain "apprehensive, quick, forgetive, full of nimble, fiery, and delectable shapes." And being less aware of the life and substantiality of words, we are probably less aware of the things . . . that these words stand for.

"Every word which is used to express a moral or intellectual fact," said Emerson in *The Conduct of Life,* "if traced to its root, is found to be borrowed from some material appearance. *Right* means straight; *wrong* means twisted. *Spirit* primarily means wind; *transgression,* the crossing of a line; *supercilious,* the raising of an eyebrow." Browse in a dictionary and you will discover such original concretenesses. These are revealed in your dictionary's etymologies, or brief notes on the derivation of words, given in most dictionaries near the beginning of an entry on a word; in some dictionaries, at the end of the entry. Look up *squirrel,* for instance, and you will find it comes from two Greek words meaning "shadow-tail." For another example of a common word that originally contained a poetic metaphor, look up the origin of the word *daisy.*

EXPERIMENT: *Seeing Words' Origins*

Much of the effect of the following poem depends upon our awareness of the precision with which the poet has selected his words. We can better see this by knowing their derivations. For instance, *potpourri* comes from French: *pot* plus *pourri.* What do these words mean? (If you do not know French, look up the etymology of the word in a dictionary.) Look up the definitions and etymologies of *revenance, circumstance, inspiration, conceptual, commotion, cordial,* and *azure;* and try to state the meanings these words have in Wilbur's poem.

Richard Wilbur (b. 1921)

IN THE ELEGY SEASON   1950

Haze, char, and the weather of All Souls':
A giant absence mopes upon the trees:
Leaves cast in casual potpourris
Whisper their scents from pits and cellar-holes.

Or brewed in gulleys, steeped in wells, they spend   5
In chilly steam their last aromas, yield

From shallow hells a revenance of field
And orchard air. And now the envious mind

Which could not hold the summer in my head
While bounded by that blazing circumstance 10
Parades these barrens in a golden trance,
Remembering the wealthy season dead,

And by an autumn inspiration makes
A summer all its own. Green boughs arise
Through all the boundless backward of the eyes, 15
And the soul bathes in warm conceptual lakes.

Less proud than this, my body leans an ear
Past cold and colder weather after wings'
Soft commotion, the sudden race of springs,
The goddess' tread heard on the dayward stair, 20

Longs for the brush of the freighted air, for smells
Of grass and cordial lilac, for the sight
Of green leaves building into the light
And azure water hoisting out of wells.

An **allusion** is an indirect reference to any person, place, or thing
— fictitious, historical, or actual. Sometimes, to understand an allusion
in a poem, we have to find out something we didn't know before. But
usually the poet asks of us only common knowledge. When Edgar Allan
Poe refers to "the glory that was Greece / And the grandeur that was
Rome," he assumes that we have heard of those places, and that we will
understand his allusion to the cultural achievement of those nations
(implicit in *glory* and *grandeur*).

Allusions not only enrich the meaning of a poem, they also save
space. In "The Love Song of J. Alfred Prufrock" (page 336), T. S. Eliot, by
giving a brief introductory quotation from the speech of a damned soul
in Dante's *Inferno,* is able to suggest that his poem will be the confession of a soul in torment, who sees no chance of escape.

Often in reading a poem you will meet a name you don't recognize, on which the meaning of a line (or perhaps a whole poem) seems
to depend. In this book, most such unfamiliar references and allusions
are glossed or footnoted, but when you venture out on your own in
reading poems, you may find yourself needlessly perplexed unless you
look up such names, the way you look up any other words. Unless the
name is one that the poet made up, you will probably find it in one of
the larger desk dictionaries, such as *Webster's New Collegiate Dictionary,*
The American Heritage Dictionary, or *The American College Dictionary.* If
you don't solve your problem there, try an encyclopedia, a world atlas,
or *The New Century Cyclopedia of Names.*

Some allusions are quotations from other poems. In L. E. Sissman's "In and Out: A Home Away from Home," the narrator, a male college student, describes his sleeping love,

> This Sally now does like a garment wear
> The beauty of the evening; silent, bare,
> Hips, shoulders, arms, tresses, and temples lie.

(For the source of these lines, see Wordsworth's "Composed upon Westminster Bridge," page 414.)

EXERCISE: *Catching Allusions*

From your knowledge, supplemented by a dictionary or other reference work if need be, explain the allusions in the following poems.

Cid Corman (b. 1924)

THE TORTOISE   1964

Always to want to
go back, to correct
an error, ease a

guilt, see how a friend
is doing. And yet   5
one doesnt, except

in memory, in
dreams. The land remains
desolate. Always

the feeling is of   10
terrible slowness
overtaking haste.

J. V. Cunningham (b. 1911)

FRIEND, ON THIS SCAFFOLD THOMAS MORE LIES DEAD   1960

Friend, on this scaffold Thomas More lies dead
Who would not cut the Body from the Head.

Herman Melville (1819–1891)

THE PORTENT   (1859)

Hanging from the beam,
  Slowly swaying (such the law),
Gaunt the shadow on your green,
  Shenandoah!

The cut is on the crown   5
    (Lo, John Brown),
And the stabs shall heal no more.

Hidden in the cap
    Is the anguish none can draw;
So your future veils its face,   10
    Shenandoah!

But the streaming beard is shown
    (Weird John Brown),
The meteor of the war.

John Clare (1793–1864)

MOUSE'S NEST   (about 1835)

I found a ball of grass among the hay
And progged it as I passed and went away;
And when I looked I fancied something stirred,
And turned again and hoped to catch the bird—
When out an old mouse bolted in the wheats   5
With all her young ones hanging at her teats;
She looked so odd and so grotesque to me,
I ran and wondered what the thing could be,
And pushed the knapweed bunches where I stood;
Then the mouse hurried from the craking° brood.   *crying* 10
The young ones squeaked, and as I went away
She found her nest again among the hay.
The water o'er the pebbles scarce could run
And broad old cesspools glittered in the sun.

QUESTIONS

1. "To prog" (line 2) means "to poke about for food, to forage." In what ways
   does this word fit more exactly here than *prodded, touched,* or *searched*?
2. Is *craking* (line 10) better than *crying*? Which word better fits the poem? Why?
3. What connections do you find between the last two lines and the rest of the
   poem? To what are water that *scarce could run* and *broad old cesspools* (lines 13
   and 14) likened?

Lewis Carroll
[Charles Lutwidge Dodgson] (1832–1898)

JABBERWOCKY   1871

'Twas brillig, and the slithy toves
    Did gyre and gimble in the wabe:
All mimsy were the borogoves,
    And the mome raths outgrabe.

"Beware the Jabberwock, my son!   5
    The jaws that bite, the claws that catch!
Beware the Jubjub bird, and shun
    The frumious Bandersnatch!"

He took his vorpal sword in hand;
    Long time the manxome foe he sought—   10
So rested he by the Tumtum tree
    And stood awhile in thought.

And, as in uffish thought he stood,
    The Jabberwock, with eyes of flame,
Came whiffling through the tulgey wood,   15
    And burbled as it came!

One, two! One, two! And through and through
    The vorpal blade went snicker-snack!
He left it dead, and with its head
    He went galumphing back.   20

"And hast thou slain the Jabberwock?
    Come to my arms, my beamish boy!
O frabjous day! Callooh, Callay!"
    He chortled in his joy.

'Twas brillig, and the slithy toves   25
    Did gyre and gimble in the wabe:
All mimsy were the borogoves,
    And the mome raths outgrabe.

Questions

1. Look up *chortled* (line 24) in your dictionary and find out its definition and
   origin.
2. In *Through the Looking-Glass,* Alice seeks the aid of Humpty Dumpty to deci-
   pher the meaning of this nonsense poem. *"Brillig,"* he explains, "means four
   o'clock in the afternoon—the time when you begin *broiling* things for dinner." Does *brillig* sound like any other familiar word?
3. *"Slithy,"* the explanation goes on, "means 'lithe and slimy.' 'Lithe' is the
   same as 'active.' You see it's like a portmanteau—there are two meanings
   packed up into one word." *Mimsy* is supposed to pack together both
   "flimsy" and "miserable." In the rest of the poem, what other portmanteau—
   or packed suitcase—words can you find?

Wallace Stevens (1879–1955)

Metamorphosis   1942

Yillow, yillow, yillow,
Old worm, my pretty quirk,
How the wind spells out
Sep - tem - ber. . . .

Summer is in bones. 5
Cock-robin's at Caracas.
Make o, make o, make o,
Oto - otu - bre.

And the rude leaves fall.
The rain falls. The sky 10
Falls and lies with the worms.
The street lamps

Are those that have been hanged.
Dangling in an illogical
To and to and fro 15
Fro Niz - nil - imbo.

QUESTIONS

1. Explain the title. Of the several meanings of *metamorphosis* given in a dictionary, which best applies to the process that Stevens sees in the natural world?
2. What metamorphosis is also taking place in the *language* of the poem? How does it continue from line 4 to line 8 to line 16?
3. In the last line, which may recall the thickening drone of a speaker lapsing into sleep, *Niz - nil - imbo* seems not only a pun on the name of a month, but also a portmanteau word into which at least two familiar words are packed. Say it aloud. What are they?
4. What dictionary definitions of the word *quirk* seem relevant to line 2? How can a worm be a quirk? What else in this poem seems quirky?

J. V. Cunningham (b. 1911)

MOTTO FOR A SUN DIAL   1947

I who by day am function of the light
Am constant and invariant by night.

QUESTION

In mathematics, what do the words *function* and *constant* mean?

WORD CHOICE AND WORD ORDER

Even if Samuel Johnson's famous *Dictionary* of 1755 had been as thick as Webster's unabridged, an eighteenth-century poet searching through it for words to use would have had a narrower choice. For in English literature of the **neoclassical period** or **Augustan age**—that period from about 1660 into the late eighteenth century—many poets subscribed to a belief in **poetic diction:** "A system of words," said Dr. Johnson, "refined from the grossness of domestic use." The system admitted into a serious poem only certain words and subjects, excluding others as violations of **decorum** (propriety). Accordingly such common words as *rat, cheese, big, sneeze,* and *elbow,* although admissible to satire, were thought inconsistent with the loftiness of tragedy, epic, ode, and elegy. Dr. Johnson's biographer, James Boswell, tells how a poet writing an epic reconsidered the word "rats" and instead wrote "the whiskered vermin race." Johnson himself objected to Lady Macbeth's allusion to her "keen knife," saying that "we do not immediately conceive that any crime of importance is to be committed with a knife; or who does not, at last, from the long habit of connecting a knife with sordid offices, feel aversion rather than terror?" Probably Johnson was here the victim of his age, and Shakespeare was right, but Johnson in one of his assumptions was right too: there are inappropriate words as well as appropriate ones.

Neoclassical poets chose their classical models more often from Roman writers than from Greek, as their diction suggests by the frequency of Latin derivatives. For example, a *net,* according to Dr. Johnson's dictionary, is "any thing reticulated or decussated, at equal distances, with interstices between the intersections." In company with Latinate words often appeared fixed combinations of adjective and noun ("finny prey" for "fish"), poetic names (a song to a lady named Molly might rechristen her Parthenia), and allusions to classical mythology. Neoclassical poetic diction was evidently being abused when, instead of saying "uncork the bottle," a poet could write,

> Apply thine engine to the spongy door,
> Set *Bacchus* from his glassy prison free,

in some bad lines ridiculed by Alexander Pope in *Peri Bathous, or, Of the Art of Sinking in Poetry.*

Not all poetic diction is excess baggage. To a reader who knew at first hand both living sheep and the pastoral poems of Virgil — as most readers nowadays do not — such a fixed phrase as "the fleecy care," which seems stilted to us, conveyed pleasurable associations. But "fleecy care" was more than a highfalutin way of saying "sheep"; as one scholar has pointed out, "when they wished, our poets could say 'sheep' as clearly and as often as anybody else. In the first place, 'fleecy' drew attention to wool, and demanded the appropriate visual image of sheep; for aural imagery the poets would refer to 'the bleating kind'; it all depended upon what was happening in the poem."[3]

Other poets have found some special kind of poetic language valuable: Anglo-Saxon poets, with their standard figures of speech, or **kennings** ("whale-road" for the sea, "ring-giver" for a ruler); makers of folk ballads who, no less than neoclassicists, love fixed epithet-noun combi-

[3] Bonamy Dobrée, *English Literature in the Early Eighteenth Century, 1700–1740* (New York: Oxford University Press, 1959), p. 161.

nations ("milk-white steed," "blood-red wine," "steel-driving man");
and Edmund Spenser, whose example made popular the adjective ending in -y (*fleecy, grassy, milky*).

When Wordsworth, in his Preface to *Lyrical Ballads*, asserted that "the language really spoken by men," especially by humble rustics, is plainer, more emphatic, and conveys "elementary feelings . . . in a state of greater simplicity," he was, in effect, advocating a new poetic diction. Wordsworth's ideas invited freshness into English poetry and, by admitting words that neoclassical poets would have called "low" ("His poor old *ankles* swell"), helped rid poets of the fear of being thought foolish for mentioning a commonplace.

This theory of the superiority of rural diction was, as Coleridge pointed out, hard to adhere to, and, in practice, Wordsworth was occasionally to write a language as Latinate and citified as these lines on yew trees:

> Huge trunks! — and each particular trunk a growth
> Of intertwisted fibers serpentine
> Up-coiling, and inveterately convolved . . .

Language so Latinate sounds pedantic to us, especially the phrase *inveterately convolved*. In fact, some poets, notably Gerard Manley Hopkins, have subscribed to the view that English words derived from Anglo-Saxon (Old English) have more force and flavor than their Latin equivalents. *Kingly*, one may feel, has more power than *regal*. One argument for this view is that so many words of Old English origin — *man, wife, child, house, eat, drink, sleep* — are basic to our living speech. It may be true that a language closer to Old English is particularly fit for rendering abstract notions concretely — as does the memorable title of a medieval work of piety, the *Ayenbite of Inwit* ("again-bite of inner wit" or "remorse of conscience"). And yet this view, if accepted at all, must be accepted with reservations. Some words of Latin origin carry meanings both precise and physical. In the King James Bible is the admonition, "See then that ye walk circumspectly, not as fools, but as wise" (Ephesians 5:15). To be *circumspect* (a word from two Latin roots meaning "to look" and "around") is to be watchful on all sides — a meaning altogether lost in a modernized wording of the passage once printed on a subway poster for a Bible society: "Be careful how you live, not thoughtlessly but thoughtfully."

When E. E. Cummings begins a poem, "mr youse needn't be so spry / concernin questions arty," we recognized another kind of diction available to poetry: **vulgate** (speech not much affected by schooling). Handbooks of grammar sometimes distinguish various **levels of usage.** A sort of ladder is imagined, on whose rungs words, phrases, and sentences may be ranked in an ascending order of formality, from the curses of an illiterate thug to the commencement-day address of a doctor of divinity. These levels range from vulgate through **colloquial** (the casual conversation or informal writing of literate people) and **general English** (most literate speech and writing, more studied than colloquial but not pretentious), up to **formal English** (the impersonal language of educated persons, usually only written, possibly spoken on dignified occasions). Recently, however, lexicographers have been shunning such labels. The designation *colloquial* has been expelled (*bounced* would be colloquial; *trun out*, vulgate) from *Webster's Third New International Dictionary* on the grounds that "it is impossible to know whether a word out of context is colloquial or not" and that the diction of Americans nowadays is more fluid than the labels suggest. Aware that we are being unscientific, we may find the labels useful. They may help roughly to describe what happens when, as in the following poem, a poet shifts from one level of usage to another. This poem employs, incidentally, a colloquial device throughout: omitting the subjects of sentences. In keeping the characters straight, it may be helpful to fill in the speaker for each *said* and for the verbs *saw* and *ducked* (lines 9 and 10).

Josephine Miles (b. 1911)

REASON   1955

Said, Pull her up a bit will you, Mac, I want to unload there.
Said, Pull her up my rear end, first come first serve.
Said, Give her the gun, Bud, he needs a taste of his own bumper.

Then the usher came out and got into the act:
Said, Pull her up, pull her up a bit, we need this space, sir.   5
Said, For God's sake, is this still a free country or what?
You go back and take care of Gary Cooper's horse
And leave me handle my own car.

Saw them unloading the lame old lady,
Ducked out under the wheel and gave her an elbow,   10
Said, All you needed to do was just explain;
Reason, Reason is my middle name.

Language on more than one level enlivens this miniature comedy; the vulgate of the resentful driver ("Pull her up my rear end," "leave me handle my own car") and the colloquial of the bystander ("Give her the gun"). There is also a contrast in formality between the old lady's driver, who says "Mac," and the usher, who says "sir." These varied levels of language distinguish the speakers in the poem from one another.

The diction of "Reason" is that of speech; that of Coleridge's "Kubla Khan" (p. 320) is more bookish. Coleridge is not at fault, however: the language of Josephine Miles's reasonable driver might not have contained Kubla Khan's stately pleasure dome. At present, most poetry in English appears to be shunning expressions such as "fleecy care" in favor of general English and the colloquial. In Scotland, there has been an interesting development: the formation of an active group of poets who write in Scots, a **dialect** (variety of language spoken by a social group or spoken in a certain locality). Perhaps, whether poets write in language close to speech or in language of greater formality, their poems will ring true if they choose appropriate words.

EXPERIMENT: *Wheeshts into Hushes*

Reword the following poem from Scots dialect into general English, using the closest possible equivalents. Then try to assess what the poem has gained or lost. (In line 4, a "ploy," as defined by *Webster's Third New International Dictionary*, is a pursuit or activity, "especially one that requires eagerness or finesse.")

Hugh MacDiarmid
[Christopher Murray Grieve] (1892–1978)

WHEESHT, WHEESHT   1926

Wheest°, wheesht, my foolish hert,	*hush*
For weel ye ken°	*know*
I widna ha'e ye stert	
Auld ploys again.	

It's guid to see her lie	
Sae snod° an' cool,	*smooth*
A' lust o' lovin' by —	
Wheesht, wheesht, ye fule!	

Not only the poet's choice of words makes a poem seem more formal, or less, but also the way the words are arranged into sentences. Compare these lines,

> Jack and Jill went up the hill
> To fetch a pail of water.
> Jack fell down and broke his crown
> And Jill came tumbling after.

with Milton's account of a more significant downfall:

> Earth trembled from her entrails, as again
> In pangs, and Nature gave a second groan;
> Sky loured, and, muttering thunder, some sad drops
> Wept at completing of the mortal sin
> Original; while Adam took no thought

Eating his fill, nor Eve to iterate
Her former trespass feared, the more to soothe
Him with her loved society, that now
As with new wine intoxicated both
They swim in mirth, and fancy that they feel
Divinity within them breeding wings
Wherewith to scorn the Earth.

Not all the words in Milton's lines are bookish: indeed, many of them can be found in nursery rimes. What helps, besides diction, to distinguish this account of the Biblical fall from "Jack and Jill" is that Milton's nonstop sentence seems farther removed from usual speech in its length (83 words), in its complexity (subordinate clauses), and in its word order ("with new wine intoxicated both" rather than "both intoxicated with new wine"). Should we think less (or more highly) of Milton for choosing a style so elaborate and formal? No judgment need be passed: both Mother Goose and the author of *Paradise Lost* use language appropriate to their purposes.

Among the languages of humankind, English is by no means the most flexible. English words must be used in fairly definite and inviolable patterns, and whoever departs too far from them will not be understood. In the sentence "Cain slew Abel," if you change the word order, you change the meaning: "Abel slew Cain." Such inflexibility was not true of Latin, in which a poet could lay down words in almost any sequence and, because their endings (inflections) showed what parts of speech they were, could trust that no reader would mistake a subject for an object or a noun for an adjective. (E. E. Cummings has striven, in certain of his poems, for the freedom of Latin. One such poem, "anyone lived in a pretty how town," appears on page 49.)

The rigidity of English word order invites the poet to defy it and to achieve unusual effects by inverting it. It is customary in English to place adjective in front of noun (*a blue mantle, new pastures*). But an unusual emphasis is achieved when Milton ends "Lycidas" by reversing the pattern:

At last he rose, and twitched his mantle blue:
Tomorrow to fresh woods, and pastures new.

Perhaps the inversion in *mantle blue* gives more prominence to the color associated with heaven (and in "Lycidas," heaven is of prime importance). Perhaps the inversion in *pastures new,* stressing the *new,* heightens the sense of a rebirth.

Coleridge offered two "homely definitions of prose and poetry; that is, *prose:* words in their best order; *poetry:* the best words in the best order." If all goes well, a poet may fasten the right word into the right place, and the result may be — as T. S. Eliot said in "Little Gidding" — a "complete consort dancing together."

Reed Whittemore (b. 1919)

THE FALL OF THE HOUSE OF USHER

1970

It was a big boxy wreck of a house
Owned by a classmate of mine named Rod Usher,
Who lived in the thing with his twin sister.
He was a louse and she was a souse.

While I was visiting them one wet summer, she died.   5
We buried her,
Or rather we stuck her in a back room for a bit, meaning to bury her
When the graveyard dried.

But the weather got wetter.
One night we were both waked by a twister,   10
Plus a screeching and howling outside that turned out to be sister
Up and dying again, making it hard for Rod to forget her.

He didn't. He and she died in a heap, and I left quick,
Which was lucky since the house fell in right after,
                              Like a ton of brick.   15

QUESTIONS

1. Identify the story to which this poem makes allusion.
2. How is the tone of the original version of the Usher tragedy (if you know the story) different from that of Whittemore's retelling of it?
3. To say that something falls "like a ton of brick" is ordinarily to use a cliché. Does Whittemore's last line seem a cliché? What is novel about it?
4. How formal is the language of Whittemore's speaker? Why is the diction of this poem essential to its effectiveness?

E. E. Cummings (1894–1962)

ANYONE LIVED IN A PRETTY HOW TOWN

1940

anyone lived in a pretty how town
(with up so floating many bells down)
spring summer autumn winter
he sang his didn't he danced his did.

Women and men(both little and small)   5
cared for anyone not at all
they sowed their isn't they reaped their same
sun moon stars rain

children guessed(but only a few
and down they forgot as up they grew   10
autumn winter spring summer)
that noone loved him more by more

when by now and tree by leaf
she laughed his joy she cried his grief
bird by snow and stir by still   15
anyone's any was all to her

someones married their everyones
laughed their cryings and did their dance
(sleep wake hope and then)they
said their nevers they slept their dream   20

stars rain sun moon
(and only the snow can begin to explain
how children are apt to forget to remember
with up so floating many bells down)

one day anyone died i guess   25
(and noone stooped to kiss his face)
busy folk buried them side by side
little by little and was by was

all by all and deep by deep
and more by more they dream their sleep   30
noone and anyone earth by april
wish by spirit and if by yes.

Women and men(both dong and ding)
summer autumn winter spring
reaped their sowing and went their came   35
sun moon stars rain

Questions

1. Summarize the story told in this poem. Who are the main characters?
2. Rearrange the words in the two opening lines into the order you would expect them usually to follow. What effect does Cummings obtain by his unconventional word order?
3. Another of Cummings's strategies is to use one part of speech as if it were another; for instance, in line 4, *didn't* and *did* ordinarily are verbs, but here they are used as nouns. What other words in the poem perform functions other than their expected ones?

Richard Eberhart (b. 1904)

The Fury of Aerial Bombardment   1947

You would think the fury of aerial bombardment
Would rouse God to relent; the infinite spaces
Are still silent. He looks on shock-pried faces.
History, even, does not know what is meant.

You would feel that after so many centuries   5
God would give man to repent; yet he can kill

As Cain could, but with multitudinous will,
No farther advanced than in his ancient furies.

Was man made stupid to see his own stupidity?
Is God by definition indifferent, beyond us all?   10
Is the eternal truth man's fighting soul
Wherein the Beast ravens in its own avidity?

Of Van Wettering I speak, and Averill,
Names on a list, whose faces I do not recall
But they are gone to early death, who late in school   15
Distinguished the belt feed lever from the belt holding pawl.

QUESTIONS

1. As a naval officer during World War II, Richard Eberhart was assigned for a time as an instructor in a gunnery school. How has this experience apparently contributed to the diction of his poem?
2. In his *Life of John Dryden*, complaining about a description of a sea fight Dryden had filled with nautical language, Samuel Johnson argued that technical terms should be excluded from poetry. Is this criticism applicable to Eberhart's last line? Can a word succeed for us in a poem, even though we may not be able to define it? (For more evidence, see also the technical terms in Henry Reed's "Naming of Parts," p. 384.)
3. Some readers have found a contrast in tone between the first three stanzas of this poem and the last stanza. How would you describe this contrast? What does diction contribute to it?

EXERCISE: *Different Kinds of English*

Read the following poems and see what kinds of diction and word order you find in them. Which poems are least formal in their language and which most formal? Is there any use of vulgate English? Any dialect? What does each poem achieve that its own kind of English makes possible?

Anonymous (American)

AS I WAS LAYING ON THE GREEN   (late nineteenth century)

As I was laying on the green,
A small English book I seen.
Carlyle's *Essay on Burns* was the edition,
So I left it laying in the same position.

A. R. Ammons (b. 1926)

SPRING COMING   1970

The caryophyllaceae
like a scroungy
frost are
rising through the lawn:

many-fingered as leggy   5
  copepods:
a suggestive delicacy,
lacework, like
the scent of wild plum
  thickets: 10
also the grackles
with their incredible
vertical, horizontal,
reversible
tails have arrived: 15
such nice machines.

William Wordsworth (1770–1850)

MY HEART LEAPS UP WHEN I BEHOLD   1807

My heart leaps up when I behold
  A rainbow in the sky:
So was it when my life began;
So is it now I am a man;
So be it when I shall grow old,
  Or let me die!
The Child is father of the Man;
And I could wish my days to be
Bound each to each by natural piety.

William Wordsworth (1770–1850)

MUTABILITY   1822

From low to high doth dissolution climb,
And sink from high to low, along a scale
Of awful notes, whose concord shall not fail;
A musical but melancholy chime,
Which they can hear who meddle not with crime,   5
Nor avarice, nor over-anxious care.
Truth fails not; but her outward forms that bear
The longest date do melt like frosty rime°,   *frozen dew*
That in the morning whitened hill and plain
And is no more; drop like the tower sublime   10
Of yesterday, which royally did wear
His crown of weeds, but could not even sustain
Some casual shout that broke the silent air,
Or the unimaginable touch of Time.

Anonymous

SCOTTSBORO   1936

Paper come out—done strewed de news
Seven po' chillun moan deat' house blues,
Seven po' chillun moanin' deat' house blues.
Seven nappy° heads wit' big shiny eye   *kinky*
All boun' in jail and framed to die,   5
All boun' in jail and framed to die.

Messin' white woman—snake lyin' tale
Hang and burn and jail wit' no bail.
Dat hang and burn and jail wit' no bail.
Worse ol' crime in white folks' lan'   10
Black skin coverin' po' workin' man,
Black skin coverin' po' workin' man.

Judge and jury—all in de stan'
Lawd, biggety name for same lynchin' ban',
Lawd, biggety name for same lynchin' ban'.   15
White folks and nigger in great co't house
Like cat down cellar wit' nohole mouse.
Like cat down cellar wit' nohole mouse.

SCOTTSBORO. This folk blues, collected by Lawrence Gellert in *Negro Songs of Protest* (New York: Carl Fischer, Inc., 1936), is a comment on the Scottsboro case. In 1931 nine black youths of Scottsboro, Alabama, were arrested and charged with the rape of two white women. Though eventually, after several trials, they were found not guilty, some of them at the time this song was composed had been convicted and sentenced to death.

4 Imagery

Ezra Pound (1885–1972)

IN A STATION OF THE METRO   1916

The apparition of these faces in the crowd;
Petals on a wet, black bough.

Pound said he wrote this poem to convey an experience: emerging one day from a train in the Paris subway (*Métro*), he beheld "suddenly a beautiful face, and then another and another." Originally he had described his impression in a poem thirty lines long. In this final version, each line contains an **image,** which, like a picture, may take the place of a thousand words.

Though the term *image* suggests a thing seen, when speaking of images in poetry we generally mean *a word or sequence of words that refers to any sensory experience.* Often this experience is a sight (**visual imagery,** as in Pound's poem), but it may be a sound (**auditory imagery**) or a touch (**tactile imagery,** as a perception of roughness or smoothness). It may be an odor or a taste or perhaps a bodily sensation such as pain, the prickling of gooseflesh, the quenching of thirst, or—as in the following brief poem—the perception of something cold.

Taniguchi Buson (1715–1783)

THE PIERCING CHILL I FEEL   (about 1760)

The piercing chill I feel:
  my dead wife's comb, in our bedroom,
    under my heel . . .

—Translated by Harold G. Henderson

As in this **haiku** (in Japanese, a poem of seventeen syllables) an image can convey—in a flash—understanding. Had he wished, the poet might have spoken of the dead woman, of the contrast between her death and his memory of her, of his feelings toward death in general. But such a discussion would be quite different from the poem he actually wrote. Striking his bare foot against the comb, now cold and motionless but associated with the living wife (perhaps worn in her hair), the widower feels a shock as if he had touched the woman's corpse. A literal, physical sense of death is conveyed; the abstraction "death" is understood through the senses. To render the abstract in concrete terms is what poets often try to do; in this attempt, an image can be valuable.

An image may occur in a single word, a phrase, a sentence, or, as in this case, an entire short poem. To speak of the **imagery** of a poem— all its images taken together—is often more useful than to speak of separate images. To divide Buson's haiku into five images—*chill, wife, comb, bedroom, heel*—is possible, for any noun that refers to a visible object or a sensation is an image, but this is to draw distinctions that in themselves mean little and to disassemble a single experience.

Does an image cause a reader to experience a sense impression? Not quite. Reading the word *petals,* no one literally sees petals; but the occasion is given for imagining them. The image asks to be seen with the mind's eye. And although "In a Station of the Metro" records what Ezra Pound saw, it is of course not necessary for a poet actually to have lived through a sensory experience in order to write it. Keats may never have seen a newly discovered planet through a telescope, despite the image in his sonnet on Chapman's Homer (p. 361).

It is tempting to think of imagery as mere decoration, particularly when we read Keats, who fills his poems with an abundance of sights, sounds, odors, and tastes. But a successful image is not just a dab of paint or a flashy bauble. When Keats opens "The Eve of St. Agnes" with what have been called the coldest lines in literature, he evokes by a series of images a setting and a mood:

> St. Agnes' eve—Ah, bitter chill it was!
> The owl, for all his feathers, was a-cold;
> The hare limped trembling through the frozen grass,
> And silent was the flock in woolly fold:
> Numb were the Beadsman's fingers, while he told
> His rosary, and while his frosted breath,
> Like pious incense from a censer old,
> Seemed taking flight for heaven, without a death, . . .

Indeed, some literary critics look for much of the meaning of a poem in its imagery, wherein they expect to see the mind of the poet more truly revealed than in whatever the poet explicitly claims to believe. In his investigation of Wordsworth's "Ode: Intimations of Immortality," the critic Cleanth Brooks devotes his attention to the imagery of light and darkness, which he finds carries on and develops Wordsworth's thought.[1]

Though Shakespeare's Theseus (in *A Midsummer Night's Dream*) accuses poets of being concerned with "airy nothings," poets are usually very much concerned with what is in front of them. This concern is of use to us. Perhaps, as Alan Watts has remarked, Americans are not the materialists they are sometimes accused of being. How could anyone taking a look at an American city think that its inhabitants deeply cherish material things? Involved in our personal hopes and apprehensions, anticipating the future so hard that much of the time we see the present through a film of thought across our eyes, perhaps we need a poet occasionally to remind us that even the coffee we absentmindedly sip comes in (as Yeats put it) a "heavy spillable cup."

"The greatest poverty," wrote Wallace Stevens, "is not to live / In a physical world." In his own poems, Stevens makes us aware of our world's richness. He can take even a common object sold by the pound in supermarkets and, with precise imagery, recall to us what we had forgotten we ever knew about it.

Wallace Stevens (1879–1955)

STUDY OF TWO PEARS   1942

I

Opusculum paedagogum°.   *a little work that teaches*
The pears are not viols,
Nudes or bottles.
They resemble nothing else.

II

They are yellow forms   5
Composed of curves
Bulging toward the base.
They are touched red.

III

They are not flat surfaces
Having curved outlines.   10
They are round
Tapering toward the top.

IV

In the way they are modeled
There are bits of blue.

---

[1] "Wordsworth and the Paradox of the Imagination," in *The Well Wrought Urn* (New York: Harcourt Brace Jovanovich, 1956).

A hard dry leaf hangs   15
From the stem.

V

The yellow glistens.
It glistens with various yellows,
Citrons, oranges and greens
Flowering over the skin.   20

VI

The shadows of the pears
Are blobs on the green cloth.
The pears are not seen
As the observer wills.

QUESTIONS

1. What is Stevens's point in paying so much attention to what pears *don't* look
   like? Comment in particular on his poem's last two lines.
2. How hard is it to visualize the two pears? How clear are the poet's descriptions?

EXPERIMENT: *Illustrating a Poem*

Let an artist in the class sketch Steven's two pears in color, following the poem
as faithfully as possible, trying to add little that the poem doesn't call for. Then
let the class compare poem and picture. A question for the artist: in rendering
which details was·it necessary to use your own imagination?

Theodore Roethke (1908–1963)
ROOT CELLAR   1948

Nothing would sleep in that cellar, dank as a ditch,
Bulbs broke out of boxes hunting for chinks in the dark,
Shoots dangled and drooped,
Lolling obscenely from mildewed crates,
Hung down long yellow evil necks, like tropical snakes.   5
And what a congress of stinks! —
Roots ripe as old bait,
Pulpy stems, rank, silo-rich,
Leaf-mold, manure, lime, piled against slippery planks.
Nothing would give up life: 10
Even the dirt kept breathing a small breath.

QUESTIONS

1. As a boy growing up in Saginaw, Michigan, Theodore Roethke spent much
   of his time in a large commercial greenhouse run by his family. What details
   in his poem show more than a passing acquaintance with growing things?
2. What varieties of image does "Root Cellar" contain? Point out examples.

3. Which lines contain personifications, metaphors, or similes? How large a part of this poem is composed of these figures of speech?
4. What do you understand to be Roethke's attitude toward the root cellar? Does he view it as a disgusting chamber of horrors? Pay special attention to the last two lines.

Elizabeth Bishop (1911–1979)

THE FISH   1946

I caught a tremendous fish
and held him beside the boat
half out of water, with my hook
fast in a corner of his mouth.
He didn't fight.   5
He hadn't fought at all.
He hung a grunting weight,
battered and venerable
and homely. Here and there
his brown skin hung in strips   10
like ancient wall-paper,
and its pattern of darker brown
was like wall-paper:
shapes like full-blown roses
stained and lost through age.   15
He was speckled with barnacles,
fine rosettes of lime,
and infested
with tiny white sea-lice,
and underneath two or three   20
rags of green weed hung down.
While his gills were breathing in
the terrible oxygen
— the frightening gills,
fresh and crisp with blood,   25
that can cut so badly —
I thought of the coarse white flesh
packed in like feathers,
the big bones and the little bones,
the dramatic reds and blacks   30
of his shiny entrails,
and the pink swim-bladder
like a big peony.
I looked into his eyes
which were far larger than mine   35
but shallower, and yellowed,
the irises backed and packed
with tarnished tinfoil
seen through the lenses

of old scratched isinglass. 40
They shifted a little, but not
to return my stare.
—It was more like the tipping
of an object toward the light.
I admired his sullen face, 45
the mechanism of his jaw,
and then I saw
that from his lower lip
—if you could call it a lip—
grim, wet, and weapon-like, 50
hung five old pieces of fish-line,
or four and a wire leader
with the swivel still attached,
with all their five big hooks
grown firmly in his mouth. 55
A green line, frayed at the end
where he broke it, two heavier lines,
and a fine black thread
still crimped from the strain and snap
when it broke and he got away. 60
Like medals with their ribbons
frayed and wavering,
a five-haired beard of wisdom
trailing from his aching jaw:
I stared and stared 65
and victory filled up
the little rented boat,
from the pool of bilge
where oil had spread a rainbow
around the rusted engine 70
to the bailer rusted orange,
the sun-cracked thwarts,
the oarlocks on their strings,
the gunnels—until everything
was rainbow, rainbow, rainbow! 75
And I let the fish go.

QUESTIONS

1. How many abstract words does this poem contain? What proportion of the poem is imagery?
2. What is the speaker's attitude toward the fish? Comment in particular on lines 61–64.
3. What attitude do the images of the rainbow of oil (line 69), the orange bailer (bailing bucket, line 71), the *sun-cracked thwarts* (line 72) convey? Does the poet expect us to feel mournful because the boat is in such sorry condition?
4. What is meant by *rainbow, rainbow, rainbow*?
5. How do these images prepare us for the conclusion? Why does the speaker let the fish go?

MORE ABOUT HAIKU

On the one-ton temple bell
a moonmoth, folded into sleep,
sits still.

— Taniguchi Buson

Few words, many suggestions. By its nature, a haiku starts us thinking and feeling. Its name means "beginning-verse," perhaps because the haiku form may have originated in a game: players, given a haiku, were supposed to extend its three lines into a longer poem. Haiku tend to consist mainly of imagery, but as we saw in Buson's lines on the cold comb, their imagery is not always pictorial.

Heat-lightning streak —
through darkness pierces
the heron's shriek.

— Matsuo Basho

In the poet's account of his experience, are sight and sound neatly distinguished from each other?

Note that a haiku has little room for abstract thoughts or general observations. The following attempt, though in seventeen syllables, is far from haiku in spirit:

Now that our love is gone
I feel within my soul
a nagging distress.

Unlike the author of those lines, haiku poets look out upon a literal world, seldom looking inward to *discuss* their feelings. Japanese haiku tend to be seasonal in subject, but because they are so highly compressed, they usually just *imply* a season: a blossom indicates spring; a crow on a branch, autumn; snow, winter. Not just pretty little sketches of nature (as some Westerners think), haiku assume a view of the universe in which observer and nature are not separated.

A haiku in Japanese is rimeless, its seventeen syllables arranged in a five-seven-five pattern. Haiku written in English frequently ignore any strict syllable-count; they may be rimed or unrimed as the poet likes.

If you care to try your hand at haiku-writing, here are a few suggestions. Make every word matter. Include few adjectives; shun needless conjunctions. Set your haiku in the present moment. Confine your poem to what can be seen, heard, smelled, tasted, or touched. Mere sensory reports, however, will be meaningless unless they make the reader feel something — as a contemporary American writer points out in this spoof.

Richard Brautigan (b. 1935)

Haiku Ambulance

A piece of green pepper
  fell
off the wooden salad bowl:
  so what?

Here, freely translated, are two more Japanese haiku to inspire you. Both are by Basho (1644–1694), the greatest master of the form. Classic haiku sometimes gain from our knowing when and where they were written: the first was composed on Basho's finding the site of a famous castle, which the hero Yoshitsune and his warriors had died trying to storm, reduced to wilderness.

Green weeds of summer
grow where swordsmen's dreams
once used to shimmer.

In the old stone pool
a frogjump:
splishhhhh.

Finally, here are four more untitled haiku written in English, of recent origin.

Sprayed with strong poison
my roses are crisp this year
  in the crystal vase
       — Paul Goodman

Clap!
the coffin lid
shelters the fly
       — Raymond Roseliep

A great freight truck
    lit like a town
through the dark stony desert
    — Gary Snyder

After weeks of watching the roof leak
    I fixed it tonight
by moving a single board
       — Gary Snyder

FOR REVIEW AND FURTHER STUDY

Jean Toomer (1894–1967)

Reapers

1923

Black reapers with the sound of steel on stones
Are sharpening scythes. I see them place the hones
In their hip-pockets as a thing that's done,
And start their silent swinging, one by one.

Black horses drive a mower through the weeds,
And there, a field rat, startled, squealing bleeds,
His belly close to ground. I see the blade,
Blood-stained, continue cutting weeds and shade.

QUESTIONS

1. Imagine the scene Jean Toomer describes. Which particulars most vividly strike the mind's eye?
2. What kind of image is *silent swinging*?
3. Read the poem aloud. Notice especially the effect of the words *sound of steel on stones* and *field rat, startled, squealing bleeds*. What interesting sounds are present in the very words that contain these images?
4. What feelings do you get from this poem as a whole? Would you agree with someone who said, "This poem gives us a sense of happy, carefree life down on the farm, close to nature"? Exactly what in "Reapers" makes you feel the way you do? Besides appealing to our auditory and visual imagination, what do the images contribute?

Gerard Manley Hopkins (1844–1889)

PIED BEAUTY   (1877)

Glory be to God for dappled things —
   For skies of couple-color as a brinded° cow;   *streaked*
     For rose-moles all in stipple upon trout that swim;
Fresh-firecoal chestnut-falls; finches' wings;
   Landscape plotted and pieced — fold, fallow, and plow;   5
     And áll trádes, their gear and tackle and trim°.   *equipment*

All things counter, original, spare, strange;
   Whatever is fickle, freckled (who knows how?)
     With swift, slow; sweet, sour; adazzle, dim;
He fathers-forth whose beauty is past change: 10
        Praise him.

QUESTIONS

1. What does the word *pied* mean? (Hint: what does a Pied Piper look like?)
2. According to Hopkins, what do *skies, cow, trout, ripe chestnuts, finches' wings,* and *landscapes* all have in common? What landscapes can the poet have in mind? (Have you ever seen any *dappled* landscape while looking down from an airplane, or from a mountain or high hill?)
3. What do you make of line 6: what can carpenters' saws and ditch-diggers' spades possibly have in common with the dappled things in lines 2–4?
4. Does Hopkins refer only to contrasts that meet the eye? What other kinds of variation interest him?
5. Try to state in your own words the theme of this poem. How essential to our understanding of this theme are Hopkins's images?

John Keats (1795–1821)

BRIGHT STAR! WOULD I WERE STEADFAST AS THOU ART

(1819)

Bright star! would I were steadfast as thou art —
  Not in lone splendor hung aloft the night,
And watching, with eternal lids apart,
  Like nature's patient, sleepless Eremite°   *hermit*
The moving waters at their priest-like task   5
  Of pure ablution round earth's human shores,
Or gazing on the new soft-fallen mask
  Of snow upon the mountains and the moors —
No — yet still steadfast, still unchangeable,
  Pillowed upon my fair love's ripening breast,   10
To feel for ever its soft fall and swell,
  Awake for ever in a sweet unrest,
Still, still to hear her tender-taken breath,
And so live ever — or else swoon to death.

QUESTIONS

1. Stars are conventional symbols for love and a loved one. (Love, Shakespeare tells us in a sonnet, "is the star to every wandering bark.") In this sonnet, why is it not possible for the star to have this meaning? How does Keats use it?
2. What seems concrete and particular in the speaker's observations?
3. Suppose Keats had said *slow and easy* instead of *tender-taken* in line 13? What would have been lost?

Carl Sandburg (1878–1967)

FOG

1916

The fog comes
on little cat feet.
It sits looking
over harbor and city
on silent haunches
and then moves on.

QUESTION

In lines 15–22 of "The Love Song of J. Alfred Prufrock" (p. 336), T. S. Eliot also likens fog to a cat. Compare Sandburg's lines and Eliot's. Which passage tells us more about fogs and cats?

EXPERIMENT: *Writing with Images*

Taking the following poems as examples from which to start rather than as models to be slavishly copied, try to compose a brief poem that consists largely of imagery.

Walt Whitman (1819–1892)
THE RUNNER

1867

On a flat road runs the well-train'd runner;
He is lean and sinewy, with muscular legs;
He is thinly clothed—he leans forward as he runs,
With lightly closed fists, and arms partially rais'd.

T. E. Hulme (1883–1917)
IMAGE

(about 1910)

Old houses were scaffolding once
            and workmen whistling.

William Carlos Williams (1883–1963)
THE GREAT FIGURE

1921

Among the rain
and lights
I saw the figure 5
in gold
on a red   5
firetruck
moving
tense
unheeded
to gong clangs   10
siren howls
and wheels rumbling
through the dark city.

Robert Bly (b. 1926)
DRIVING TO TOWN LATE TO MAIL A LETTER

1962

It is a cold and snowy night. The main street is deserted.
The only things moving are swirls of snow.
As I lift the mailbox door, I feel its cold iron.
There is a privacy I love in this snowy night.
Driving around, I will waste more time.

H. D. [Hilda Doolittle] (1886–1961)

HEAT   1916

O wind, rend open the heat,
cut apart the heat,
rend it to tatters.

Fruit cannot drop
through this thick air—   5
fruit cannot fall into heat
that presses up and blunts
the points of pears
and rounds the grapes.

Cut the heat—   10
plough through it,
turning it on either side
of your path.

5 Saying and Suggesting

To write so clearly that they might bring "all things as near the mathe-matical plainness" as possible — that was the goal of scientists according to Bishop Thomas Sprat, who lived in the seventeenth century. Such an effort would seem bound to fail, because words, unlike numbers, are ambiguous indicators. Although it may have troubled Bishop Sprat, the tendency of a word to have multiplicity of meaning rather than mathe-matical plainness opens broad avenues to poetry.

Every word has at least one **denotation:** a meaning as defined in a dictionary. But the English language has many a common word with so many denotations that a reader may need to think twice to see what it means in a specific context. The noun *field*, for instance, can denote a piece of ground, a sports arena, the scene of a battle, part of a flag, a pro-fession, and a number system in mathematics. Further, the word can be used as a verb ("he fielded a grounder") or an adjective ("field trip," "field glasses").

A word also has **connotations:** overtones or suggestions of addi-tional meaning that it gains from all the contexts in which we have met it in the past. The word *skeleton*, according to a dictionary, denotes "the bony framework of a human being or other vertebrate animal, which supports the flesh and protects the organs." But by its associations, the word can rouse thoughts of war, of disease and death, or (possibly) of one's plans to go to medical school. Think, too, of the difference be-tween "Old Doc Jones" and "Abner P. Jones, M.D." In the mind's eye, the former appears in his shirtsleeves; the latter has a gold nameplate on his door. That some words denote the same thing but have sharply dif-ferent connotations is pointed out in this anonymous Victorian jingle:

> Here's a little ditty that you really ought to know:
> Horses "sweat" and men "perspire," but ladies only "glow."

The terms *druggist, pharmacist,* and *apothecary* all denote the same oc-cupation, but apothecaries lay claim to special distinction.

Poets aren't the only people who care about the connotations of language. Advertisers know that connotations make money. Recently a Boston automobile dealer advertised his secondhand cars not as "used" but as "pre-owned," as if fearing that "used car" would connote an old heap with soiled upholstery and mysterious engine troubles that somebody couldn't put up with. "Pre-owned," however, suggests that the previous owner has taken the trouble of breaking in the car for you. Not long ago prune-packers, alarmed by a slump in sales, sponsored a survey to determine the connotations of prunes in the public consciousness. Asked, "What do you think of when you hear the word *prunes*?" most people replied, "dried up," "wrinkled," or "constipated." Dismayed, the packers hired an advertising agency to create a new image for prunes, in hopes of inducing new connotations. Soon, advertisements began to show prunes in brightly colored settings, in the company of bikinied bathing beauties.[1]

In imaginative writing, connotations are as crucial as they are in advertising. Consider this sentence: "A new brand of journalism is being born, or spawned" (Dwight Macdonald writing in *The New York Review of Books*). The last word, by its associations with fish and crustaceans, suggests that this new journalism is scarcely the product of human beings. And what do we make of Romeo's assertion that Juliet "is the sun"? Surely even a lovesick boy cannot mean that his sweetheart is "the incandescent body of gases about which the earth and other planets revolve" (a dictionary definition). He means, of course, that he thrives in her sight, that he feels warm in her presence or even at the thought of her, that she illumines his world and is the center of his universe. Because in the mind of the hearer these and other suggestions are brought into play, Romeo's statement, literally absurd, makes excellent sense.

Here is a famous poem that groups together things with similar connotations: certain ships and their cargoes. (A quinquireme, by the way, was an ancient Assyrian vessel propelled by sails and oars.)

John Masefield (1878–1967)

CARGOES   1902

Quinquireme of Nineveh from distant Ophir,
Rowing home to haven in sunny Palestine,
With a cargo of ivory,
And apes and peacocks,
Sandalwood, cedarwood, and sweet white wine.   5

---

[1] For this and other instances of connotation-engineering, see Vance Packard's *The Hidden Persuaders* (New York: McKay, 1958), chap. 13.

Stately Spanish galleon coming from the Isthmus,
Dipping through the Tropics by the palm-green shores,
With a cargo of diamonds,
Emeralds, amethysts,
Topazes, and cinnamon, and gold moidores°.   *Portuguese coins* 10

Dirty British coaster with a salt-caked smoke stack,
Butting through the Channel in the mad March days,
With a cargo of Tyne coal,
Road-rails, pig-lead,
Firewood, iron-ware, and cheap tin trays.   15

To us, as well as to the poet's original readers, the place-names in the
first two stanzas suggest the exotic and faraway. Ophir, a vanished
place, may have been in Arabia; according to the Bible, King Solomon
sent there for its celebrated pure gold, also for ivory, apes, peacocks,
and other luxury items. (See I Kings 9–10.) In his final stanza, Masefield
groups commonplace things (mostly heavy and metallic), whose
suggestions of crudeness, cheapness, and ugliness he deliberately contrasts with those of the precious stuffs he has listed earlier. For British
readers, the Tyne is a stodgy and familiar river; the English Channel in
March, choppy and likely to upset a stomach. The quinquireme is *rowing*, the galleon is *dipping*, but the dirty British freighter is *butting*,
aggressively pushing. Conceivably, the poet could have described
firewood and even coal as beautiful, but evidently he wants them to
convey sharply different suggestions here, to go along with the rest of
the coaster's cargo. In drawing such a sharp contrast between past and
present, Masefield does more than merely draw up bills-of-lading.
Perhaps he even implies a wry and unfavorable comment upon life in
the present day. His meaning lies not so much in the dictionary definitions of his words (*"moidores:* Portuguese gold coins formerly worth approximately five pounds sterling") as in their rich and vivid connotations.

William Blake (1757–1827)

LONDON   1794

I wander through each chartered street,
Near where the chartered Thames does flow,
And mark in every face I meet
Marks of weakness, marks of woe.

In every cry of every man,   5
In every infant's cry of fear,
In every voice, in every ban,
The mind-forged manacles I hear.

How the chimney-sweeper's cry
Every black'ning church appalls;   10
And the hapless soldier's sigh
Runs in blood down palace walls.

But most through midnight streets I hear
How the youthful harlot's curse
Blasts the new born infant's tear,   15
And blights with plagues the marriage hearse.

Here are only a few of the possible meanings of four of Blake's
words:

chartered (lines 1, 2)

> Denotations: Established by a charter (a written grant or a certifi-
> cate of incorporation); leased or hired.
>
> Connotations: Defined, limited, restricted, channeled, mapped,
> bound by law; bought and sold (like a slave or an inanimate ob-
> ject); Magna Charta; charters given crown colonies by the King.
>
> Other Words in the Poem with Similar Connotations: *Ban; man-
> acles; chimney-sweeper, soldier, harlot* (all hirelings).
>
> Interpretation of the Lines: The street has had mapped out for it
> the direction in which it must go; the Thames has had laid down
> to it the course it must follow. Street and river are channeled,
> imprisoned, enslaved (like every inhabitant of London).

black'ning (line 10)

> Denotation: Becoming black.
>
> Connotations: The darkening of something once light, the defile-
> ment of something once clean, the deepening of guilt, the gath-
> ering of darkness at the approach of night.
>
> Other Words in the Poem with Similar Connotations: Objects
> becoming marked or smudged (*marks of weakness, marks of woe*
> in the faces of passers-by; bloodied walls of a palace; marriage
> blighted with plagues); the word *appalls* (suggesting not only
> "to overcome with horror" but "to cast a pall or shroud over
> something"); *midnight streets.*
>
> Interpretation of the Line: Literally, every London church grows
> black from soot and hires a chimney-sweeper (a small boy) to
> help clean it. But Blake suggests too that by profiting from the
> suffering of the child laborer, the church is soiling its original
> purity.

Blasts, blights (lines 15–16)

> Denotations: Both *blast* and *blight* mean "to cause to wither" or "to
> ruin and destroy." Both are terms from horticulture. Frost *blasts*
> a bud and kills it; disease *blights* a growing plant.

Connotations: Sickness and death; gardens shriveled and dying;
gusts of wind and the ravages of insects; things blown to pieces
or rotted and warped.

Other Words in the Poem with Similar Connotations: Faces
marked with weakness and woe; the child become a chimney-
sweep; the soldier killed by war; blackening church and blood-
ied palace; young girl turned harlot; wedding carriage transformed into a hearse.

Interpretation of the Lines: Literally, the harlot spreads the plague
of syphilis, which, carried into marriage, can cause a baby to be
born blind. In a larger and more meaningful sense, Blake sees
the prostitution of even one young girl corrupting the entire in-
stitution of matrimony and endangering every child.

Some of these connotations are more to the point than others; the reader
of a poem nearly always has the problem of distinguishing relevant associations from irrelevant ones. We need to read a poem in its entirety
and, when a word leaves us in doubt, look for other things in the poem
to corroborate or refute what we think it means. Relatively simple and
direct in its statement, Blake's account of his stroll through the city at
night becomes an indictment of a whole social and religious order. The
indictment could hardly be this effective if it were "mathematically
plain," its every word restricted to one denotation clearly spelled out.

Wallace Stevens (1879–1955)
DISILLUSIONMENT OF TEN O'CLOCK   1923

The houses are haunted
By white night-gowns.
None are green,
Or purple with green rings,
Or green with yellow rings,   5
Or yellow with blue rings.
None of them are strange,
With socks of lace
And beaded ceintures.
People are not going   10
To dream of baboons and periwinkles.
Only, here and there, an old sailor,
Drunk and asleep in his boots,
Catches tigers
In red weather.   15

QUESTIONS

1. What are *beaded ceintures*? What does the phrase suggest?

2. What meanings do you find in the colors mentioned in this poem?
3. What contrast does Stevens draw between the people who live in these houses and the old sailor? What do the connotations of *white night-gowns* and *sailor* add to this contrast?
4. What is lacking in these people who wear white night-gowns? Why should the poet's view of them be a "disillusionment"?

Guy Owen (b. 1925)

THE WHITE STALLION   1969

The Runaway

A white horse came to our farm once
Leaping like dawn the backyard fence.
In dreams I heard his shadow fall
Across my bed. A miracle,
I woke beneath his mane's surprise;   5
I saw my face within his eyes,
The dew ran down his nose and fell
Upon the bleeding window quince. . . .

But long before I broke the spell
My father's curses sped him on,   10
Four flashing hooves that bruised the lawn.
And as I stumbled into dawn
I saw him scorn a final hedge,
I heard his pride upon the bridge,
Then through the wakened yard I went   15
To read the rage the stallion spent.

QUESTIONS

1. What do these words denote in Owen's poem: *scorn, pride, wakened, rage*? (What does the stallion do when he *scorns* the hedge? How can *pride* be heard? What has *wakened* in the yard? From what evidence can the stallion's *rage* be read?)
2. What words in the poem seem especially rich in connotations?
3. Here is one paraphrase of the poem: "A runaway horse wakes a boy up and does some damage." Make a better paraphrase, one that more accurately reflects the feelings you are left with after reading the poem.

Samuel Johnson (1709–1784)

A SHORT SONG OF CONGRATULATION   (1780)

Long-expected one and twenty
    Ling'ring year at last is flown,
Pomp and pleasure, pride and plenty,
    Great Sir John, are all your own.

Loosened from the minor's tether;   5
    Free to mortgage or to sell,
Wild as wind, and light as feather
    Bid the slaves of thrift farewell.

Call the Bettys, Kates, and Jennys
    Every name that laughs at care,   10
Lavish of your grandsire's guineas,
    Show the spirit of an heir.

All that prey on vice and folly
    Joy to see their quarry fly:
Here the gamester light and jolly,   15
    There the lender grave and sly.

Wealth, Sir John, was made to wander,
    Let it wander as it will;
See the jockey, see the pander,
    Bid them come, and take their fill.   20

When the bonny blade carouses,
    Pockets full, and spirits high,
What are acres? What are houses?
    Only dirt, or° wet or dry.   *either*

If the guardian or the mother   25
    Tell the woes of willful waste,
Scorn their counsel and their pother,
    You can hang or drown at last.

QUESTIONS

1. In line 5, what does *tether* denote? What does the word suggest?
2. Why are *Bettys, Kates,* and *Jennys* more meaningful names as Johnson uses
   them than Elizabeths, Katherines, and Genevieves would be?
3. Johnson states in line 24 the connotations that *acres* and *houses* have for the
   young heir. What connotations might these terms have for Johnson himself?

Denise Levertov (b. 1923)

SUNDAY AFTERNOON   1958

After the First Communion
and the banquet of mangoes and
bridal cake, the young daughters
of the coffee merchant lay down
for a long siesta, and their white dresses   5
lay beside them in quietness
and the white veils floated
in their dreams as the flies buzzed.
But as the afternoon
burned to a close they rose   10

and ran about the neighborhood
among the halfbuilt villas
alive, alive, kicking a basketball, wearing
other new dresses, of bloodred velvet.

QUESTIONS

1. What contrasts do you find between the scene in lines 1–8 and that in the rest
   of this poem?
2. What suggestions do you derive from *white dresses* and *white veils*? From
   other new dresses, of bloodred velvet?
3. In line 10, what is interesting in the word *burned*? Why is it a more meaningful word than *drew*, or *came to a close*, or *closed*?

James Camp (b. 1923)
AT THE FIRST AVENUE REDEMPTION CENTER   1975

I enter the Plaidland Redemption Center
And, whistling a descant on a Handel theme,
Look for a sign.

The sign says:
"There is only one line.
Wait here."

AT THE FIRST AVENUE REDEMPTION CENTER. 1. *Plaidland:* a brand of trading stamps. 2. *descant:* in music, a melody or counterpoint played at the same time as a theme. *Handel:*
George Frederick Handel (1685–1759), German-born composer of oratorios, musical
dramas based on Bible stories. *Messiah* is Handel's best-known oratorio, in which solo
voices and choruses sing of the annunciation, birth, life, death, and resurrection of Christ.
3. *Look for a sign:* In both Old and New Testaments, many persons look for some visible
message from God: Noah, whose dove brings back an olive branch (Genesis 8); the doubting Pharisees who ask Christ to perform a miracle: "Master, we would see a sign from
thee" (Matthew 12:38).

QUESTIONS

1. What suggestions do you find in the phrase *Redemption Center*?
2. What do the allusions to Handel and to the Bible lend to the poem? How do
   they help the message on the sign to appear more meaningful?

Richard Snyder (b. 1925)
A MONGOLOID CHILD HANDLING SHELLS ON THE BEACH   1971

She turns them over in her slow hands,
as did the sea sending them to her;
broken bits from the mazarine maze,
they are the calmest things on this sand.

The unbroken children splash and shout,
rough as surf, gay as their nesting towels.
But she plays soberly with the sea's
small change and hums back to it its slow vowels.

QUESTIONS

1. In what ways is the phrase *the mazarine maze* more valuable to this poem than if the poet had said "the deep blue sea"?
2. What is suggested by calling the other children *unbroken*? By saying that their towels are *nesting*?
3. How is the mongoloid child like the sea? How are the other children like the surf? What do the differences between sea and surf contribute to Richard Snyder's poem?
4. What is the poet's attitude toward the mongoloid child? How can you tell?

Elizabeth Bishop (1911–1979)

LATE AIR   1946

From a magician's midnight sleeve
    the radio-singers
distribute all their love-songs
over the dew-wet lawns.
    And like a fortune-teller's   5
their marrow-piercing guesses are whatever you believe.

But on the Navy-Yard aerial I find
    better witnesses
for love on summer nights.
Five remote red lights   10
    keep their nests there; Phoenixes
burning quietly, where the dew cannot climb.

QUESTIONS

1. To what kind of air, besides the kind we breathe, does the title refer?
2. What do you recall about phoenixes and their habits that lends meaning to this poem?
3. In the first stanza, what suggestions do you find in the *magician* and the *fortune-teller*? What do the two have in common? Are they likened to — or contrasted with — the *phoenixes* in stanza two?
4. Does line 4 contain a literal fact, a meaningful suggestion, or both? Comment also on the poet's reference to *dew* in the last line.
5. What can lights on an aerial in a shipyard possibly have to do with love?
6. Comment on this comment: "In 'Late Air' Elizabeth Bishop doesn't like vague, soggy language that can mean just any old thing the hearer wants it to — the language of pop songs and penny-in-the-slot fortune tickets. She likes language to be precise and mechanical, like an aerial. She doesn't want language to be rich in suggestions."

W. S. Merwin (b. 1927)

Dead Hand   1963

Temptations still nest in it like basilisks.
Hang it up till the rings fall.

Dead Hand. The basilisk, a fabled lizard of the Sahara, could crack rock with its look and (according to the Roman poet Lucan) could poison the hand of an attacker and cause death unless the hand was quickly severed from the body. (For more details see Jorge Luis Borges, *The Book of Imaginary Beings*. New York: E. P. Dutton, 1969.)

Questions

1. What are we told about the owner of the hand?
2. What is suggested?

Geoffrey Hill (b. 1932)

Merlin   1959

I will consider the outnumbering dead:
For they are the husks of what was rich seed.
Now, should they come together to be fed,
They would outstrip the locusts' covering tide.

Arthur, Elaine, Mordred; they are all gone
Among the raftered galleries of bone.
By the long barrows of Logres they are made one,
And over their city stands the pinnacled corn.

Merlin. In medieval legend, Merlin was a powerful magician and a seer, an aide of King Arthur. 5. *Elaine:* in Arthurian romance, the beloved of Sir Launcelot. *Mordred:* Arthur's treacherous nephew by whose hand the king died. 7. *barrows:* earthworks for burial of the dead. *Logres:* name of an ancient British kingdom, according to the twelfth-century historian Geoffrey of Monmouth, who gathered legends of King Arthur.

Questions

1. What does the title "Merlin" contribute to this poem? Do you prefer to read the poem as though it is Merlin who speaks to us—or the poet?
2. Line 4 alludes to the plague of locusts that God sent upon Egypt (Exodus 10): "For they covered the face of the whole earth, so that the land was darkened . . ." With this allusion in mind, explain the comparison of the dead to locusts.
3. Why are the suggestions inherent in the names of *Arthur, Elaine,* and *Mordred* more valuable to this poem than those we might find in the names of other dead persons called, say, Gus, Tessie, and Butch?
4. Explain the phrase in line 6: *the raftered galleries of bone.*
5. In the last line, what *city* does the poet refer to? Does he mean some particular city, or is he making a comparison?
6. What is interesting in the adjective *pinnacled*? How can it be applied to corn?

Wallace Stevens (1879–1955)

The Emperor of Ice-Cream

1923

Call the roller of big cigars,
The muscular one, and bid him whip
In kitchen cups concupiscent curds.
Let the wenches dawdle in such dress
As they are used to wear, and let the boys   5
Bring flowers in last month's newspapers.
Let be be finale of seem.
The only emperor is the emperor of ice-cream.

Take from the dresser of deal,
Lacking the three glass knobs, that sheet   10
On which she embroidered fantails once
And spread it so as to cover her face.
If her horny feet protrude, they come
To show how cold she is, and dumb.
Let the lamp affix its beam.   15
The only emperor is the emperor of ice-cream.

The Emperor of Ice-Cream. 9. *deal:* fir or pine wood used to make cheap furniture.

Questions

1. What scene is taking place in the first stanza? Describe it in your own words. What are your feelings about it?
2. Who do you suppose to be the dead person in the second stanza? What can you infer about her? What do you know about her for sure?
3. Make a guess about this mysterious emperor. Who do you take him to be?
4. What does ice cream mean to you? In this poem, what do you think it means to Stevens?

Robert Frost (1874–1963)

Fire and Ice

1923

Some say the world will end in fire,
Some say in ice.
From what I've tasted of desire
I hold with those who favor fire.
But if it had to perish twice,
I think I know enough of hate
To say that for destruction ice
Is also great
And would suffice.

Questions

1. To whom does Frost refer in line 1? In line 2?
2. What connotations of *fire* and *ice* contribute to the richness of Frost's comparison?

6 Figures of Speech

WHY SPEAK FIGURATIVELY?

"I will speak daggers to her, but use none," says Hamlet, preparing to confront his mother. His statement makes sense only because we realize that *daggers* is to be taken two ways: literally (denoting sharp, pointed weapons) and nonliterally (referring to something that can be used *like* weapons — namely, words). Reading poetry, we often meet comparisons between two things whose similarity we have never noticed before. When Marianne Moore observes that a fir tree has "an emerald turkey-foot at the top," the result is a pleasure that poetry richly affords: the sudden recognition of likenesses.

A treetop like a turkey-foot, words like daggers — such comparisons are called **figures of speech.** In its broadest definition, a figure of speech may be said to occur whenever a speaker or writer, for the sake of freshness or emphasis, departs from the usual denotations of words. Certainly, when Hamlet says he will speak daggers, no one expects him to release pointed weapons from his lips, for *daggers* is not to be read solely for its denotation. Its connotations — sharp, stabbing, piercing, wounding — also come to mind, and we see ways in which words and daggers work alike. (Words too can hurt: by striking through pretenses, possibly, or by wounding their hearer's self-esteem.) In the statement "A razor is sharper than an ax," there is no departure from the usual denotations of *razor* and *ax,* and no figure of speech results. Both objects are of the same class; the comparison is not offensive to logic. But in "How sharper than a serpent's tooth it is to have a thankless child," the objects — snake's tooth (fang) and ungrateful offspring — are so unlike that no reasonable comparison may be made between them. To find similarity, we attend to the connotations of *serpent's tooth* — biting, piercing, pain — rather than to its denotations. If we are aware of the connotations of *red rose* (beauty, softness, freshness, and so forth), then the line "My love is like a red, red rose" need not call to mind a woman with a scarlet face and a thorny neck.

Figures of speech are not devices to state what is demonstrably untrue. Indeed they often state truths that more literal language cannot communicate; they call attention to such truths; they lend them emphasis.

Alfred, Lord Tennyson (1809–1892)
THE EAGLE   1851

He clasps the crag with crooked hands;
Close to the sun in lonely lands,
Ringed with the azure world, he stands.

The wrinkled sea beneath him crawls;
He watches from his mountain walls,
And like a thunderbolt he falls.

This brief poem is rich in figurative language. In the first line, the phrase *crooked hands* may surprise us. An eagle does not have hands, we might protest; but the objection would be a quibble, for evidently Tennyson is indicating exactly how an eagle clasps a crag, in the way that human fingers clasp a thing. By implication, too, the eagle is a person. *Close to the sun,* if taken literally, is an absurd exaggeration, the sun being a mean distance of 93,000,000 miles from the earth. For the eagle to be closer to it by the altitude of a mountain is an approach so small as to be insignificant. But figuratively, Tennyson conveys that the eagle stands above the clouds, perhaps silhouetted against the sun, and for the moment belongs to the heavens rather than to the land and sea. The word *ringed* makes a circle of the whole world's horizons and suggests that we see the world from the eagle's height; the sea becomes an aged, sluggish animal; *mountain walls,* possibly literal, also suggests a fort or castle; and finally the eagle itself is likened to a thunderbolt in speed and in power, perhaps also in that its beak is — like our abstract conception of a lightning bolt — pointed. How much of the poem can be taken literally? Only *he clasps the crag, he stands, he watches, he falls.* (And even *he* is scarcely literal, for the poet cannot know the sex of the eagle; *it* would be the more likely word in an ornithologist's description of the bird.) The rest is made of figures of speech. The result is that, reading Tennyson's poem, we gain a bird's-eye view of sun, sea, and land — and even of bird. Like imagery, figurative language refers us to the physical world.

William Shakespeare (1564–1616)
SHALL I COMPARE THEE TO A SUMMER'S DAY?   1609

Shall I compare thee to a summer's day?
Thou art more lovely and more temperate.

Rough winds do shake the darling buds of May,
And summer's lease hath all too short a date.
Sometime too hot the eye of heaven shines,   5
And often is his gold complexion dimmed;
And every fair from fair sometimes declines,
By chance, or nature's changing course, untrimmed.
But thy eternal summer shall not fade,
Nor lose possession of that fair thou ow'st°;   *ownest, have*   10
Nor shall death brag thou wand'rest in his shade,
When in eternal lines to time thou grow'st.
  So long as men can breathe or eyes can see,
  So long lives this, and this gives life to thee.

Howard Moss (b. 1922)

SHALL I COMPARE THEE TO A SUMMER'S DAY?   1976

Who says you're like one of the dog days?
You're nicer. And better.
Even in May, the weather can be gray,
And a summer sub-let doesn't last forever.
Sometimes the sun's too hot;   5
Sometimes it is not.
Who can stay young forever?
People break their necks or just drop dead!
But you? Never!
If there's just one condensed reader left   10
Who can figure out the abridged alphabet,
    After you're dead and gone,
    In this poem you'll live on!

QUESTIONS

1. In Howard Moss's streamlined version of Shakespeare, from a series called "Modified Sonnets (Dedicated to adapters, abridgers, digesters, and condensers everywhere)," to what extent does he use figurative language? In Shakespeare's original sonnet, how high a proportion of Shakespeare's language is figurative?
2. Compare some of Moss's lines to the corresponding lines in Shakespeare's sonnet. Why is *Even in May, the weather can be gray* less interesting than the original? In the lines on the sun (5–6 in both versions), what has Moss's modification deliberately left out? Why is Shakespeare's seeing death as a braggart memorable? Why aren't you greatly impressed by Moss's last two lines?
3. Can you explain Shakespeare's play on the word *untrimmed* (line 8)? Evidently the word can mean "divested of trimmings," but what other suggestions do you find in it?
4. How would you answer someone who argued, "Maybe Moss's language isn't as good as Shakespeare's, but the meaning is still there. What's wrong with putting Shakespeare into up-to-date words that can be understood by everybody?"

METAPHOR AND SIMILE

> Life, like a dome of many-colored glass,
> Stains the white radiance of Eternity.

The first of these lines (from Shelley's "Adonais") is a **simile:** a comparison of two things, indicated by some connective, usually *like, as, than,* or a verb such as *resembles.* The things compared have to be dissimilar in kind for a simile to exist: it is no simile to say "Your fingers are like mine"; it is a literal observation. But to say "Your fingers are like sausages" is to use a simile. Omit the connective — say "Your fingers are sausages" — and the result is a **metaphor,** a statement that one thing *is* something else, which, in a literal sense, it is not. In the second of Shelley's lines, it is *assumed* that Eternity is light or radiance, and we have an **implied metaphor,** one that uses neither a connective nor the verb *to be.* Here are examples:

Oh, my love is like a red, red rose.	*Simile*
Oh, my love resembles a red, red rose.	*Simile*
Oh, my love is redder than a rose.	*Simile*
Oh, my love is a red, red rose.	*Metaphor*
Oh, my love has red petals and sharp thorns.	*Implied metaphor*
Oh, I placed my love into a long-stem vase	
And I bandaged my bleeding thumb.	*Implied metaphor*

Often you can tell a metaphor from a simile by much more than just the presence or absence of a connective. In general, a simile refers to only one characteristic that two things have in common, while a metaphor is not plainly limited in the number of resemblances it may indicate. To use the simile "He eats like a pig" is to compare man and animal in one respect: eating habits. But to say "He's a pig" is to use a metaphor that might involve comparisons of appearance and morality as well.

In everyday speech, simile and metaphor occur frequently. We use metaphors ("She's a doll"), and similes ("The tickets are selling like hotcakes") without being fully conscious of them. If, however, we are aware that words possess literal meanings as well as figurative ones, we do not write *died in the wool* for *dyed in the wool* or *tow the line* for *toe the line,* nor do we use **mixed metaphors** as did the writer who advised, "Water the spark of knowledge and it will bear fruit," or the speaker who urged, "To get ahead, keep your nose to the grindstone, your shoulder to the wheel, your ear to the ground, and your eye on the ball." Perhaps the unintended humor of these statements comes from our seeing that the writer, busy stringing together stale metaphors, was not aware that they had any physical reference.

Unlike a writer who thoughtlessly mixes metaphors, a good poet can join together incongruous things and still keep the reader's respect.

In his ballad "Thirty Bob a Week," John Davidson has a British working-man tell how it feels to try to support a large family on small wages:

> It's a naked child against a hungry wolf;
>   It's playing bowls upon a splitting wreck;
> It's walking on a string across a gulf
>   With millstones fore-and-aft about your neck;
> But the thing is daily done by many and many a one;
>   And we fall, face forward, fighting, on the deck.

Like the man with his nose to the grindstone, Davidson's wage-earner is in an absurd fix; but his balancing act seems far from merely nonsensical. For every one of the poet's comparisons—of workingman to child, to bowler, to tight-rope walker, and to seaman—offer suggestions of a similar kind. All help us see (and imagine) the workingman's hard life: a brave and unyielding struggle against impossible odds.

A poem may make a series of comparisons, like Davidson's, or the whole poem may be one extended comparison:

Richard Wilbur (b. 1917)
A SIMILE FOR HER SMILE   1950

Your smiling, or the hope, the thought of it,
Makes in my mind such pause and abrupt ease
As when the highway bridgegates fall,
Balking the hasty traffic, which must sit
On each side massed and staring, while   5
Deliberately the drawbridge starts to rise:

Then horns are hushed, the oilsmoke rarifies,
Above the idling motors one can tell
The packet's smooth approach, the slip,
Slip of the silken river past the sides,   10
The ringing of clear bells, the dip
And slow cascading of the paddle wheel.

How much life metaphors bring to poetry may be seen by comparing two poems by Tennyson and Blake.

Alfred, Lord Tennyson (1809–1892)
FLOWER IN THE CRANNIED WALL   1869

Flower in the crannied wall,
I pluck you out of the crannies,
I hold you here, root and all, in my hand,
Little flower—but *if* I could understand
What you are, root and all, and all in all,
I should know what God and man is.

How many metaphors does this poem contain? None. Compare it with a briefer poem on a similar theme: the quatrain that begins Blake's "Auguries of Innocence." (We follow here the opinion of W. B. Yeats who, in editing Blake's poems, thought the lines ought to be printed separately.)

William Blake (1757–1827)

TO SEE A WORLD IN A GRAIN OF SAND   (about 1803)

To see a world in a grain of sand
And a heaven in a wild flower,
Hold infinity in the palm of your hand
And eternity in an hour.

Set beside Blake's poem, Tennyson's — short though it is — seems lengthy. What contributes to the richness of "To see a world in a grain of sand" is Blake's use of a metaphor in every line. And every metaphor is loaded with suggestion. Our world does indeed resemble a grain of sand: in being round, in being stony, in being one of a myriad (the suggestions go on and on). Like Blake's grain of sand, a metaphor holds much, within a small circumference.

Sylvia Plath (1932–1963)

METAPHORS   1960

I'm a riddle in nine syllables,
An elephant, a ponderous house,
A melon strolling on two tendrils.
O red fruit, ivory, fine timbers!
This loaf's big with its yeasty rising.
Money's new-minted in this fat purse.
I'm a means, a stage, a cow in calf.
I've eaten a bag of green apples,
Boarded the train there's no getting off.

QUESTIONS

1. To what central fact do all the metaphors in this poem refer?
2. In the first line, what has the speaker in common with a riddle? Why does she say she has *nine* syllables?
3. How would you describe the tone of this poem? (Perhaps the poet expresses more than one attitude.) What attitude is conveyed in the metaphors of an elephant, "a ponderous house," "a melon strolling on two tendrils"? By the metaphors of red fruit, ivory, fine timbers, new-minted money? By the metaphor in the last line?

Emily Dickinson (1830–1886)

It dropped so low—in my Regard   (about 1863)

It dropped so low–in my Regard–
I heard it hit the Ground–
And go to pieces on the Stones
At bottom of my Mind–

Yet blamed the Fate that flung it–*less*
Than I denounced Myself,
For entertaining Plated Wares
Upon My Silver Shelf–

Questions

1. What is *it*? What two things are compared?
2. How much of the poem develops and amplifies this comparison?

Anonymous (English)

There was a man of double deed   1783

There was a man of double deed
Who sowed his garden full of seed.
When the seed began to grow
'Twas like a garden full of snow,
When the snow began to melt   5
'Twas like a ship without a belt,
When the ship began to sail
'Twas like a bird without a tail,
When the bird began to fly
'Twas like an eagle in the sky,   10
When the sky began to roar
'Twas like a lion at the door,
When the door began to crack
'Twas like a stick across my back,
When my back began to smart   15
'Twas like a penknife in my heart,
And when my heart began to bleed
'Twas death and death and death indeed.

THERE WAS A MAN OF DOUBLE DEED. This traditional nursery rime may have originated as a chant to the rhythm of a bouncing ball. Its opening lines echo an old proverb: "A man of words and not of deeds is like a garden full of weeds." 6. *belt:* a series of armored plates at a ship's water line.

Question

Does this seem no more than rigmarole or do you find it making any sense? Consider possible meanings of the phrase *double deed* and ways in which the objects joined in similes might be truly similar.

Ruth Whitman (b. 1922)

Castoff Skin   1973

She lay in her girlish sleep at ninety-six,
small as a twig.
Pretty good figure

for an old lady, she said to me once.
Then she crawled away, leaving
a tiny stretched transparence

behind her. When I kissed her paper cheek
I thought of the snake,
of his quick motion.

Questions

1. Explain the central metaphor in "Castoff Skin."
2. What other figures of speech does the poem contain?

Denise Levertov (b. 1923)

Leaving Forever   1964

He says the waves in the ship's wake
are like stones rolling away.
I don't see it that way.
But I see the mountain turning,
turning away its face as the ship
takes us away.

Questions

1. What do you understand to be the man's feelings about leaving forever?
   How does the speaker feel? With what two figures of speech does the poet
   express these conflicting views?
2. Suppose that this poem had ended in another simile (instead of its three last
   lines):

   I see the mountain as a suitcase
   left behind on the shore
   as the ship takes us away.

   How is Denise Levertov's choice of a figure of speech a much stronger one?

Exercise: *What Is Similar?*

Each of these quotations contains a simile or a metaphor. In each of these figures of speech, what two things is the poet comparing? Try to state exactly what
you understand the two things to have in common: the most striking similarity
or similarities that the poet sees.

1. Think of the storm roaming the sky uneasily
   like a dog looking for a place to sleep in,
   listen to it growling.
   > —Elizabeth Bishop, "Little Exercise"

2. When the hounds of spring are on winter's traces . . .
   > —Algernon Charles Swinburne, "Atalanta in Calydon"

3. The scarlet of the maples can shake me like a cry
   Of bugles going by.
   > —Bliss Carman, "A Vagabond Song"

4. "Hope" is the thing with feathers—
   That perches in the soul—
   And sings the tune without the words—
   And never stops—at all—
   > —Emily Dickinson, an untitled poem

5. Work without Hope draws nectar in a sieve . . .
   > —Samuel Taylor Coleridge, "Work Without Hope"

6. The finish of his hands
   shows oil, grain, knots
   where his growth scarred him.
   > —Carolyn Forché, "Dulcimer Maker"

OTHER FIGURES

When Shakespeare asks, in a sonnet,

> O! how shall summer's honey breath hold out
> Against the wrackful siege of batt'ring days,

it might seem at first that he mixes metaphors. How can a *breath* confront the battering ram of an invading army? But it is summer's breath and, by giving it to summer, Shakespeare makes the season a man or woman. It is as if the fragrance of summer were the breath within a person's body, and winter were the onslaught of old age.

Such is one instance of **personification:** a figure of speech in which a thing, an animal, or an abstract term (*truth, nature*) is made human. A personification extends throughout this whole short poem:

James Stephens (1882–1950)
THE WIND   1915

The wind stood up and gave a shout.
He whistled on his fingers and

Kicked the withered leaves about
And thumped the branches with his hand

And said he'd kill and kill and kill,
And so he will and so he will.

The wind is a wild man, and evidently it is not just any autumn breeze but a hurricane or at least a stiff gale. In poems that do not work as well as this one, personification may be employed mechanically. Hollow-eyed personifications walk the works of lesser English poets of the eighteenth century: Coleridge has quoted the beginning of one such neoclassical ode, "Inoculation! heavenly Maid, descend!" It is hard for the contemporary reader to be excited by William Collins's "The Passions, An Ode for Music" (1747), which personifies, stanza by stanza, Fear, Anger, Despair, Hope, Revenge, Pity, Jealousy, Love, Hate, Melancholy, and Cheerfulness, and has them listen to Music, until even "Brown Exercise rejoiced to hear, / And Sport leapt up, and seized his beechen spear." Still, the portraits of the Seven Deadly Sins in the four-teenth-century *Vision of Piers Plowman* remain memorable: "Thanne come Slothe al bislabered, with two slimy eiyen. . . ." In "Two Sonnets on Fame" John Keats makes an abstraction come alive in seeing Fame as "a wayward girl."

Hand in hand with personification often goes **apostrophe:** a way of addressing someone or something invisible or not ordinarily spoken to. In an apostrophe, a poet (in these examples Wordsworth) may address an inanimate object ("Spade! with which Wilkinson hath tilled his lands"), some dead or absent person ("Milton! thou shouldst be living at this hour"), an abstract thing ("Return, Delights!"), or a spirit ("Thou Soul that art the eternity of thought"). More often than not, the poet uses apostrophe to anounce a lofty and serious tone. An "O" may even be put in front of it ("O moon!") since, according to W. D. Snodgrass, every poet has a right to do so at least once in a lifetime. But apostrophe doesn't have to be highfalutin. It is a means of giving life to the inanimate. It is a way of giving body to the intangible, a way of speaking to it person to person, as in the words of a moving American spiritual: "Death, ain't you got no shame?"

Most of us, from time to time, emphasize a point with a statement containing exaggeration: "Faster than greased lightning," "I've told him a thousand times." We speak, then, not literal truth but use a figure of speech called **overstatement** (or **hyperbole**). Poets too, being fond of emphasis, often exaggerate for effect. Instances are Marvell's profession of a love that should grow "Vaster than empires, and more slow" and Burgon's description of Petra: "A rose-red city, half as old as Time." Overstatement can be used also for humorous purposes, as in a fat woman's boast (from a blues song): "Every time I shake, some skinny gal loses her home."[1] The opposite is **understatement,** implying more than is said. Mark Twain in *Life on the Mississippi* recalls how, as an ap-

---

[1] Quoted by LeRoi Jones in *Blues People* (New York: Wm. Morrow, 1963).

prentice steamboat-pilot asleep when supposed to be on watch, he was roused by the pilot and sent clambering to the pilot house: "Mr. Bixby was close behind, commenting." Another example is Robert Frost's line "One could do worse than be a swinger of birches" — the conclusion of a poem that has suggested that to swing on a birch tree is one of the most deeply satisfying activities in the world.

In **metonymy,** the name of a thing is substituted for that of another closely associated with it. For instance, we say "The White House decided," and mean the president did. When John Dyer writes in "Grongar Hill,"

> A little rule, a little sway,
> A sun beam on a winter's day,
> Is all the proud and might have
> Between the cradle and the grave,

we recognize that *cradle* and *grave* signify birth and death. A kind of metonymy, **synecdoche** is the use of a part of a thing to stand for the whole of it or vice versa. We say "She lent a hand," and mean that she lent her entire presence. Similarly, Milton in "Lycidas" refers to greedy clergymen as "blind mouths." Another kind of metonymy is the **transferred epithet:** a device of emphasis in which the poet attributes some characteristic of a thing to another thing closely associated with it. When Thomas Gray observes that, in the evening pastures, "drowsy tinklings lull the distant folds," he well knows that sheep's bells do not drowse, but sheep do. When Hart Crane, describing the earth as seen from an airplane, speaks of "nimble blue plateaus," he attributes the airplane's motion to the earth.

Paradox occurs in a statement that at first strikes us as self-contradictory but that on reflection makes some sense. "The peasant," said G. K. Chesterton, "lives in a larger world than the globe-trotter." Here, two different meanings of *larger* are contrasted: "greater in spiritual values" versus "greater in miles." Some paradoxical statements, however, are much more than plays on words. In a moving sonnet, the blind John Milton tells how one night he dreamed he could see his dead wife. The poem ends in a paradox:

> But oh, as to embrace me she inclined,
> I waked, she fled, and day brought back my night.

EXERCISE: *Paradox*

What paradoxes do you find in the following poem? For each, explain the sense that underlies the statement.

Chidiock Tichborne (1558?–1586)

ELEGY, WRITTEN WITH HIS OWN HAND
IN THE TOWER BEFORE HIS EXECUTION   1586

My prime of youth is but a frost of cares,
  My feast of joy is but a dish of pain,
My crop of corn is but a field of tares°,   *weeds*
  And all my good is but vain hope of gain:
The day is past, and yet I saw no sun,   5
And now I live, and now my life is done.

My tale was heard, and yet it was not told,
  My fruit is fall'n, and yet my leaves are green,
My youth is spent, and yet I am not old,
  I saw the world, and yet I was not seen: 10
My thread is cut, and yet it is not spun,
And now I live, and now my life is done.

I sought my death, and found it in my womb,
  I looked for life, and saw it was a shade,
I trod the earth, and knew it was my tomb,   15
  And now I die, and now I was but made:
My glass is full, and now my glass is run,
And now I live, and now my life is done.

Asked to define the difference between men and women, Samuel Johnson replied, "I can't conceive, madam, can you?" The great dictionary-maker was using a figure of speech known to classical rhetoricians as *paranomasia*, better known to us as a **pun** or play on words. How does a pun operate? It reminds us of another word (or other words) of similar or identical sound but of very different denotation. Although puns at their worst can be mere piddling quibbles, at best they can sharply point to surprising but genuine resemblances. The name of a dentist's country estate, Tooth Acres, is accurate: aching teeth paid for the land. In poetry, a pun may be facetious, as in Thomas Hood's ballad of "Faithless Nelly Gray":

> Ben Battle was a soldier bold,
>   And used to war's alarms;
> But a cannon-ball took off his legs,
>   So he laid down his arms!

Or it may be serious, as in these lines on war by E. E. Cummings:

> the bigness of cannon
> is skilful,

(*is skilful* becoming *is kill-ful* when read aloud), or perhaps, as in

Shakespeare's song in *Cymbeline*, "Fear no more the heat o' th' sun," both facetious and serious at once:

> Golden lads and girls all must,
> As chimney-sweepers, come to dust.

George Herbert (1593–1633)

THE PULLEY   1633

> When God at first made man,
> Having a glass of blessings standing by—
> Let us (said he) pour on him all we can;
> Let the world's riches, which dispersèd lie,
>   Contract into a span.   5
>
> So strength first made a way,
> Then beauty flowed, then wisdom, honor, pleasure:
> When almost all was out, God made a stay,
> Perceiving that, alone of all His treasure,
>   Rest in the bottom lay.   10
>
> For if I should (said he)
> Bestow this jewel also on My creature,
> He would adore My gifts instead of Me,
> And rest in Nature, not the God of Nature:
>   So both should losers be.   15
>
> Yet let him keep the rest,
> But keep them with repining restlessness;
> Let him be rich and weary, that at least,
> If goodness lead him not, yet weariness
>   May toss him to My breast.   20

QUESTIONS

1. What different senses of the word *rest* does Herbert bring into this poem?
2. How do God's words in line 16, *Yet let him keep the rest,* seem paradoxical?
3. What do you feel to be the tone of Herbert's poem? Does the punning make the poem seem comic?
4. Why is the poem called "The Pulley"? What is its implied metaphor?

To sum up: even though figures of speech are not to be taken *only* literally, they refer us to a tangible world. By *personifying* an eagle, Tennyson reminds us that the bird and humankind have certain characteristics in common. Through *metonymy*, a poet can focus our attention on a particular detail in a larger object; through *hyperbole* and *understatement*, make us see the physical actuality in back of words. *Pun* and *paradox* cause us to realize this actuality, too, and probably surprise us enjoyably at the same time. Through *apostrophe*, the poet animates the inanimate and asks it to listen — speaks directly to an immediate god or to the revivified dead. Put to such uses, figures of speech have power. They are more than just ways of playing with words.

Edmund Waller (1606–1687)

ON A GIRDLE   1645

That which her slender waist confined,
Shall now my joyful temples bind;
No monarch but would give his crown,
His arms might do what this has done.

It was my heaven's extremest sphere,   5
The pale° which held that lovely deer;   *enclosure*
My joy, my grief, my hope, my love,
Did all within this circle move!

A narrow compass! and yet there
Dwelt all that's good, and all that's fair!   10
Give me but what this riband bound,
Take all the rest the sun goes round!

ON A GIRDLE. Lines 1–2. *That which . . . temples bind:* A courtly lover might bind his brow with a lady's ribbon, to signify he was hers. 5. *extremest sphere:* In Ptolemaic astronomy, the outermost of the concentric spheres that surround the earth. In its wall the farthest stars are set.

QUESTIONS

1. To what things is the girdle compared?
2. Explain the pun in line 4. What effect does it have upon the tone of the poem?
3. Why is the effect of this pun different from that of Thomas Hood's play on the same word in "Faithless Nelly Gray" (quoted on p. 88)?
4. What does *compass* denote in line 9?
5. What paradox occurs in lines 9–10?
6. How many of the poem's statements are hyperbolic? Is the compliment the speaker pays his lady too grandiose to be believed? Explain.

John Donne (1572–1631)

A HYMN TO GOD THE FATHER   (1623)

Wilt Thou forgive that sin where I begun,
    Which is my sin, though it were done before?
Wilt Thou forgive those sins through which I run,
    And do them still, though still I do deplore?
        When Thou hast done, Thou hast not done,   5
            For I have more.

Wilt Thou forgive that sin by which I have won
  Others to sin? and made my sin their door?
Wilt Thou forgive that sin which I did shun
  A year or two, but wallowed in a score?   10
    When Thou hast done, Thou hast not done,
      For I have more.

I have a sin of fear, that when I have spun
  My last thread, I shall perish on the shore;
Swear by Thyself that at my death Thy Sun   15
  Shall shine as it shines now, and heretofore;
    And, having done that, Thou hast done,
      I have no more.

A HYMN TO GOD THE FATHER. According to his biographer Izaak Walton, Donne wrote
this poem during an illness which brought him close to death.

QUESTIONS

1. Donne's wife, who had died in 1617, was named Anne More. Do you think
   he is punning on her name? Would that interpretation make sense?
2. For what different meanings can we read lines 5–6, 11–12, 17–18?
3. Discuss how fairly it can be charged that, because of its puns, Donne's poem
   is not serious.

Theodore Roethke (1908–1963)

I KNEW A WOMAN   1958

I knew a woman, lovely in her bones,
When small birds sighed, she would sigh back at them;
Ah, when she moved, she moved more ways than one:
The shapes a bright container can contain!
Of her choice virtues only gods should speak,   5
Or English poets who grew up on Greek
(I'd have them sing in chorus, cheek to cheek).

How well her wishes went! She stroked my chin,
She taught me Turn, and Counter-turn, and Stand;
She taught me Touch, that undulant white skin;   10
I nibbled meekly from her proffered hand;
She was the sickle; I, poor I, the rake,
Coming behind her for her pretty sake
(But what prodigious mowing we did make).

Love likes a gander, and adores a goose: 15
Her full lips pursed, the errant note to seize;
She played it quick, she played it light and loose;
My eyes, they dazzled at her flowing knees;
Her several parts could keep a pure repose,
Or one hip quiver with a mobile nose   20
(She moved in circles, and those circles moved).

Let seed be grass, and grass turn into hay:
I'm martyr to a motion not my own;
What's freedom for? To know eternity.
I swear she cast a shadow white as stone.   25
But who would count eternity in days?
These old bones live to learn her wanton ways:
(I measure time by how a body sways).

QUESTIONS

1. What outrageous puns do you find in Roethke's poem? Describe the effect of them.
2. What kind of figure of speech occurs in all three lines: *Of her choice virtues only gods should speak; My eyes, they dazzled at her flowing knees;* and *I swear she cast a shadow white as stone?*
3. What sort of figure is the poet's reference to himself as *old bones?*
4. Do you take *Let seed be grass, and grass turn into hay* as figurative language, or literal statement?
5. If you agree that the tone of this poem is witty and playful, do you think the poet is making fun of the woman? What is his attitude toward her? What part do figures of speech play in communicating it?

FOR REVIEW AND FURTHER STUDY

Robert Frost (1874–1963)

TREE AT MY WINDOW   1928

Tree at my window, window tree,
My sash is lowered when night comes on;
But let there never be curtain drawn
Between you and me.

Vague dream-head lifted out of the ground,   5
And thing next most diffuse to cloud,
Not all your light tongues talking aloud
Could be profound.

But, tree, I have seen you taken and tossed,
And if you have seen me when I slept,   10
You have seen me when I was taken and swept
And all but lost.

That day she put our heads together,
Fate had her imagination about her,
Your head so much concerned with outer,   15
Mine with inner, weather.

QUESTIONS

1. What is the central metaphor of this poem? Is it explicit or implied?

2. What is meant by *light tongues* (line 7)? What resemblances does this comparison point out?
3. What do you understand from the *inner weather* (line 16) by which the speaker was *taken and swept*?
4. What use does Frost make of personification? What does it contribute to the poem?

James C. Kilgore (b. 1928)

THE WHITE MAN PRESSED THE LOCKS   1970

Driving down the concrete vein,
Away from the smoky heart,
Through the darkening, blighted body,
Pausing at clotted arteries,
The white man pressed the locks
   on all the sedan's doors,
Sped toward the white corpuscles
   in the white arms
     hugging the black city.

QUESTIONS

1. Explain the two implied metaphors in this poem: what are the two bodies?
2. How do you take the word *hugging*? Is this a loving embrace or a stranglehold?
3. What, in your own words, is the poet's theme?

Elizabeth Jennings (b. 1926)

DELAY   1953

The radiance of that star that leans on me
Was shining years ago. The light that now
Glitters up there my eye may never see
And so the time lag teases me with how

Love that loves now may not reach me until
Its first desire is spent. The star's impulse
Must wait for eyes to claim it beautiful
And love arrived may find us somewhere else.

QUESTIONS

1. What is the poet comparing in this metaphor?
2. Why would the metaphor not have been available to a poet in Shakespeare's time?
3. What is the tone of the poem? How does the speaker feel about the *radiance of that star*—simply joyous and glad, as we might expect?

4. What connotations has the word *impulse* (line 6)? What is the implied metaphor here?

EXERCISE: *Figure Spotting*

In each of these poems, what figures of speech do you notice? For each metaphor or simile, try to state what is compared. In any use of metonymy, what is represented?

Richard Wilbur (b. 1921)
SLEEPLESS AT CROWN POINT   1976

All night, this headland
Lunges into the rumpling
Capework of the wind.

Anonymous (English)
THE FORTUNES OF WAR, I TELL YOU PLAIN   (1854–1856)

The fortunes of war, I tell you plain,
Are a wooden leg – or a golden chain.

A. E. Housman (1859–1936)
FROM THE WASH THE LAUNDRESS SENDS   1922

From the wash the laundress sends
My collars home with raveled ends:
I must fit, now these are frayed,
My neck with new ones London-made.

Homespun collars, homespun hearts,
Wear to rags in foreign parts.
Mine at least's as good as done,
And I must get a London one.

Robert Frost (1874–1963)
THE SECRET SITS   1936

We dance round in a ring and suppose,
But the Secret sits in the middle and knows.

Charles Simic (b. 1938)

FORK 1971

This strange thing must have crept
Right out of hell.
It resembles a bird's foot
Worn around the cannibal's neck.

As you hold it in your hand,
As you stab with it into a piece of meat,
It is possible to imagine the rest of the bird:
Its head which like your fist
Is large, bald, beakless and blind.

Ishmael Reed (b. 1938)

.05 1973

If i had a nickel
For all the women who've
Rejected me in my life
I would be the head of the
World Bank with a flunkie 5
To hold my derby as i
Prepared to fly chartered
Jet to sign a check
Giving India a new lease
On life 10

If i had a nickel for
All the women who've loved
Me in my life i would be
The World Bank's assistant
Janitor and wouldn't need 15
To wear a derby
All i'd think about would
Be going home

A. R. Ammons (b. 1926)

AUTO MOBILE 1971

For the bumps bangs & scratches of
collisive encounters
madam
I through time's ruts and weeds
sought you, metallic, your 5

stainless steel flivver:
I have banged you, bumped
and scratched, side-swiped,
momocked & begommed you &
your little flivver still   10
works so well.

W. S. Merwin (b. 1927)
Song of Man Chipping an Arrowhead   1973

Little children you will all go
but the one you are hiding
will fly

Robert Burns (1759–1796)
Oh, my love is like a red, red rose   (about 1788)

Oh, my love is like a red, red rose
    That's newly sprung in June;
My love is like the melody
    That's sweetly played in tune.

So fair art thou, my bonny lass,   5
    So deep in love am I;
And I will love thee still, my dear,
    Till a' the seas gang° dry.   *go*

Till a' the seas gang dry, my dear,
    And the rocks melt wi' the sun;   10
And I will love thee still, my dear,
    While the sands o' life shall run.

And fare thee weel, my only love!
    And fare thee weel awhile!
And I will come again, my love   15
    Though it were ten thousand mile.

Ogden Nash (1902–1971)
Very Like a Whale   1934

One thing that literature would be greatly the better for
Would be a more restricted employment by authors of simile and meta-
        phor.
Authors of all races, be they Greeks, Romans, Teutons or Celts,
Can't seem just to say that anything is the thing it is but have to go out of
        their way to say that it is like something else.

What does it mean when we are told   5
That the Assyrian came down like a wolf on the fold?
In the first place, George Gordon Byron had had enough experience
To know that it probably wasn't just one Assyrian, it was a lot of As-
  syrians.
However, as too many arguments are apt to induce apoplexy and thus
  hinder longevity,
We'll let it pass as one Assyrian for the sake of brevity.   10
Now then, this particular Assyrian, the one whose cohorts were gleaming
  in purple and gold,
Just what does the poet mean when he says he came down like a wolf on
  the fold?
In heaven and earth more than is dreamed of in our philosophy there are a
  great many things,
But I don't imagine that among them there is a wolf with purple and gold
  cohorts or purple and gold anythings.
No, no, Lord Byron, before I'll believe that this Assyrian was actually like
  a wolf I must have some kind of proof;   15
Did he run on all fours and did he have a hairy tail and a big red mouth
  and big white teeth and did he say Woof woof woof?
Frankly I think it very unlikely, and all you were entitled to say, at the
  very most,
Was that the Assyrian cohorts came down like a lot of Assyrian cohorts
  about to destroy the Hebrew host.
But that wasn't fancy enough for Lord Byron, oh dear me no, he had to in-
  vent a lot of figures of speech and then interpolate them,
With the result that whenever you mention Old Testament soldiers to
  people they say'Oh yes, they're the ones that a lot of wolves dressed
  up in gold and purple ate them.   20
That's the kind of thing that's being done all the time by poets, from
  Homer to Tennyson;
They're always comparing ladies to lilies and veal to venison.
How about the man who wrote,
Her little feet stole in and out like mice beneath her petticoat?
Wouldn't anybody but a poet think twice   25
Before stating that his girl's feet were mice?
Then they always say things like that after a winter storm
The snow is a white blanket. Oh it is, is it, all right then, you sleep under a
  six-inch blanket of snow and I'll sleep under a half-inch blanket of
  unpoetical blanket material and we'll see which one keeps warm,
And after that maybe you'll begin to comprehend dimly
What I mean by too much metaphor and simile.   30

VERY LIKE A WHALE. The title is from *Hamlet* (Act III, scene 2): Feigning madness, Hamlet
likens the shape of a cloud to a whale. "Very like a whale," says Polonius, who, to humor
his prince, will agree to the accuracy of any figure at all. Nash's art has been described by
Max Eastman in *Enjoyment of Laughter* (New York: Simon and Schuster, 1936):

> If you have ever tried to write rimed verse, you will recognize in Nash's writing
> every naïve crime you were ever tempted to commit—artificial inversions, pre-
> tended rimes, sentences wrenched and mutilated to bring the rime-word to the end

of the line, words assaulted and battered into riming whether they wanted to or not, ideas and whole dissertations dragged in for the sake of a rime, the metrical beat delayed in order to get all the necessary words in, the metrical beat speeded up unconscionably because there were not enough words to put in.

QUESTIONS

1. Nash alludes to the opening lines of Byron's poem "The Destruction of Sennacherib" (see page 152):

The Assyrian came down like the wolf on the fold,
And his cohorts were gleaming in purple and gold;

and to Sir John Suckling's portrait of a bride in "A Ballad Upon a Wedding":

Her feet beneath her petticoat,
Like little mice stole in and out,
As if they feared the light: . . .

How can these metaphors be defended against Nash's quibbles?
2. What valuable functions of simile and metaphor in poetry is Nash pretending to ignore?

7 Song

SINGING AND SAYING

Most poems are more memorable than most ordinary speech, and when music is combined with poetry the result can be more memorable still. The differences between speech, poetry, and song may appear if we consider, first of all, this fragment of an imaginary conversation between two lovers:

> Let's not drink; let's just sit here and look at each other. Or put a kiss inside my goblet and I won't want anything to drink.

Forgettable language, we might think; but let's try to make it a little more interesting:

> Drink to me only with your eyes, and I'll pledge my love to you with my
>   eyes;
> Or leave a kiss within the goblet, that's all I'll want to drink.

The passage is closer to poetry, but still has a distance to go. At least we now have a figure of speech — the metaphor that love is wine, implied in the statement that one lover may salute another by lifting an eye as well as by lifting a goblet. But the sound of the words is not yet especially interesting. Here is another try, by Ben Jonson:

> Drink to me only with thine eyes,
>   And I will pledge with mine;
> Or leave a kiss but in the cup,
>   And I'll not ask for wine.

In these opening lines from Jonson's poem "To Celia," the improvement is noticeable. These lines are poetry; their language has become special. For one thing, the lines rime (with an additional rime sound on *thine*). There is interest, too, in the proximity of the words *kiss* and *cup:* the repetition (or alliteration) of the *k* sound. The rhythm of the lines has become regular; generally every other word (or syllable) is stressed:

> DRINK to me ON-ly WITH thine EYES,
>   And I will PLEDGE with MINE;
> OR LEAVE a KISS but IN the CUP,
>   And I'LL not ASK for WINE.

All these devices of sound and rhythm, together with metaphor, produce a pleasing effect — more pleasing than the effect of "Let's not drink; let's look at each other." But the words became more pleasing still when later set to music:

Drink to me on-ly with thine eyes, and I will pledge with mine,

Or leave a kiss but in the cup, and I'll not ask for wine.

In this memorable form, the poem is still alive today.

Ben Jonson (1573?–1637)

To Celia   1616

Drink to me only with thine eyes,
    And I will pledge with mine;
Or leave a kiss but in the cup,
    And I'll not ask for wine.
The thirst that from the soul doth rise   5
    Doth ask a drink divine;
But might I of Jove's nectar sup,
    I would not change for thine.

I sent thee late a rosy wreath,
    Not so much honoring thee   10
As giving it a hope that there
    It could not withered be.
But thou thereon didst only breathe,
    And sent'st it back to me;
Since when it grows, and smells, I swear,   15
    Not of itself but thee.

A compliment to a lady has rarely been put in language more graceful, more wealthy with interesting sounds. Other figures of speech besides metaphor make them unforgettable: for example, the hyperbolic tributes to the power of the lady's sweet breath, which can start picked roses growing again, and her kisses, which even surpass the nectar of the gods.

This song falls into stanzas—as many poems that resemble songs also do. A **stanza** (Italian for "station," "stopping-place," or "room") is a group of lines whose pattern is repeated throughout the poem. Most songs have more than one stanza. When printed, the stanzas of songs and poems usually are set off from one another by space. When sung, stanzas of songs are indicated by a pause or by the introduction of a refrain, or chorus (a line or lines repeated). The word **verse,** which strictly refers to one line of a poem, is sometimes loosely used to mean a whole stanza: "All join in and sing the second verse!" In speaking of a stanza, whether sung or read, it is customary to indicate by a convenient algebra its **rime scheme,** the order in which rimed words recur. For instance, the rime scheme of this stanza by Herrick is *a b a b;* the first and third lines rime and so do the second and fourth:

> Round, round, the roof doth run;
>   And being ravished thus,
> Come, I will drink a tun
>   To my Propertius.

Refrains are words, phrases, or lines repeated at intervals in a song or songlike poem. A refrain usually follows immediately after a stanza, and when it does, it is called **terminal refrain.** A refrain whose words change slightly with each recurrence is called an **incremental refrain,** as in "Frankie and Johnny" (p. 112). Sometimes we also hear an **internal refrain:** one that appears within a stanza, generally in a position that stays fixed throughout a poem. Both internal refrains and terminal refrains are used to great effect in the traditional song "The Cruel Mother":

Anonymous (traditional Scottish ballad)

The Cruel Mother

She sat down below a thorn,
  Fine flowers in the valley,
And there she has her sweet babe born
  And the green leaves they grow rarely.

"Smile na sae° sweet, my bonny babe,"   *so* 5
  Fine flowers in the valley,
"And° ye smile sae sweet, ye'll smile me dead."   *if*
  And the green leaves they grow rarely.

She's taen out her little pen-knife,
  Fine flowers in the valley,   10
And twinned° the sweet babe o' its life,   *severed*
  And the green leaves they grow rarely.

She's howket° a grave by the light o' the moon,   *dug*
  Fine flowers in the valley,
And there she's buried her sweet babe in   15
  And the green leaves they grow rarely.

As she was going to the church,
  Fine flowers in the valley,
She saw a sweet babe in the porch
  And the green leaves they grow rarely.   20

"O sweet babe, and thou were mine,"
  Fine flowers in the valley,
"I wad cleed° thee in the silk so fine."   *dress*
  And the green leaves they grow rarely.

"O mother dear, when I was thine,"   25
  Fine flowers in the valley,
"You did na prove to me sae kind."
  And the green leaves they grow rarely.

Taken by themselves, the refrain lines might seem mere pretty nonsense. But interwoven with the story of the murdered child, they form a
terrible counterpoint. What do they come to mean? Possibly that Nature
keeps going about her chores, unmindful of sin and suffering. The effect is an ironic contrast. It is the repetitiveness of a refrain, besides,
that helps to give it power.

Songs tend to be written in language simple enough to be understood on first hearing. Recently, however, song-writers have been able
to assume that their audiences would pay close attention to their words.
Bob Dylan, Leonard Cohen, Don McLean, and others have employed
words more complicated and difficult than have most previous writers
of popular songs, requiring listeners sometimes to play their recordings
many times over, with trebles turned up all the way.

Many poems began life as songs but today, their tunes forgotten,
survive in poetry anthologies. Shakespeare studded his plays with
songs, and many of his contemporaries wrote verse to fit existing tunes.
Some poets, themselves musicians (like Thomas Campion), composed
both words and music. In Shakespeare's day, **madrigals,** short secular
songs for three or more voice-parts arranged in counterpoint, enjoyed
great favor. A madrigal by Chidiock Tichborne is given on page 88; and
another, an anonymous English madrigal, "The Silver Swan," on page
115.

Some poets who were not composers printed their work in madrigal books for others to set to music. In the seventeenth century, however, poetry and song seem to have fallen away from each other. By the end of the century, much new poetry, other than songs for plays, was written to be printed and to be silently read. Poets who wrote popular songs—like Thomas D'Urfey, compiler of the collection *Pills to Purge Melancholy*—were considered somewhat disreputable. With the notable exceptions of John Gay, who took existing popular tunes for *The Beggar's Opera*, and Robert Burns, who rewrote folk songs or made completely new words for them, few important English poets since Campion have been first-rate song-writers.

Occasionally, a poet has learned a thing or two from music. "But for the opera I could never have written *Leaves of Grass*," said Walt Whitman, who loved the Italian art form for its expansiveness. Coleridge, Hardy, Auden, and many others have learned from folk ballads, and T. S. Eliot patterned his thematically repetitive *Four Quartets* after the structure of a quartet in classicial music. "Poetry," said Ezra Pound, "begins to atrophy when it gets too far from music." Still, even in the twentieth century, the poet has been more often a corrector of printer's proofs than a tunesmith or performer.

Some people think that to make a poem and to travel about singing it, as many rock singer-composers now do, is a return to the venerable tradition of the **troubadours,** minstrels of the late Middle Ages. But there are differences. No doubt the troubadours had to please their patrons, but for better or worse their songs were not affected by a stopwatch in a producer's hand or by the technical resources of a sound studio. Bob Dylan has denied that he is a poet, and Paul Simon once told an interviewer, "If you want poetry read Wallace Stevens." Nevertheless, much has been made lately of current song lyrics as poetry.[1] Are rock songs poems? Clearly some, but not all, are. That the lyrics of a song cannot stand the scrutiny of a reader does not necessarily invalidate them, though; song-writers do not usually write in order to be read. Pete Seeger has quoted a saying of his father: "A printed folk song is like a photograph of a bird in flight." Still there is no reason not to photograph birds, or to read song lyrics. If the words seem rich and interesting, we may possibly increase our enjoyment of them and perhaps be able to sing them more accurately. Like most poems and songs of the past, most current songs may end in the trash can of time. And yet, certain memorable rimed and rhythmic lines may live on, especially if music has served them for a base and if singers have given them wide exposure.

[1] See the paperback anthologies *The Poetry of Rock,* Richard Goldstein, ed. (New York: Bantam, 1969), and *Rock Is Beautiful,* Stephanie Spinner, ed. (New York: Dell, 1970).

Compare the following poem by Edwin Arlington Robinson and a popular song lyric based on it. Notice what Paul Simon had to do to Robinson's original in order to make it into a song, and how Simon altered Robinson's conception.

Edwin Arlington Robinson (1869–1935)

RICHARD CORY   1897

Whenever Richard Cory went down town,
We people on the pavement looked at him:
He was a gentleman from sole to crown,
Clean favored, and imperially slim.

And he was always quietly arrayed,   5
And he was always human when he talked;
But still he fluttered pulses when he said,
"Good-morning," and he glittered when he walked.

And he was rich—yes, richer than a king—
And admirably schooled in every grace: 10
In fine°, we thought that he was everything   *in short*
To make us wish that we were in his place.

So on we worked, and waited for the light,
And went without the meat, and cursed the bread;
And Richard Cory, one calm summer night,   15
Went home and put a bullet through his head.

Paul Simon (b. 1942)

RICHARD CORY   1966

With Apologies to E. A. Robinson

They say that Richard Cory owns
One half of this old town,
With elliptical connections
To spread his wealth around.
Born into Society,   5
A banker's only child,
He had everything a man could want:
Power, grace and style.

Refrain:

But I, I work in his factory
And I curse the life I'm livin'   10

RICHARD CORY, by Paul Simon. If possible, listen to the ballad sung by Simon and Garfunkel on *Sounds of Silence* (Columbia recording CL 2469, stereo CS 9269).
© 1966 by Paul Simon. Used by permission.

And I curse my poverty
And I wish that I could be
Oh I wish that I could be
Oh I wish that I could be
Richard Cory.   15

The papers print his picture
Almost everywhere he goes:
Richard Cory at the opera,
Richard Cory at a show
And the rumor of his party   20
And the orgies on his yacht—
Oh he surely must be happy
With everything he's got.   *(Refrain.)*

He really gave to charity,
He had the common touch,   25
And they were grateful for his patronage
And they thanked him very much,
So my mind was filled with wonder
When the evening headlines read:
   "Richard Cory went home last night   30
   And put a bullet through his head."   *(Refrain.)*

BALLADS

Any narrative song, like Paul Simon's "Richard Cory," may be called a **ballad.** In English, some of the most famous ballads are **folk ballads,** loosely defined as anonymous story-songs transmitted orally before they were ever written down. Sir Walter Scott, a pioneer collector of Scottish folk ballads, drew the ire of an old woman whose songs he had transcribed: "They were made for singing and no' for reading, but ye ha'e broken the charm now and they'll never be sung mair." The old singer had a point. Print freezes songs and tends to hold them fast to a single version. However, if Scott and others had not written them down, many would have been lost.

In his monumental work *The English and Scottish Popular Ballads* (1882–1898), the American scholar Francis J. Child winnowed out 305 folk ballads he considered authentic — that is, creations of illiterate or semiliterate people who had preserved them orally. Child, who worked by insight as well as by learning, did such a good job of telling the difference between folk ballads and other kinds that later scholars have added only about a dozen ballads to his count. Often called **Child ballads,** his texts include "The Three Ravens," "Sir Patrick Spence," "The Twa Corbies," "Edward," "The Cruel Mother," and many others still on the lips of singers. Here is one of the best-known Child ballads.

Anonymous (traditional Scottish ballad)

BONNY BARBARA ALLAN

It was in and about the Martinmas time,
  When the green leaves were afalling,
That Sir John Graeme, in the West Country,
  Fell in love with Barbara Allan.

He sent his men down through the town,   5
  To the place where she was dwelling:
"O haste and come to my master dear,
  Gin° ye be Barbara Allan."   *if*

O hooly°, hooly rose she up,   *slowly*
  To the place where he was lying,   10
And when she drew the curtain by:
  "Young man, I think you're dying."

"O it's I'm sick, and very, very sick,
  And 'tis a' for Barbara Allan." —
"O the better for me ye's never be,   15
  Tho your heart's blood were aspilling.

"O dinna ye mind°, young man," said she,   *don't you remember*
  "When ye was in the tavern adrinking,
That ye made the health° gae round and round,   *toasts*
  And slighted Barbara Allan?"   20

He turned his face unto the wall,
  And death was with him dealing:
"Adieu, adieu, my dear friends all,
  And be kind to Barbara Allan."

And slowly, slowly raise she up,   25
  And slowly, slowly left him,
And sighing said she could not stay,
  Since death of life had reft him.

She had not gane a mile but twa,
  When she heard the dead-bell ringing,   30
And every jow° that the dead-bell geid,   *stroke*
  It cried, "Woe to Barbara Allan!"

"O mother, mother, make my bed!
  O make it saft and narrow!
Since my love died for me today,   35
  I'll die for him tomorrow."

BONNY BARBARA ALLAN. 1. *Martinmas:* Saint Martin's day, November 11.

QUESTIONS

1. In any line does the Scottish dialect cause difficulty? If so, try reading the line aloud.

2. Without ever coming out and explicitly calling Barbara hard-hearted, this ballad reveals that she is. In which stanza and by what means is her cruelty demonstrated?
3. At what point does Barbara evidently have a change of heart? Again, how does the poem dramatize this change without explicitly talking about it?
4. In many American versions of this ballad, noble knight John Graeme becomes an ordinary citizen. The gist of the story is the same, but at the end are these further stanzas, incorporated from a different ballad:

They buried Willie in the old churchyard
  And Barbara in the choir;
And out of his grave grew a red, red rose,
  And out of hers a briar.

They grew and grew to the steeple top
  Till they could grow no higher;
And there they locked in a true love's knot,
  The red rose round the briar.

Do you think this appendage heightens or weakens the final impact of the story? Can the American ending be defended as an integral part of a new song? Explain.
5. Paraphrase lines 9, 15–16, 22, 25–28. By putting these lines into prose, what has been lost?

As you can see from "Bonny Barbara Allan," in a traditional English or Scottish folk ballad the storyteller speaks of the lives and feelings of others. Even if the pronoun "I" occurs, it rarely has much personality. Characters often exchange dialogue, but no one character speaks all the way through. Events move rapidly, perhaps because some of the dull transitional stanzas have been forgotten. The events themselves, as ballad scholar Albert B. Friedman has said, are frequently "the stuff of tabloid journalism — sensational tales of lust, revenge and domestic crime. Unwed mothers slay their newborn babes; lovers unwilling to marry their pregnant mistresses brutally murder the poor women, for which, without fail, they are justly punished."[2] There are also many ballads about people who converse with the dead ("The Unquiet Grave") or with supernatural beings ("Thomas the Rimer") and about gallant knights ("Sir Patrick Spence"), and there are a few humorous ballads, usually about unhappy marriages.

The ballad-spinner has at hand a fund of ready-made epithets: steeds are usually "milk-white" or "berry-brown," lips "rosy" or "ruby-red," corpses and graves "clay-cold," beds (like Barbara Allan's) "soft and narrow." At the least, these conventional phrases are terse and understandable. Sometimes they add meaning: the king who sends Sir Patrick Spence to his doom drinks "blood-red wine." The clothing,

[2] Introduction to *The Viking Book of Folk Ballads of the English-Speaking World*, edited by Albert B. Friedman (New York: Viking Press, 1956).

steeds, and palaces of ladies and lords are always luxurious: a queen may wear "grass-green silk" or "Spanish leather" and ride a horse with "fifty silver bells and nine." Such descriptions are naive, for as Friedman points out, ballad-singers were probably peasants imagining what they had seen only from afar: the life of the nobility. This may be why the skin of ladies in folk ballads is ordinarily "milk-white," "lily-white," or "snow-white." In an agrarian society, where most people worked in the fields, not to be suntanned was a sign of gentility.

A favorite pattern of ballad-makers is the so-called **ballad stanza,** four lines rimed *a b c b*, tending to fall into 8, 6, 8, and 6 syllables:

> Clerk Saunders and Maid Margaret
> Walked owre yon garden green,
> And deep and heavy was the love
> That fell thir twa between°.   *between those two*

Though not the only possible stanza for a ballad, this easily singable quatrain has continued to attract poets since the Middle Ages. Close kin to the ballad stanza is **common meter,** a stanza found in hymns, such as "Amazing Grace," by the eighteenth-century English hymnist John Newton:

> Amazing grace! how sweet the sound
> That saved a wretch like me!
> I once was lost, but now am found,
> Was blind, but now I see.

Notice that its pattern is that of the ballad stanza except for its *two* pairs of rimes. That all its lines rime is probably a sign of more literate artistry than we usually hear in folk ballads. Another sign of schoolteachers' influence is that Newton's rimes are exact. (Rimes in folk ballads are often rough-and-ready, as if made by ear, rather than polished and exact, as if the riming words had been matched for their similar spellings. In "Barbara Allan," for instance, the hard-hearted lover's name rimes with *afalling, dwelling, aspilling, dealing,* and even with *ringing* and *adrinking.*) That so many hymns were written in common meter may have been due to convenience. If a congregation didn't know the tune to a hymn in common meter, they readily could sing its words to the tune of another such hymn they knew. Besides hymnists, many poets have favored common meter, among them A. E. Housman and Emily Dickinson.

Obviously, whatever stanza a folk ballad may have is determined not by any printed shape its poet wishes for it but by the demands of music. Here, for instance, is a folk ballad (one of the few Child overlooked) with a stanza much more complicated than the ballad stanza.[3]

---

[3] Collected by Cecil Sharp in *Folksongs from Somerset* (London: Novello & Co., Ltd., 1904–09).

Anonymous (traditional English ballad)

STILL GROWING

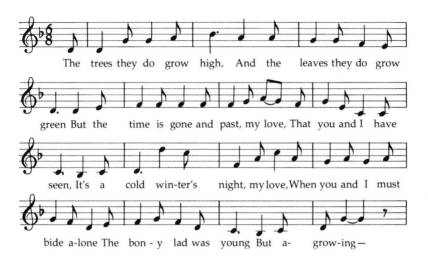

The trees they do grow high, and the leaves they do grow green;
    But the time is gone and past, my love, that you and I have seen:
It's a cold winter's night, my love, when you and I must bide alone.
    The bonny lad was young,
        But a-growing.   5

"O father, dear father, I'm feared you've done me harm
    You've married me a boy and I fear he is too young."
"O daughter, dear daughter, and if you stay at home and wait along o' me
    A lady you shall be,
        While he's a-growing.   10

"We'll send him to the college for one year or two
    And then perhaps in time, my love, a man he will grow.
I will buy you a bunch of white ribbons to tie about his bonny, bonny
        waist
    To let the ladies know
        That he's married."   15

At the age of sixteen, he was a married man,
    At the age of seventeen, she brought him a son;
At the age of eighteen, my love, O his grave was growing green,
    And so she put an end
        To his growing.   20

"I made my love a shroud of the holland so fine,"
    And every stitch she put in it the tears came trickling down;
"O once I had a sweetheart, but now I have got never a one
    So fare you well my own true love
        For ever."   25

QUESTIONS

1. What are the features of this stanza pattern?
2. If you know music, sing or hum the melody. How has this tune apparently helped to shape words to it?
3. Consider in particular the fourth stanza, in which the action of the story is so greatly condensed and accelerated. Do you find it meaningless that the poor lad is so abruptly yanked from marriage to fatherhood and then into his grave? Do you find this brevity on the part of the storyteller in any way effective?

Related to traditional folk ballads but displaying characteristics of their own, **broadside ballads** (so called because they were printed on one sheet of paper) often were set to traditional tunes. Most broadside ballads were an early form of journalism made possible by the development of cheap printing and by the growth of audiences who could read, just barely. Sometimes merely humorous or tear-jerking, often they were rimed accounts of sensational news events. That they were widespread and often scorned in Shakespeare's day is attested by the character of Autolycus in *A Winter's Tale,* an itinerant hawker of ballads about sea monsters and strange pregnancies ("a usurer's wife was brought to bed of twenty money-bags"). Although many broadsides tend to be **doggerel** (verse full of irregularities due not to skill but to incompetence), many excellent poets had their work taken up and peddled in the streets — among them Marvell, Swift, and Byron.[4]

Because they stick in the mind and because they were inexpensive to publish and to purchase, broadsides in the nineteenth century often were used to convey social or political messages. Some of the best are **protest songs,** like "Song of the Lower Classes" (about 1848) by Ernest Jones. A stanza follows:

> We're low — we're low — we're very very low,
>   Yet from our fingers glide
> The silken flow — and the robes that glow
>   Round the limbs of the sons of pride.
> And what we get — and what we give —
>   We know, and we know our share;
> We're not too low the cloth to weave,
>   But too low the Cloth to wear!

Compare those lines with this modern protest ballad:

---

[4] A generous collection of broadsides has been assembled by Vivian de Sola Pinto and A. E. Rodway in *The Common Muse: An Anthology of Popular British Ballad Poetry, XVth-XXth Century* (St. Clair Shores, Mich.: Scholarly Press, 1957). See also *Irish Street Ballads,* edited by Colm O. Lochlainn (New York: Corinth Books, 1960), and Olive Woolley Burt, *American Murder Ballads and Their Stories* (New York: Oxford University Press, 1958).

Woody Guthrie (1912–1967)

PLANE WRECK AT LOS GATOS (DEPORTEE) 1961

The crops are all in and the peaches are rotting,
The oranges are piled in their creosote dumps;
You're flying them back to the Mexican border
To pay all their money to wade back again.

Refrain:

Goodbye to my Juan, Goodbye Rosalita;   5
Adiós mes amigos, Jesús and Marie,
You won't have a name when you ride the big airplane:
All they will call you will be deportee.

My father's own father he waded that river;
They took all the money he made in his life;   10
My brothers and sisters come working the fruit trees
And they rode the truck till they took down and died.

Some of us are illegal and some are not wanted,
Our work contract's out and we have to move on;
Six hundred miles to that Mexico border,   15
They chase us like outlaws, like rustlers, like thieves.

We died in your hills, we died in your deserts,
We died in your valleys and died on your plains;
We died neath your trees and we died in your bushes,
Both sides of this river we died just the same.   20

The sky plane caught fire over Los Gatos Canyon,
A fireball of lightning and shook all our hills.
Who are all these friends all scattered like dry leaves?
The radio says they are just deportees.

Is this the best way we can grow our big orchards?   25
Is this the best way we can grow our good fruit?
To fall like dry leaves to rot on my top soil
And be called by no name except deportees?

PLANE WRECK AT LOS GATOS (DEPORTEE), lyric by Woody Guthrie, music by Martin Hoffman, TRO. This song pays tribute to twenty-eight deported migrant workers killed when the airplane returning them to Mexico crashed on January 28, 1948, near Coalinga, California.

In making a song out of a news event, "Plane Wreck at Los Gatos" resembles a broadside ballad; but it is more like a folk ballad in that the singer, instead of sticking around to comment on the action, disappears and lets the characters speak for themselves. That is the way of most Child ballads: people in them may wail and mourn, but not the singer, who usually remains impersonal.

Literary ballads, not meant for singing, are written by sophisticated poets for book-educated readers who enjoy being reminded of folk ballads. Literary ballads imitate certain features of folk ballads: they may tell of tragic love affairs or of mortals who confront the supernatural; they may use conventional figures of speech, old-fangled diction, or ballad stanzas. Well-known poems of this kind include Keats's "La Belle Dame sans Merci" (page 222) and Coleridge's "Rime of the Ancient Mariner."

Anonymous (American ballad)

Frankie and Johnny

Frankie she was a good woman, Johnny he was her man,
And every silver dollar Frankie made went straight to her Johnny's hand.
He was her man, but he done her wrong.

Frankie and Johnny went walking, Johnny in a brand new suit.
"Cost me a hundred," says Frankie, "but don't my Johnny look cute?"   5
He was her man, but he done her wrong.

Frankie went down to the corner, she called for a thimble of gin,
She says to the fat bartender, "Has my lovin' Johnny been in?
I can't believe he's been doing me wrong."

"Ain't going to tell you no story, ain't going to tell you no lie,   10
Mister Johnny was in her 'bout an hour ago with a floozy named Ella Fly.
He is your man, but I believe he's doing you wrong."

Frankie ran down to the pawn shop, she didn't go there for fun.
She turned in her doorknob diamonds, she took out a forty-four gun.
He was her man, but he done her wrong.   15

Frankie ran down to the parlor-house, she leaned on the parlor-house bell.
"Stand out of my way, you floozies, or I'll splash you all over Hell!
I want my man, he's been doing me wrong."

Frankie looked over the transom, the tears ran out of her eyes.
There was her lovin' Johnny a-lovin' up Ella Fly.   20
He was her man, but he was doing her wrong.

She threw back her red silk kimono, she whipped out that old forty-four.
Rooty-toot-toot, three times she did shoot, right through that hardwood door.
He was her man, but he done her wrong.

Johnny grabbed off his Stetson, "O Lord no, Frankie, don't shoot!" 25
But Frankie squeezed the trigger three times more and he fell down like a
    stick of wood.
He was her man, but he done her wrong.

The first shot, Johnny staggered; the second shot, he fell;
The third shot took him through the heart and his face started coming out
    in Hell.
He was her man, but he done her wrong. 30

"O roll me over easy, roll me over slow,
Roll me over on my right side, honey, so my heart don't overflow.
I was your man, but I done you wrong."

Bring on your rubber-tired hearses, bring on your rubber-tired hacks.
There's eight men going to the burying yard and only seven of 'em com-
    ing back. 35
He was her man, but he done her wrong.

The judge look hard at the jury, says, "It's plain as plain can be.
This woman put some daylight through her man, it's murder in the sec-
    ond degree.
He was her man, and she done him wrong."

Now it wasn't murder in the second degree, it wasn't murder in the third, 40
All Frankie did was drop her man like a hunter drops a bird.
He was her man, but he done her wrong.

The jury went out on Frankie, sat under an electric fan,
Came back and said, "You're a free woman, go kill yourself another man
If he does you wrong, if he does you wrong." 45

"O put me away in a dungeon, put me in a cold, cold cell,
Put me where the north wind blows from the southeast corner of Hell.
I shot my man, 'cause he done me wrong."

Frankie she heard a rumbling, away down under the ground.
Maybe it was little Johnny where she had shot him down. 50
He was her man, but he done her wrong.

Frankie went out to the burying yard, just to look her Johnny in the face.
"Ain't it hard to see you, Johnny, in this lonesome place?"
He was her man, but he done her wrong.

Well, I looked down the lonesome street, Lord, as far off as I could see, 55
All I could hear was a two-string fiddle playing "Nearer, My God, to
    Thee."
He was her man, but he done her wrong.

FRANKIE AND JOHNNY. Hundreds of versions of this ballad exist; this one is a composite of many. In the 1890s a murder that took place either in St. Louis or in Kansas City, Missouri, became famous in folk song as the story of Frankie and Albert. About 1911, vaudeville singers changed Albert's name to Johnny and introduced other elements. 16. *parlor-house:* a brothel fancy enough to have a waiting room.

1. How would you describe the tone of this ballad?
2. Compare its account of Frankie's trial with these stanzas from an earlier "Frankie and Albert" version:

> They took little Frankie to the courthouse,
> They sat her in a big arm chair.
> She was waiting for the judge to say,
> "We will give her ninety-nine year,
> Because she killed her man in the first degree."
>
> But the judge he said to the jury,
> "It's plain as plain can be
> Why she shot the man she loved.
> I think she ought to go free
> Because a gambling man won't treat you right."
>
> Frankie walked out on the scaffold
> As brave as she could be:
> "When I shot the man I loved
> I murdered in the first degree.
> He was my man and I loved him so."

How is this earlier version different in tone?
3. How can it be claimed that "Frankie and Johnny" is composed in the ballad stanza (illustrated on page 518)? It is hardly likely that whoever wrote it knew Child ballads. Why do you suppose this stanza has been so popular for five hundreds years or more?

EXPERIMENT: *Seeing the Traits of Ballads*

In the anthology at the back of this book, read the Child ballads "Edward," "Sir Patrick Spence," "The Three Ravens," and "The Twa Corbies" (pages 713–716). With these ballads in mind, consider one or more of these modern poems:

> W. H. Auden, "As I Walked Out One Evening" (page 720)
> E. E. Cummings, "All in green went my love riding" (page 733)
> Walter de la Mare, "The Listeners" (page 734)
> Bob Dylan, "Subterranean Homesick Blues" (page 743)
> Dudley Randall, "Ballad of Birmingham" (page 792)
> William Jay Smith, "American Primitive" (page 808)
> William Butler Yeats, "Crazy Jane Talks with the Bishop" (page 828).

What characteristics of folk ballads do you find in them? In what ways do these modern poets depart from the traditions of folk ballads of the Middle Ages?

FOR REVIEW AND FURTHER STUDY

EXERCISE: *Songs or Poems or Both?*

Consider each of the following song lyrics. Which do you think can stand not only to be sung but to be read as poetry? Which probably should not be seen but only heard?

Anonymous (English madrigal)

FA, MI, FA, RE, LA, MI

Fa, mi, fa, re, la, mi,
Begin, my son, and follow me;
   Sing flat, fa mi,
   So shall we well agree.
      Hey tro loly lo.
      Hold fast, good son,
   With hey tro lily lo.
O sing this once again, lustily.

Anonymous (English madrigal)

THE SILVER SWAN, WHO LIVING HAD NO NOTE

The silver swan, who living had no note,
When death approached unlocked her silent throat;
Leaning her breast against the reedy shore,
Thus sung her first and last, and sung no more.
Farewell, all joys; O death, come close mine eyes;
More geese than swans now live, more fools than wise.

Ern Alpaugh (b. 1914)
Dewey G. Pell (b. 1917)

SWINGING CHICK

Swinging chick
You know she does the trick
Sho ba ba dee ba
She's so swinging
Always singing   5
She's my swinging chick

Swinging chick
Boy are we ever nice and thick
When she starts to doin' that swing and sway
The man in the moon's gotta get out of her way   10

Oh, swinging chick
Sho ba ba dee ba
She's my swing it
Pick it up and fling it
Swinging hum-a-dinging chick   15

For Review and Further Study   115

John Lennon (b. 1940)
Paul McCartney (b. 1942)

ELEANOR RIGBY   1966

Ah, look at all the lonely people!
Ah, look at all the lonely people!

Eleanor Rigby
Picks up the rice in the church where a wedding has been,
Lives in a dream,   5
Waits at the window
Wearing the face that she keeps in a jar by the door.
Who is it for?

All the lonely people,
Where do they all come from?   10
All the lonely people,
Where do they all belong?

Father McKenzie,
Writing the words of a sermon that no one will hear,
No one comes near   15
Look at him working,
Darning his socks in the night when there's nobody there.
What does he care?

All the lonely people
Where do they all come from?   20
All the lonely people
Where do they all belong?

Eleanor Rigby
Died in the church and was buried along with her name.
Nobody came.   25
Father McKenzie,
Wiping the dirt from his hands as he walks from the grave,
No one was saved.

All the lonely people,
Where do they all come from?   30
All the lonely people,
Where do they all belong?

Ah, look at all the lonely people!
Ah, look at all the lonely people!

Joni Mitchell (b. 1943)

BLACK CROW

1976

There's a crow flying
Dark and ragged
Tree to tree
He's black as the highway that's leading me
Now he's diving down   5
To pick up on something shiny
I feel like that black crow
Flying
In a blue sky.

I took a ferry to the highway   10
Then I drove to a pontoon plane
I took a plane to a taxi
And a taxi to a train
I've been travelling so long
How'm I ever going to know my home   15
When I see it again
I'm like a black crow flying
In a blue, blue sky.

In search of love and music
My whole life has been   20
Illumination
Corruption
And diving, diving, diving, diving,
Diving down to pick up on every shiny thing
Just like that black crow flying   25
In a blue sky.

I looked at the morning
After being up all night
I looked at my haggard face in the bathroom light
I looked out the window   30
And I saw that ragged soul take flight
I saw a black crow flying
In a blue sky
Oh I'm like a black crow flying
In a blue sky.   35

Anonymous (American song)

Good Mornin', Blues   1959

I woke up this mornin' with the blues all round my bed,
Yes, I woke up this morning with the blues all round my bed,
Went to eat my breakfast, had the blues all in my bread.

"Good mornin', blues, blues, how do you do?" (2)
"I'm feelin' pretty well, but, pardner, how are you?"   5

Yes, I woke up this morning, 'bout an hour 'fore day, (2)
Reached and grabbed the pillow where my baby used to lay.

If you ever been down, you know just how I feel, (2)
Feel like an engine, ain't got no drivin' wheel.

If I feel tomorrow, like I feel today, (2)   10
I'll stand right here, look a thousand miles away.

If the blues was whisky, I'd stay drunk all the time, (2)
Stay drunk, baby, just to wear you off my mind.

I got the blues so bad, it hurts my feet to walk, (2)
I got the blues so bad, it hurts my tongue to talk.   15

The blues jumped a rabbit, run him a solid mile, (2)
When the blues overtaken him, he hollered like a newborn child.

Good Mornin', Blues. This folk song has been adapted by Alan Lomax from a version by singer Huddie Ledbetter (Leadbelly). The number (2) indicates a line to be sung twice.

8 Sound

SOUND AS MEANING

Isak Dinesen, in a memoir of her life on a plantation in East Africa, tells how some Kikuyu tribesmen reacted to their first hearing of rimed verse:

> The Natives, who have a strong sense of rhythm, know nothing of verse, or at least did not know anything before the times of the schools, where they were taught hymns. One evening out in the maize-field, where we had been harvesting maize, breaking off the cobs and throwing them on to the ox-carts, to amuse myself, I spoke to the field laborers, who were mostly quite young, in Swahili verse. There was no sense in the verses, they were made for the sake of rime—"Ngumbe na-penda chumbe, Malaya mbaya. Wakamba na-kula mamba." The oxen like salt—whores are bad—The Wakamba eat snakes. It caught the interest of the boys, they formed a ring round me. They were quick to understand that meaning in poetry is of no consequence, and they did not question the thesis of the verse, but waited eagerly for the rime, and laughed at it when it came. I tried to make them themselves find the rime and finish the poem when I had begun it, but they could not, or would not, do that, and turned away their heads. As they had become used to the idea of poetry, they begged: "Speak again. Speak like rain." Why they should feel verse to be like rain I do not know. It must have been, however, an expression of applause, since in Africa rain is always longed for and welcomed.[1]

What the tribesmen had discovered is that poetry, like music, appeals to the ear. However limited it may be in comparison with the sound of an orchestra—or a tribal drummer—the sound of words in itself gives pleasure. However, we might doubt Isak Dinesen's assumption that "meaning in poetry is of no consequence." "Hey nonny-nonny" and such nonsense has a place in song lyrics and other poems, and we might take pleasure in hearing rimes in Swahili; but most good poetry has meaningful sound as well as musical sound. Certainly the words of a song have an effect different from that of wordless music: they go along

[1] Isak Dinesen, *Out of Africa* (New York: Random House, 1972).

with their music and, by making statements, add more meaning. The French poet Isodore Isou, founder of a literary movement called *lettrisme*, maintained that poems can be written not only in words but in letters (sample lines: *xyl, xyl, / prprali dryl / znglo trpylo pwi*). But the sound of letters alone, without denotation and connotation, has not been enough to make Letterist poems memorable. In the response of the Kikuyu tribesmen, there may have been not only the pleasure of hearing sounds but also the agreeable surprise of finding that things not usually associated had been brought together.

More powerful when in the company of meaning, not apart from it, the sounds of consonants and vowels can contribute greatly to a poem's effect. The sound of *s*, which can suggest the swishing of water, has rarely been used more accurately than in Surrey's line "Calm is the sea, the waves work less and less." When, in a poem, the sound of words working together with meaning pleases mind and ear, the effect is **euphony,** as in the following lines from Tennyson's "Come down, O maid":

> Myriads of rivulets hurrying through the lawn,
> The moan of doves in immemorial elms,
> And murmuring of innumerable bees.

Its opposite is **cacophony:** a harsh, discordant effect. It too is chosen for the sake of meaning. We hear it in Milton's scornful reference in "Lycidas" to corrupt clergymen whose songs "Grate on their scrannel pipes of wretched straw." (Read that line and one of Tennyson's aloud and see which requires lips, teeth, and tongue to do more work.) But note that although Milton's line is harsh in sound, the line (when we meet it in his poem) is pleasing because it is artful. Pope has illustrated both euphony and cacophony in his *Essay on Criticism*, insisting that sound must echo sense:

> Soft is the strain when Zephyr gently blows,
> And the smooth stream in smoother numbers° flows;   *metrical rhythm*
> But when loud surges lash the sounding shore,
> The harsh, rough verse should like the torrent roar . . .

Not merely sound but also rhythm contributes to the effect of this passage.

Is sound in those examples identical with meaning? Not quite. In Tennyson's lines, for instance, the cooing of doves is not *exactly* a moan. As John Crowe Ransom has pointed out, the sound would be almost the same but the meaning entirely different in "The murdering of innumerable beeves." While it is true that the consonant sound *sl-* will often begin a word that conveys ideas of wetness and smoothness — *slick, slimy, slippery, slush* — we are so used to hearing it in words that convey nothing of the kind — *slave, sledgehammer, sleeve, slow* — that it is doubtful that the sound all by itself communicates anything very definite. Asked to nominate the most beautiful word in the English language, a wit once suggested not *sunrise* or *silvery* but *syphilis*.

Relating sound more closely to meaning, the device called **onomatopoeia** is an attempt to represent a thing or action by a word that imitates the sound associated with it: *zoom, whiz, crash, bang, ding-dong, pitter-patter, yakety-yak*. Onomatopoeia is often effective in poetry, as in Emily Dickinson's line about the fly with its "uncertain stumbling Buzz," in which the nasal sounds *n, m, ng* and the sibilants *c, s,* help make a droning buzz, and in Robert Lowell's transciption of a birdcall, "yuck-a, yuck-a, yuck-a" (in "Falling Asleep over the Aeneid").

Like the Kikuyu tribesmen, others who care for poetry have discovered in the sound of words something of the refreshment of cool rain. Dylan Thomas, telling how he began to write poetry, said that from early childhood words were to him "as the notes of bells, the sounds of musical instruments, the noises of wind, sea, and rain, the rattle of milkcarts, the clopping of hooves on cobbles, the fingering of branches on the window pane, might be to someone, deaf from birth, who has miraculously found his hearing."[2] For readers, too, the sound of words can have a magical spell, most powerful when it points to meaning. James Weldon Johnson in *God's Trombones* has told of an old-time preacher who began his sermon, "Brothers and sisters, this morning I intend to explain the unexplainable — find out the indefinable — ponder over the imponderable — and unscrew the inscrutable!" The repetition of sound in *unscrew* and inscrutable has appeal, but the magic of the words is all the greater if they lead us to imagine the mystery of all Creation as an enormous screw that the preacher's mind, like a screw-driver, will loosen. Though the sound of a word or the meaning of a word may have value all by itself, both become more memorable when taken together.

William Butler Yeats (1865–1939)

WHO GOES WITH FERGUS? 1892

Who will go drive with Fergus now,
And pierce the deep wood's woven shade,
And dance upon the level shore?
Young man, lift up your russet brow,

---

[2] "Notes on the Art of Poetry," *The Texas Quarterly*, 1961; reprinted in *Modern Poetics*, James Scully, ed. (New York: McGraw-Hill, 1965).

And lift your tender eyelids, maid,   5
And brood on hopes and fear no more.

And no more turn aside and brood
Upon love's bitter mystery;
For Fergus rules the brazen cars,
And rules the shadows of the wood,   10
And the white breast of the dim sea
And all dishevelled wandering stars.

WHO GOES WITH FERGUS? *Fergus:* Irish king who gave up his throne to be a wandering
poet.

QUESTIONS

1. In what lines do you find euphony?
2. In what line do you find cacophony?
3. How do the sounds of these lines stress what is said in them?

EXERCISE: *Listening to Meaning*

Read aloud the following brief poems. In the sounds of which particular words
are meanings well captured? In which of the poems below do you find onomatopoeia?

John Updike (b. 1932)
WINTER OCEAN   1960

Many-maned scud-thumper, tub
of male whales, maker of worn wood, shrub-
ruster, sky-mocker, rave!
portly pusher of waves, wind-slave.

Frances Cornford (1886–1960)
THE WATCH   1923

I wakened on my hot, hard bed,
Upon the pillow lay my head;
Beneath the pillow I could hear
My little watch was ticking clear.
I thought the throbbing of it went   5
Like my continual discontent.
I thought it said in every tick:
I am so sick, so sick, so sick.
O death, come quick, come quick, come quick,
Come quick, come quick, come quick, come quick!   10

William Wordsworth (1770–1850)

A SLUMBER DID MY SPIRIT SEAL

1800

A slumber did my spirit seal;
  I had no human fears —
She seemed a thing that could not feel
  The touch of earthly years.

No motion has she now, no force;
  She neither hears nor sees;
Rolled round in earth's diurnal course,
  With rocks, and stones, and trees.

Emanuel diPasquale (b. 1943)

RAIN

1971

Like a drummer's brush,
the rain hushes the surface of tin porches.

ALLITERATION AND ASSONANCE

Listening to a symphony in which themes are repeated throughout each movement, we enjoy both their recurrence and their variation. We take similar pleasure in the repetition of a phrase or a single chord. Something like this pleasure is afforded us frequently in poetry.

Analogies between poetry and wordless music, it is true, tend to break down when carried far, since poetry — to mention a single difference — has denotation. But like musical compositions, poems have patterns of sounds. Among such patterns long popular in English poetry is **alliteration,** which has been defined as a succession of similar sounds. Alliteration occurs in the repetition of the same consonant sound at the beginning of successive words — "round and round the rugged rocks the ragged rascal ran" — or inside the words, as in Milton's description of the gates of Hell:

> On a sudden open fly
> With impetuous recoil and jarring sound
> The infernal doors, and on their hinges grate
> Harsh thunder, that the lowest bottom shook
> Of Erebus.

The former kind is called **initial alliteration,** the latter **internal alliteration** or **hidden alliteration.** We recognize alliteration by sound, not by spelling: *know* and *nail* alliterate, *know* and *key* do not. In a line by E. E. Cummings, "colossal hoax of clocks and calendars," the sound of *x* within *hoax* alliterates with the *cks* in *clocks*. Incidentally, the letter *r* does not *always* lend itself to cacophony: elsewhere in *Paradise Lost* Milton said that

> Heaven opened wide
> Her ever-during gates, harmonious sound
> On golden hinges moving . . .

By itself, a letter-sound has no particular meaning. This is a truth forgotten by people who would attribute the effectiveness of Milton's lines on the Heavenly Gates to, say, "the mellow *o*'s and liquid *l* of *harmonious* and *golden*." Mellow *o*'s and liquid *l*'s occur also in the phrase *moldy cold oatmeal*, which may have a quite different effect. Meaning depends on larger units of language than letters of the alphabet.

Today good prose writers usually avoid alliteration; in the past, some cultivated it. "There is nothing more swifter than time, nothing more sweeter," wrote John Lyly in *Euphues* (1579), and he went on — playing especially with the sounds of *v, n, t, s, l,* and *b* — "we have not, as Seneca saith, little time to live, but we lose much; neither have we a short life by nature, but we make it shorter by naughtiness." Poetry, too, formerly contained more alliteration than it usually contains today. In Old English verse, each line was held together by alliteration, a basic pattern still evident in the fourteenth century, as in the following description of the world as a "fair field" in *Piers Plowman:*

> A *f*eir *f*eld *f*ul of *f*olk *f*ond I ther bi-twene,
> Of alle *m*aner of *m*en, the *m*ene and the riche . . .

(For modern imitations of Old English verse, see Ezra Pound's "The Seafarer," page 380, and Richard Wilbur's "Junk," page 410.) Most poets nowadays save alliteration for special occasions. They may use it to give emphasis, as Edward Lear does: "*F*ar and *f*ew, *f*ar and *f*ew, / Are the *l*ands where the Jumblies *l*ive." With its aid they can point out the relationship between two things placed side by side, as in Pope's line on things of little worth: "The courtier's *p*romises, and sick man's *p*rayers." Alliteration, too, can be a powerful aid to memory. It is hard to forget such tongue twisters as "Peter Piper picked a peck of pickled peppers," or common expressions like "green as grass," "tried and true," and "from stem to stern." In fact, because alliteration directs our attention to something, it had best be used neither thoughtlessly nor merely for decoration, lest it call attention to emptiness. A case in point may be a line by Philip James Bailey, a reaction to a lady's weeping: "I saw, but *sp*ared to *sp*eak." If the poet chose the word *spared* for any meaningful reason other than that it alliterates with *speak,* the reason is not clear.

As we have seen, to repeat the sound of a consonant is to produce alliteration, but to repeat the sound of a *vowel* is to produce **assonance.** Like alliteration, assonance may occur either initially — "*a*ll the *aw*ful *auguries*"[3] — or internally — Spenser's "Her goodly *eyes* like sapph*i*res sh*i*ning br*i*ght, / Her forehead *i*vory wh*i*te . . ." and it can help make common phrases unforgettable: "eager beaver," "holy smoke." Like alliteration, it slows the reader down and focuses attention.

A. E. Housman (1859–1936)

EIGHT O'CLOCK   1922

He stood, and heard the steeple
  Sprinkle the quarters on the morning town.
One, two, three, four, to market-place and people
  It tossed them down.

Strapped, noosed, nighing his hour,
  He stood and counted them and cursed his luck;
And then the clock collected in the tower
  Its strength, and struck.

QUESTIONS

1. Why does the protagonist in this brief drama curse his luck? What is his situation?
2. For so short a poem, "Eight O'Clock" carries a great weight of alliteration. What patterns of initial alliteration do you find? What patterns of internal alliteration? What effect is created by all this heavy emphasis?

Alexander Pope (1688–1744)

EPITAPH, INTENDED FOR SIR ISAAC NEWTON
IN WESTMINSTER ABBEY   1730

Nature and Nature's laws lay hid in night.
God said, *Let Newton be!* and all was light.

QUESTIONS

1. What patterns of alliteration and assonance does Pope employ?
2. How are they useful to his poem?

J. C. Squire (1884–1958)

IT DID NOT LAST   1933

It did not last: the Devil, howling *Ho!*
Let Einstein be! restored the status quo.

[3] Some prefer to call the repetition of an initial vowel-sound by the name of alliteration: "apt alliteration's artful aid."

Which of these translations of the same passage from Petrarch do you think is better poetry? Why? What do assonance and alliteration have to do with your preference?

1. Love that liveth and reigneth in my thought,
   That built his seat within my captive breast,
   Clad in the arms wherein with me he fought,
   Oft in my face he doth his banner rest.
   —Henry Howard, Earl of Surrey (1517?–1547)

2. The long love that in my thought doth harbor,
   And in mine heart doth keep his residence,
   Into my face presseth with bold pretense
   And therein campeth, spreading his banner.
   —Sir Thomas Wyatt (1503?–1542)

EXPERIMENT: *Reading for Assonance*

Try reading aloud as rapidly as possible the following poem by Tennyson. From the difficulties you encounter, you may be able to sense the slowing effect of assonance. Then read the poem aloud a second time, with consideration.

Alfred, Lord Tennyson (1809–1892)

THE SPLENDOR FALLS ON CASTLE WALLS   1850

The splendor falls on castle walls
  And snowy summits old in story;
The long light shakes across the lakes,
  And the wild cataract leaps in glory.
Blow, bugle, blow, set the wild echoes flying,   5
Blow, bugle; answer, echoes, dying, dying, dying.

O hark, O hear! how thin and clear,
  And thinner, clearer, farther going!
O sweet and far from cliff and scar
  The horns of Elfland faintly blowing!   10
Blow, let us hear the purple glens replying:
Blow, bugle; answer, echoes, dying, dying, dying.

O love, they die in yon rich sky,
  They faint on hill or field or river;
Our echoes roll from soul to soul,   15
  And grow for ever and for ever.
Blow, bugle, blow, set the wild echoes flying,
And answer, echoes, answer, dying, dying, dying.

RIME

Isak Dinesen's tribesmen, to whom rime was a new phenomenon, recognized at once that rimed language is special language. So do we, for, although much English poetry is unrimed, rime is one means to set poetry apart from ordinary conversation and bring it closer to music. A **rime** (or rhyme), defined most narrowly, occurs when two or more words or phrases contain an identical or similar vowel-sound, usually accented, and the consonant-sounds (if any) that follow the vowel-sound are identical: *hay* and *sleigh, prairie schooner* and *piano tuner.*[4] From these examples it will be seen that rime depends not on spelling but on sound.

Excellent rimes surprise. It is all very well that a reader may anticipate which vowel-sound is coming next, for patterns of rime give pleasure by satisfying expectations; but riming becomes dull clunking if, at the end of each line, the reader can predict the word that will end the next. Hearing many a jukebox song for the first time, a listener can do so: *charms* lead to *arms, skies above* to *love.* As Alexander Pope observes of the habits of dull rimesters,

> Where'er you find "the cooling western breeze,"
> In the next line it "whispers through the trees";
> If crystal streams "with pleasing murmurs creep,"
> The reader's threatened (not in vain) with "sleep" . . .

But who—given the opening line of this children's jingle—could predict the lines that follow?

Anonymous (English)

JULIUS CAESAR   (about 1940?)

> Julius Caesar,
> The Roman geezer,
> Squashed his wife with a lemon-squeezer.

Here rimes combine things unexpectedly. Robert Herrick, too, made good use of rime to indicate a startling contrast:

> Then while time serves, and we are but decaying,
> Come, my Corinna, come, let's go a-Maying.

Though good rimes seem fresh, not all will startle, and probably few will call to mind things so unlike as *May* and *decay, Caesar* and *lemon-squeezer.* Some masters of rime often link words that, taken out of context, might seem common and unevocative. Here, for instance, is Alexander Pope's comment on a trifling courtier:

> Yet let me flap this bug with gilded wings,
> This painted child of dirt, that stinks and stings;

---

[4] Some definitions of *rime* would apply the term to the repetition of any identical or similar sound, not only a vowel-sound. In this sense, assonance is a kind of rime; so is alliteration (called **initial rime**).

Whose buzz the witty and the fair annoys,
Yet wit ne'er tastes, and beauty ne'er enjoys:
So well-bred spaniels civilly delight
In mumbling of the game they dare not bite.
Eternal smiles his emptiness betray,
As shallow streams run dimpling all the way.

Pope's rime-words are not especially memorable — and yet these lines are, because (among other reasons) they rime. Wit may be driven home without rime, but it is rime that rings the doorbell. Admittedly, some rimes wear thin from too much use. More difficult to use freshly than before the establishment of Tin Pan Alley, rimes such as *moon, June, croon* seem leaden and to ring true would need an extremely powerful context. *Death* and *breath* are a rime that poets have used with wearisome frequency; another is *birth, earth, mirth.* And yet we cannot exclude these from the diction of poetry, for they might be the very words a poet would need in order to say something new and original. Both the following brief poems seem fresher than their rimes (if taken out of context) would lead us to expect.

William Blake (1757–1827)
THE ANGEL THAT PRESIDED O'ER MY BIRTH (1808–1811)

The Angel that presided o'er my birth
Said, "Little creature, formed of Joy and Mirth,
Go love without the help of any thing on earth."

John Frederick Nims (b. 1914)
PERFECT RHYME 1967

Life, that struck up his cocky tune with *breath,*
Finds, to conclude in music, only *death.*

What matters to rime is freshness — not of a word but of the poet's way of seeing.

Good poets, said John Dryden, learn to make their rime "so properly a part of the verse, that it should never mislead the sense, but itself be led and governed by it." The comment may remind us that skillful rime — unlike poor rime — is never a distracting ornament. "Rime the rudder is of verses, / With which, like ships, they steer their courses," wrote the seventeenth-century poet Samuel Butler. Like other patterns of sound, rime can help a poet to group ideas, emphasize particular words, and weave a poem together. It can start reverberations between words and can point to connections of meaning.

To have an **exact rime,** sounds following the vowel sound have to be the same: *red* and *bread, wealthily* and *stealthily, walk to her* and *talk to her*. If final consonant sounds are the same but the vowel sounds are different, the result is **slant rime,** also called **near rime, off rime,** or **partial rime:** *stone* riming with *sun, moon, rain, green, gone, thin*. By not satisfying the reader's expectation of an exact chime, but instead giving a clunk, a slant rime can help a poet say some things in a particular way. It works especially well for disappointed let-downs, negations, and denials, as in Blake's couplet:

> He who the ox to wrath has moved
> Shall never be by woman loved.

Consonance, a kind of slant rime, occurs when the rimed words or phrases have the same consonant sounds but a different vowel, as in *chitter* and *chatter*. It is used in a traditional nonsense poem, "The Cutty Wren": " 'O where are you going?' says *Milder* to *Malder*." (W. H. Auden wrote a variation on it that begins, " 'O where are you going?' said *reader* to *rider*," thus keeping the consonance.)

End rime, as its name indicates, comes at the ends of lines, **internal rime** within them. Most rime tends to be end rime. Few recent poets have used internal rime so heavily as Wallace Stevens in the beginning of "Bantams in Pine-Woods": "Chieftain Iffucan of Azcan in caftan / Of tan with henna hackles, halt!" (lines also heavy on alliteration). A poet may employ both end rime and internal rime in the same poem, as in Robert Burn's satiric ballad "The Kirk's Alarm":

> Orthodox, Orthodox, wha believe in John Knox,
>> Let me sound an alarm to your conscience:
> There's a heretic blast has been blawn i' the wast°,   *west*
>> "That what is not sense must be nonsense."

Masculine rime is a rime of one-syllable words (*jail, bail*) or (in words of more than one syllable) stressed final syllables: *di-VORCE, re-MORSE,* or *horse, re-MORSE*. **Feminine rime** is a rime of two or more syllables, with stress on a syllable other than the last: *TUR-tle, FER-tile,* or (to take an example from Byron) *in-tel-LECT-u-al, hen-PECKED you all*. Often it lends itself to comic verse, but can occasionally be valuable to serious poems, as in Wordsworth's "Resolution and Independence":

> We poets in our youth begin in gladness,
> But thereof come in the end despondency and madness.

or as in Anne Sexton's "Eighteen Days Without You":

> and of course we're not married, we are a pair of scissors
> who come together to cut, without towels saying His. Hers.

Serious poems containing feminine rimes of three syllables have been attempted, notably by Thomas Hood in "The Bridge of Sighs":

Take her up tenderly,
Lift her with care;
Fashioned so slenderly,
Young, and so fair!

But the pattern is hard to sustain without lapsing into unintended comedy, as in the same poem:

Still, for all slips of hers,
One of Eve's family —
Wipe those poor lips of hers,
Oozing so clammily.

It works better when comedy is wanted:

Hilaire Belloc (1870–1953)

THE HIPPOPOTAMUS   1896

I shoot the Hippopotamus
   with bullets made of platinum,
Because if I use leaden ones
   his hide is sure to flatten 'em.

In **eye rime,** spellings look alike but pronunciations differ — *rough* and *dough, idea* and *flea*. Strictly speaking, eye rime is not rime at all.

In recent years American poetry has seen a great erosion of faith in rime, with Louis Simpson, James Wright, Robert Lowell, W. S. Merwin, and others quitting it for open forms. Indeed, it has been suggested that rime in the English language is exhausted. Such a view may be a reaction against the wearing-thin of rimes by overuse or the mechanical and meaningless application of a rime scheme. Yet anyone who listens to children skipping rope in the street, making up rimes to delight themselves as they go along, may doubt that the pleasures of rime are ended; and certainly the practice of Yeats and Emily Dickinson, to name only two, suggests that the possibilities of slant rime may be nearly infinite. If successfully employed, as it has been at times by a majority of English-speaking poets whose work we care to save, rime runs through its poem like a spine: the creature moves by means of it.

William Butler Yeats (1865–1939)

LEDA AND THE SWAN   1924

A sudden blow: the great wings beating still
Above the staggering girl, her thighs caressed
By the dark webs, her nape caught in his bill,
He holds her helpless breast upon his breast.

How can those terrified vague fingers push
The feathered glory from her loosening thighs?
And how can body, laid in that white rush,
But feel the strange heart beating where it lies?

A shudder in the loins engenders there
The broken wall, the burning roof and tower
And Agamemnon dead.
                                        Being so caught up,
So mastered by the brute blood of the air,
Did she put on his knowledge with his power
Before the indifferent beak could let her drop?

QUESTIONS

1. According to Greek mythology, the god Zeus in the form of a swan descended upon Leda, a Spartan queen. Among the offspring of this union were
   Clytemnestra, Agamemnon's unfaithful wife who conspired in his murder,
   and Helen, on whose account the Trojan war was fought. What does a knowledge of these allusions contribute to our understanding of the poem's last
   two lines?
2. The slant rime *up* / *drop* (lines 11, 14) may seem accidental or inept. Is it?
   Would this poem have ended nearly so well if Yeats had made an exact rime
   like *up* / *cup* or like *stop* / *drop*?

Allen Ginsberg (b. 1926)
POSTCARD TO D----

1975

Chuggling along in an old open bus
        past the green sugarfields
                down a dusty dirt road
                        overlooking the ocean in Fiji,
thinking of your big Macdougal street house
        & the old orange peels
                in your mail-garbage load,
                        smoggy windows you clean with a squeejee——

March 3, 1972

QUESTIONS

1. Which lines end in slant rimes and which end in exact rimes?
2. What is the effect of riming *Fiji* and *squeejee*? Comic or serious?
3. Who do you suppose D---- is?

Gerard Manley Hopkins (1844–1889)
GOD'S GRANDEUR

(1877)

The world is charged with the grandeur of God.
    It will flame out, like shining from shook foil;

It gathers to a greatness, like the ooze of oil
Crushed. Why do men then now not reck his rod?
Generations have trod, have trod, have trod; 5
   And all is seared with trade; bleared, smeared with toil;
   And wears man's smudge and shares man's smell: the soil
Is bare now, nor can foot feel, being shod.

And for all this, nature is never spent;
   There lives the dearest freshness deep down things; 10
And though the last lights off the black West went
   Oh, morning, at the brown brink eastward, springs —
Because the Holy Ghost over the bent
   World broods with warm breast and with ah! bright wings.

QUESTIONS

1. In a letter Hopkins explained *shook foil* (line 2): "I mean foil in its sense of leaf or tinsel . . . . Shaken goldfoil gives off broad glares like sheet lightning and also, and this is true of nothing else, owing to its zigzag dints and creasings and network of small many cornered facets, a sort of fork lightning too." What do you think he meant by *ooze of oil* (line 3)? Is this phrase an example of alliteration?
2. What instances of internal rime does the poem contain? How would you describe their effects?
3. Point out some of the poet's uses of alliteration and assonance. Does Hopkins go too far in his heavy use of devices of sound, or would you defend his practice?
4. Why do you suppose Hopkins, in the last two lines, says *over the bent / World* instead of (as we might expect) *bent over the world*? How can the world be bent? Can you make any sense out of this wording, or is Hopkins just trying to get his rime scheme to work out?

READING AND HEARING POEMS ALOUD

Thomas Moore's "The light that lies in women's eyes" — a line rich in internal rime, alliteration, and assonance — is harder to forget than "The light burning in the gaze of a woman." Because of sound, it is possible to remember the obscure line Christopher Smart wrote while in an insane asylum: "Let Ross, house of Ross rejoice with the Great Flabber Dabber Flat Clapping Fish with hands." Such lines, striking as they are even when read silently, become still more effective when said out loud. Reading poems aloud is a way to understand them. For this reason, practice the art of lending poetry your voice.

Before trying to read a poem aloud to other people, understand its meaning as thoroughly as possible. If you know what the poet is saying and the poet's attitude toward it, you will be able to find an appropriate tone of voice and to give each part of the poem a proper emphasis.

Except in the most informal situations and in some class exercises, read a poem to yourself before trying it on an audience. No actor goes before the footlights without first having studied the script, and the language of poems usually demands even more consideration than the language of most contemporary plays. Prepare your reading in advance. Check pronunciations you are not sure of. Underline things to be emphasized.

Read deliberately, more slowly than you would read aloud from a newspaper. Keep in mind that you are saying something to somebody. Don't race through the poem as if you are eager to get it over with.

Don't lapse into singsong. A poem may have a definite swing, but swing should never be exaggerated at the cost of sense. If you understand what the poem is saying and utter the poem as if you do, the temptation to fall into such a mechanical intonation should not occur. Observe the punctuation, making slight pauses for commas, longer pauses for full stops (periods, question marks, exclamation points).

If the poem is rimed, don't raise your voice and make the rimes stand out unnaturally. They should receive no more volume than other words in the poem, though a faint pause at the end of each line will call the listener's attention to them. This advice is contrary to a school that holds that, if a line does not end in any punctuation, one should not pause but run it together with the line following. The trouble is that, from such a reading, a listener may not be able to identify the rimes; besides, the line, that valuable unit of rhythm, is destroyed.

In some older poems rimes that look like slant rimes may have been exact rimes in their day:

> Still so perverse and opposite,
> As if they worshiped God for spite.
> —Samuel Butler, *Hudibras* (1663)

> Soft yielding minds to water glide away,
> And sip, with nymphs, their elemental tea.
> —Alexander Pope, "The Rape of the Lock" (1714)

You may wish to establish a consistent policy toward such shifting usage: is it worthwhile to distort current pronunciation for the sake of the rime?

Listening to a poem, especially if it is unfamiliar, calls for concentration. Merciful people seldom read poetry uninterruptedly to anyone for more than a few minutes at a time. Robert Frost, always kind to his audiences, used to intersperse poems with many silences and seemingly casual remarks—shrewdly giving his hearers a chance to rest from their labors and giving his poems a chance to settle in.

If, in first listening to a poem, you don't take in all its meaning, don't be discouraged. With more practice in listening, your attention span and your ability to understand poems read aloud will increase. Incidentally, following the text of poems in a book while hearing them read aloud may increase your comprehension, but it may not necessarily help you to *listen*. At least some of the time, close your book and let your ears make the poems welcome. That way, their sounds may better work for you.

Hearing recordings of poets reading their work can help both your ability to read aloud and your ability to listen. Not all poets read their poems well, but there is much to be relished in both the highly dramatic reading style of a Dylan Thomas and the quiet underplay of a Robert Frost. You need feel no obligation, of course, to imitate the poet's reading of a poem. You have to feel about the poem in your own way, in order to read it with conviction and naturalness.

Even if you don't have an audience, the act of speaking poetry can have its own rewards. Perhaps that is what James Wright is driving at in the following brief prose poem.

James Wright (b. 1927)
SAYING DANTE ALOUD   1976

You can feel the muscles and veins rippling in widening and rising circles, like a bird in flight under your tongue.

EXERCISE: *Reading for Sound and Meaning*

Read these two brief poems aloud. What devices of sound do you find in each of them? Try to explain what sound contributes to the total effect of the poem and how it reinforces what the poet is saying.

A. E. Housman (1859–1936)
WITH RUE MY HEART IS LADEN   1896

With rue my heart is laden
  For golden friends I had,
For many a rose-lipt maiden
  And many a lightfoot lad.

By brooks too broad for leaping
  The lightfoot boys are laid;
The rose-lipt girls are sleeping
  In fields where roses fade.

T. S. Eliot (1888–1965)
VIRGINIA   1934

Red river, red river,
Slow flow heat is silence

No will is still as a river
Still. Will heat move
Only through the mocking-bird   5
Heard once? Still hills
Wait. Gates wait. Purple trees,
White trees, wait, wait,
Delay, decay. Living, living,
Never moving. Ever moving   10
Iron thoughts came with me
And go with me:
Red river, river, river.

VIRGINIA. This poem is one of a series entitled "Landscapes."

9 Rhythm

STRESSES AND PAUSES

Rhythms affect us powerfully. We are lulled by a hammock's sway, awakened by an alarm clock's repeated yammer. Long after we come home from a beach, the rising and falling of waves and tides continue in memory. How powerfully the rhythms of poetry also move us may be felt in folk songs of railroad workers and chain gangs whose words were chanted in time to the lifting and dropping of a sledgehammer, and in verse that marching soldiers shout, putting a stress on every word that coincides with a footfall:

> Your LEFT! TWO! THREE! FOUR!
> Your LEFT! TWO! THREE! FOUR!
> You LEFT your WIFE and TWEN-ty-one KIDS
> And you LEFT! TWO! THREE! FOUR!
> You'll NEV-er get HOME to-NIGHT!

A rhythm is produced by a series of recurrences: the returns and departures of the seasons, the repetitions of an engine's stroke, the beats of the heart. A rhythm may be produced by the recurrence of a sound (the throb of a drum, a telephone's busy-signal), but rhythm and sound are not identical. A totally deaf man at a parade can sense rhythm from the motions of the marchers' arms and feet, from the shaking of the pavement as they tramp. Rhythms inhere in the motions of the moon and stars, even though they move without a sound.

In poetry, several kinds of recurrent *sound* are possible, including (as we saw in the last chapter) rime, alliteration, and assonance. But most often when we speak of the **rhythm** of a poem we mean the recurrence of stresses and pauses in it. When we hear a poem read aloud, stresses and pauses are, of course, part of its sound. It is possible to be aware of rhythms in poems read silently, too.

A **stress** (or **accent**) is a greater amount of force given to one syllable in speaking than is given to another. We favor a stressed syllable with a little more breath and emphasis, with the result that it comes out slightly louder, higher in pitch, or longer in duration than other syllables. In this manner we place a stress on the first syllable of words such as *eagle, impact, open,* and *statue,* and on the second syllable in *cigar, mystique, precise,* and *until.* Each word in English carries at least one stress, except (usually) for the articles *a, an,* and *the,* and one-syllable prepositions: *at, by, for, from, of, to, with.* Even these, however, take a stress once in a while: "Get WITH it!" "You're not THE Farrah Fawcett-Majors?" One word by itself is seldom long enough for us to notice a rhythm in it. Usually a sequence of at least a few words is needed for stresses to establish their pattern: a line, a passage, a whole poem. Strong rhythms may be seen in most Mother Goose rimes, to which children have been responding for hundreds of years. This rime is for an adult to chant while jogging a child up and down on a knee:

> Here goes my lord
> A trot, a trot, a trot, a trot!
> Here goes my lady
> A canter, a canter, a canter, a canter!
> Here goes my young master
> Jockey-hitch, jockey-hitch, jockey-hitch, jockey-hitch!
> Here goes my young miss
> An amble, an amble, an amble, an amble!
> The footman lags behind to tipple ale and wine
> And goes gallop, a gallop, a gallop, to make up his time.

More than one rhythm occurs in these lines, as the make-believe horse changes pace. How do these rhythms differ? From one line to the next, the interval between stresses lengthens or grows shorter. In "a TROT a TROT a TROT a TROT," the stress falls on every other syllable. But in the middle of the line "A CAN-ter a CAN-ter a CAN-ter a CAN-ter," the stress falls on every third syllable. When stresses recur at fixed intervals as in these lines, the resulting pattern is called a **meter.** The line "A trot a trot a trot a trot" is in **iambic** meter, a pattern of alternate unstressed and stressed syllables.[1] Of all patterns of rhythm in the English language, this one is most familiar; most of our traditional poetry is written in it and ordinary speech tends to resemble it. Most poems, less obvious in rhythm than nursery rimes are, rarely stick to their meters with such jog-trot regularity. The following lines also contain a horseback-riding rhythm. (The poet, Gerard Manley Hopkins, is comparing the pell-mell plunging of a burn — Scottish word for a brook — to the motion of a wild horse.)

> This darksome burn, horseback brown,
> His rollrock highroad roaring down,

---

[1] Another kind of meter is possible, in which the intervals between stresses vary. This is **accentual** meter, not often found in contemporary poetry. It is discussed in the second section of this chapter.

In coop and in comb the fleece of his foam
Flutes and low to the lake falls home.

In the third line, when the brook courses through coop and comb
("hollow" and "ravine"), the passage breaks into a gallop; then, with
the two-beat *falls home,* almost seems reined to a sudden halt.

Stresses embody meanings. Whenever two or more fall side by
side, words gain in emphasis. Consider these hard-hitting lines from
John Donne, in which accent marks have been placed, dictionary-
fashion, to indicate the stressed syllables:

Bat'ter my heart', three'-per'soned God', for You'
As yet' but knock', breathe', shine', and seek' to mend';
That I may rise' and stand', o'er'throw' me, and bend'
Your force' to break', blow', burn', and make' me new'.

Unstressed (or **slack**) syllables also can direct our attention to what the
poet means. In a line containing few stresses and a great many unstressed syllables, there can be an effect not of power and force but of
hesitation and uncertainty. Yeats asks in "Among School Children"
what young mother, if she could see her baby grown to be an old man,
would think him

A com'pen·sa'tion for the pang' of his birth'
Or the un·cer'tain·ty of his set'ting forth'?

When unstressed syllables recur in pairs, the result is a rhythm that
trips and bounces, as in Robert Service's rollicking line:

A bunch' of the boys' were whoop'ing it up'in the Mal'a·mute sa·loon'. . .

or in Poe's lines — also light but probably supposed to be serious:

For the moon' nev'er beams' with·out' bring'ing me dreams'
Of the beau'ti·ful An'na·bel Lee'.

Apart from the words that convey it, the rhythm of a poem has no
meaning. There are no essentially sad rhythms, nor any essentially
happy ones. But some rhythms enforce certain meanings better than
others do. The bouncing rhythm of Service's line seems fitting for an account of a merry night in a Klondike saloon; but it may be distracting
when encountered in Poe's wistful elegy.

EXERCISE: *Appropriate and Inappropriate Rhythms*

In each of the following passages, decide whether rhythm enforces meaning
and tone or works against these elements and consequently against the poem's
effectiveness.

1. Alfred, Lord Tennyson, "Break, break, break":

Break, break, break,
On thy cold gray stones, O Sea!

2. Edgar Allan Poe, "Ulalume":

Then my heart it grew ashen and sober
  As the leaves that were crispèd and sere—
  As the leaves that were withering and sere,
And I cried: "It was surely October
      On *this* very night of last year
      That I journey—I journeyed down here—
      That I brought a dread burden down here—
      On this night of all nights in the year,
      Ah, what demon has tempted me here?"

3. A. A. Milne, "Disobedience":

James James
Morrison Morrison
Weatherby George Dupree
Took great
Care of his Mother,
Though he was only three.
James James
Said to his Mother,
"Mother," he said, said he;
"You must never go down to the end of the town, if you don't go
  down with me."

4. Eliza Cook, "Song of the Sea-Weed":

Many a lip is gaping for drink,
  And madly calling for rain;
And some hot brains are beginning to think
  Of a messmate's opened vein.

5. William Shakespeare, song from *The Tempest:*

The master, the swabber, the boatswain, and I,
The gunner and his mate
Loved Moll, Meg, and Marian, and Margery,
But none of us cared for Kate;
For she had a tongue with a tang
Would cry to a sailor "Go hang!"—
She loved not the savor of tar nor of pitch
Yet a tailor might scratch her where'er she did itch;
Then to sea, boys, and let her go hang!

Rhythms in poetry are due not only to stresses but also to pauses. "Every nice ear," observed Alexander Pope (*nice* meaning "finely tuned"), "must, I believe, have observed that in any smooth English verse of ten syllables, there is naturally a pause either at the fourth, fifth, or sixth syllable." Such a light but definite pause within a line is called a **cesura** (or caesura), "a cutting." More liberally than Pope, we apply the name to any pause in a line of any length, after any word in the line. In studying a poem, we often indicate a cesura by double lines (∥). Usually, a cesura will occur at a mark of punctuation, but there can be a cesura even if no punctuation is present. Sometimes you will find it at the end of a phrase or clause or, as in these lines by William Blake, after an internal rime:

> And priests in black gowns‖were walking their rounds
> And binding with briars‖my joys and desires.

Lines of ten or twelve syllables (as Pope knew) tend to have just one cesura, though sometimes there are more:

> Cover her face:‖mine eyes dazzle:‖she died young.

Pauses also tend to recur at more prominent places — namely, after each line. At the end of a verse (from *versus*, "a turning"), the reader's eye, before turning to go on to the next line, makes a pause, however brief. If a line ends in a full pause — usually indicated by some mark of punctuation — we call it **end-stopped.** All the lines in this stanza by Theodore Roethke are end-stopped:

> Let seed be grass and grass turn into hay:
> I'm martyr to a motion not my own;
> What's freedom for? To know eternity.
> I swear she cast a shadow white as stone.
> But who would count eternity in days?
> These old bones live to learn her wanton ways:
> (I measure time by how a body sways).[2]

A line that does not end in punctuation and that therefore is read with only a slight pause after it is called **run-on;** the running-on of its thought into the next line is **enjambment.** A run-on line gives us only part of a phrase, clause, or sentence. All these lines from Robert Browning are run-on lines, despite the fact that the lines are pairs of rimes:

>   . . . Sir, 'twas not
> Her husband's presence only, called that spot
> Of joy into the Duchess' cheek: perhaps
> Frà Pandolf chanced to say "Her mantle laps
> Over my lady's wrist too much," or "Paint
> Must never hope to reproduce the faint
> Half-flush that dies along her throat." Such stuff
> Was courtesy, she thought . . .[3]

A passage in run-on lines has a rhythm different from that of a passage like Roethke's in end-stopped lines. When emphatic pauses occur in the quotation from Browning, they fall within a line rather than at the end of one. The passage by Roethke and that by Browning are in lines of the same meter (iambic) and the same length (ten syllables). What makes the big difference in their rhythms is enjambment, or lack of it.

---

[2] The complete poem, "I Knew a Woman," appears on page 91.
[3] The complete poem, "My Last Duchess," appears on page 316.

To sum up: rhythm is recurrence. In poems, it is made of stresses and pauses. The poet can produce it by doing any of several things: making the intervals between stresses fixed or varied, long or short; indicating pauses (cesuras) within lines; end-stopping lines or running them over; writing in short or long lines. Rhythm in itself cannot convey meaning. And yet if a poet's words have meaning, their rhythm must be one with it.

Gwendolyn Brooks (b. 1917)

WE REAL COOL 1960

The Pool Players.
Seven at the Golden Shovel.

We real cool. We
Left school. We

Lurk late. We
Strike straight. We

Sing sin. We
Thin gin. We

Jazz June. We
Die soon.

QUESTION

Describe the rhythms of this poem. By what techniques are they produced?

Robert Frost (1874–1963)

NEVER AGAIN WOULD BIRDS' SONG BE THE SAME 1942

He would declare and could himself believe
That the birds there in all the garden round
From having heard the daylong voice of Eve
Had added to their own an oversound,
Her tone of meaning but without the words.   5
Admittedly an eloquence so soft
Could only have had an influence on birds
When call or laughter carried it aloft.
Be that as may be, she was in their song.
Moreover her voice upon their voices crossed   10
Had now persisted in the woods so long
That probably it never would be lost.
Never again would birds' song be the same.
And to do that to birds was why she came.

1. Who is *he*?
2. In reading aloud line 9, do you stress *may*? (Do you say "as MAY be" or "as may BE"?) What guide do we have to the poet's wishes here?
3. Which lines does Frost cast mostly or entirely into monosyllables? How would you describe the impact of these lines?
4. In his *Essay on Criticism*, Alexander Pope made fun of poets who wrote mechanically, without wit: "And ten low words oft creep in one dull line." Do you think this criticism applicable to Frost's lines of monosyllables? Explain.

Ben Jonson (1573?–1637)

SLOW, SLOW, FRESH FOUNT, KEEP TIME
WITH MY SALT TEARS   1600

Slow, slow, fresh fount, keep time with my salt tears;
   Yet slower yet, oh faintly, gentle springs;
List to the heavy part the music bears,
    Woe weeps out her division° when she sings.   *a part in a song*
     Droop herbs and flowers,   5
     Fall grief in showers;
     Our beauties are not ours;
       Oh, I could still,
Like melting snow upon some craggy hill,
   Drop, drop, drop, drop,   10
Since nature's pride is now a withered daffodil.

SLOW, SLOW, FRESH FOUNT. The nymph Echo sings this lament over the youth Narcissus in Jonson's play *Cynthia's Revels*. In mythology, Nemesis, goddess of vengeance, to punish Narcissus for loving his own beauty, caused him to pine away and then transformed him into a narcissus (another name for a *daffodil*, line 11).

QUESTIONS

1. Read the first line aloud rapidly. Why is it difficult to do so?
2. Which lines rely most heavily on stressed syllables?
3. In general, how would you describe the rhythm of this poem? How is it appropriate to what is said?

Robert Lowell (1917–1977)

AT THE ALTAR   1946

I sit at a gold table with my girl
Whose eyelids burn with brandy. What a whirl
Of Easter eggs is colored by the lights,
As the Norwegian dancer's crystalled tights
Flash with her naked leg's high-booted skate,   5
Like Northern Lights upon my watching plate.

The twinkling steel above me is a star;
I am a fallen Christmas tree. Our car
Races through seven red-lights — then the road
Is unpatrolled and empty, and a load   10
Of ply-wood with a tail-light makes us slow.
I turn and whisper in her ear. You know
I want to leave my mother and my wife,
You wouldn't have me tied to them for life . . .
Time runs, the windshield runs with stars. The past   15
Is cities from a train, until at last
Its escalating and black-windowed blocks
Recoil against a Gothic church. The clocks
Are tolling. I am dying. The shocked stones
Are falling like a ton of bricks and bones   20
That snap and splinter and descend in glass
Before a priest who mumbles through his Mass
And sprinkles holy water; and the Day
Breaks with its lightning on the man of clay,
Dies amara valde. Here the Lord   25
Is Lucifer in harness: hand on sword,
He watches me for Mother, and will turn
The bier and baby-carriage where I burn.

AT THE ALTAR. In a public reading of this poem, Robert Lowell made some remarks cited
by George P. Elliott in *Fifteen Modern American Poets* (New York: Holt, Rinehart & Winston, 1956). Lit up like a Christmas tree, the speaker finds himself in a Boston nightclub,
watching a skating floorshow. Then he and his girl drive (or does he only dream they
drive?) to a church where a priest saying a funeral Mass sprinkles a corpse with holy
water. 23. *the Day:* the Day of Judgment. 25. *Dies amara valde:* "day bitter above all
others," a phrase from a funeral hymn, the *Dies Irae,* in which sinners are warned to fear
God's wrath. 28. *baby-carriage:* the undertaker's silver dolly, supporting a coffin.

QUESTIONS

1. Which lines in this poem are end-stopped?
2. What effects does Lowell obtain by so much enjambment?
3. What besides enjambment contributes to the rhythm of the poem?
4. How is this rhythm appropriate to what the poet is saying? Explain.

Alexander Pope (1688–1744)

ATTICUS   1735

How did they fume, and stamp, and roar, and chafe!
And swear, not Addison himself was safe.
    Peace to all such! but were there one whose fires
True genius kindles, and fair fame inspires;
Blest with each talent, and each art to please,   5
And born to write, converse, and live with ease,
Should such a man, too fond to rule alone,

Bear, like the Turk, no brother near the throne,
View him with scornful, yet with jealous eyes,
And hate for arts that caused himself to rise;   10
Damn with faint praise, assent with civil leer,
And, without sneering, teach the rest to sneer;
Willing to wound, and yet afraid to strike,
Just hint a fault, and hesitate dislike;
Alike reserved to blame, or to commend,   15
A timorous foe, and a suspicious friend;
Dreading e'en fools, by flatterers besieged,
And so obliging, that he ne'er obliged;
Like Cato, give his little Senate laws,
And sit attentive to his own applause: 20
While wits and Templars every sentence raise,
And wonder with a foolish face of praise —
Who but must laugh, if such a man there be?
Who would not weep, if Atticus were he?

ATTICUS. In this selection from "An Epistle to Dr. Arbuthnot," Pope has been referring to dull versifiers and their angry reception of his satiric thrusts at them. With *Peace to all such!* (line 3) he turns to his celebrated portrait of a rival man of letters, Joseph Addison. 19. *Cato:* Roman senator about whom Addison had written a tragedy. 21. *Templars:* London lawyers who dabbled in literature.

QUESTIONS

1. In these lines — one of the most famous damnations in English poetry — what positive virtues, in Pope's view, does Addison lack?
2. Read aloud from Robert Lowell's "At the Altar," then read aloud a few lines from Pope. Although both poets write in rimed couplets, in lines ten syllables long, how do the rhythms of the two poems compare? To what do you attribute the differences?

EXERCISE: *Two Kinds of Rhythm*

The following compositions in verse have lines of similar length, yet they differ greatly in rhythm. Explain how they differ and why.

Sir Thomas Wyatt (1503?–1542)

WITH SERVING STILL   (1528–1536)

With serving still°   *continually*
    This have I won,
For my goodwill
    To be undone;

And for redress   5
    Of all my pain,

Disdainfulness
   I have again;

And for reward
   Of all my smart   10
Lo, thus unheard,
   I must depart!

Wherefore all ye
   That after shall
By fortune be,   •   15
   As I am, thrall,

Example take
   What I have won,
Thus for her sake
   To be undone!   20

Dorothy Parker (1893–1967)

RÉSUMÉ   1926

Razors pain you;
Rivers are damp;
Acids stain you;
And drugs cause cramp.
Guns aren't lawful;
Nooses give;
Gas smells awful;
You might as well live.

METER

To enjoy the rhythms of a poem, no special knowledge of meter is necessary. All you need do is pay attention to stresses and where they fall;
and you will perceive the basic pattern, if there is any. However, there
is nothing occult about the study of meter. Most people find they can
master its essentials in no more time than it takes to learn a complicated
game such as chess. If you take the time, you will then have the pleasure
of knowing what is happening in the rhythms of many a fine poem, and
pleasurable knowledge may even deepen your insight into poetry.

   Far from being artificial constructions found only in the minds of
poets, meters occur in everyday speech and prose. As the following example will show, they may need only a poet to recognize them. The
English satirist Max Beerbohm, after contemplating the title page of his
first book, took his pen and added two more lines.

Max Beerbohm (1872–1956)

On the Imprint of the First English Edition of "The Works of Max Beerbohm" (1896)

"London: JOHN LANE, *The Bodley Head*
  New York: CHARLES SCRIBNER'S SONS."
This plain announcement, nicely read,
  Iambically runs.

In everyday life, nobody speaks or writes in perfect iambic rhythm, except in occasional brief remarks: "a HAM on RYE." (As we have seen, iambic rhythm consists of a series of syllables alternately unstressed and stressed.) Poets rarely speak in it for very long either, and seldom with exactitude. If you read aloud Max Beerbohm's lines, you will hear an iambic rhythm but not an absolutely invariable one. And yet all of us speak with a rising and falling of stress somewhat like iambic meter. Perhaps, as the poet and scholar John Thompson has maintained, "The iambic metrical pattern has dominated English verse because it provides the best symbolic model of our language."[4]

A meter supplies a pattern for a poet's speech to depart from or to follow. To make ourselves aware of this pattern, we can **scan** a line or a poem by indicating the stresses in it. **Scansion,** the art of so doing, is not just a matter of pointing to syllables; it is also a matter of listening to a poem and making sense of it. To scan a poem is one way to indicate how to read it aloud; in order to see where stresses fall, you have to see the places where the poet wishes to put emphasis. That is why, when scanning a poem, you may find yourself suddenly understanding it.

An objection might be raised against scanning: isn't it too simple to pretend that all language (and poetry) can be divided neatly into stressed syllables and unstressed syllables? Indeed it is. As the linguist Otto Jespersen has said, "In reality there are infinite gradations of stress, from the most penetrating scream to the faintest whisper."[5] However, the idea in scanning a poem is not to reproduce the sound of a human voice. For that we would do better to buy a tape recorder. To scan a poem, rather, is to make a diagram of the stresses (and absences of stress) we find in it. Various marks are used in scansion; in this book we use ' for a stressed syllable and ⌣ for an unstressed syllable. Some scanners, wishing a little more precision, also use the **half-stress** (`); this device can be helpful in many instances when a syllable usually not

---

[4] *The Founding of English Metre* (New York: Columbia University Press, 1966), p. 12.
[5] "Notes on Metre," (1933), reprinted in *The Structure of Verse: Modern Essays on Prosody,* edited by Harvey Gross (Greenwich, Conn.: Fawcett, 1966).

stressed comes at a place where it takes some emphasis, as in the last syllable in a line:

> ˘ ′ ˘ ′ ˘ ′ ˘ ˘ ′˘'
> Bound each to each with nat·u·ral pi·e·ty.

Here, with examples, are some of the principal meters we find in English poetry. For each is given its basic **foot,** or molecule (usually one stressed and one or two unstressed syllables);

1. **Iambic** (foot: the **iamb,** ˘ ′):

   > ˘ ′ ˘ ′ ˘ ′ ˘ ′ ˘ ′ ˘ ′
   > The fall·ing out of faith·ful friends, re·new·ing is of love

2. **Anapestic** (foot: the **anapest,** ˘ ˘ ′):

   > ˘ ˘ ′ ˘ ˘ ′ ˘ ˘ ′
   > I am mon·arch of all I sur·vey

3. **Trochaic** (foot: the **trochee,** ′ ˘):

   > ′ ˘ ′ ˘ ′ ˘ ′ ˘
   > Dou·ble, dou·ble, toil and trou·ble

4. **Dactylic** (foot: the **dactyl,** ′ ˘ ˘):

   > ′ ˘ ˘ ′ ˘ ˘
   > Take her up ten·der·ly

Iambic and anapestic meters are called **rising** meters because their movement rises from unstressed syllable (or syllables) to stress; trochaic and dactylic meters are called **falling.** In the twentieth century, the bouncing meters—anapestic and dactylic—have been used more often for comic verse than for serious poetry. Called feet, though they contain no unaccented syllables, are the **monosyllabic foot** (′) and the **spondee** (″). Meters are not ordinarily made up of them; if one were, it would be like the steady impact of nails being hammered into a board—no pleasure to hear or to dance to. But inserted now and then, they can lend emphasis and variety to a meter, as Yeats well knew when he broke up the predominantly iambic rhythm of "Who Goes with Fergus?" (p. 121) with the line,

> ˘ ˘ ′ ′ ˘ ˘ ′ ′
> And the white breast of the dim sea,

in which occur two spondees.

Metrical patterns are classified also by line lengths: **trochaic monometer,** for instance, is a line one trochee long, as in this anonymous brief comment on microbes:

> Adam
> Had 'em.

A frequently heard metrical description is **iambic pentameter:** a line of five iambs, a pattern especially familiar because it occurs in all blank verse (such as Shakespeare's plays and Milton's *Paradise Lost*), heroic couplets, and sonnets. The commonly used names for line lengths follow:

monometer	one foot	**pentameter**	five feet
dimeter	two feet	**hexameter**	six feet
trimeter	three feet	**heptameter**	seven feet
tetrameter	four feet	**octameter**	eight feet

Lines of more than eight feet are possible but are rare. They tend to break up into shorter lengths in the listening ear.

When Yeats chose the spondees *white breast* and *dim sea,* he was doing what poets who write in meter do frequently for variety — using a foot other than the expected one. Often such a substitution will be made at the very beginning of a line, as in the third line of this passage from Christopher Marlowe's *Tragical History of Doctor Faustus:*

> ⌣ ′ ⌣ ′ ⌣ ′ ⌣ ′ ⌣ ′
> Was this the face that launched a thou·sand ships
> ⌣ ′ ⌣ ′ ⌣ ′ ⌣ ′ ⌣ ‵
> And burnt the top·less tow'rs of Il·i·um?
> ′ ′ ⌣ ′ ⌣⌣ ′ ⌣ ⌣ ⌣ ′
> Sweet Hel·en, make me im·mor·tal with a kiss.

How, we might wonder, can that last line be called iambic at all? But it is, just as a waltz that includes an extra step or two, or leaves a few steps out, remains a waltz. In the preceding lines the basic iambic pentameter is established, and though in the third line the pattern is varied from, it does not altogether disappear. It continues for a while to run on in the reader's mind, where (if the poet does not stay away from it for too long) the meter will be there when the poem comes back to it.

Like a basic dance step, a metrical pattern is not to be slavishly adhered to. The fun in reading a metrical poem often comes from watching the poet continually departing from a pattern, giving a few heel-kicks to display a bit of joy or ingenuity, then easing back into the basic step again. Because meter is orderly and the rhythms of living speech are unruly, poets can play one against the other, in a sort of counterpoint. Robert Frost, a master at pitting a line of iambs against a very natural-sounding and irregular sentence, declared, "I am never more pleased than when I can get these into strained relation. I like to drag and break the intonation across the meter as waves first comb and then break stumbling on a shingle."[6]

Evidently Frost's skilled effects would be lost to a reader who, scanning a Frost poem or reading it aloud, distorted its rhythms to fit the words exactly to the meter. With rare exceptions, a good poem can

---

[6] Letter to John Cournos in 1914, in *Selected Letters of Robert Frost,* edited by Lawrance Thompson (New York: Holt, Rinehart & Winston, 1964), p. 128.

be read and scanned the way we would speak its sentences if they were ours. This, for example, is an unreal scansion:

> ⌣ ′ ⌣ ′ ⌣ ′ ⌣ ′ ⌣ ′
> That's my last Duch·ess paint·ed on the wall.

—because no speaker of English would say that sentence in that way. We are likely to stress *That's* and *last*.

Departure from metrical pattern is not merely desirable in poetry, it is a necessity: woe be to the poet who fails to depart from pattern often enough. Allowing the beat of words to slip into mechanical regularity, the poet sets a poem marching robot-like right over a precipice. Luckily, few poets, except writers of greeting cards, favor rhythms that go "a TROT a TROT a TROT a TROT" for very long. Robert Frost told an audience one time that if when writing a poem he found its rhythm becoming monotonous, he knew that the poem was going wrong and that he himself didn't believe what it was saying.

Although in good poetry we seldom meet a very long passage of absolute metrical regularity, we sometimes find (in a line or so) a monotonous rhythm that is effective. Words fall meaningfully in Macbeth's famous statement of world-weariness: "Tomorrow and tomorrow and tomorrow . . ." and in the opening lines of Thomas Gray's "Elegy":

> ⌣ ′ ⌣ ′ ⌣ ′ ⌣ ′ ⌣ ′
> The cur·few tolls the knell of part·ing day,
> ⌣ ′ ⌣ ′ ′ ′ ⌣ ′ ⌣ ′
> The low·ing herd wind slow·ly o'er the lea,
> ⌣ ′ ⌣ ′ ⌣ ′ ⌣ ′ ⌣ ′
> The plow·man home·ward plods his wear·y way,
> ⌣ ′ ⌣ ′ ⌣ ′ ⌣ ⌣ ⌣ ′
> And leaves the world to dark·ness and to me.[7]

Here the almost unvarying iambic rhythm seems appropriate to convey the tolling of a bell and the weary setting down of one foot after the other.

Besides the two rising meters (iambic, anapestic) and the two falling meters (trochaic, dactylic), English poets have another valuable meter. It is **accentual meter,** in which the poet does not write in feet (as in the other meters) but instead counts accents (stresses). The idea is to have the same number of stresses in every line. The poet may place them anywhere in the line and may include practically any number of unstressed syllables, which do not count. In "Christabel," for instance, Coleridge keeps four stresses to a line, though the first line has only eight syllables and the last line has eleven:

> ′ ′ ′ ′
> There is not wind e·nough to twirl
> ′ ′ ′ ′
> The one red leaf, the last of its clan,

[7] The complete poem, "Elegy Written in a Country Churchyard," appears on page 258.

That dan·ces as óf·ten as dánce it cán,

Háng·ing so líght, and háng·ing so hígh,

On the tóp-most twíg that looks úp at the ský.

The history of accentual meter is long and honorable. Old English poetry was written in a kind of accentual meter, but its line was more rule-
bound than Coleridge's: four stresses arranged two on either side of a
cesura, plus alliteration of three of the stressed syllables. In "Junk" (p.
410), Richard Wilbur revives the pattern:

An áxe án·gles ‖ from my néigh·bor's ásh·can . . .

Many poets, from the authors of Mother Goose rimes to Gerard Manley
Hopkins, have sometimes found accentual meters congenial.

It has been charged that the importation of Greek names for
meters and of the classical notion of feet was an unsuccessful attempt to
make a Parthenon out of English wattles. The charge is open to debate,
but at least it is certain that Greek names for feet cannot mean to us
what they meant to Aristotle. Greek and Latin poetry is measured not
by stressed and unstressed syllables but by long and short vowel
sounds. An iamb in classical verse is one short vowel followed by a long
vowel. Such a meter constructed on the principle of vowel length is
called a **quantitative** meter. Campion's "Rose-cheeked Laura" was an
attempt to demonstrate it in English, but probably we enjoy the rhythm
of the poem's well-placed stresses whether or not we notice its pattern
of vowel sounds.

Thomas Campion (1567–1620)
ROSE-CHEEKED LAURA, COME   1602

Rose-cheeked Laura, come,
Sing thou smoothly with thy beauty's
Silent music, either other
    Sweetly gracing.

Lovely forms do flow   5
From concent° divinely framèd;   *harmony*
Heav'n is music, and thy beauty's
    Birth is heavenly.

These dull notes we sing
Discords need for helps to grace them;   10
Only beauty purely loving
    Knows no discord,

But still moves delight,
Like clear springs renewed by flowing,
Ever perfect, ever in them-   15
        Selves eternal.

Less popular among poets today than formerly, the use of meter
endures. Major poets from Shakespeare through Yeats have fashioned
their poems by it, and if we are to read their work with full enjoyment,
we need to be aware of it. Another argument in favor of meter is
expressed in an old jazz song: "It don't mean a thing if you ain't got that
swing." Or, as critic Paul Fussell, Jr., has put it: "No element of a poem
is more basic — and I mean physical — in its effect upon the reader than
the metrical element, and perhaps no technical triumphs reveal more
readily than the metrical the poet's sympathy with that universal
human nature . . . which exists outside his own."[8]

Walter Savage Landor (1775–1864)

ON SEEING A HAIR OF LUCRETIA BORGIA   (1825)

Borgia, thou once wert almost too august
And high for adoration; now thou'rt dust.
All that remains of thee these plaits unfold,
Calm hair, meandering in pellucid gold.

QUESTIONS

1. Who was Lucretia Borgia and when did she live? What connotations that add
   meaning to Landor's poem has her name?
2. What does *meander* mean? How can a hair meander?
3. Scan the poem, indicating stressed syllables. What is the basic meter of most
   of the poem? What happens to this meter in the last line? Note especially
   meandering in pel-. How many light, unstressed syllables are there in a row?
   Does rhythm in any way reinforce what Landor is saying?

EXERCISE: *Meaningful Variation*

At what place or places in each of these passages does the poet depart from
basic iambic meter? How does each departure help underscore the meaning?

1. John Dryden, "Mac Flecknoe" (speech of Flecknoe, prince of Nonsense, referring to Thomas Shadwell, poet and playwright):

   Shadwell alone of all my sons is he
   Who stands confirmed in full stupidity.
   The rest to some faint meaning make pretense,
   But Shadwell never deviates into sense.

---

[8] Paul Fussell, Jr., *Poetic Meter and Poetic Form* (New York: Random House, 1965), p. 110.

2. Alexander Pope, *An Essay on Criticism:*

A needless Alexandrine ends the song
That, like a wounded snake, drags its slow length along.

3. Henry King, "The Exequy" (an apostrophe to his wife):

'Tis true, with shame and grief I yield,
Thou like the van° first tookst the field,   *vanguard*
And gotten hath the victory
In thus adventuring to die
Before me, whose more years might crave
A just precedence in the grave.
But hark! my pulse like a soft drum
Beats my approach, tells thee I come;
And slow howe'er my marches be,
I shall at last sit down by thee.

4. Henry Wadsworth Longfellow, "Mezzo Cammin":

Half-way up the hill, I see the Past
Lying beneath me with its sounds and sights,—
A city in the twilight dim and vast,
With smoking roofs, soft bells, and gleaming lights,—
And hear above me on the autumnal blast
The cataract of Death far thundering from the heights.

5. Wallace Stevens, "Sunday Morning":

Deer walk upon our mountains, and the quail
Whistle about us their spontaneous cries;
Sweet berries ripen in the wilderness;
And, in the isolation of the sky,
At evening, casual flocks of pigeons make
Ambiguous undulations as they sink,
Downward to darkness, on extended wings.

EXERCISE: *Recognizing Rhythms*

Which of the following poems contain predominant meters? Which poems are
not wholly metrical, but are metrical in certain lines? Point out any such lines.
What reasons do you see, in such places, for the poet's seeking a metrical effect?

George Gordon, Lord Byron (1788–1824)

THE DESTRUCTION OF SENNACHERIB   1815

The Assyrian came down like the wolf on the fold,
And his cohorts were gleaming in purple and gold;
And the sheen of their spears was like stars on the sea,
When the blue wave rolls nightly on deep Galilee.

Like the leaves of the forest when summer is green,   5
That host with their banners at sunset were seen:
Like the leaves of the forest when autumn hath blown,
That host on the morrow lay withered and strown.

For the Angel of Death spread his wings on the blast,
And breathed in the face of the foe as he passed;   10
And the eyes of the sleepers waxed deadly and chill,
And their hearts but once heaved—and for ever grew still!

And there lay the steed with his nostril all wide,
But through it there rolled not the breath of his pride;
And the foam of his gasping lay white on the turf,   15
And cold as the spray of the rock-beating surf.

And there lay the rider distorted and pale,
With the dew on his brow, and the rust on his mail;
And the tents were all silent, the banners alone,
The lances unlifted, the trumpet unblown.   20

And the widows of Ashur are loud in their wail,
And the idols are broke in the temple of Baal;
And the might of the Gentile, unsmote by the sword,
Hath melted like snow in the glance of the Lord!

THE DESTRUCTION OF SENNACHERIB. Byron retells the Bible story of King Sennacherib of Assyria who, while leading an invasion of Jerusalem, suddenly lost his army: "And it came to pass that night, that the angel of the Lord went out, and smote in the camp of the Assyrians a hundred fourscore and five thousand: and when they arose early in the morning, behold, they were all dead corpses" (II Kings 19:35). 21–22: *Ashur . . . Baal:* Assyria and the Assyrian deity. 23. *Gentile:* Sennacherib (a non-Hebrew).

Edna St. Vincent Millay (1892–1950)

COUNTING-OUT RHYME   1928

Silver bark of beech, and sallow
Bark of yellow birch and yellow
    Twig of willow.

Stripe of green in moosewood maple,
Colour seen in leaf of apple,   5
    Bark of popple.

Wood of popple pale as moonbeam,
Wood of oak for yoke and barn-beam,
    Wood of hornbeam.

Silver bark of beech, and hollow   10
Stem of elder, tall and yellow
    Twig of willow.

A. E. Housman (1859–1936)

WHEN I WAS ONE-AND-TWENTY   1896

When I was one-and-twenty
    I heard a wise man say,

"Give crowns and pounds and guineas
    But not your heart away;
Give pearls away and rubies   5
    But keep your fancy free."
But I was one-and-twenty,
    No use to talk to me.

When I was one-and-twenty
    I heard him say again,   10
"The heart out of the bosom
    Was never given in vain;
'Tis paid with sighs a plenty
    And sold for endless rue."
And I am two-and-twenty,   15
    And oh, 'tis true, 'tis true.

William Carlos Williams (1883–1963)

THE DESCENT OF WINTER (SECTION 10/30)   1934

To freight cars in the air

all the slow
    clank, clank
    clank, clank
moving about the treetops   5

the
    wha, wha
of the hoarse whistle

    pah,   pah,   pah
    pah, pah, pah, pah, pah   10
    piece and piece
    piece and piece
moving still trippingly
through the morningmist

long after the engine   15
has fought by
            and disappeared
in silence
            to the left

Walt Whitman (1819–1892)

BEAT! BEAT! DRUMS!   (1861)

Beat! beat! drums! — blow! bugles! blow!
Through the windows — through doors — burst like a ruthless force,
Into the solemn church, and scatter the congregation,
Into the school where the scholar is studying;

Leave not the bridegroom quiet—no happiness must he have now with
　　his bride, 5
Nor the peaceful farmer any peace, ploughing his field or gathering his
　　grain,
So fierce you whirr and pound you drums—so shrill you bugles blow.

Beat! beat! drums!—blow! bugles! blow!
Over the traffic of cities—over the rumble of wheels in the streets;
Are beds prepared for sleepers at night in the houses? no sleepers must
　　sleep in those beds, 10
No bargainer's bargains by day—no brokers or speculators—would they
　　continue?
Would the talkers be talking? would the singer attempt to sing?
Would the lawyer rise in the court to state his case before the judge?
Then rattle quicker, heavier drums—you bugles wilder blow.

Beat! beat! drums!—blow! bugles! blow! 15
Make no parley—stop for no expostulation,
Mind not the timid—mind not the weeper or prayer,
Mind not the old man beseeching the young man,
Let not the child's voice be heard, nor the mother's entreaties,
Make even the trestles to shake the dead where they lie awaiting the
　　hearses. 20
So strong you thump O terrible drums—so loud you bugles blow.

10 Closed Form, Open Form

Form, as a general idea, is the design of a thing as a whole, the configuration of all its parts. No poem can escape having some kind of form, whether its lines are as various in length as broomstraws, or all in hexameter. To put this point another way: if you were to listen to a poem read aloud in a language unknown to you, or if you saw the poem printed in that foreign language, whatever in the poem you could see or hear would be the form of it.[1]

Of late, poets and critics debating the relative merits of "closed" and "open" form have worn out many miles of typewriter ribbon. Writing in **closed form,** a poet follows (or finds) some sort of pattern, such as that of a sonnet with its rime scheme and its fourteen lines of iambic pentameter. On a page, poems in closed form tend to look regular and symmetrical. Along with William Butler Yeats, who held that a successful poem will "come shut with a click, like a closing box," the poet who writes in closed form apparently strives for a kind of perfection — seeking, perhaps, to lodge words so securely in place that no word can be budged without a worsening.

The poet who writes in **open form** usually seeks no final click. Often, such a poet views the writing of a poem as a process, rather than a quest for an absolute. Free to use white space for emphasis, able to shorten or lengthen lines as the sense seems to require, the poet lets the poem discover its shape as it goes along, moving as water flows downhill, adjusting to its terrain, engulfing obstacles.

Right now, most American poets prefer open form to closed. But although less fashionable than they were, rime and meter are still in evidence. Most poetry of the past is in closed form. The reader who seeks a wide understanding of poetry will want to know both closed and open varieties.

---

[1] For a good summary of the uses of the term **form** in criticism of poetry, see the article "Form" by G. N. G. Orsini in *Princeton Encyclopedia of Poetry and Poetics*, 2nd ed., eds. Preminger, Warnke, and Hardison (Princeton: Princeton University Press, 1975).

CLOSED FORM:
BLANK VERSE, STANZA, SONNET

Closed form gives some poems a valuable advantage: it makes them more easily memorable. The **epic** poems of nations—long narratives tracing the adventures of popular heroes: the Greek *Iliad* and *Odyssey*, the French *Song of Roland*, the Spanish *Cid*—tend to occur in patterns of fairly consistent line length or number of stresses because these works were sometimes transmitted orally. Sung to the music of a lyre or chanted to a drumbeat, they may have been easier to memorize because of their patterns. If a singer forgot something, the song would have a noticeable hole in it, so rime or fixed meter probably helped prevent an epic from deteriorating when passed along from one singer to another. It is no coincidence that so many English playwrights of Shakespeare's day favored iambic pentameter. Companies of actors, often called upon to perform a different play daily, could count on a fixed line length to aid their burdened memories.

Some poets complain that closed form is a straitjacket, a limit to free expression. Other poets, however, feel that, like fires held fast in a narrow space, thoughts stated in a tightly binding form may take on a heightened intensity. "Limitation makes for power," according to one contemporary practitioner of closed form, Richard Wilbur; "the strength of the genie comes of his being confined in a bottle." Compelled by some strict pattern to arrange and rearrange words, delete, and exchange them, poets must focus on them the keenest attention. Often they stand a chance of discovering words more meaningful than the ones they started out with. And at times, in obedience to a rime scheme, the poet may be surprised by saying something quite unexpected. Composing a poem is like walking blindfolded down a dark road, with one's hand in the hand of an inexorable guide. With the conscious portion of the mind, the poet may wish to express what seems to be a good idea. But a line ending in *year* must be followed by another ending in *atmosphere, beer, bier, bombardier, cashier, deer, friction-gear, frontier*, or some other rime word that otherwise might not have entered the poem. That is why rime schemes and stanza patterns can be mighty allies and valuable disturbers of the unconscious. As Rolfe Humphries has said about a strict form: "It makes you think of better things than you would all by yourself."

The best-known one-line pattern for a poem in English is **blank verse:** unrimed iambic pentameter. (This pattern is not a stanza: stanzas have more than one line.) Most portions of Shakespeare's plays are in blank verse, and so are Milton's *Paradise Lost*, Tennyson's "Ulysses," certain dramatic monologues of Browning and Frost, and thousands of other poems. Here is a poem in blank verse that startles us by dropping out of its pattern in the final line. Keats appears to have written it late in his life to his fiancée Fanny Brawne.

John Keats (1795–1821)

THIS LIVING HAND, NOW WARM AND CAPABLE   (1819?)

This living hand, now warm and capable
Of earnest grasping, would, if it were cold
And in the icy silence of the tomb,
So haunt thy days and chill thy dreaming nights
That thou wouldst wish thine own heart dry of blood
So in my veins red life might stream again,
And thou be conscience-calmed — see here it is —
I hold it towards you.

The **couplet** is a two-line stanza, usually rimed. Its lines often tend to be equal in length, whether short or long. Here are two examples:

Blow,
Snow!

As I in hoary winter's night stood shivering in the snow,
Surprised I was with sudden heat which made my heart to glow.

(Actually, any pair of rimed lines that contains a complete thought is called a couplet, even if it is not a stanza, such as the couplet that ends a sonnet by Shakespeare.) Unlike other stanzas, couplets are often printed solid, not separated one couplet from the next by white space. This practice is usual in printing the **heroic couplet** — or **closed couplet** — two rimed lines of iambic pentameter, the first ending in a light pause, the second more heavily end-stopped. George Crabbe, in *The Parish Register*, described a shotgun wedding:

Next at our altar stood a luckless pair,
Brought by strong passions and a warrant there:
By long rent cloak, hung loosely, strove the bride,
From every eye, what all perceived, to hide;
While the boy bridgegroom, shuffling in his place,
Now hid awhile and then exposed his face.
As shame alternately with anger strove
The brain confused with muddy ale to move,
In haste and stammering he performed his part,
And looked the rage that rankled in his heart.

Though employed by Chaucer, the heroic couplet was named from its later use by Dryden and others in poems, translations of classical epics, and verse plays of epic heroes. It continued in favor through most of the eighteenth century. Much of our pleasure in reading good heroic couplets comes from the seemingly easy precision with which a skilled poet unites statements and strict pattern. In doing so, the poet may place a pair of words, phrases, clauses, or sentences side by side in agreement or similarity, forming a **parallel,** or in contrast and opposition, forming an **antithesis.** The effect is neat. For such skill in manipulating parallels and antitheses, John Denham's lines on the river Thames were much admired:

> O could I flow like thee, and make thy stream
> My great example, as it is my theme!
> Though deep, yet clear; though gentle, yet not dull;
> Strong without rage, without o'erflowing full.

These lines were echoed by Pope, ridiculing a poetaster, in two heroic couplets in *The Dunciad:*

> Flow, Welsted, flow! like thine inspirer, Beer:
> Though stale, not ripe; though thin, yet never clear;
> So sweetly mawkish, and so smoothly dull;
> Heady, not strong; o'erflowing, though not full.

Reading long poems in so exact a form, one may feel like a spectator at a ping-pong match unless the poet skillfully keeps varying rhythms. (Among much else, this skill distinguishes the work of Dryden and Pope from that of a lockstep horde of coupleteers who followed them.) One way of escaping such metronome-like monotony is to keep the cesura (see p. 139) shifting about from place to place — now happening early in a line, now happening late — and at times unexpectedly to hurl in a second or third cesura. Try working through George Crabbe's lines (on p. 158) and observe where the cesuras fall.

The **tercet** is a three-line stanza that, if rimed, usually keeps to one rime sound. **Terza rima,** the form Dante employs for *The Divine Comedy,* is made of tercets linked together by the rime scheme *a b a, b c b, c d c, d e d, e f e,* and so on. Harder to do in English than in Italian — with its greater resources of riming words — the form nevertheless has been managed by Shelley in "Ode to the West Wind" (with the aid of some slant rimes):

> Make me thy lyre, even as the forest is:
> What if my leaves are falling like its own!
> The tumult of thy mighty harmonies
>
> Will take from both a deep, autumnal tone,
> Sweet though in sadness. Be thou, spirit fierce,
> My spirit! Be thou me, impetuous one![2]

The workhorse of English stanzas is the **quatrain,** used for more

---

[2] The complete poem appears on pages 394–396.

rimed poems than any other form. It comes in many line lengths, and sometimes contains lines of varying length, as in the ballad stanza (see Chapter Seven).

Longer and more complicated stanzas are, of course, possible, but couplet, tercet, and quatrain have been called the building blocks of our poetry because most longer stanzas are made up of them. What short stanzas does John Donne mortar together to make the longer stanza of his "Song"?

John Donne (1572–1631)

SONG   1633

Go and catch a falling star
  Get with child a mandrake root,
Tell me where all past years are,
  Or who cleft the Devil's foot,
Teach me to hear mermaids singing,   5
  Or to keep off envy's stinging,
      And find
      What wind
Serves to advance an honest mind.

If thou be'st borne to strange sights,   10
  Things invisible to see,
Ride ten thousand days and nights,
  Till age snow white hairs on thee,
Thou, when thou return'st, wilt tell me
  All strange wonders that befell thee,   15
      And swear
      Nowhere
Lives a woman true, and fair.

If thou findst one, let me know,
  Such a pilgrimage were sweet —   20
Yet do not, I would not go,
  Though at next door we might meet;
Though she were true, when you met her,
  And last, till you write your letter,
      Yet she   25
      Will be
False, ere I come, to two, or three.

Recently in vogue is a form known as **syllabic verse** in which the poet establishes a pattern of a certain number of syllables to a line. Either rimed or rimeless but usually stanzaic, syllabic verse has been hailed as a way for poets to escape "the tyranny of the iamb" and discover less conventional rhythms, since, if they take as their line length an *odd* number of syllables, then iambs, being feet of *two* syllables, cannot fit perfectly into it. Offbeat victories have been scored in syllabics by such poets as W. H. Auden, W. D. Snodgrass, Donald Hall, Thom Gunn, and Marianne Moore. A well-known syllabic poem is Dylan Thomas's "Fern Hill" (page 407). Notice its shape on the page, count the syllables in its lines, and you'll perceive its perfect symmetry. Although like playing a game, the writing of such a poem is apparently more than finger exercise: the discipline can help a poet to sing well, though (with Thomas) singing "in . . . chains like the sea."

Poets who write in demanding forms seem to enjoy taking on an arbitrary task for the fun of it, as ballet dancers do, or weightlifters. Much of our pleasure in reading such poems comes from watching words fall into a shape. It is the pleasure of seeing any hard thing done skillfully—a leap executed in a dance, a basketball swished through a basket. Still, to be excellent, a poem needs more than skill; and to enjoy a poem it isn't always necessary for the reader to be aware of the skill that went into it. Unknowingly, the editors of *The New Yorker* once printed an **acrostic**—a poem in which the initial letter of each line, read downwards, spells out a word or words—that named (and insulted) a well-known anthologist. Evidently, besides being ingenious, the acrostic was a printable poem. In the Old Testament book of Lamentations, profoundly moving songs tell of the sufferings of the Jews after the destruction of Jerusalem. Four of the songs are written as an alphabetical acrostic, every stanza beginning with a letter of the Hebrew alphabet. However ingenious, such sublime poetry cannot be dismissed as merely witty; nor can it be charged that a poet who writes in such a form does not express deep feeling.

Patterns of sound and rhythm can, however, be striven after in a dull mechanical way, for which reason many poets today think them dangerous. Swinburne, who loved alliterations and tripping meters, had enough detachment to poke fun at his own excessive patterning:

> From the depth of the dreamy decline of the dawn through a notable
>   nimbus of nebulous noonshine,
>   Pallid and pink as the palm of the flag-flower that flickers with fear of
>   the flies as they float,
>   Are the looks of our lovers that lustrously lean from a marvel of mystic mi-
>   raculous moonshine,
>   These that we feel in the blood of our blushes that thicken and threaten
>   with throbs through the throat?

This is bad, but bad deliberately. If any good at all, a poem in a fixed pattern, such as a sonnet, is created not only by the craftsman's chipping away at it but by the explosion of a sonnet-shaped *idea*. Viewed mechanically, as so many empty boxes somehow to be filled up, stanzas can impose the most hollow sort of discipline, and a poem written in these stanzas becomes no more than finger-exercise. This comment (although on fiction) may be appropriate:

Roy Campbell (1901–1957)

ON SOME SOUTH AFRICAN NOVELISTS   1930

You praise the firm restraint with which they write—
 I'm with you there, of course.
They use the snaffle and the curb all right;
 But where's the bloody horse?

Not only firm restraint marks the rimed poems of Shakespeare, Emily Dickinson, and William Butler Yeats, but also strong emotion. Such poets ride with certain hand upon a sturdy horse.

Ronald Gross (b. 1935)

YIELD   1967

Yield.
No Parking.
Unlawful to Pass.
Wait for Green Light.
Yield.   5

Stop.
Narrow Bridge.
Merging Traffic Ahead
Yield.

Yield.   10

QUESTIONS

1. This poem by Ronald Gross is a "found poem." After reading it, how would you define **found poetry?**
2. Does "Yield" have a theme? If so, how would you state it?
3. What makes "Yield" mean more than traffic signs ordinarily mean to us?

EXPERIMENT: *Finding a Poem*

In a newspaper, magazine, catalogue, textbook, or advertising throwaway, find a sentence or passage that (with a little artistic manipulation on your part) shows promise of becoming a poem. Copy it into lines like poetry, being careful to place what seem to be the most interesting words at the ends of lines to give them greatest emphasis. According to the rules of found poetry, you may excerpt, delete, repeat, and rearrange elements but not add anything. What does this experiment tell you about poetric form? About ordinary prose?

Ronald Gross, who produces his "found poetry" by arranging prose from such unlikely places as traffic signs and news stories into poem-like lines, has told of making a discovery:

> As I worked with labels, tax forms, commercials, contracts, pin-up captions, obituaries, and the like, I soon found myself rediscovering all the traditional verse forms in found materials: ode, sonnet, epigram, haiku, free verse. Such finds made me realize that these forms are not mere artifices, but shapes that language naturally takes when carrying powerful thoughts or feelings.[3]

Though Gross is a playful experimenter, his remark is true of serious poetry. Traditional verse forms like sonnets and haiku aren't a lot of hollow pillowcases for a poet to stuff with verbiage. At best, in the hands of a skilled poet, they can be shapes into which living language seems to fall naturally.

It is fun to see words tumble gracefully into such a shape. Consider, for instance, one famous "found poem," a sentence discovered in a physics textbook: "And so no force, however great, can stretch a cord, however fine, into a horizontal line which shall be absolutely straight."[4] What a good clear sentence containing effective parallels ("however great . . . however fine"), you might say, taking pleasure in it. Yet this plain statement gives extra pleasure if arranged like this:

> And so no force, however great,
>   Can stretch a cord, however fine,
>   Into a horizontal line
> Which shall be absolutely straight.

So spaced, in lines that reveal its built-in rimes and rhythms, the sentence would seem one of those "shapes that language naturally takes" that Ronald Gross finds everywhere. (It is possible, of course, that the textbook writer was gleefully planting a quatrain for someone to find; but perhaps it is more likely that he knew much rimed, metrical poetry by heart and couldn't help writing it unconsciously.)

When we speak, with Ronald Gross, of "traditional verse forms," we usually mean **fixed forms.** If written in a fixed form, a poem inherits from other poems certain familiar elements of structure: an unvarying number of lines, say, or a stanza pattern. In addition, it may display certain **conventions:** expected features such as themes, subjects, attitudes, or figures of speech. In medieval folk ballads a "milk-white steed" is a

[3] "Speaking of Books: Found Poetry," *The New York Times Book Review*, June 11, 1967. Inspired by pop artists who reveal fresh vistas in Brillo boxes and comic strips, found poetry has had a recent vogue. Earlier practitioners include William Carlos Williams, whose long poem *Paterson* (New York: New Directions, 1963) quotes historical documents and statistics. Prose, said Williams in a letter, can be a "laboratory" for poetry: "It throws up jewels which may be cleaned and grouped."
[4] William Whewell, *Elementary Treatise on Mechanics* (Cambridge, England, 1819).

conventional figure of speech; and if its rider be a cruel and beautiful witch who kidnaps mortals, she is a conventional character. (*Conventional* doesn't necessarily mean uninteresting.)

In the poetry of western Europe and America, the **sonnet** is the fixed form that has attracted for the longest time the largest number of noteworthy practitioners. Originally an Italian form (*sonnetto:* "little song"), the sonnet owes much of its prestige to Petrarch (1304–1374), who wrote in it of his love for the unattainable Laura. So great was the vogue for sonnets in England at the end of the sixteenth century that a gentleman might have been thought a boor if he couldn't turn out a decent one. Not content to adopt merely the sonnet's fourteen-line pattern, English poets also tried on its conventional mask of the tormented lover. They borrowed some of Petrarch's similes (a lover's heart, for instance, is like a storm-tossed boat) and invented others. (If you would like more illustrations of Petrarchan conventions, see pages 254–256.)

Soon after English poets imported the sonnet in the middle of the sixteenth century, they worked out their own rime scheme — one easier for them to follow than Petrarch's, which calls for a greater number of riming words than English can readily provide. (In Italian, according to an exaggerated report, practically everything rimes.) In the following **English sonnet,** sometimes called a **Shakespearean sonnet,** the rimes cohere in four clusters: *a b a b, c d c d, e f e f, g g.* Because a rime scheme tends to shape the poet's statements to it, the English sonnet has three places where the procession of thought is likely to turn in another direction. Within its form, a poet may pursue one idea throughout the three quatrains and then in the couplet end with a surprise.

Michael Drayton (1563–1631)

SINCE THERE'S NO HELP, COME LET US KISS
AND PART   1619

Since there's no help, come let us kiss and part;
Nay, I have done, you get no more of me,
And I am glad, yea, glad with all my heart
That thus so cleanly I myself can free;
Shake hands for ever, cancel all our vows,   5
And when we meet at any time again,
Be it not seen in either of our brows
That we one jot of former love retain.
Now at the last gasp of Love's latest breath,
When, his pulse failing, Passion speechless lies,   10
When Faith is kneeling by his bed of death,
And Innocence is closing up his eyes,
    Now if thou wouldst, when all have given him over,
    From death to life thou mightst him yet recover.

Less frequently met in English poetry, the **Italian sonnet,** or **Petrarchan sonnet,** follows the rime scheme *a b b a, a b b a* in its first eight lines, the **octave,** and then adds new rime sounds in the last six lines, the **sestet.** The sestet may rime *c d c d c d, c d e c d e, c d c c d c,* or in almost any other variation that doesn't end in a couplet. This organization into two parts sometimes helps arrange the poet's thoughts. In the octave, the poet may state a problem, and then, in the sestet, may offer a resolution. A lover, for example, may lament all octave long that a loved one is neglectful, then in line 9 begin to foresee some outcome: the speaker will die, or accept unhappiness, or trust that the beloved will have a change of heart.

Elizabeth Barrett Browning (1806–1861)

GRIEF   1844

I tell you, hopeless grief is passionless;
   That only men incredulous of despair,
   Half-taught in anguish, through the midnight air
Beat upward to God's throne in loud access
Of shrieking and reproach. Full desertness   5
   In souls, as countries, lieth silent-bare
   Under the blanching, vertical eye-glare
Of the absolute Heavens. Deep-hearted man, express
Grief for the Dead in silence like to death:
   Most like a monumental statue set   10
In everlasting watch and moveless woe
Till itself crumble to the dust beneath.
   Touch it: the marble eyelids are not wet—
If it could weep, it could arise and go.

In this Italian sonnet, the division in thought comes a bit early—in the middle of line 8. Few English-speaking poets who have used the form seem to feel strictly bound by it.

   "The sonnet," in the view of Robert Bly, a modern critic, "is where old professors go to die." And yet the use of the form by such twentieth-century poets as Yeats, Frost, Auden, Thomas, Pound, Cummings, Berryman, and Lowell suggests that it may be far from exhausted. Like the hero of the popular ballad "Finnegan's Wake," literary forms (though not professors) declared dead have a habit of springing up again.

EXERCISE: *Knowing Two Kinds of Sonnet*
Find other sonnets in this book. Which are English in form? Which are Italian?

Which are variations on either form or combinations of the two? You may wish to try your hand at writing both kinds of sonnet and experience the difference for yourself.

Oscar Wilde said that a cynic is "a man who knows the price of everything and the value of nothing." Such a terse, pointed statement is called an epigram. In poetry, however, an **epigram** is a form: "A short poem ending in a witty or ingenious turn of thought, to which the rest of the composition is intended to lead up" (according to the *Oxford English Dictionary*). Often it is a malicious gibe with an unexpected stinger in the final line—perhaps in the very last word:

Alexander Pope (1688–1744)
Epigram Engraved on the Collar of a Dog Which I Gave to His Royal Highness 1738

I am his Highness' dog at Kew;
Pray tell me, sir, whose dog are you?

Cultivated by the Roman poet Martial—for whom the epigram was a short poem, sometimes satiric but not always—this form has been especially favored by English poets who love Latin. Few characteristics of the English epigram seem fixed. Its pattern tends to be brief and rimed, its tone playfully merciless.

Martial (A.D. 40?–102?)
You serve the best wines always, my dear sir A.D. 90

You serve the best wines always, my dear sir,
And yet they say your wines are not so good.
They say you are four times a widower.
They say . . . A drink? I don't believe I would.

— Translated by J. V. Cunningham

Sir John Harrington (1561?–1612)
Of Treason 1618

Treason doth never prosper; what's the reason?
For if it prosper, none dare call it treason.

William Blake (1757–1827)
HER WHOLE LIFE IS AN EPIGRAM (1793)

Her whole life is an epigram: smack smooth°, and   *perfectly smooth*
    neatly penned,
Platted° quite neat to catch applause, with a sliding   *plaited, woven*
    noose at the end.

E. E. Cummings (1894–1962)
A POLITICIAN 1944

a politician is an arse upon
which everyone has sat except a man

J. V. Cunningham (b. 1911)
THIS HUMANIST WHOM NO BELIEFS CONSTRAINED 1947

This *Humanist* whom no beliefs constrained
Grew so broad-minded he was scatter-brained.

Keith Waldrop (b. 1932)
ON MEASURE 1968

The delicate foot of
Phoebe Isolde Farmer
taps meters acceptable to, among others, the
* * * *Poetry Journal* and the
University of * * * * * * *Review* and to   5
her brother, a minister, who is paying
for the printing of a small
volume — while he should be
praying, "Lord, grant her
wings."   10

EXPERIMENT: *Expanding an Epigram*

Rewrite any of the preceding epigrams, taking them out of rime (if they are in rime) and adding a few more words to them. See if your revisions have nearly the same effect as the originals.

EXERCISE: *Reading for Couplets*

Read all the sonnets by Shakespeare in this book. How do the final couplets of some of them resemble epigrams? Does this similarity diminish their effect of "seriousness"?

In English the only other fixed form to rival the sonnet and the epigram in favor is the **limerick:** five anapestic lines usually riming *a a b b a.*

There was an old man of Pantoum
Who kept a live sheep in his room.
    "It reminds me," he said,
    "Of a loved one long dead,
But I never can quite recall whom."

The limerick was made popular by Edward Lear (1812–1888), English humorist and painter, whose own practice was to make the last line hark back to the first: "That oppressive old man of Pantoum."

EXPERIMENT: *Contriving a Clerihew*

The **clerihew,** a fixed form named for its inventor, Edmund Clerihew Bentley (1875–1956), has straggled behind the limerick in popularity. Here are four examples: how would you define the form and what are its rules? Who or what is its conventional subject matter? Try writing your own example.

James Watt
Was the hard-boiled kind of Scot:
He thought any dream
Sheer waste of steam.

—W. H. Auden

Sir Christopher Wren
Said, "I am going to dine with some men.
If anybody calls
Say I am designing St. Paul's."

—Edmund Clerihew Bentley

Etienne de Silhouette
(It's a good bet)
Has the shadiest claim
To fame.

—Cornelius J. Ter Maat

Dylan Thomas
Showed early promise.
His name's no dimmer, man,
On old Bob Zimmerman.

—T. O. Maglow

Dylan Thomas (1914–1953)

DO NOT GO GENTLE INTO THAT GOOD NIGHT   1952

Do not go gentle into that good night,
Old age should burn and rave at close of day;
Rage, rage against the dying of the light.

Though wise men at their end know dark is right,
Because their words had forked no lightning they   5
Do not go gentle into that good night.

Good men, the last wave by, crying how bright
Their frail deeds might have danced in a green bay,
Rage, rage against the dying of the light.

Wild men who caught and sang the sun in flight,   10
And learn, too late, they grieved it on its way,
Do not go gentle into that good night.

Grave men, near death, who see with blinding sight
Blind eyes could blaze like meteors and be gay,
Rage, rage against the dying of the light.   15

And you, my father, there on the sad height,
Curse, bless, me now with your fierce tears, I pray,
Do not go gentle into that good night.
Rage, rage against the dying of the light.

QUESTIONS

1. "Do not go gentle into that good night" is a **villanelle:** a fixed form originated by French courtly poets of the Middle Ages. (For another villanelle, see Theodore Roethke's "The Waking," page 389.) What are its rules?
2. Is Thomas's poem, like many another villanelle, just an elaborate and trivial exercise? Whom does the poet address? What is he saying?

OPEN FORM

Writing in **open form,** a poet seeks to discover a fresh and individual arrangement for words in every poem. Such a poem, generally speaking, has neither a rime scheme nor a basic meter informing the whole of it. Doing without those powerful (some would say hypnotic) elements, the poet who writes in open form relies on other means to engage and to sustain the reader's attention. Novice poets often think that open form looks easy, not nearly so hard as riming everything; but in truth, formally open poems are easy to write only if written carelessly. To compose lines with keen awareness of open form's demands, and of its infinite possibilities, calls for skill: at least as much as that needed to write in meter and rime, if not more. Should the poet succeed, then the discovered arrangement will seem exactly right for what the poem is saying. Words will seem at home in their positions, as naturally as the words of a decent sonnet.

Denise Levertov (b. 1923)

Six Variations (part iii)   1961

Shlup, shlup, the dog
as it laps up
water
makes intelligent
music, resting
now and then to take breath in irregular
measure.

Open form, in this brief poem, affords Denise Levertov certain advantages. Able to break off a line at whatever point she likes (a privilege not available to the poet writing, say, a conventional sonnet, who has to break off each line after its tenth syllable), she selects her pauses artfully. Line-breaks lend emphasis: a word or phrase at the end of a line takes a little more stress (and receives a little more attention), because the ending of the line compels the reader to make a slight pause, if only for the brief moment it takes to sling back one's eyes (like a typewriter carriage) and fix them on the line following. Slight pauses, then, follow the words and phrases *the dog / laps up / water / intelligent / resting / irregular / measure* — all of these being elements that apparently the poet wishes to call our attention to. (The pause after a line-break also casts a little more weight upon the *first* word or phrase of each succeeding line.) Levertov makes the most of white space — another means of calling attention to things, as any good picture-framer knows. By setting a word all alone on a line (*water / measure*), she makes it stand out more than it would do in a line of pentameter. She feels free to include a bit of rime (*Shlup, shlup / up*). She creates rhythms: if you will read aloud the phrases *intelligent / music* and *irregular / measure*, you will sense that in each phrase the arrangement of pauses and stresses is identical. Like the dog's halts to take breath, the lengths of the lines seem naturally irregular. The result is a fusion of meaning and form: indeed, an "intelligent music."

Poetry in open form used to be called **free verse** (from the French *vers libre*), suggesting a kind of verse liberated from the shackles of rime and meter. "Writing free verse," said Robert Frost, who wasn't interested in it, "is like playing tennis with the net down." And yet, as Denise Levertov and many other poets demonstrate, high scores can be made in such an unconventional game, provided it doesn't straggle all over the court. For a successful poem in open form, the term *free verse* seems inaccurate. "Being an art form," said William Carlos Williams, "verse cannot be 'free' in the sense of having *no* limitations or guiding principles."[5] Various substitute names have been suggested: organic poetry, composition by field, raw (as against cooked) poetry, open form poetry. "But what does it matter what you call it?" remark the editors of an anthology called *Naked Poetry*. The best poems of the last twenty years "don't rhyme (usually) and don't move on feet of more or less equal duration (usually). That nondescription moves toward the only technical principle they all have in common."[6]

And yet many poems in open form have much more in common than absences and lacks. One positive principle has been Ezra Pound's famous suggestion that poets "compose in the sequence of the musical phrase, not in the sequence of the metronome" — good advice, perhaps, even for poets who write inside fixed forms. In Charles Olson's influential theory of **projective verse,** poets compose by listening to their own breathing. On paper, they indicate the rhythms of a poem by using a little white space or a lot, a slight indentation or a deep one, depending on whether a short pause or a long one is intended. Words can be grouped in clusters on the page (usually no more words than a lungful of air can accommodate). Heavy cesuras are sometimes shown by breaking a line in two and lowering the second part of it.[7] (An Olson poem appears on page 186.)

To the poet working in open form, no less than to the poet writing a sonnet, line length can be valuable. Walt Whitman, who loved to expand vast sentences for line after line, knew well that an impressive rhythm can accumulate if the poet will keep long lines approximately the same length, causing a pause to recur at about the same interval after every line. Sometimes, too, Whitman repeats the same words at each line's opening. An instance is the masterful sixth section of "When Lilacs Last in the Dooryard Bloom'd," an elegy for Abraham Lincoln:

> Coffin that passes through lanes and streets,
> Through day and night with the great cloud darkening the land,
> With the pomp of the inloop'd flags with the cities draped in black,
> With the show of the States themselves as of crape-veil'd women stand-
>   ing,
> With processions long and winding and the flambeaus of the night,
> With the countless torches lit, with the silent sea of faces and the unbared
>   heads,

[5] "Free Verse," article in *Princeton Encyclopedia of Poetry and Poetics.*
[6] Stephen Berg and Robert Mezey, eds., foreword to *Naked Poetry: Recent American Poetry in Open Forms* (Indianapolis: Bobbs-Merrill, 1969).
[7] See Olson's essays "Projective Verse" and "Letter to Elaine Feinstein" in *Selected Writings,* edited by Robert Creeley (New York: New Directions, 1966). Olson's letters to Cid Corman are fascinating: *Letters for Origin, 1950–1955,* edited by Albert Glover (New York: Grossman, 1970).

With the waiting depot, the arriving coffin, and the somber faces,
With dirges through the night, with the thousand voices rising strong and
   solemn,
With all the mournful voices of the dirges pour'd around the coffin,
The dim-lit churches and the shuddering organs — where amid these you
   journey,
With the tolling tolling bells' perpetual clang,
Here, coffin that slowly passes,
I give you my sprig of lilac.

There is music in such solemn, operatic arias. Whitman's lines echo another model: the Hebrew **psalms,** or sacred songs, as translated in the King James Version of the Bible. In Psalm 150, repetition also occurs inside of lines:

Praise ye the Lord. Praise God in his sanctuary: praise him in the firmament of his power.
Praise him for his mighty acts: praise him according to his excellent greatness.
Praise him with the sound of the trumpet: praise him with the psaltery and harp.
Praise him with the timbrel and dance: praise him with stringed instruments and organs.
Praise him upon the loud cymbals: praise him upon the high sounding cymbals.
Let every thing that hath breath praise the Lord. Praise ye the Lord.

In Biblical Psalms, we are in the presence of (as Robert Lowell has said) "supreme poems, written when their translators merely intended prose and were forced by the structure of their originals to write poetry."[8]

Whitman was a more deliberate craftsman than he let his readers think, and to anyone interested in writing in open form, his work will repay close study. He knew that repetitions of any kind often make memorable rhythms, as in this passage from "Song of Myself," with every line ending on an *-ing* word (a stressed syllable followed by an unstressed syllable):

Here and there with dimes on the eyes walking,
To feed the greed of the belly the brains liberally spooning,
Tickets buying, taking, selling, but in to the feast never once going,
Many sweating, ploughing, thrashing, and then the chaff for payment
   receiving,
A few idly owning, and they the wheat continually claiming.

Much more than simply repetition, of course, went into the music of those lines — the internal rime *feed, greed,* the use of assonance, the

---

[8] "On Freedom in Poetry," in Berg and Mezey, *Naked Poetry.*

trochees that begin the third and fourth lines, whether or not they were calculated.

In such classics of open form poetry, sound and rhythm are positive forces. When speaking a poem in open form, you often may find that it makes a difference for the better if you pause at the end of each line. Try pausing there, however briefly; but don't allow your voice to drop. Read just as you would normally read a sentence in prose (except for the pauses, of course). Why do the pauses matter? Open form poetry usually has no meter to lend it rhythm. *Some* lines in an open form poem, as we have seen in Whitman's "dimes on the eyes" passage, do fall into metrical feet; sometimes the whole poem does. Usually lacking meter's aid, however, open form, in order to have more and more noticeable rhythms, has need of all the recurring pauses it can get. When reading their own work aloud, open form poets like Robert Creeley and Allen Ginsberg often pause very definitely at each line break. Such a habit makes sense only in reading artful poems.

No law requires a poet to split thoughts into irregular lines at all. Charles Baudelaire, Rainer Maria Rilke, Jorge Luis Borges, Alexander Solzhenitsyn, T. S. Eliot, and many others have written **prose poems,** in which, without caring that eye appeal and some of the rhythm of a line structure may be lost, the poet prints words in a block like a prose paragraph. For an example see Karl Shapiro's "The Dirty Word" (page 394).[9]

The great majority of poems appearing at present in American literary magazines are in open form. "Farewell, pale skunky pentameters (the only honest English meter, gloop! gloop!)," Kenneth Koch has gleefully exclaimed. Many poets have sought reasons for turning away from patterns and fixed forms. Some hold that it is wrong to fit words into any pattern that already exists and instead believe in letting a poem seek its own shape as it goes along. (Traditionalists might say that that is what all good poems do anyway: sonnets rarely know they are going to be sonnets until the third line has been written. However, there is no doubt that the sonnet form already exists, at least in the back of the head of any poet who has ever read sonnets.) Some open form poets offer a historical motive: they want to reflect the nervous, staccato, disconnected pace of our bumper-to-bumper society. Others see open form as an attempt to suit thoughts and words to a more spontaneous order than the traditional verse forms allow. "Better," says Gary Snyder, quoting from Zen, "the perfect, easy discipline of the swallow's dip and swoop, 'without east or west.' "[10]

[9] For more examples see *The Prose Poem, An International Anthology,* edited by Michael Benedikt (New York: Dell, 1976).
[10] "Some Yips & Barks in the Dark," in Berg and Mezey, *Naked Poetry.*

E. E. Cummings (1894–1962)

BUFFALO BILL'S   1923

Buffalo Bill's
defunct
        who used to
        ride a watersmooth-silver
                                stallion   5
and break onetwothreefourfive pigeonsjustlikethat
                                        Jesus

he was a handsome man
                        and what i want to know is
how do you like your blueeyed boy   10
Mister Death

QUESTION

Cummings's poem would look like this if given conventional punctuation and set in a solid block like prose:

Buffalo Bill's defunct, who used to ride a water-smooth silver stallion and break one, two, three, four, five pigeons just like that. Jesus, he was a handsome man. And what I want to know is: "How do you like your blue-eyed boy, Mister Death?"

If this were done, by what characteristics would it still be recognizable as poetry? But what would be lost?

Emily Dickinson (1830–1886)

VICTORY COMES LATE   (1861)

Victory comes late–
And is held low to freezing lips–
Too rapt with frost
To take it–
How sweet it would have tasted–   5
Just a Drop–
Was God so economical?
His Table's spread too high for Us–
Unless We dine on tiptoe–
Crumbs–fit such little mouths–   10
Cherries–suit Robins–
The Eagle's Golden Breakfast strangles–Them–
God keep His Oath to Sparrows–
Who of little Love–know how to starve–

QUESTIONS

1. In this specimen of poetry in open form, can you see any other places at
   which the poet might have broken off any of her lines? To place a word last in

a line gives it a greater emphasis; she might, for instance, have ended line 12 with *Breakfast* and begun a new line with the word *strangles*. Do you think she knows what she is doing here or does the pattern of this poem seem decided by whim? Discuss.

2. Read the poem aloud. Try pausing for a fraction of a second at every dash. Is there any justification for the poet's unorthodox punctuation?

William Carlos Williams (1883–1963)

THE DANCE   1944

In Breughel's great picture, The Kermess,
the dancers go round, they go round and
around, the squeal and the blare and the
tweedle of bagpipes, a bugle and fiddles
tipping their bellies (round as the thick-   5
sided glasses whose wash they impound)
their hips and their bellies off balance
to turn them. Kicking and rolling about
the Fair Grounds, swinging their butts, those
shanks must be sound to bear up under such   10
rollicking measures, prance as they dance
in Breughel's great picture, The Kermess.

THE DANCE. Pieter Breughel (1520?–1569), a Flemish painter known for his scenes of peasant activities, represented in "The Kermess" a celebration on the feast day of a local patron saint.

1. Scan this poem and try to describe the effect of its rhythms.
2. Williams, widely admired for his free verse, insisted for many years that what he sought was a form not in the least bit free. What effect does he achieve by ending lines on such weak words as the articles *and* and *the*? By splitting *thick- / sided*? By splitting a prepositional phrase with the break at the end of line 8? By using line breaks to split *those* and *such* from what they modify? What do you think he is trying to convey?
3. Is there any point in his making line 12 a repetition of the opening line?
4. Look at the reproduction of Breughel's painting "The Kermess" (also called "Peasants Dancing"). Aware that the rhythms of dancers, the rhythms of a painting, and the rhythms of a poem are not all the same, can you put in your own words what Breughel's dancing figures have in common with Williams's descriptions of them?

Robert Herrick (1591–1674)
UPON A CHILD THAT DIED   1648

Here she lies, a pretty bud,
Lately made of flesh and blood.
Who as soon fell fast asleep
As her little eyes did peep.
Give her strewings, but not stir
The earth that lightly covers her.

Saint Geraud [Bill Knott] (b. 1940)
POEM   1968

The only response
to a child's grave is
to lie down before it and play dead

What differences do you find between the effect of Herrick's poem and that of Saint Geraud's? Try to explain how the pattern (or lack of pattern) in each poem contributes to these differences.

Stephen Crane (1871–1900)
THE HEART   1895

In the desert
I saw a creature, naked, bestial,
Who, squatting upon the ground,
Held his heart in his hands,
And ate of it.   5

I said, "Is it good, friend?"
"It is bitter—bitter," he answered;
"But I like it
Because it is bitter,
And because it is my heart."   10

Walt Whitman (1819–1892)

CAVALRY CROSSING A FORD   (1865)

A line in long array where they wind betwixt green islands,
They take a serpentine course, their arms flash in the sun—hark to the
    musical clank,
Behold the silvery river, in it the splashing horses loitering stop to drink,
Behold the brown-faced men, each group, each person a picture, the
    negligent rest on the saddles,
Some emerge on the opposite bank, others are just entering the ford—
    while,
Scarlet and blue and snowy white,
The guidon flags flutter gayly in the wind.

QUESTIONS

The following nit-picking questions are intended to help you see exactly what
makes these two open form poems by Crane and Whitman so different in their
music.

1. What devices of sound occur in Whitman's phrase *silvery river* (line 3)?
   Where else in his poem do you find these devices?
2. Does Crane use any such devices? Try picking out, for instance, all syllables
   that end with the sound of the letter *t*.(There are a surprising number for a
   poem so short.)
3. In number of syllables, Whitman's poem is almost twice as long as Crane's.
   Which poem has more pauses in it? (Count pauses at the ends of lines, at
   marks of punctuation.)
4. Read the two poems aloud. In general, how would you describe the effect of
   their sounds and rhythms? Is Crane's poem necessarily an inferior poem for
   having less music?

Gary Gildner (b. 1938)

FIRST PRACTICE   1969

After the doctor checked to see
we weren't ruptured,
the man with the short cigar took us
under the grade school,
where we went in case of attack   5
or storm, and said

he was Clifford Hill, he was
a man who believed dogs
ate dogs, he had once killed
for his country, and if   10
there were any girls present
for them to leave now.
                              No one
left. OK, he said, he said I take
that to mean you are hungry
men who hate to lose as much   15
as I do. OK. Then
he made two lines of us
facing each other,
and across the way, he said,
is the man you hate most   20
in the world,
and if we are to win
that title I want to see how.
But I don't want to see
any marks when you're dressed,   25
he said. He said, *Now.*

Questions

1. What do you make of Hill and his world-view?
2. How does the speaker reveal his own view? Why, instead of quoting Hill directly ("This is a dog-eat-dog world"), does he call him *a man who believed dogs ate dogs* (lines 8–9)?
3. What effect is made by breaking off and lowering *No one* at the end of line 12?
4. What is gained by having a rime on the poem's last word?
5. For the sake of understanding how right the form of Gildner's poem is for it, imagine the poem in meter and a rime scheme, and condensed into two stanzas:

   Then he made two facing lines of us
   And he said, Across the way,
   Of all the men there are in the world
   Is the man you most want to slay,

   And if we are to win that title, he said,
   I want you to show me how.
   But I don't want to see any marks when you're dressed,
   He said. Go get him. *Now.*

   Why would that rewrite be so unfaithful to what Gildner is saying?
6. How would you answer someone who argued, "This can't be a poem — its subject is ugly and its language isn't beautiful"?

Leigh Hunt (1784–1859)

RONDEAU   1838

Jenny kissed me when we met,
   Jumping from the chair she sat in;
Time, you thief, who love to get
   Sweets into your list, put that in:
Say I'm weary, say I'm sad,
   Say that health and wealth have missed me,
Say I'm growing old, but add,
   Jenny kissed me.

QUESTION

Here is a fresh contemporary version of Hunt's "Rondeau" that yanks open the
form of the rimed original:

Jenny kissed me when we met,
jumping from her chair;
Time, you thief, who love to add
sweets into your list, put that in:
say I'm weary, say I'm sad,
say I'm poor and in ill health,
say I'm growing old — but note, too,
Jenny kissed me.

That revised version says approximately the same thing as Hunt's original,
doesn't it? Why is it less effective?

Frank Sidgwick (1879–1939)

THE AERONAUT TO HIS LADY   1921

I
   Through
   Blue
Sky
Fly   5
   To
   You.
Why?

Sweet
   Love,   10
Feet
   Move
      So
      Slow!

1. Describe the form in which this poem is written.
2. Would you guess that anybody could dash off a poem in this form with ease, or that Sidgwick is a skilled poet who had to overcome difficulty? (To find out, try writing a poem in this form and see what difficulties you meet.)
3. An opinion in a recent little magazine: "The form of a poem is the poet's business, not the reader's. Reading a poem, all you have to do is get the message." How well does this opinion apply to "The Aeronaut to his Lady"? Would you take as much pleasure from this poem if you weren't aware of its form? How important is its message?
4. How highly would you rate this poem in comparison to other poems you know? Do you think it a bit of trash? A clever doodad? A deathless masterpiece?
5. Here is a larger question to mull, if you didn't think Sidgwick's poem a masterpiece. What, *in addition to* mastery of form (whether open or closed), do you expect of the finest poetry?

Stevie Smith (1902–1971)

I REMEMBER   1957

It was my bridal night I remember,
An old man of seventy-three
I lay with my young bride in my arms,
A girl with t.b.
It was wartime, and overhead   5
The Germans were making a particularly heavy raid on Hampstead.
What rendered the confusion worse, perversely
Our bombers had chosen that moment to set out for Germany.
Harry, do they ever collide?
I do not think it has ever happened,   10
Oh my bride, my bride.

QUESTIONS

1. From the opening three lines, you might expect a rollicking, roughly metrical ballad or song. But as this poem goes on, how does its form surprise you?
2. What besides form, by the way, is odd or surprising here? Why can't this be called a conventional love lyric?
3. Lewis Turco has proposed the name *Nashers* for a certain kind of line (or couplet) found in the verse of Ogden Nash (whose "Very Like a Whale" appears on page 96). Nashers, according to Turco, are "usually long, of flat free verse or prose with humorous, often multisyllabic endings utilizing wrenched rhymes" (Lewis Turco, *The Book of Forms*, New York: E. P. Dutton, 1968). What Nashers can you find in "I Remember"?
4. What does the poet achieve by ending her poem in an exact rime (*collide/bride*)? Suppose she had ended it with another long, sprawling, unrimed line; for example, "As far as I know from reading the newspapers, O my poor coughing dear." What would be lost?
5. What do you understand to be the *tone* of this poem (the poet's implied attitude toward her material)? Would you call it tender and compassionate? Sorrowful? Grim? Playful and humorous? Earnest?

6. How does noticing the form of this poem help you to understand the tone of it?

Thomas Hardy (1840–1928)

AT A HASTY WEDDING   1901

If hours be years the twain are blest,
For now they solace swift desire
By bonds of every bond the best,
If hours be years. The twain are blest
Do eastern stars slope never west,
Nor pallid ashes follow fire:
If hours be years the twain are blest,
For now they solace swift desire.

QUESTIONS

1. A challenge that a poet faces in writing a **triolet** (another French courtly form) is that, obliged to devote five out of eight lines to repetitions, the poet has little room to say anything. In this triolet, what has Hardy succeeded in saying? Sum up his theme.
2. Why is the image of fire that dies to "pallid ashes" especially appropriate? (Compare the effect of this image to that of other images of pale things in Hardy's "Neutral Tones," page 202, a poem about the aftermath of a love affair.)

Geoffrey Chaucer (1340?–1400)

YOUR YEN TWO WOL SLEE ME SODENLY   (late fourteenth century)

Your yen° two wol slee° me sodenly;   *eyes, slay*
I may the beautee of hem° not sustene°,   *them, resist*
So woundeth hit thourghout my herte kene.

And but° your word wol helen° hastily   *unless, heal*
My hertes wounde, while that hit is grene°,   *new*   5
    Your yen two wol slee me sodenly;
    I may the beautee of hem not sustene.

Upon my trouthe° I sey you feithfully   *word*
That ye ben of my lyf and deeth the quene;
For with my deeth the trouthe° shal be sene.   *truth*   10
    Your yen two wol slee me sodenly;
    I may the beautee of hem not sustene,
    So woundeth it thourghout my herte kene.

YOUR YEN TWO WOL SLEE ME SODENLY. This poem is one of a group of three in the same fixed form, entitled "Merciles Beaute." 3. *so woundeth . . . kene:* "So deeply does it wound me through the heart."

1. This is a **roundel** (or **rondel**), an English form. What are its rules? How does it remind you of French courtly forms such as the villanelle and the triolet?
2. Try writing a roundel of your own in modern English. Although tricky, the form isn't extremely difficult: write only three lines and your poem is already eight-thirteenths finished. Here are some possible opening lines:

Baby, your eyes will slay me. Shut them tight.
Against their glow, I can't hold out for long. . . .

Your eyes present a pin to my balloon:
One pointed look and I start growing small. . . .

Since I escaped from love, I've grown so fat,
I barely can remember being thin. . . .

Wallace Stevens (1879–1955)

THIRTEEN WAYS OF LOOKING AT A BLACKBIRD   1923

I

Among twenty snowy mountains,
The only moving thing
Was the eye of the blackbird.

II

I was of three minds,
Like a tree   5
In which there are three blackbirds.

III

The blackbird whirled in the autumn winds.
It was a small part of the pantomime.

IV

A man and a woman
Are one.   10
A man and a woman and a blackbird
Are one.

V

I do not know which to prefer,
The beauty of inflections
Or the beauty of innuendoes,   15
The blackbird whistling
Or just after.

VI

Icicles filled the long window
With barbaric glass.
The shadow of the blackbird   20

Crossed it, to and fro.
The mood
Traced in the shadow
An indecipherable cause.

VII

O thin men of Haddam,   25
Why do you imagine golden birds?
Do you not see how the blackbird
Walks around the feet
Of the women about you?

VIII

I know noble accents   30
And lucid, inescapable rhythms;
But I know, too,
That the blackbird is involved
In what I know.

IX

When the blackbird flew out of sight,   35
It marked the edge
Of one of many circles.

X

At the sight of blackbirds
Flying in a green light,
Even the bawds of euphony   40
Would cry out sharply.

XI

He rode over Connecticut
In a glass coach.
Once, a fear pierced him,
In that he mistook   45
The shadow of his equipage
For blackbirds.

XII

The river is moving.
The blackbird must be flying.

XIII

It was evening all afternoon.   50
It was snowing
And it was going to snow.
The blackbird sat
In the cedar-limbs.

THIRTEEN WAYS OF LOOKING AT A BLACKBIRD. 25. *Haddam:* This Biblical-sounding name is
that of a town in Connecticut.

1. What is the speaker's attitude toward the men of Haddam? What attitude toward this world does he suggest they lack? What is implied by calling them *thin* (line 25)?
2. What do the landscapes of winter contribute to the poem's effectiveness? If Stevens had chosen images of summer lawns, what would have been lost?
3. In which sections of the poem does Stevens suggest that a unity exists between human being and blackbird, between blackbird and the entire natural world? Can we say that Stevens "philosophizes"? What role does imagery play in Steven's statement of his ideas?
4. What sense can you make of Part X? Make an enlightened guess.
5. Consider any one of the thirteen parts. What patterns of sound and rhythm do you find in it? What kind of structure does it have?
6. If the thirteen parts were arranged in some different order, would the poem be just as good? Or can we find a justification for its beginning with Part I and ending with Part XIII?
7. Does the poem seem an arbitrary combination of thirteen separate poems? Or is there any reason to call it a whole?

EXERCISE: *Seeing the Logic of Open Form Verse*

Read the following poems in open form silently to yourself, noticing what each poet does with white space, repetitions, line breaks, and indentations. Then read the poems aloud, trying to indicate by slight pauses where lines end and also pausing slightly at any space inside a line. Can you see any reasons for the poet's placing his words in this arrangement rather than in a prose paragraph? Do any of these poets seem to care also about visual effect? (As is the case with other kinds of poetry, there may not be any obvious logical reason for everything that happens in these poems.)

E. E. Cummings (1894–1962)

IN JUST-   1923

in Just-
spring   when the world is mud-
luscious the little
lame balloonman

whistles   far   and wee   5

and eddieandbill come
running from marbles and
piracies and it's
spring

when the world is puddle-wonderful   10

the queer
old balloonman whistles
far   and   wee
and bettyandisbel come dancing

from hop-scotch and jump-rope and   15

it's
spring
and
   the

      goat-footed   20

balloonMan   whistles
far
and
wee

Myra Cohn Livingston (b. 1926)

DRIVING   1972

Smooth it feels
    wheels
        in the groove of the gray
            roadway
            speedway   5
            freeway

long along the in and out
of gray car
    red car
    blue car   10

catching up and overtaking into
        one lane
        two lane
        three lane

            it feels   15

over and over and ever and along

Donald Finkel (b. 1929)

GESTURE   1970

My arm sweeps down
    a pliant arc
        whatever I am
            streams through my
                negligent wrist: 5

the poem
        uncoils
            like a
                whip, and
snaps   10
softly   an inch from your enchanted face.

Charles Olson (1910–1970)

LA CHUTE

1967

my drum, hollowed out thru the thin slit,
carved from the cedar wood, the base I took
when the tree was felled

o my lute, wrought from the tree's crown

my drum, whose lustiness   5
was not to be resisted
                my lute,
from whose pulsations
not one could turn away

                         They   10
are where the dead are, my drum fell
where the dead are, who
will bring it up, my lute
who will bring it up where it fell in the face of them
where they are, where my lute and drum have fallen?   15

LA CHUTE. The French title means "The Fall."

11 Poems for the Eye

Let's look at a famous poem with a distinctive visible shape. In the seventeenth century, ingenious poets trimmed their lines into the silhouettes of altars and crosses, pillars and pyramids. Here is one. Is it anything more than a demonstration of ingenuity?

George Herbert (1593–1633)

EASTER WINGS   1633

Lord, who createdst man in wealth and store,
Though foolishly he lost the same,
Decaying more and more
Till he became
Most poor;
With thee
Oh, let me rise
As larks, harmoniously,
And sing this day thy victories;
Then shall the fall further the flight in me.

My tender age in sorrow did begin;
And still with sicknesses and shame
Thou didst so punish sin,
That I became
Most thin.
With thee
Let me combine,
And feel this day thy victory;
For if I imp my wing on thine,
Affliction shall advance the flight in me.

In the next-to-last line, *imp* is a term from falconry meaning to repair the wing of an injured bird by grafting feathers into it.

If we see it merely as a picture, we will have to admit that Herbert's word design does not go far. It renders with difficulty shapes that a sketcher's pencil could set down in a flash. The pencil sketch might have more detail, might be more accurate. Was Herbert's effort wasted? It might have been, were there not more to his poem than meets the eye. The mind, too, is engaged by the visual pattern, by the realization that the words *most thin* are given emphasis by their narrow form. Here, visual pattern points out meaning. Heard aloud, too, "Easter Wings" takes on additional depths. Its rimes, its pattern of rhythm are perceptible. It gives pleasure as any poem in a symmetrical stanza may do: by establishing a pattern that leads the reader to anticipate when another rime or a pause will arrive and then fulfilling that expectation.

Ever since the invention of the alphabet, poems have existed not only as rhythmic sounds upon the air but also as visual patterns made of words. At least some of our pleasure in silently reading a poem derives from the way it looks upon its page. A poem in an open form can engage the eye with snowfields of white space and thickets of close-set words. A poem in stanzas can please us by its visual symmetry. And, far from being merely decorative, the visual devices of a poem can be meaningful, too. White space — as poets demonstrate who work in open forms — can indicate pauses. If white space entirely surrounds a word or phrase or line, then that portion of the poem obviously takes special emphasis. Typographical devices such as capital letters and italics also can lay stress upon words. In most traditional poems, a capital letter at the beginning of each new line helps indicate the importance the poet places upon line-divisions, whose regular intervals make a rhythm out of pauses. And the poet may be trying to show us that certain lines rime by indenting them.

Ever since George Herbert's day, writers have continued to experiment with the appearances of printed poetry. Notable efforts to entertain the eye are Lewis Carroll's rimed mouse's tail in *Alice in Wonderland;* and the *Calligrammes* of Guillaume Apollinaire, who arranged words in the shapes of a necktie, of the Eiffel Tower, and of spears of falling rain. Here is a shaped poem of more recent inspiration:

John Hollander (b. 1929)

SKELETON KEY

1969

Opening and starting key for a
1954 Dodge junked last year.

```
           O with what key
         shall I unlock this
        heart Tight in a coffer
     of chest something awaits a
   jab a click a sharp turn yes an
 opening Out with it then Let it
 pour into forms it molds itself
 Much like an escape of dreaming
 prisoners taking shape out in a
 relenting air in bright volumes
 unimaginable even amid anterior
 blacknesses let mine run out in
     the sunny roads Let them be
       released by modulations
         of point by bend of
           line too tiny for
         planning out back
           in hopeful dark
           times or places
          How to hold on
           to a part flat
          or wide enough
            to grasp was
            not too hard
           formerly and
             patterned
             edges cut
            themselves
           What midget
           forms shall
              fall in
              line or
            row beyond
            this wall
            of self A
             key can
          open a car
          Why not me
            O let me
             get in
```

Evidently the shape of Hollander's car key agrees with what is said in it. A whole poem, of course, does not need to be such a verbal silhouette to have a meaningful appearance. In part of a longer poem, William Carlos Williams has conveyed the way a bellhop runs downstairs:

> ta tuck a
> > ta tuck a
> > > ta tuck a
> > > > ta tuck a
> > > > > ta tuck a

This is not only good onomatopoeia and an accurate description of a rhythm; the steplike appearance of the lines goes together with their meaning.

Sometimes an unconventional-looking poem represents no familiar object but is an attempt to make the eye follow an unaccustomed path, as in this experiment by E. E. Cummings.

E. E. Cummings (1894–1962)

R-P-O-P-H-E-S-S-A-G-R   1935

                         r-p-o-p-h-e-s-s-a-g-r
                 who
a)s w(e loo)k
upnowgath
                 PPEGORHRASS
                                         eringint(o-
aThe):l
         eA
             !p:
S   a
                 (r
     rIvInG   .gRrEaPsPhOs)
                             to
rea(be)rran(com)gi(e)ngly
,grasshopper;

However startling it may be to eyes accustomed to poems in conventional line arrangements, this experiment is not a shaped poem. What matters is the grasshopperish leaps and backtracks that our eyes must make in unscrambling letters and words, rearranging them into a more usual order.

Though too much importance can be given to the visual element of poetry and though many poets seem hardly to care about it, it can be another dimension that sets apart poetry from prose. It is at least arguable that some of Walt Whitman's long-line, page-filling descriptions of the wide ocean, open landscapes, and broad streets of his America, which meet the eye as wide expanses of words, would lose something — besides rhythm — if couched in lines only three or four syllables long. Another poet who deeply cared about visual appearance was William Blake, graphic artist and engraver as well as a master artist in words. By publishing his *Songs of Innocence* and *Songs of Experience* (among other works) with illustrations and accompanying hand-lettered poems, often interwoven with the lines of the poems, Blake apparently strove to make poem and appearance of poem a unity, striking mind and eye at the same time.

The way a poem looks, while significant, is hardly enough in itself to make a poem succeed. To pour just any old words into a silhouette of the Taj Mahal would be as likely to result in a dismal poem as to arrange them into the pattern of a sonnet. Like other good poems, good shaped poems appeal not only to sight but to our other faculties, and they depend upon sound, rhythm, imagery, denotation, and connotation. May Swenson, a poet who has written poems of both kinds, has insisted that for her the visual arrangement of a poem can be discovered only after the poem's "whole language structure and behavior" have been completed: "What the poems say or show, their way of doing it with *language*, is the main thing."[1] Clearly, if a poem has other virtues, its visual pattern can be one more means for the poet to speak to us.

May Swenson (b. 1919)

Stone Gullets   1970

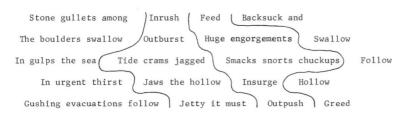

Questions

1. What do the three curving lines drawn into this poem suggest?
2. Besides depicting something, do they have any other uses to the poem?
3. Read "Stone Gullets" aloud. By what other devices (besides visual ones) does the poet communicate meanings?

[1] From an explanatory note at the end of her book of poems, *Iconographs* (New York: Scribners, 1970).

Some poets who write in English have envied poets who write in Chinese, a language in which certain words look like the things they represent. Consider this Chinese poem:

Wang Wei (701–761)

Bird-Singing Stream   (about 750)

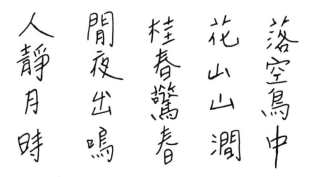

Substituting English words for ideograms, the poem becomes:

man	leisure	cassia	flower	fall
quiet	night	spring	mountain	empty
moon	rise	startle	mountain	bird
at times	sing	spring	stream	middle

Even without the aid of English crib-notes, all of us can read some Chinese if we can recognize a picture of a man. What resemblances can you see between any of the other ideograms and the things they stand for?[2]

Wai-lim Yip, the poet and critic who provided the Chinese text and translation, has also translated the poem into more usual English word order, still keeping close to the original sequence of ideas:

Man at leisure. Cassia flowers fall.
Quiet night. Spring mountain is empty.
Moon rises. Startles—a mountain bird.
It sings at times in the spring stream.

One envious Western poet was Ezra Pound, who included a few Chinese ideograms in his *Cantos* as illustrations. From the scholar Ernest Fenollosa, Pound said he had come to understand why a language written in ideograms "simply *had to stay poetic*; simply couldn't help being and staying poetic in a way that a column of English type might

---

[2] To help you compare English and Chinese, the Chinese original has been arranged in Western word-order. (Ordinarily, in Chinese, the word for "man" would appear at the upper right.)

192   Poems for the Eye

very well not stay poetic."[3] Having an imperfect command of Chinese, Pound greatly overestimated the tendency of the language to depict things. (Only a small number of characters in modern Chinese are pictures; Chinese characters, like Western alphabets, also indicate the sounds of words.) Still, Pound's misunderstanding was fruitful. Thanks to his influence, many other recent poets were encouraged to consider the appearance of words.[4] E. E. Cummings, in a poem that begins "mOOn Over tOwns mOOn," has reveled in the fact that O's are moon-shaped. Aram Saroyan, in a poem entitled "crickets," makes capital of the fact that the word *cricket* somewhat resembles the snub-nosed insect of approximately the same length. The poem begins,

 crickets
 crickets
 crickets
 crickets

and goes on down its page like that, for thirty-seven lines. (Read aloud, by the way, the poem sounds somewhat like crickets chirping!) In recent years, a movement called **concrete poetry** has traveled far and wide. Though practitioners of the art disagree over its definition, what most concretists seem to do is make designs out of letters and words.

Reinhard Döhl (b. 1934)

1965

---

[3] *The ABC of Reading* (Norfolk, Conn., 1960), p. 22.
[4] For a good brief discussion of Pound's misunderstanding and its influence, see Milton Klonsky's introduction to his anthology *Speaking Pictures: A Gallery of Pictorial Poetry from the Sixteenth Century to the Present* (New York: Harmony, 1975).

QUESTIONS

1. Translate this concrete poem.
2. Do you think we should call it a poem? Why? Or why not?

Other concrete poets wield typography like a brush dipped in paint, using such techniques as blow-up, montage, and superimposed elements (the same words printed many times on top of the same impression, so that the result is blurriness). They may even keep words in a usual order, perhaps employing white space as freely as any writer of open form verse. According to Mary Ellen Solt, an American concretist, we can tell a concrete poem by its "concentration upon the physical material from which the poem or text is made."[5] Still another practitioner, Richard Kostelanetz, has suggested that a more accurate name for concrete poetry might be "word-imagery." He sees it occupying an area somewhere between conventional poetry and visual art.[6]

What makes concretism look foolish or impossible to understand (to those who approach it as if it ought to be traditional poetry) may be that concretists often use words without placing them in context with any other words. Aram Saroyan has a concrete poem consisting of a page blank except for one word: *oxygen.*

Much concrete poetry is clearly "something to look at rather than to read," Louis Untermeyer has said unsympathetically. And yet certain concrete poems can please as good poems always do: by their connotations, figures of speech, sounds, and metaphors — not to mention their rewards to the eye.

Ian Hamilton Finlay (b. 1925)

THE HORIZON OF HOLLAND   1963

[5] Introduction to her anthology *Concrete Poetry: A World View* (Bloomington, Ind.: Indiana University Press, 1969).
[6] Introduction to his anthology *Imaged Words and Worded Images* (New York: Outerbridge and Dienstfrey, 1970).

Like E. E. Cummings's grasshoppers (p. 190), Finlay's verbal windmills make us search out a familiar word order. But in Finlay's poem our pleasure lies not only in puzzling out a sentence ("The horizon of Holland is all ears"), but also in beholding a shape that strikes the eye and in making a connection between it and an image that the title brings to mind. This is something other than what happens in a shaped poem such as "Skeleton Key" (p. 189) and "Easter Wings" (p. 187), where individual letters of the alphabet are not in themselves especially important.

Admittedly, some concrete poems mean less than meets the eye. In this fact, they seem more rigidly confined to the printed page than shaped poems such as "Easter Wings." A good shaped poem, though it would lose much if heard and not seen, still might be a satisfying poem. That many pretentious doodlers have taken up concretism may have caused a *Time* writer to sneer: did Joyce Kilmer miss all that much by never having seen a poem lovely as a

```
     t
    ttt
   rrrrr
  rrrrrrr
eeeeeeeee
   ???
```

However, like other structures of language, concrete poems evidently can have the effect of poetry, if written by poets. Whether or not it ought to be dubbed "poetry," this art can do what poems traditionally have done: use language in delightful ways that reveal meanings to us.

Edwin Morgan (b. 1920)

SIESTA OF A HUNGARIAN SNAKE   1968

s   sz   sz   SZ   sz   SZ   sz   ZS   zs   ZS   zs   zs   z

QUESTIONS

1. What do you suppose Morgan is trying to indicate by reversing the order of the two letters in mid line?
2. What, if anything, about this snake seems Hungarian?
3. Does the sound of its consonants matter?

Dorthi Charles (b. 1960)

CONCRETE CAT 1971

A   A
e ɾ   e ɾ

eYe   eYe   stripestripestripestripe
                    stripestripestripe
whisker   whisker   stripestripestripestripes
         m   h whisker   stripestripestripe
whisker   o   ʇ   stripestripestripe
         U   stripestripestripestripe

paw paw   paw paw   ǝsnoɯ

dishdish   litterbox
                            litterbox

QUESTIONS

1. What does this writer indicate by capitalizing the *a* in *ear*? The *y* in *eye*? The *u* in *mouth*? By using spaces between the letters in the word *tail*?
2. Why is the word *mouse* upside down?
3. What possible pun might be seen in the cat's middle stripe?
4. What is the tone of "Concrete Cat"? How is it made evident?
5. Do these words seem chosen for their connotations or only for their denotations? Would you call this work of art a poem?

EXPERIMENT: *Do It Yourself*

Make a concrete poem of your own. If you need inspiration, pick some familiar object or animal and try to find words that look like it. For more ideas, study the typography of a magazine or newspaper; cut out interesting letters and numerals and try pasting them into arrangements. What (if anything) do your experiments tell you about familiar letters and words? You might also find it helpful to read a book of concrete poetry. Some are mentioned in this chapter. Another useful anthology is that of Emmett Williams, *Anthology of Concrete Poetry* (New York: Something Else Press, 1967).

12 Symbol

The national flag is supposed to bestir our patriotic feelings. When a black cat crosses his path, a superstitious man shivers, foreseeing bad luck. To each of these, by custom, our society expects a standard response. A flag, a black cat's crossing one's path — each is a **symbol:** a visible object or action that suggests some further meaning in addition to itself. In literature, a symbol might be the word *flag* or the words *a black cat crossed his path* or every description of flag or cat in an entire novel, story, play, or poem.

A flag and the crossing of a black cat may be called **conventional symbols,** since they can have a conventional or customary effect on us. Conventional symbols are also part of the language of poetry, as we know when we meet the red rose, emblem of love, in a lyric, or the Christian cross in the devotional poems of George Herbert. More often, however, symbols in literature have no conventional, long-established meaning, but particular meanings of their own. In Melville's novel *Moby Dick,* to take a rich example, whatever we associate with the great white whale is *not* attached unmistakably to white whales by custom. Though Melville tells us that men have long regarded whales with awe and relates Moby Dick to the celebrated fish that swallowed Jonah, the reader's response is to one particular whale, the creature of Herman Melville. Only the experience of reading the novel in its entirety can give Moby Dick his particular meaning.

We should say *meanings,* for as Eudora Welty has observed, it is a good thing Melville made Moby Dick a whale, a creature large enough to contain all that critics have found in him. A symbol in literature, if not conventional, has more than just one meaning. In "The Raven," by Edgar Allan Poe, the appearance of a strange black bird in the narrator's study is sinister; and indeed, if we take the poem seriously, we may even respond with a sympathetic shiver of dread. Does the bird mean death, fate, melancholy, the loss of a loved one, knowledge in the service of evil? All these, perhaps. Like any well-chosen symbol, Poe's raven sets going within the reader an unending train of feelings and associations.

We miss the value of a symbol, however, if we think it can mean absolutely anything we wish. If a poet has any control over our reactions, the poem will guide our responses in a certain direction.

T. S. Eliot (1888–1965)
THE BOSTON EVENING TRANSCRIPT   1917

The readers of the *Boston Evening Transcript*
Sway in the wind like a field of ripe corn.

When evening quickens faintly in the street,
Wakening the appetites of life in some
And to others bringing the *Boston Evening Transcript*,
I mount the steps and ring the bell, turning
Wearily, as one would turn to nod good-bye to La Rochefoucauld,
If the street were time and he at the end of the street,
And I say, "Cousin Harriet, here is the *Boston Evening Transcript*."

The newspaper, whose name Eliot purposely repeats so monotonously, indicates what this poem is about. Now defunct, the *Transcript* covered in detail the slightest activity of Boston's leading families and was noted for the great length of its obituaries. Eliot, then, uses the newspaper as a symbol for an existence of boredom, fatigue (*Wearily*), petty and unvarying routine (since an evening newspaper, like night, arrives on schedule). The *Transcript* evokes a way of life without zest or passion, for, opposed to people who read it, Eliot sets people who do not: those whose desires revive, not expire, when the working day is through. Suggestions abound in the ironic comparison of the *Transcript*'s readers to a cornfield late in summer. To mention only a few: the readers sway because they are sleepy; they vegetate; they are drying up; each makes a rattling sound when turning a page. It is not necessary that we know the remote and similarly disillusioned friend to whom the speaker might nod: La Rochefoucauld, whose cynical *Maxims* entertained Parisian society under Louis XIV (sample: "All of us have enough strength to endure the misfortunes of others"). We understand that the nod is symbolic of an immense weariness of spirit. We know nothing about Cousin Harriet, whom the speaker addresses, but imagine from the greeting she inspires that she is probably a bore.

If Eliot wishes to say that certain Bostonians lead lives of sterile boredom, why does he couch his meaning in symbols? Why doesn't he tell us directly what he means? These questions imply two assumptions not necessarily true: first, that Eliot has a message to impart; second, that he is concealing it. We have reason to think that Eliot did not usually have a message in mind when beginning a poem, for as he once told a critic: "The conscious problems with which one is concerned in the actual writing are more those of a quasi musical nature . . . than of a conscious exposition of ideas." Poets sometimes discover what they have to say while in the act of saying it. And it may be that in his *Transcript* poem, Eliot is saying exactly what he means. By communicating his meaning through symbols instead of statements, he may be choosing the only kind of language appropriate to an idea of great subtlety and complexity. (The paraphrase "Certain Bostonians are bored" hardly begins to describe the poem in all its possible meaning.) And by his use of symbolism, Eliot affords us the pleasure of finding our own entrances to his poem. Another great strength of a symbol is that, like some figures of speech, it renders the abstract in concrete terms, and, like any other image, refers to what we can perceive — an object like a newspaper, a gesture like a nod. Eliot might, like Robert Frost, have called himself a "synecdochist." Frost explained: "Always a larger significance. A little thing touches a larger thing."

This power of suggestion that a symbol contains is, perhaps, its greatest advantage. Sometimes, as in the following poem by Emily Dickinson, a symbol will lead us from a visible object to something too vast to be perceived.

Emily Dickinson (1830–1886)

THE LIGHTNING IS A YELLOW FORK   (about 1870)

The Lightning is a yellow Fork
From Tables in the sky
By inadvertent fingers dropt
The awful Cutlery

Of mansions never quite disclosed
And never quite concealed
The Apparatus of the Dark
To ignorance revealed.

If the lightning is a fork, then whose are the fingers that drop it, the table from which it slips, the household to which it belongs? The poem implies this question without giving an answer. An obvious answer is "God," but can we be sure? We wonder, too, about these partially lighted mansions: if our vision were clearer, what would we behold?[1]

---

[1] In its suggestion of an infinite realm that mortal eyes cannot quite see, but whose nature can be perceived fleetingly through things visible, Emily Dickinson's poem, by coincidence, resembles the work of late-nineteenth-century French poets called **symbolists.** To a symbolist the shirt-tail of Truth is continually seen disappearing around a corner. With their Neoplatonic view of ideal realities existing in a great beyond, whose corresponding symbols are the perceptible cats that bite us and tangible stones we stumble over, French poets such as Charles Baudelaire, Jules Laforgue, and Stéphane Mallarmé were profoundly to affect poets writing in English, notably Yeats (who said a poem "entangles . . . a part of the Divine essence") and Eliot. But we consider in this chapter symbolism as an element in certain poems, not Symbolism, the literary movement.

"But how am I supposed to know a symbol when I see one?" The best approach is to read poems closely, taking comfort in the likelihood that it is better not to notice symbols at all than to find significance in every literal stone and huge meanings in every thing. In looking for the symbols in a poem, pick out all the references to concrete objects — newspapers, black cats, twisted pins. Consider these with special care. Note any that the poet emphasizes by detailed description, by repetition, or by placing at the very beginning or end of the poem. Ask: What is the poem about, what does it add up to? If, when the poem is paraphrased, the paraphrase depends primarily upon the meaning of certain concrete objects, these richly suggestive objects may be the symbols.

There are some things a literary symbol usually is *not*. A symbol is not an abstraction. Such terms as *truth, death, love,* and *justice* cannot work as symbols (unless personified, as in the traditional figure of Justice holding a scale). Most often, a symbol is something we can see in the mind's eye: a newspaper, a lightning bolt, a gesture of nodding good-bye.

In narratives, a well-developed character who speaks much dia-·logue and is not the least bit mysterious is usually not a symbol. But watch out for an executioner in a black hood; a character, named for a Biblical prophet, who does little but utter a prophecy; a trio of old women who resemble the Three Fates. (It has been argued, with good reason, that Milton's fully rounded character of Satan in *Paradise Lost* is a symbol embodying evil and human pride, but a narrower definition of symbol is more frequently useful.) A symbol *may* be a part of a person's body (the baleful eye of the murder victim in Poe's story "The Tell-Tale Heart") or a look, a voice, a mannerism.

A symbol usually is not the second term of a metaphor. In the line "The lightning is a yellow fork," the symbol is the lightning, not the fork.

Sometimes a symbol addresses a sense other than sight: the sound of a mysterious harp at the end of Chekhov's play *The Cherry Orchard;* or, in William Faulkner's tale "A Rose for Emily," the odor of decay that surrounds the house of the last survivor of a town's leading family — suggesting not only physical dissolution but also the decay of a social order. A symbol is a special kind of image, for it exceeds the usual image in the richness of its connotations. The dead wife's cold comb in the haiku of Buson (discussed on p. 54) works symbolically, suggesting among other things the chill of the grave, the contrast between the living and the dead.

Holding a narrower definition than thaι used in this book, some readers of poetry prefer to say that a symbol is always a concrete object, never an act. They would deny the label "symbol" to Ahab's breaking his tobacco pipe before setting out to pursue Moby Dick (suggesting, perhaps, his determination to allow no pleasure to distract him from the chase) or to any large motion (as Ahab's whole quest). This distinction, while confining, does have the merit of sparing one from seeing all motion to be possibly symbolic. Some would call Ahab's gesture not a symbol but a **symbolic act.**

To sum up: a symbol radiates hints or casts long shadows (to use Henry James's metaphor). We are unable to say it "stands for" or "represents" a meaning. It evokes, it suggests, it manifests. It demands no single necessary interpretation, such as the interpretation a driver gives to a red traffic light. Rather, like Emily Dickinson's lightning bolt, it points toward an indefinite meaning, which may lie in part beyond the reach of words. In a symbol, as Thomas Carlyle said in *Sartor Resartus,* "the Infinite is made to blend with the Finite, to stand visible, and as it were, attainable there."

Emily Dickinson (1830–1886)

I HEARD A FLY BUZZ—WHEN I DIED   (about 1862)

I heard a Fly buzz–when I died–
The Stillness in the Room
Was like the Stillness in the Air–
Between the Heaves of Storm—

The Eyes around–had wrung them dry–
And Breaths were gathering firm
For that last Onset–when the King
Be witnessed–in the Room—

I willed my Keepsakes–Signed away
What portion of me be   10
Assignable–and then it was
There interposed a Fly–

With Blue–uncertain stumbling Buzz–
Between the light–and me–
And then the Windows failed–and then   15
I could not see to see–

QUESTIONS

1. Why is the poem written in the past tense? Where is the speaker at present?
2. What do you understand from the repetition of the word *see* in the last line?
3. What does the poet mean by *Eyes around* (line 5), *that last Onset* (line 7), *the King* (line 7), and *What portion of me be / Assignable* (lines 10–11)?
4. In line 13, how can a sound be called *Blue* and *stumbling?*
5. What further meaning might *the Windows* (line 15) suggest, in addition to denoting the windows of the room?
6. What connotations of the word *fly* seem relevant to an account of a death?
7. Summarize your interpretation of the poem. What does the fly mean?

Thomas Hardy (1840–1928)

NEUTRAL TONES   1898

We stood by a pond that winter day,
And the sun was white, as though chidden of God,
And a few leaves lay on the starving sod;
   — They had fallen from an ash, and were gray.

Your eyes on me were as eyes that rove   5
Over tedious riddles of years ago;
And some words played between us to and fro
   On which lost the more by our love.

The smile on your mouth was the deadest thing
Alive enough to have strength to die;   10
And a grin of bitterness swept thereby
   Like an ominous bird a-wing. . . .

Since then, keen lessons that love deceives,
And wrings with wrong, have shaped to me
Your face, and the God-curst sun, and a tree,   15
   And a pond edged with grayish leaves.

QUESTIONS

1. Sum up the story told in this poem. In lines 1–12, what is the dramatic situation? What has happened in the interval between the experience related in these lines and the reflection in the last stanza?
2. What meanings do you find in the title?
3. Explain in your own words the metaphor in line 2.
4. What connotations appropriate to this poem does the *ash* (line 4) have, that *oak* or *maple* would lack?
5. What visible objects in the poem function symbolically? What actions or gestures?

If we read of a ship, its captain, its sailors, and the rough seas, and we realize we are reading about a commonwealth and how its rulers and workers keep it going even in difficult times, then we are reading an **allegory.** Closely akin to symbolism, allegory is a description — usually narrative — in which persons, places, and things are employed in a continuous system of equivalents.

Although more strictly limited in its suggestions than symbolism, allegory need not be thought inferior. Few poems continue to interest readers more than Dante's allegorical *Divine Comedy.* Sublime evidence of the appeal of allegory may be found in Christ's use of the **parable:** a brief narrative — usually allegorical but sometimes not — that teaches a moral.

Matthew 13:24–30 (Authorized or King James Version, 1611)
THE PARABLE OF THE GOOD SEED

The kingdom of heaven is likened unto a man which sowed good seed in his field:

But while men slept, his enemy came and sowed tares among the wheat, and went his way.

But when the blade was sprung up, and brought forth fruit, then appeared the tares also.

So the servants of the householder came and said unto him, Sir, didst not thou sow good seed in thy field? From whence then hath it tares?

He said unto them, An enemy hath done this. The servants said unto him, Wilt thou then that we go and gather them up?

But he said, Nay; lest while ye gather up the tares, ye root up also the wheat with them.

Let both grow together until the harvest: and in the time of harvest I will say to the reapers, Gather ye together first the tares, and bind them in bundles to burn them: but gather the wheat into my barn.

The sower is the Son of man, the field is the world, the good seed are the children of the Kingdom, the tares are the children of the wicked one, the enemy is the devil, the harvest is the end of the world, the reapers are angels. "As therefore the tares are gathered and burned in the fire; so shall it be in the end of this world" (Matthew 13:36–42).

Usually, as in this parable, the meanings of an allegory are plainly labeled or thinly disguised. In John Bunyan's allegorical narrative *The Pilgrim's Progress*, it is clear that the hero Christian, on his journey through places with such pointed names as Vanity Fair, the Valley of the Shadow of Death, and Doubting Castle, is the soul, traveling the road of life on the way toward Heaven. An allegory, when carefully built, is systematic. It makes one principal comparison, the working out of whose details may lead to further comparisons, then still further comparisons: Christian, thrown by Giant Despair into the dungeon of Doubting Castle, escapes by means of a key called Promise. Such a complicated design may take great length to unfold, as in Spenser's *Faerie Queene*; but, the method may be seen in a short poem:

George Herbert (1593–1633)
REDEMPTION   1633

Having been tenant long to a rich Lord,
  Not thriving, I resolvèd to be bold,
And make a suit unto him to afford
  A new small-rented lease and cancel th' old.

In Heaven at his manor I him sought.   5
    They told me there that he was lately gone
About some land which he had dearly bought
    Long since on earth, to take possessiòn.
I straight returned, and knowing his great birth,
    Sought him accordingly in great resorts,   10
    In cities, theaters, gardens, parks, and courts.
At length I heard a ragged noise and mirth
    Of thieves and murderers; there I him espied,
    Who straight "Your suit is granted," said, and died.

Questions

1. In this allegory, what equivalents does Herbert give each of these terms:
   *tenant, Lord, not thriving, suit, new lease, old lease, manor, land, dearly bought,
   take possession, his great birth?*
2. What scene is depicted in the last three lines?

An object in allegory is like a bird whose cage is clearly lettered
with its identity — "RAVEN, *Corvus corax*; habitat of specimen, Maine."
A symbol, by contrast, is a bird with piercing eyes that mysteriously appears one evening in your library. It is there; you can touch it. But what
does it mean? You look at it. It continues to look at you.

Whether an object in literature is a symbol, part of an allegory, or
no such thing at all, it has at least one sure meaning. Moby Dick is first a
whale, the *Boston Evening Transcript* a newspaper. Besides deriving a
multitude of intangible suggestions from the title symbol in Eliot's long
poem *The Waste Land*, its readers cannot fail to carry away a sense of the
land's physical appearance: a river choked with sandwich papers and
cigarette ends, London Bridge "under the brown fog of a winter dawn."
A virtue of *The Pilgrim's Progress* is that its walking abstractions are no
mere abstractions but are also human: Giant Despair is a henpecked
husband. The most vital element of a literary work may pass us by,
unless before seeking further depths in a thing, we look to the thing itself.

Sir Philip Sidney (1554–1586)

You that with allegory's curious frame   1591

You that with allegory's curious frame
    Of others' children changelings use to make,
    With me those pains, for God's sake, do not take;
    I list not° dig so deep for brazen fame.   *I do not choose to*
When I say Stella, I do mean the same   5
    Princess of beauty for whose only sake
    The reins of love I love, though never slake,
    And joy therein, though nations count it shame.

I beg no subject to use eloquence,
  Nor in hid ways do guide philosophy;   10
  Look at my hands for no such quintessence,
But know that I in pure simplicity
  Breathe out the flames which burn within my heart,
  Love only reading unto me this art.

Mina Loy (1881–1966)

OMEN OF VICTORY   1958

Women in uniform

relaxed for tea

under a shady garden tree

discover

a dove's feather

fallen in the sugar.

QUESTIONS

1. What does the conventional symbol of a dove usually indicate?
2. What do you understand from the symbol of the dove's feather in the sugar
   bowl? Do you take it to be an omen of something desirable, an evil omen of
   something the women in uniform don't wish, or aren't you sure?

Hart Crane (1899–1932)

BLACK TAMBOURINE   1926

The interests of a black man in a cellar
Mark tardy judgment on the world's closed door.
Gnats toss in the shadow of a bottle,
And a roach spans a crevice in the floor.

Aesop, driven to pondering, found
Heaven with the tortoise and the hare;
Fox brush and sow ear top his grave
And mingling incantations on the air.

The black man, forlorn in the cellar,
Wanders in some mid-kingdom, dark, that lies,   10
Between his tambourine, stuck on the wall,
And, in Africa, a carcass quick with flies.

QUESTIONS

1. According to tradition, Aesop, the Greek author of fables, was a slave. Do
   you think Crane means that Aesop's condition and the black man's are iden-

tical? What suggestions arise from the animals that Aesop "found Heaven with"? From the creatures that keep the black man company (lines 3–4)?
2. What do you make of the symbol of the tambourine? Of the symbol in the last line: the slain animal?
3. What *mid-kingdom* do you think the poet means? What do you understand by *the world's closed door*? If the black man is being kept in the cellar, what is this house?

EXERCISE: *Symbol Hunting*

After you have read each of these poems, decide which description best suits it:
1. The poem has a central symbol.
2. The poem contains no symbolism, but is to be taken literally.

William Carlos Williams (1883–1963)

POEM   1934

As the cat
climbed over
the top of

the jamcloset
first the right   5
forefoot

carefully
then the hind
stepped down

into the pit of   10
the empty
flowerpot

Theodore Roethke (1908–1963)

NIGHT CROW   1948

When I saw that clumsy crow
Flap from a wasted tree,
A shape in the mind rose up:
Over the gulfs of dream
Flew a tremendous bird
Further and further away
Into a moonless black,
Deep in the brain, far back.

John Donne (1572–1631)
A Burnt Ship   1633

Out of a fired ship which by no way
But drowning could be rescued from the flame
Some men leaped forth, and ever as they came
Near the foe's ships, did by their shot decay;
So all were lost, which in the ship were found,
    They in the sea being burnt, they in the burnt ship drowned.

Wallace Stevens (1879–1955)
Anecdote of the Jar   1923

I placed a jar in Tennessee,
And round it was, upon a hill.
It made the slovenly wilderness
Surround that hill.

The wilderness rose up to it,   5
And sprawled around, no longer wild.
The jar was round upon the ground
And tall and of a port in air.

It took dominion everywhere.
The jar was gray and bare.   10
It did not give of bird or bush,
Like nothing else in Tennessee.

T. S. Eliot (1888–1965)
Rhapsody on a Windy Night   1917

Twelve o'clock.
Along the reaches of the street
Held in a lunar synthesis,
Whispering lunar incantations
Dissolve the floors of memory   5
And all its clear relations
Its divisions and precisions,
Every street-lamp that I pass
Beats like a fatalistic drum,
And through the spaces of the dark   10
Midnight shakes the memory
As a madman shakes a dead geranium.

Half-past one,
The street-lamp sputtered,
The street-lamp muttered,
The street-lamp said, "Regard that woman
Who hesitates toward you in the light of the door
Which opens on her like a grin.
You see the border of her dress
Is torn and stained with sand,
And you see the corner of her eye
Twists like a crooked pin."

The memory throws up high and dry
A crowd of twisted things;
A twisted branch upon the beach
Eaten smooth, and polished
As if the world gave up
The secret of its skeleton,
Stiff and white.
A broken spring in a factory yard,
Rust that clings to the form that the strength has left
Hard and curled and ready to snap.

Half-past two,
The street-lamp said,
"Remark the cat which flattens itself in the gutter,
Slips out its tongue
And devours a morsel of rancid butter."
So the hand of the child, automatic,
Slipped out and pocketed a toy that was running along the quay.
I could see nothing behind that child's eye.
I have seen eyes in the street
Trying to peer through lighted shutters,
And a crab one afternoon in a pool,
An old crab with barnacles on his back,
Gripped the end of a stick which I held him.

Half-past three,
The lamp sputtered,
The lamp muttered in the dark.
The lamp hummed:
"Regard the moon,
La lune ne garde aucune rancune,
She winks a feeble eye,
She smiles into corners.
She smooths the hair of the grass.
The moon has lost her memory.

A washed-out smallpox cracks her face,
Her hand twists a paper rose,
That smells of dust and eau de Cologne,

She is alone
With all the old nocturnal smells   60
That cross and cross across her brain."
The reminiscence comes
Of sunless dry geraniums
And dust in crevices,
Smells of chestnuts in the streets,   65
And female smells in shuttered rooms,
And cigarettes in corridors
And cocktail smells in bars.

The lamp said,
"Four o'clock,   70
Here is the number on the door.
Memory!
You have the key,
The little lamp spreads a ring on the stair.
Mount.   75
The bed is open; the tooth-brush hangs on the wall,
Put your shoes at the door, sleep, prepare for life."

The last twist of the knife.

QUESTIONS

1. Comment on the title. What sort of utterance is a rhapsody? What does the term mean in musical composition? Is it any more appropriate that the speaker's experience occurs on a windy night instead of on, say, a clear day at noon?
2. What happens to *memory* in the first twelve lines? What uses of memory are made throughout the remainder of the poem?
3. Into what sections or episodes can the poem clearly be divided? What marks the beginning of each episode?
4. In each episode, what happens? What parallel organization do the second and succeeding episodes have?
5. In general, how would you describe the process by which, in the second and each succeeding episode, one image leads to others?
6. In lines 33–45, what do cat, child, peering eyes, and crab have in common?
7. The description of a street lamp in lines 8–9 is not a hallucination. Gas-burning street lamps *did* pulsate and make a drumming sound. What other symbols in the poem also seem products of exact observation?
8. How do you visualize the comparison in lines 21–22?
9. Line 51 is a quotation from the French symbolist poet Laforgue: "The moon holds no grudge." What does the moon, as personified in this episode, have in common with the woman in the doorway (lines 16–22)? What does it have in common with the street lamp?
10. What patterns of sound and rhythm help bind the poem together?
11. What do you make of the tooth-brush on the wall (line 76)? What does it have to do with the *last twist of the knife* (line 78)?
12. Compare this poem with "The *Boston Evening Transcript*" (p. 198) and with "The Love Song of J. Alfred Prufrock" (p. 336). Do the symbols in these poems point to any mutual themes?

13 Myth

Poets have long been fond of retelling **myths,** narrowly defined as traditional stories of immortal beings. Such stories taken collectively may also be called **myth** or **mythology.** In one of the most celebrated collections of myth ever assembled, the *Metamorphoses*, the poet Ovid has told — to take one example from many — how Phaeton, child of the sun god, rashly tried to drive his father's fiery chariot on its daily round, lost control of the horses, and caused disaster both to himself and to the world. Our use of the term *myth* in discussing poetry, then, differs from its use in expressions such as "the myth of communism" and "the myth of democracy." In these examples, myth, in its broadest sense, is any idea people believe in, whether true or false. Nor do we mean — to take another familiar use of the word — a cock-and-bull story: "Judge Rapp doesn't roast speeders alive; that's just a *myth.*" In the following discussion, *myth* will mean — as critic Northrop Frye has put it — "the imitation of actions near or at the conceivable limits of desire." Myths tell us of the exploits of the gods — their battles, the ways in which they live, love, and perhaps suffer — all on a scale of magnificence larger than our life. We envy their freedom and power; they enact our wishes and dreams. Whether we believe in them or not, their adventures are myths: Ovid, it seems, placed no credence in the stories he related, for he declared, "I prate of ancient poets' monstrous lies."

And yet it is characteristic of a myth that it *can* be believed. Throughout history, myths have accompanied religious doctrines and rituals. They have helped sanction or recall the reasons for religious observances. A sublime instance is the New Testament account of the Last Supper. Because of it and its record of the words of Jesus, "This do in remembrance of Me," Christians have continued to re-enact the offering and partaking of the body and blood of their Lord, under the appearances of bread and wine. It is essential to recall that, just because a myth narrates the acts of a god, we do not necessarily mean by the term a false or fictitious narrative. When we speak of the "myth of Islam" or "the Christian myth," we do so without implying either belief or disbelief. Myths can also help sanction customs and institutions other than religious ones. At the same time the baking of bread was introduced to ancient Greece — one theory goes — there was introduced the myth of Demeter, goddess of grain, who had kindly sent her emissary Triptolemus to teach humankind this valuable art — thus helping to persuade the distrustful that bread was a good thing. Some myths seem made to divert and regale, not to sanction anything. Such may be the story of the sculptor Pygmalion, who fell in love with his statue of a woman; so exquisite was his work, so deep was his feeling, that Aphrodite brought the statue to life. And yet perhaps the story goes deeper than mere diversion: perhaps it is a way of saying that works of art achieve a reality of their own, that love can transform or animate its object.

How does a myth begin? Several theories have been proposed, none universally accepted. One is that a myth is a way to explain some natural phenomenon. Winter comes and the vegetation perishes because Persephone, child of Demeter, must return to the underworld for four months every year. This theory, as classical scholar Edith Hamilton has pointed out, may lead us to think incorrectly that Greek mythology was the creation of a primitive people. Tales of the gods of Mount Olympus may reflect an earlier inheritance, but Greek myths known to us were transcribed in an era of high civilization. Anthropologists have questioned whether primitive people generally find beauty in the mysteries of nature. "From my own study of living myths among savages," wrote Bronislaw Malinowski, "I should say that primitive man has to a very limited extent the purely artistic or scientific interest in nature; there is but little room for symbolism in his ideas and tales; and myth, in fact, is not an idle rhapsody . . . but a hard-working, extremely important cultural force."[1] Such a practical function was seen by Sir James Frazer in *The Golden Bough:* myths were originally expressions of human hope that nature would be fertile. Still another theory is that, once upon a time, heroes of myth were human prototypes. The Greek philosopher Euhemerus declared myths to be tales of real persons, which poets had exaggerated. Most present-day historians of myth would seek no general explanation but would say that different myths probably have different origins.

Poets have many coherent mythologies on which to draw; perhaps those most frequently consulted by British and American poets are the classical, the Christian, the Norse, and folk myth of the American frontier (embodying the deeds of superhuman characters such as Paul Bunyan). Some poets have taken inspiration from other myths as well: T. S. Eliot's *The Waste Land,* for example, is enriched by allusions to Buddhism and to pagan vegetation-cults.

As a tour through any good art museum will demonstrate, myth

---

[1] Bronislaw Malinowski, *Myth in Primitive Psychology* (1926); reprinted in *Magic, Science and Religion* (New York: Doubleday, 1954), p. 97.

pervades much of the graphic art of Western civilization. In literature, one evidence of its continuing value to recent poets and storytellers is the frequency with which myths—both primitive and civilized—are retold. William Faulkner's story "The Bear" recalls tales of Indian totem animals; John Updike's novel *The Centaur* presents the horse-man Chiron as a modern high school teacher; Hart Crane's poem "For the Marriage of Faustus and Helen" unites two figures of different myths, who dance to jazz; T. S. Eliot's plays bring into the drawing-room the myths of Alcestis (*The Cocktail Party*) and the Eumenides (*The Family Reunion*); Jean Cocteau's film *Orphée* shows us Eurydice riding to the underworld with an escort of motorcycles. Popular interest in such works may testify to the profound appeal myths continue to hold for us. Like any other large body of knowledge that can be alluded to, myth offers the poet an instant means of communication—if the reader also knows the particular myth cited. Writing "Lycidas," John Milton could depend upon his readers—mostly persons of similar classical learning—to understand him without footnotes. Today, a poet referring to a traditional myth must be sure to choose a reasonably well known one, or else write as well as T. S. Eliot, whose work has compelled his readers to single out his allusions and look them up. Like other varieties of poetry, myth is a kind of knowledge, not at odds with scientific knowledge but existing in addition to it.

D. H. Lawrence (1885–1930)
BAVARIAN GENTIANS   1932

Not every man has gentians in his house
In soft September, at slow, sad Michaelmas.

Bavarian gentians, big and dark, only dark
darkening the daytime, torch-like with the smoking blueness of Pluto's
    gloom,
ribbed and torch-like, with their blaze of darkness spread blue   5
down flattening into points, flattened under the sweep of white day
torch-flower of the blue-smoking darkness, Pluto's dark-blue daze,
black lamps from the halls of Dis, burning dark blue,
giving off darkness, blue darkness, as Demeter's pale lamps give off light,
lead me then, lead the way.   10

Reach me a gentian, give me a torch!
let me guide myself with the blue, forked torch of this flower
down the darker and darker stairs, where blue is darkened on blueness
even where Persephone goes, just now, from the frosted September
to the sightless realm where darkness is awake upon the dark   15

and Persephone herself is but a voice
or a darkness invisible enfolded in the deeper dark
of the arms Plutonic, and pierced with the passion of dense gloom,
among the splendor of torches of darkness, shedding darkness on the lost
    bride and her groom.

BAVARIAN GENTIANS. 4. *Pluto:* Roman name for Hades, in Greek mythology the ruler of the underworld, who abducted Persephone to be his bride. Each spring Persephone returns to earth and is welcomed by her mother Demeter, goddess of fruitfulness; each winter she departs again, to dwell with her husband below. 8. *Dis:* Pluto's realm.

QUESTIONS

1. Read this poem aloud. What devices of sound do you hear in it?
2. What characteristics of gentians appear to remind Lawrence of the story of Persephone? What significance do you attach to the poem's being set in September? How does the fact of autumn matter to the gentians and to Persephone?

Thomas Hardy (1840–1928)

THE OXEN   1915

Christmas Eve, and twelve of the clock.
  "Now they are all on their knees,"
An elder said as we sat in a flock
  By the embers in hearthside ease.

We pictured the meek mild creatures where
  They dwelt in their strawy pen,   5
Nor did it occur to one of us there
  To doubt they were kneeling then.

So fair a fancy few would weave
  In these years! Yet, I feel,   10
If someone said on Christmas Eve,
  "Come; see the oxen kneel

"In the lonely barton° by yonder coomb°   *farmyard; a hollow*
  Our childhood used to know,"
I should go with him in the gloom,   15
  Hoping it might be so.

THE OXEN. This ancient belief has had wide currency among peasants and farmers of western Europe. Some also say that on Christmas eve the beasts can speak.

QUESTIONS

1. What body of myth is Hardy's subject and what are his speaker's attitudes toward it? Perhaps, in Hardy's view, the pious report about oxen is only part of it.

2. Read this poem aloud and notice its sound and imagery. What contrast do you find between the sounds of the first stanza and the sounds of the last stanza? Which words make the difference? What images enforce a contrast in tone between the beginning of the poem and its ending?
3. G. K. Chesterton, writing as a defender of Christian faith, called Hardy's writings "the mutterings of the village atheist." See other poems by Hardy (particularly "Channel Firing," p. 345). What do you think Chesterton might have meant? Can "The Oxen" be called a hostile mutter?

William Wordsworth (1770–1850)

THE WORLD IS TOO MUCH WITH US   1807

The world is too much with us; late and soon,
Getting and spending, we lay waste our powers;
Little we see in Nature that is ours;
We have given our hearts away, a sordid boon!
This Sea that bares her bosom to the moon;   5
The winds that will be howling at all hours,
And are up-gathered now like sleeping flowers;
For this, for everything, we are out of tune;
It moves us not. Great God! I'd rather be
A Pagan suckled in a creed outworn;   10
So might I, standing on this pleasant lea,
Have glimpses that would make me less forlorn;
Have sight of Proteus rising from the sea;
Or hear old Triton blow his wreathèd horn.

QUESTIONS

1. In this sonnet by Wordsworth what condition does the poet complain about? To what does he attribute this condition?
2. How does it affect him as an individual?

When Plato in *The Republic* relates the Myth of Er, he introduces supernatural characters he himself originated. Poets, too, have been inspired to make up myths of their own, for their own purposes. "I must create a system or be enslaved by another man's," said William Blake, who in his "prophetic books" peopled the cosmos with supernatural beings having names like Los, Urizen, and Vala (side by side with recognizable figures from the Old Testament and New Testament). This kind of system-making probably has advantages and drawbacks. T. S. Eliot, in his essay on Blake, wishes that the author of *The Four Zoas* had accepted traditional myths, and he compares Blake's thinking to a piece of homemade furniture whose construction diverted valuable energy from the writing of poems. Others have found Blake's untraditional cosmos an achievement—notably William Butler Yeats, himself the author of an elaborate personal mythology. Although we need not know all of Yeats's mythology to enjoy his poems, to know of its existence can make a few great poems deeper for us and less difficult.

William Butler Yeats (1865–1939)

THE SECOND COMING   1921

Turning and turning in the widening gyre°   *spiral*
The falcon cannot hear the falconer;
Things fall apart; the center cannot hold;
Mere anarchy is loosed upon the world,
The blood-dimmed tide is loosed, and everywhere   5
The ceremony of innocence is drowned;
The best lack all conviction, while the worst
Are full of passionate intensity.

Surely some revelation is at hand;
Surely the Second Coming is at hand;   10
The Second Coming! Hardly are those words out
When a vast image out of *Spiritus Mundi*
Troubles my sight: somewhere in sands of the desert
A shape with lion body and the head of a man,
A gaze blank and pitiless as the sun,   15
Is moving its slow thighs, while all about it
Reel shadows of the indignant desert birds.
The darkness drops again; but now I know
That twenty centuries of stony sleep
Were vexed to nightmare by a rocking cradle,   20
And what rough beast, its hour come round at last,
Slouches towards Bethlehem to be born?

What kind of Second Coming does Yeats expect? Evidently it is not to be a Christian one. Yeats saw human history as governed by the turning of a Great Wheel, whose phases influence events and determine human personalities—rather like the signs of the Zodiac in astrology. Every two thousand years comes a horrendous moment: the Wheel completes a turn; one civilization ends and another begins. Strangely, a new age is always announced by birds and by acts of violence. Thus the Greek-Roman world arrives with the descent of Zeus in swan's form and the burning of Troy, the Christian era with the descent of the Holy Spirit—traditionally depicted as a dove—and the Crucifixion. In 1919 when Yeats wrote "The Second Coming," his Ireland was in the midst of turmoil and bloodshed; the Western Hemisphere had been severely shaken by World War I. A new millennium seemed imminent. What sphinxlike, savage deity would next appear, with birds proclaiming it angrily? Yeats thinks he imagines it emerging from *Spiritus Mundi,* Soul of the World, a collective unconscious from which a human being (since the individual soul touches it) receives dreams, nightmares, and racial memories.[2]

It is hard to say whether a poet who discovers a personal myth does so to have something to live by or to have something to write about. Robert Graves, who professes his belief in a White Goddess ("Mother of All Living, the ancient power of love and terror"), has said that he has written poetry in a trance, inspired by his Goddess-Muse.[3] Luckily, we do not have to know a poet's religious affiliation before we can read the poems. Perhaps most personal myths that enter poems are not acts of faith but works of art: stories that resemble traditional mythology.

John Heath-Stubbs (b. 1918)

A CHARM AGAINST THE TOOTHACHE   1954

Venerable Mother Toothache
Climb down from the white battlements,
Stop twisting in your yellow fingers
The fourfold rope of nerves;
And tomorrow I will give you a tot of whiskey   5
To hold in your cupped hands,
A garland of anise-flowers,
And three cloves like nails.
And tell the attendant gnomes
It is time to knock off now,   10
To shoulder their little pick-axes,
Their cold-chisels and drills.
And you may mount by a silver ladder
Into the sky, to grind
In the cracked polished mortar   15
Of the hollow moon.

By the lapse of warm waters,
And the poppies nodding like red coals,
The paths on the granite mountains,
And the plantation of my dreams: 20

QUESTIONS

1. This poem shows us a poet inventing a mythology. What powers and characteristics does he attribute to Mother Toothache? What facts of common experience does she help account for?

[2] Yeats fully explains his system in *A Vision* (1938; reprinted New York: Macmillan, 1956).
[3] See Graves's *The White Goddess*, rev. ed. (New York: Farrar, Straus & Giroux, 1966), or for a terser statement of his position, see his lecture "The Personal Muse" in *On Poetry: Collected Talks and Essays* (New York: Doubleday, 1969).

2. What is the tone of the poem?
3. In what ways does the poem recall any existing myths and rituals?

Earlier, looking at symbols, we saw that certain concrete objects in poetry can convey suggestions to which we respond without quite being able to tell why. Such, perhaps, are Emily Dickinson's forked lightning bolt dropped from celestial tables and her buzzing fly that arrives with death. Indefinite power may be present also in an **archetype** (Greek: "first-molded"), which can mean "an original model or pattern from which later things are made." The word acquired a special denotation through the work of the Swiss psychologist Carl Gustav Jung (1875–1961). Recently, it has occurred so frequently in literary criticism that students of poetry may wish to be aware of it.

An archetype, in Jung's view, is generally a story, character, symbol, or situation that recurs again and again in worldwide myth, literature, and dream. Some of these — as defined by Jung and others — might be figures such as the cruel mother (Cinderella's stepmother), the creature half human and half animal (centaurs, satyrs, mermaids), the beautiful garden (Eden, Arcadia, the myth of the Golden Age), the story of the hero who by slaying a monster delivers a country from its curse (the romance of Parsifal, the Old English heroic narrative *Beowulf*, the myth of Perseus, the legend of Saint George and the dragon), the story of the beast who yearns for the love of a woman (the fairy tale of "Beauty and the Beast," the movie *King Kong*), the story of the fall from innocence and initiation into life (the account in Genesis of the departure from Eden, J. D. Salinger's novel *The Catcher in the Rye*).

Like Sigmund Freud, Jung saw myth as an aid to the psychiatrist seeking to understand patients' dreams. But Jung went further and postulated the existence of a "collective unconscious" or racial memory in which archetypes lie. "These fantasy-images," said Jung, referring to dreams not traceable to anything a patient has ever experienced, "correspond to certain *collective* (not personal) structural elements in the human psyche in general, and, like the morphological elements of the human body, are *inherited*. . . . The archetype — let us never forget this — is a psychic organ present in all of us."[4]

What this means to the study of poetry is that, if we accept Jung's view, poems containing recognizable archetypes are likely to stir us more profoundly than those that do not. Archetypes being our inheritance from what Shakespeare called "the dark backward and abysm of time," most people can perceive them and respond to them. Some critics have found Jung's theory helpful in fathoming poems. In *Archetypal Patterns in Poetry* (1934), Maud Bodkin found similar archetypes in such dissimilar poems as "Kubla Khan" and *Paradise Lost*.

---

[4] Carl Jung, "The Psychology of the Child Archetype," in *Psyche and Symbol*, edited by Violet S. de Laszlo (New York: Doubleday, 1958), pp. 117, 123.

Recall Yeats's poem "The Second Coming," only one manifestation of the monstrous Sphinx in literature. There are clear resemblances between the *Spiritus Mundi* in Yeats's poem and Jung's idea of the collective unconscious. As early as 1900, Yeats felt sure of the existence of symbols much like archetypes:

> Any one who has any experience of any mystical state of the soul knows how there float up in the mind profound symbols, whose meaning, if indeed they do not delude one into the dream that they are meaningless, one does not perhaps understand for years. Nor I think has anyone, who has known that experience with any constancy, failed to find some day, in some old book or on some old monument, a strange or intricate image that had floated up before him, and to grow perhaps dizzy with the sudden conviction that our little memories are but part of some great Memory that renews the world and men's thoughts age after age, and that our thoughts are not, as we suppose, the deep, but a little foam upon the deep.[5]

Not all psychologists and students of literature agree with Jung. Some maintain that archetypes, because they tend to disappear with the disintegration of a culture in which they had prospered, are transmitted by word of mouth, not by racial memory.[6] Not all poets are as fond of the notion of great Memory as Yeats was. Recently the English poet Philip Larkin has observed:

> As a guiding principle I believe that every poem must be its own sole freshly created universe, and therefore have no belief in "tradition" or a common myth-kitty. . . . To me the whole of the ancient world, the whole of classical and biblical mythology means very little, and I think that using them today not only fills poems full of dead spots but dodges the writer's duty to be original.[7]

Larkin is probably reacting against bookishness. However, even readers who took no stock in Jung's theories may find *archetype* a useful name for something that, since antiquity, has exerted appeal to makers of myth — including some poets and storytellers.

David Wagoner (b. 1926)

MUSE   1974

Cackling, smelling of camphor, crumbs of pink icing
Clinging to her lips, her lipstick smeared
Halfway around her neck, her cracked teeth bristling

---

[5] William B. Yeats, "The Philosophy of Shelley's Poetry," *Essays and Introductions* (New York: Macmillan, 1968), pp. 78–79.
[6] See J. S. Lincoln, *The Dream in Primitive Cultures* (1935, p. 24; reprinted New York: Johnson Reprints, 1970).
[7] Statements made on two different occasions, quoted by John Press, *A Map of Modern English Verse* (New York: Oxford University Press, 1969), pp. 258–59.

With bloody splinters, she leans over my shoulder.
Oh my only hope, my lost dumfounding baggage,
My gristle-breasted, slack-jawed zealot, kiss me again.

QUESTIONS

1. To what ancient belief about the source of a poet's inspiration does Wagoner refer?
2. In what respects does his version of this myth seem untraditional?

Edward Allen (b. 1948)

THE BEST LINE YET   1972

In Stamford, at the edge of town, a giant statue stands:
An iron eagle sternly clasps the crag with crooked hands.
His pedestal is twenty feet, full thirty feet is he.
His head alone weighs many times as much as you or me.
All day, all night he keeps his watch and never stirs a feather.   5
His frowning brow glares straight ahead into the foulest weather.
They say this noble bird will spread his iron wings and fly
The day a virgin graduates from Stamford Senior High.
O, evil day when he shall rise above the peaceful town,
Endanger airplanes, frighten children, drop foul tonnage down!   10
So let not this accipiter° desert his silent vigil,   *bird of prey*
But yield to me my darling, Stamford's finest, Susan Kitchell.

QUESTIONS

1. How would you describe the tone of this myth-making poem (written when the author was a high school student)? Is it humorous, half-serious, or serious? How is the tone indicated?
2. What does it have in common with John Heath-Stubbs's "A Charm Against the Toothache" (page 216)?

Anonymous (traditional Scottish ballad)

THOMAS THE RIMER

True Thomas lay on Huntlie bank,
   A ferlie° he spied wi' his ee,   *wondrous thing*
And there he saw a lady bright,
   Come riding down by the Eildon Tree.

Her shirt was o' the grass-green silk,   5
   Her mantle o' the velvet fine,
At ilka tett° of her horse's mane   *every lock*
   Hang fifty siller bells and nine.

True Thomas, he pulled aff his cap,
   And louted° low down to his knee: *bowed* 10
"All hail, thou mighty Queen of Heaven!
   For thy peer on earth I never did see."

"O no, O no, Thomas," she said,
   "That name does not belang to me;
I am but the queen of fair Elfland,   15
   That am hither come to visit thee.

"Harp and carp°, Thomas," she said,   *sing ballads*
   "Harp and carp along wi' me,
And if ye dare to kiss my lips,
   Sure of your body I will be."   20

"Betide me weal, betide me woe,
   That weird° shall never daunton me";   *fate*
Syne° he has kissed her rosy lips,   *then*
   All underneath the Eildon Tree.

"Now, ye maun° go wi' me," she said,   *must* 25
   "True Thomas, ye maun go wi' me,
And ye maun serve me seven years,
   Thro weal or woe, as may chance to be."

She mounted on her milk-white steed,
   She's taen True Thomas up behind,   30
And aye° whene'er her bridle rung,   *always*
   The steed flew swifter than the wind.

O they rade on, and farther on —
   The steed gaed swifter than the wind —
Until they reached a desart wide,   35
   And living land was left behind.

"Light down, light down, now, True Thomas,
   And lean your head upon my knee;
Abide and rest a little space,
   And I will shew you ferlies three.   40

"O see ye not yon narrow road,
   So thick beset with thorns and briars?
That is the path of righteousness,
   Though after it but few enquires.

"And see not ye that braid° braid road,   *broad* 45
   That lies across that lily leven°?   *lovely lawn*
That is the path of wickedness,
   Though some call it the road to heaven.

"And see not ye that bonny road,
   That winds about the ferny brae°?   *hillside* 50

That is the road to fair Elfland,
    Where thou and I this night maun gae.

"But, Thomas, ye maun hold your tongue,
    Whatever ye may hear or see,
For, if you speak word in Elfyn land,   55
    Ye'll ne'er get back to your ain countrie."

O they rade on, and farther on,
    And they waded thro rivers aboon the knee,
And they saw neither sun nor moon,
    But they heard the roaring of the sea.   60

It was mirk° mirk night, and there was nae stern° light,   *murky; star*
    And they waded thro red blude to the knee;
For a' the blude that's shed on earth
    Rins thro the springs o' that countrie.

Syne they came on to a garden green,   65
    And she pu'd an apple frae a tree:
"Take this for thy wages, True Thomas,
    It will give the tongue that can never lie."

"My tongue is mine ain," True Thomas said;
    "A gudely gift ye wad gie to me!   70
I neither dought° to buy or sell,   *would be able*
    At fair or tryst° where I may be.   *market*

"I dought neither speak to prince or peer,
    Nor ask of grace from fair ladye":
"Now hold thy peace," the lady said,   75
    "For as I say, so must it be."

He has gotten a coat of the even cloth,
    And a pair of shoes of velvet green,
And till seven years were gane and past
    True Thomas on earth was never seen.   80

THOMAS THE RIMER. Thomas of Erceldoune, popularly called True Thomas or Thomas the Rimer, was an actual Scottish minstrel of the thirteenth century. He was said to have received the power of prophecy as a gift from the queen of the elves.

QUESTIONS

1. From what kinds of traditional myth does the poem derive? Point out Christian and pagan elements.
2. What impression do we receive of the queen? Is she benevolent or sinister? What popular attitudes toward the supernatural might this characterization reveal?
3. What do you make of the magic apple in lines 66–68? What other celebrated apples does it recall?
4. What statements seem ironies?

John Keats (1795–1821)

LA BELLE DAME SANS MERCI

(1819)

O what can ail thee, knight-at-arms,
  Alone and palely loitering?
The sedge has withered from the lake,
  And no birds sing.

O what can ail thee, knight-at-arms,   5
  So haggard and so woe-begone?
The squirrel's granary is full,
  And the harvest's done.

I see a lily on thy brow
  With anguish moist and fever dew,   10
And on thy cheek a fading rose
  Fast withereth too.

"I met a lady in the meads,
  Full beautiful — a faery's child;
Her hair was long, her foot was light,   15
  And her eyes were wild.

"I made a garland for her head,
  And bracelets too, and fragrant zone°;   *belt, sash*
She looked at me as she did love,
  And made sweet moan.   20

"I set her on my pacing steed,
  And nothing else saw all day long,
For sidelong would she bend, and sing
  A faery's song.

"She found me roots of relish sweet,   25
  And honey wild, and manna dew,
And sure in language strange she said —
  'I love thee true!'

"She took me to her elfin grot,
  And there she wept and sighed full sore,   30
And there I shut her wild wild eyes
  With kisses four.

"And there she lullèd me asleep,
  And there I dreamed — ah! woe betide!
The latest dream I ever dreamed   35
  On the cold hill's side.

"I saw pale kings and princes too,
  Pale warriors, death-pale were they all;
They cried — 'La Belle Dame sans Merci
  Hath thee in thrall!'   40

"I saw their starved lips in the gloam,
  With horrid warning gapèd wide,
And I awoke and found me here,
  On the cold hill's side.

"And this is why I sojourn here,   45
  Alone and palely loitering,
Though the sedge is withered from the lake
  And no birds sing."

LA BELLE DAME SANS MERCI. Keats borrowed this title, "The Lovely Merciless Beauty,"
from a medieval French poem. The text given above is his earliest version.

QUESTIONS

1. What happens in this ballad? What is indicated by the contrast between the
   imagery from nature in lines 17, 18, 25, and 26 and that in lines 3–4, 7–8, 44,
   and 47–48? How do you interpret the knight's *latest dream* (line 35)?
2. What do we know about this beautiful lady without pity? What supernatural
   powers does she possess?
3. In what respects does she resemble the Queen of Elfland in the ballad of
   "Thomas the Rimer"? In what respects does she differ?
4. What other *dames sans merci* do you find in other poems in this book? In what
   respects are they similar? In what respects, if any, is Keats's lady an individual?
5. What other relentless beauties with supernatural powers do you know from
   myth, folklore, literature, movies, or television? In what respects, if any, do
   they resemble the *Belle Dame* or Thomas the Rimer's queen?

John Milton (1608–1674)

LYCIDAS   1637

*In this monody the author bewails a learned friend, unfortunately drowned in his passage
from Chester on the Irish Seas, 1637. And by occasion foretells the ruin of our corrupted
clergy then in their height.*

Yet once more, O ye laurels, and once more,
Ye myrtles brown°, with ivy never sere,   *dark*
I come to pluck your berries harsh and crude°,   *immature*
And with forced fingers rude
Shatter your leaves before the mellowing year.   5
Bitter constraint and sad occasion dear
Compels me to disturb your season due;

LYCIDAS. Milton's "learned friend" was Edward King, scholar and poet, a fellow student
at Cambridge, who had planned to enter the ministry. In calling him Lycidas, Milton
employs a conventional name for a young shepherd in **pastoral poetry** (which either por-
trays the world of shepherds with some realism, as in Virgil's *Eclogues,* or makes it a pret-
tified Eden, as in Marlowe's "The Passionate Shepherd to His Love"). A *monody,* in the
epigraph, is a song for a single voice. 1–2. *laurels, myrtles:* Evergreens in the crowns traditionally bestowed upon poets.

For Lycidas is dead, dead ere his prime,
Young Lycidas, and hath not left his peer.
Who would not sing for Lycidas? he knew   10
Himself to sing, and build the lofty rhyme.
He must not float upon his wat'ry bier
Unwept, and welter° to the parching wind,   *toss about*
Without the meed° of some melodious tear.   *tribute*
   Begin, then, Sisters of the Sacred Well   15
That from beneath the seat of Jove doth spring,
Begin, and somewhat loudly sweep the string.
Hence with denial vain and coy excuse:
So may some gentle Muse°   *poet*
With lucky words favor my destined urn,   20
And, as he passes, turn,
And bid fair peace be to my sable shroud!
For we were nursed upon the self-same hill,
Fed the same flocks, by fountain, shade, and rill;
   Together both, ere the high lawns appeared   25
Under the opening eyelids of the Morn,
We drove a-field, and both together heard
What time the gray-fly winds° her sultry horn,   *sounds*
Batt'ning° our flocks with the fresh dews of night, *feeding*
Oft till the star that rose at evening bright   30
Toward Heav'n's descent had sloped his westering wheel.
Meanwhile the rural ditties were not mute,
Tempered to the oaten° flute,   *made of an oat stalk*
Rough satyrs danced, and fauns with cloven heel
From the glad sound would not be absent long;   35
And old Damoetas loved to hear our song.
   But, O the heavy change, now thou art gone,
Now thou art gone, and never must return!
Thee, Shepherd, thee the woods and desert caves,
With wild thyme and the gadding° vine o'ergrown,   *wandering* 40
And all their echoes mourn.
The willows, and the hazel copses green,
Shall now no more be seen
Fanning their joyous leaves to thy soft lays.
As killing as the canker to the rose,   45
Or taint-worm to the weanling herds that graze,
Or frost to flowers, that their gay wardrobe wear
When first the white thorn blows°;   *blossoms*
Such, Lycidas, thy loss to shepherd's ear.
   Where were ye, Nymphs, when the remorseless deep   50
Closed o'er the head of your loved Lycidas?
For neither were ye playing on the steep
Where your old bards, the famous Druids, lie,

36. *Damoetas:* Perhaps some Cambridge tutor.
53. *Druids:* priests and poets of the Celts in pre-Christian Britain.

Nor on the shaggy top of Mona high,

Nor yet where Deva spreads her wizard stream.   55

Ay me! I fondly° dream!   *foolishly*

"Had ye been there" — for what could that have done?

What could the Muse herself that Orpheus bore,

The Muse herself, for her enchanting son,

Whom universal Nature did lament,   60

When, by the rout° that made the hideous roar,   *mob*

His gory visage down the stream was sent,

Down the swift Hebrus to the Lesbian shore?

    Alas! What boots it° with uncessant care   *what good does it do*

To tend the homely, slighted shepherd's trade,   65

And strictly meditate the thankless Muse?

Were it not better done, as others use°,   *do*

To sport with Amaryllis in the shade,

Or with the tangles of Neaera's hair?

Fame is the spur that the clear spirit doth raise   70

(That last infirmity of noble mind)

To scorn delights and live laborious days;

But the fair guerdon when we hope to find,

And think to burst out into sudden blaze,

Comes the blind Fury with th' abhorrèd shears,   75

And slits the thin-spun life. "But not the praise,"

Phoebus replied, and touched my trembling ears:

"Fame is no plant that grows on mortal soil,

Nor in the glistering° foil,   *glittering*

Set off to the world, nor in broad rumor° lies,   *reputation* 80

But lives and spreads aloft by those pure eyes

And perfect witness of all-judging Jove;

As he pronounces lastly on each deed,

Of so much fame in Heav'n expect thy meed."

    O fountain Arethuse, and thou honored flood,   85

Smooth-sliding Mincius, crowned with vocal reeds,

That strain I heard was of a higher mood:

But now my oat proceeds,

And listens to the Herald of the Sea,

That came in Neptune's plea.   90

He asked the waves, and asked the felon winds,

What hard mishap hath doomed this gentle swain?

And questioned every gust of rugged wings

That blows from off each beakèd promontory:

54. *Mona:* Roman name for the Isle of Man, near which King was drowned. 55. *Deva:* the River Dee, flowing between England and Wales. Its shifts in course were said to augur good luck for one country or the other. 68–69. *Amaryllis, Neaera:* conventional names for shepherdesses. 70. *the clear spirit doth raise:* doth raise the clear spirit. 77. *touched . . . ears:* gesture signifying "Remember!" 79. *foil:* a setting of gold or silver leaf, used to make a gem appear more brilliant. 85–86. *Arethuse, Minicius:* a fountain and river near the birthplaces of Theocritus and Virgil, respectively, hence recalling the most celebrated writer of pastorals in Greek and the most celebrated in Latin. 90. *in Neptune's plea:* bringing the sea-god's plea, "not guilty."

They knew not of his story;   95
And sage Hippotades their answer brings,
That not a blast was from his dungeon strayed:
The air was calm, and on the level brine
Sleek Panope with all her sisters played.
It was that fatal and perfidious bark,   100
Built in th' eclipse, and rigged with curses dark,
That sunk so low that sacred head of thine.
    Next, Camus, reverend sire, went footing slow,
His mantle hairy, and his bonnet sedge,
Inwrought with figures dim, and on the edge   105
Like to that sanguine flower inscribed with woe.
"Ah! who hath reft," quoth he, "my dearest pledge?"
Last came, and last did go,
The pilot of the Galilean lake;
Two massy keys he bore of metals twain   110
(The golden opes, the iron shuts amain°).   *with force*
He shook his mitered locks, and stern bespake: —
"How well could I have spared for thee, young swain,
Enow° of such as for their bellies' sake,   *enough*
Creep, and intrude, and climb into the fold!   115
Of other care they little reck'ning make
Than how to scramble at the shearers' feast,
And shove away the worthy bidden guest.
Blind mouths! that scarce themselves know how to hold
A sheep-hook, or have learned aught else the least   120
That to the faithful herdsman's art belongs!
What recks it them? What need they? they are sped°;   *prosperous*
And, when they list°, their lean and flashy songs   *so incline*
Grate on their scrannel° pipes of wretched straw;   *feeble, harsh*
The hungry sheep look up, and are not fed,   125
But, swoll'n with wind and the rank mist they draw,
Rot inwardly, and foul contagion spread;
Besides what the grim wolf with privy° paw   *stealthy*
Daily devours apace, and nothing said;
But that two-handed engine at the door   130
Stands ready to smite once, and smite no more."

---

99. *Panope:* a sea nymph. Her name means "one who sees all." 101. *eclipse:* thought to be an omen of evil fortune. 103. *Camus:* spirit of the river Cam and personification of Cambridge University. 109–112. *pilot:* Saint Peter, once a fisherman in Galilee, to whom Christ gave the *keys* of Heaven (Matthew 16:19). As first Bishop of Rome, he wears the miter, a bishop's emblematic head-covering. 115. *fold:* the Church of England. 120. *sheep-hook:* a bishop's staff or crozier, which resembles a shepherd's crook. 128. *wolf:* probably the Church of Rome. Jesuits in England at the time were winning converts. 130. *two-handed engine:* This disputed phrase may refer (among other possibilities) to the punishing sword of The Word of God (Revelation 19:13–15 and Hebrews 4:12). Perhaps Milton sees it as a lightning bolt, as does Spenser, to whom Jove's wrath is a "three-forked engine" (*Faerie Queene*, VIII, 9). 131. *smite once . . . no more:* Because, in the proverb, lightning never strikes twice in the same place?

Return, Alpheus; the dread voice is past
That shrunk thy streams; return, Sicilian Muse,
And call the vales, and bid them hither cast
Their bells and flow'rets of a thousand hues.   135
Ye valleys low, where the mild whispers use°   *resort*
Of shades, and wanton winds, and gushing brooks,
On whose fresh lap the swart star sparely looks,
Throw hither all your quaint enameled eyes,
That on the green turf suck the honied showers,   140
And purple all the ground with vernal flowers.
Bring the rathe° primrose that forsaken dies,   *early*
The tufted crow-toe, and pale jessamine,
The white pink, and the pansy freaked° with jet,   *streaked*
The glowing violet,   145
The musk-rose, and the well-attired woodbine,
With cowslips wan that hang the pensive head,
And every flower that sad embroidery wears;
Bid amaranthus all his beauty shed,
And daffadillies fill their cups with tears,   150
To strew the laureate hearse where Lycid lies.
For so, to interpose a little ease,
Let our frail thoughts dally with false surmise,
Ay me! whilst thee the shores and sounding seas
Wash far away, where'er thy bones are hurled;   155
Whether beyond the stormy Hebrides,
Where thou, perhaps, under the whelming tide
Visit'st the bottom of the monstrous° world;   *full of sea monsters*
Or whether thou, to our moist vows° denied,   *prayers*
Sleep'st by the fable of Bellerus old,   160
Where the great Vision of the guarded mount
Looks toward Namancos and Bayona's hold°:   *stronghold*
Look homeward, angel, now, and melt with ruth°;   *pity*
And, O ye dolphins, waft the hapless youth.
  Weep no more, woeful shepherds, weep no more,   165
For Lycidas, your sorrow, is not dead,
Sunk though he be beneath the wat'ry floor:
So sinks the day-star in the ocean bed
And yet anon repairs his drooping head,
And tricks° his beams, and with new-spangled ore°   *arrays; gold* 170
Flames in the forehead of the morning sky:
So Lycidas sunk low, but mounted high,
Through the dear might of Him that walked the waves,

133. *Sicilian Muse:* who inspired Theocritus, a native of Sicily. 138. *swart star:* Sirius, at its
zenith in summer, was thought to turn vegetation black. 153. *false surmise:* futile hope that
the body of Lycidas could be recovered. 160. *Bellerus:* legendary giant of Land's End, the
far tip of Cornwall. 161. *guarded mount:* Saint Michael's Mount, off Land's End, said to be
under the protection of the archangel. 162. *Namancos, Bayona:* on the coast of Spain. 164.
dolphins: In Greek legend, these kindly fish carried the spirits of the dead to the Blessed
Isles.

Where, other groves and other streams along,
With nectar pure his oozy locks he laves,   175
And hears the unexpressive nuptial song,
In the blest kingdoms meek of Joy and Love.
There entertain him all the Saints above,
In solemn troops, and sweet societies,
That sing, and singing in their glory move,   180
And wipe the tears forever from his eyes.
Now, Lycidas, the shepherds weep no more;
Henceforth thou art the Genius° of the shore,   *guardian spirit*
In thy large recompense, and shalt be good
To all that wander in that perilous flood.   185

   Thus sang the uncouth° swain to th' oaks and rills,   *rustic (or little-known)*
While the still Morn went out with sandals gray;
He touched the tender stops of various quills°,   *reeds of a shepherd's pipe*
With eager thought warbling his Doric lay:
And now the sun had stretched out all the hills,   190
And now was dropped into the western bay.
At last he rose, and twitched° his mantle blue: *donned*
Tomorrow to fresh woods and pastures new.

176. *unexpressive nuptial song:* inexpressibly beautiful song for the marriage feast of the Lamb (Revelation 19:9). 189. *Doric lay:* pastoral poem. Doric is the dialect of Greek employed by Theocritus.

Questions and Exercises

1. With the aid of an encyclopedia or a handbook of classical mythology (such as Bulfinch's *Mythology*, Edith Hamilton's *Mythology*, or H. J. Rose's *Handbook of Greek Mythology*) learn more about the following myths or mythical figures and places to which Milton alludes:

   Line 15   Sisters of the Sacred Well (Muses)
        16   seat of Jove (Mount Olympus)
        58   the Muse . . . that Orpheus bore (Calliope)
    61–63   (the death of Orpheus)
        75   Fury with the . . . shears (Atropos, one of the three Fates)
        77   Phoebus
        89   Herald of the Sea (Triton)
        90   Neptune
        96   Hippotades
      106   (Hyacinthus)
      132   Alpheus

   Then reread Milton's poem. As a result of your familiarity with these myths, what details become clear?
2. Read the parable of the Good Shepherd (John 10:1–18). What relationships does Milton draw between the Christian idea of the shepherd and pastoral poetry?

3. "With these trifling fictions [allusions to classical mythology]," wrote Samuel Johnson about "Lycidas," "are mingled the most awful and sacred truths, such as ought never to be polluted with such irreverend combinations." Does this mingling of paganism and Christianity detract from Milton's poem? Discuss.
4. In "Lycidas" does Milton devise any new myth or myths?

14 Telling Good from Bad

"The bulk of English poetry is bad," a critic has said,[1] referring to all verse printed over the past six hundred years, not only that which survives in anthologies. As his comment reminds us, excellent poetry is at least as scarce as gold. Though readers who seek it for themselves can expect to pan through much shale, such labor need not discourage them from prospecting. Only the naïve reader assumes, "This poem must be good, or else why would it appear in a leading magazine?" Only the reader whose mind is coasting in neutral says, "Who knows if this poem is good? Who cares? It all depends upon your point of view." Open-minded, skeptical, and alert, the critical reader will make independent evaluations.

Why do we call some poems "bad"? We are not talking about their moral implications. Rather, we mean that, for one or more of many possible reasons, the poem has failed to move us or to engage our sympathies. Instead, it has made us doubt that the poet is in control of language and vision; perhaps it has aroused our antipathies or unwittingly appealed to our sense of the comic, though the poet is serious. Some poems can be said to succeed despite burdensome faults. But in general such faults are symptoms of deeper malady: some weakness in a poem's basic conception or in the poet's competence.

Nearly always, a bad poem reveals only a dim and distorted awareness of its probable effect on an alert reader. Perhaps the sound of words may clash with what a poem is saying, as in the jarring last word of this opening line of a tender lyric (author unknown, quoted by Richard Wilbur): "Come into the tent, my love, and close the flap." Perhaps a metaphor may fail by calling to mind more differences than similarities, as in Emily Dickinson's lines "Our lives are Swiss-- / So still--so cool." A bad poem usually overshoots or falls short of its mark by the poet's thinking too little or too much. Thinking much, a poet contrives such an excess of ingenuity as that quoted by Alexander Pope in

[1] Christopher Adams in the preface to his anthology, *The Worst English Poets* (London: Allan Wingate, 1958).

Peri Bathous, or *Of the Art of Sinking in Poetry:* a hounded stag who "Hears his own feet, and thinks they sound like more; / And fears the hind feet will o'ertake the fore." Thinking little, a poet writes redundantly, as Wordsworth in "The Thorn": "And they had fixed the wedding-day, / The morning that must wed them both."

In a poem that has a rime scheme or a set line length, when all is well, pattern and structure move inseparably with the rest of their poem, the way a tiger's skin and bones move with their tiger. But sometimes, in a poem that fails, the poet evidently has had difficulty in persuading statements to fit a formal pattern. English poets have long felt free to invert word order for a special effect, but the poet having trouble keeping to a rime scheme may invert words for no apparent reason but convenience. Needing a rime for *barge* may lead to ending a line with a *policedog large* instead of *a large policedog.* Another sign of trouble is a profusion of adjectives. If a line of iambic pentameter reads, "Her lovely skin, like dear sweet white old silk," we suspect the poet of stuffing the line to make it long enough. Whenever two or more adjectives stand together (in poetry or in good prose), they need to be charged with meaning. No one suspects Matthew Arnold of padding the last line of "To Marguerite": "The unplumbed, salt, estranging sea."

Because, over his dead body, even a poet's slightest and feeblest efforts may be collected, some lines in the canon of celebrated bards make us wonder, "How could he have written this?" Wordsworth, Shelley, Whitman, and Browning are among the great whose failures can be painful, and lapses of awareness may occur even in poems that, taken entire, are excellent. To be unwilling to read them, though, would be as ill advised as to refuse to see Venice just because the Grand Canal is said to contain impurities. The seasoned reader of poetry thinks no less of Tennyson for having written, "Form, Form, Riflemen Form! . . . Look to your butts, and take good aims!" The collected works of a duller poet may contain no such lines of unconscious double meaning, but neither do they contain, perhaps, any poem as good as "Ulysses." If the duller poet never had a spectacular failure, it may be because of failure to take risks.

We flatter ourselves if we think all imprecise poetry the work of times gone by. Poetry editors of current magazines find that about nine hundred out of a thousand unsolicited poems are, at a glance, unworthy of a second reading. Although editors may have nightmares in which they ignorantly reject the poems of some new Gerard Manley Hopkins or Emily Dickinson, they nonetheless send them back with a printed "thank you" slip, then turn to the hundred that look interesting. How are the poems winnowed so quickly? Often, inept poems fall into familiar categories. At one extreme is the poem written entirely in conventional diction, dimly echoing Shakespeare, Wordsworth, and the Bible, but garbling them. Couched in a rhythm that ticks along like a metronome, this kind of poem shows no sign that its author has ever taken a hard look at anything that can be tasted, handled, and felt. It employs loosely and thoughtlessly the most abstract of words: *love, beauty, life, death, time, eternity*. Littered with old-fashioned contractions (*'tis, o'er, where'er*), it may end in a simple platitude or preachment, as if the poet expected us to profit from his or her wisdom and moral superiority. George Orwell's complaint against much contemporary writing (not only poetry) is applicable: "As soon as certain topics are raised" — and one thinks of such standard topics for poetry as spring, a first kiss, and stars — "the concrete melts into the abstract and no one seems able to think of turns of speech that are not hackneyed." Writers, Orwell charged, too often make their sentences out of tacked-together phrases "like the sections of a prefabricated hen-house."[2] Versifiers often do likewise.

At the opposite extreme is the poem that displays no acquaintance with poetry of the past but manages, instead, to fabricate its own clichés. Slightly paraphrased, a manuscript once submitted to *The Paris Review* began:

Vile

    rottenflush

          o   *— screaming —*

           f CORPSEBLOOD!!   ooze

STRANGLE my

      eyes . . .   HELL's

        O, ghastly   stench**!!!

At most, such a work has only a private value. The writer has vented personal frustrations upon words, instead of kicking stray dogs. In its way, "Vile Rottenflush" is as self-indulgent as the oldfangled "first kiss in spring" kind of poem. Both offend, both inspire distrust. "I dislike," said John Livingston Lowes, "poems that black your eyes, or put up their mouths to be kissed."

As jewelers tell which of two diamonds is fine by seeing which scratches the other, two poems may be tested by comparing them. This method works only on poems similar in length and kind: an epigram cannot rival an epic. Most poems we meet are neither sheer trash nor obvious masterpieces. Since, however, good diamonds to be proven need softer ones to scratch, in this chapter you will find a few clear-cut gems and a few clinkers. "In poetry," said Ronsard, "mediocrity is the greatest vice."

[2] George Orwell, "Politics and the English Language," from *Shooting an Elephant and Other Essays* (New York: Harcourt Brace Jovanovich, 1945).

Anonymous (English)

O MOON, WHEN I GAZE ON THY BEAUTIFUL FACE   (about 1900)

O Moon, when I gaze on thy beautiful face,
Careering along through the boundaries of space,
The thought has often come into my mind
If I ever shall see thy glorious behind.

O MOON. Sir Edmund Gosse, the English critic (1849–1928), offered this quatrain as the
work of his maidservant, but there is reason to suspect him of having written it.

QUESTIONS

1. To what fact of astronomy does the last line refer?
2. Which words seem chosen with too little awareness of their denotations and
   connotations?
3. Even if you did not know that these lines probably were deliberately bad,
   how would you argue with someone who maintained that the opening O in
   the poem was admirable as a bit of concrete poetry? (See the quotation from
   E. E. Cummings on page 193.)

Grace Treasone

LIFE   (about 1963)

Life is like a jagged tooth
that cuts into your heart;
fix the tooth and save the root,
and laughs, not tears, will start.

William Ernest Henley (1849–1903)

MADAM LIFE'S A PIECE IN BLOOM   1908

Madam Life's a piece in bloom
  Death goes dogging everywhere:
She's the tenant of the room,
  He's the ruffian on the stair.

You shall see her as a friend,   5
  You shall bilk him once or twice;
But he'll trap you in the end,
  And he'll stick you for her price.

With his kneebones at your chest,
  And his knuckles in your throat,   10
You would reason – plead – protest!
  Clutching at her petticoat;

But she's heard it all before,
    Well she knows you've had your fun,
Gingerly she gains the door,   15
    And your little job is done.

QUESTIONS

1. Try to paraphrase the two preceding poems. What is the theme of each?
2. Which statement of theme do you find more convincing? Why?
3. Which poem is the more consistent in working out its metaphor?

Stephen Tropp (b. 1930)
MY WIFE IS MY SHIRT   1960

My wife is my shirt
I put my hands through her armpits
slide my head through her mouth
& finally button her blood around my hands

QUESTIONS

1. How consistently is the metaphor elaborated?
2. Why can this metaphor be said to work in exactly the opposite way from a
   personification?
3. A paraphrase might discover this simile: "My wife is as intimate, familiar,
   and close to me as the shirt on my back." If this is the idea and the poem is
   supposed to be a love poem, how precisely is its attitude expressed?

M. Krishnamurti (b. 1912)
THE SPIRIT'S ODYSSEY   1951

I saw her first in gleams,
As one might see in dreams
    A moonmaiden undrape
    Her opalescent shape
Midst moveless lunar streams!   5

Now fierce and sudden-truth'd,
She smites me, sabre-tooth'd:
    As sunlight, snarling, crawls
    Into the bower and mauls
The waker, slumber-sooth'd!   10

QUESTIONS

1. Can you explain the moonmaiden's abrupt transformation from a beautiful
   stripteaser to a ferocious beast? Does the title of the poem help?

2. Read this poem aloud and comment on the effectiveness of its sounds — particularly the rimes in the second stanza.

EXERCISE: *Seeing What Went Wrong*

Here is a small anthology of bad moments in poetry. For what reasons does each selection fail? In which passages do you attribute the failure to inappropriate sound or diction? To awkward word order? To inaccurate metaphor? To excessive overstatement? To forced rime? To monotonous rhythm? To redundancy? To simple-mindedness or excessive ingenuity?

1. From Sir Richard Blackmore's *Paraphrase of the Book of Job:*

   I cannot stifle this gigantic woe,
   Nor on my raging grief a muzzle throw.

2. "I'm Glad," in its entirety, author unknown:

   I'm glad the sky is painted blue,
   And the earth is painted green,
   With such a lot of nice fresh air
   All sandwiched in between.

3. A lover's lament from Harry Edward Mills's *Select Sunflowers:*

   I see her in my fondest moods,
      She haunts the parlor hallway;
   And yet her form my clasp eludes,
      Her lips my kisses alway.

4. A suffering swain makes a vow, from "the poem of a young tradesman" quoted by Coleridge in *Biographia Literaria:*

   No more will I endure love's pleasing pain,
   Or round my heart's leg tie his galling chain.

5. From an elegy for Queen Victoria by one of her subjects:

   Dust to dust, and ashes to ashes,
   Into the tomb the Great Queen dashes.

6. The opening lines of Alice Meynell's "The Shepherdess":

   She walks — the lady of my delight —
   A shepherdess of sheep.

7. From a juvenile poem of John Dryden, "Upon the Death of the Lord Hastings" (a victim of smallpox):

   Blisters with pride swelled; which through's flesh did sprout
   Like rose-buds, stuck i' th'lily-skin about.
   Each little pimple had a tear in it,
   To wail the fault its rising did commit . . .

8. A poet discusses the pity he feels for the newborn, from J. W. Scholl's *The Light-Bearer of Liberty:*

   Gooing babies, helpless pygmies,
   Who shall solve your Fate's enigmas?
   Who shall save you from Earth's stigmas?

9. A metaphor from Edgar A. Guest's "The Crucible of Life":

Sacred and sweet is the joy that must come
From the furnace of life when you've poured off the scum.

10. A stanza composed by Samuel Johnson as a deliberately bad example:

I put my hat upon my head
And walked into the Strand;
And there I met another man
Whose hat was in his hand.

11. A lover describes his lady, from Thomas Holley Chivers's "Rosalie Lee":

Many mellow Cydonian suckets,
    Sweet apples, anthosmial, divine,
From the ruby-rimmed beryline buckets,
    Star-gemmed, lily-shaped, hyaline:
Like the sweet golden goblet found growing
    On the wild emerald cucumber-tree,
Rich, brilliant, like chrysoprase glowing,
    Was my beautiful Rosalie Lee.

12. Lines on a sick gypsy, author unknown, quoted in *The Stuffed Owl, an Anthology of Bad Verse*, edited by D. B. Wyndham Lewis and Charles Lee:

There we leave her,
There we leave her,
Far from where her swarthy kindred roam,
In the Scarlet Fever,
Scarlet Fever,
Scarlet Fever Convalescent Home.

Sentimentality is the failure of writers who imply that they feel great emotion but who fail to give us sufficient grounds for sharing it. The emotion may be an anger greater than its object seems to call for, as in these lines to a girl who caused scandal (the exact nature of her act never being specified): "The gossip in each hall / Will curse your name . . . / Go! better cast yourself right down the falls!"[3] Or it may be an enthusiasm quite unwarranted by its subject: in *The Fleece* John Dyer temptingly describes the pleasures of life in a workhouse for the poor. The sentimental poet is especially prone to tenderness. Great tears fill this poet's eyes at a glimpse of an aged grandmother sitting by a hearth. For all the poet knows, she may be the well-to-do manager of a casino in Las Vegas, who would be startled to find herself an object of pity, but the sentimentalist seems not to care to know much about the woman herself. She is employed as a general excuse for feeling maudlin. Any other conventional object will serve as well: a faded valentine, the strains of an old song, a baby's cast-off pacifier. A celebrated instance of such

[3] Ali. S. Hilmi, "The Preacher's Sermon," in *Verse at Random* (Larnaca, Cyprus: Ohanian Press, 1953).

emotional self-indulgence is "The Old Oaken Bucket," by Samuel Woodworth, a stanza of which goes:

> How sweet from the green, mossy brim to receive it,
>   As, poised on the curb, it inclined to my lips!
> Not a full-flushing goblet could tempt me to leave it,
>   Tho' filled with the nectar that Jupiter sips.
> And now, far removed from the loved habitation,
>   The tear of regret will intrusively swell,
> As fancy reverts to my father's plantation,
>   And sighs for the bucket that hung in the well.

As a symbol, the bucket might conceivably be made to hold the significance of the past and the speaker's regret at being caught in the destroying grip of time. But the staleness of the phrasing and imagery (Jove's nectar, *tear of regret*) suggests that the speaker is not even seeing the actual physical bucket, and the tripping meter of the lines is inappropriate to an expression of tearful regret. Perhaps the poet's nostalgia is genuine. We need not doubt it; indeed, as Keith Waldrop has put it, "a bad poem is always sincere." However sincere in their feelings, sentimental poets are insincere in their art—otherwise, wouldn't they trouble to write better poems, or at least not print the ones they write? Woodworth, by the vagueness of his language and the monotony of his rhythms, fails to persuade us that we ought to care. Wet-eyed and sighing for a bucket, he achieves not pathos but **bathos:** a description that can move us to laughter instead of tears.[4]

Tears, of course, can be shed for good reason. A piece of sentimentality is not be confused with a well-wrought poem whose tone is tenderness. At first glance, the following poem by Burns might strike you as sentimental. If so, your suspicions are understandable, for it is a rare poet who can speak honestly or effectively on the theme that love grows deeper as lovers grow old. Many a popular song-writer has seen the process of aging as valuable: "Darling, I am growing old, / Silver threads among the gold." According to such songs, to grow decrepit is a privilege. What is fresh in Burns's poem, however, is that no attempt is made to gloss over the ravages of age and the inevitability of death. The speaker expresses no self-pity, no comment *about* her feelings, only a simple account of what has befallen her and her John and what is still to follow.

---

[4] *Bathos* in poetry can also mean an abrupt fall from the sublime to the trivial or incongruous. A sample, from Nicholas Rowe's play *The Fair Penitent:* "Is it the voice of thunder, or my father?" Another, from John Close, a minor Victorian: "Around their heads a dazzling halo shone, / No need of mortal robes, or any hat." When, however, such a letdown is used for a *desirable* effect of humor or contrast, it is usually called an **anticlimax:** as in Alexander Pope's lines on the queen's palace, "Here thou, great Anna! whom three realms obey, / Dost sometimes counsel take—and sometimes tea."

Robert Burns (1759–1796)

John Anderson my jo, John

1790

John Anderson my jo°, John,   *dear*
  When we were first acquent°,   *acquainted*
Your locks were like the raven,
  Your bonny brow was brent°;   *unwrinkled*
But now your brow is beld°, John,   *bald*   5
  Your locks are like the snaw;
But blessings on your frosty pow°,   *head*
  John Anderson my jo.

John Anderson my jo, John,
  We clamb the hill thegither;   10
And mony a canty° day, John,   *happy*
  We've had wi' ane anither:
Now we maun° totter down, John,   *must*
  And hand in hand we'll go,
And sleep together at the foot,   15
  John Anderson my jo.

EXERCISE: *Fine or Shoddy Tenderness*

Which of the following two poems do you find sentimental? Which one would you defend? Why? At least one kind of evidence to look for is minute, detailed observation of physical objects. In a successful poem, the poet is likely at least occasionally to notice the world beyond his or her own skin; in a sentimental poem, this world is likely to be ignored while the poet looks inward. So that the poet's reputation (or lack of reputation) will not distract you, the poems are printed without by-lines.

The Old Arm-Chair

1838

I love it, I love it! and who shall dare
To chide me for loving that old arm-chair?
I've treasured it long as a sainted prize,
I've bedewed it with tears, I've embalmed it with sighs,
'Tis bound by a thousand bands to my heart;   5
Not a tie will break, not a link will start.
Would you know the spell?—a mother sat there!
And a sacred thing is that old arm-chair.

In childhood's hour I lingered near
The hallowed seat with listening ear;   10
And gentle words that mother would give
To fit me to die and teach me to live.

She told me that shame would never betide
With truth for my creed, and God for my guide;
She taught me to lisp my earliest prayer, 15
As I knelt beside that old arm-chair.

I sat and watched her many a day,
When her eyes grew dim, and her locks were gray;
And I almost worshipped her when she smiled,
And turned from her Bible to bless her child. 20
Years rolled on, but the last one sped, —
My idol was shattered, my earth-star fled!
I learned how much the heart can bear,
When I saw her die in her old arm-chair.

'Tis past, 'tis past! but I gaze on it now, 25
With quivering breath and throbbing brow;
'Twas there she nursed me, 'twas there she died,
And memory flows with a lava tide.
Say it is folly, and deem me weak,
Whilst scalding drops start down my cheek; 30
But I love it, I love it! and cannot tear
My soul from a mother's old arm-chair.

PIANO 1918

Softly, in the dusk, a woman is singing to me;
Taking me back down the vista of years, till I see
A child sitting under the piano, in the boom of the tingling strings
And pressing the small, poised feet of a mother who smiles as she sings.

In spite of myself, the insidious mastery of song 5
Betrays me back, till the heart of me weeps to belong
To the old Sunday evenings at home, with winter outside
And hymns in the cozy parlor, the tinkling piano our guide.

So now it is vain for the singer to burst into clamor
With the great black piano appassionato. The glamor 10
Of childish days is upon me, my manhood is cast
Down in the flood of remembrance, I weep like a child for the past.

Rod McKuen (b. 1933)
THOUGHTS ON CAPITAL PUNISHMENT 1954

There ought to be capital punishment for cars
that run over rabbits and drive into dogs
and commit the unspeakable, unpardonable crime
of killing a kitty cat still in his prime.

Purgatory, at the very least   5
          should await the driver
    driving over a beast.

Those hurrying headlights coming out of the dark
that scatter the scampering squirrels in the park
should await the best jury that one might compose   10
of fatherless chipmunks and husbandless does.

And then found guilty, after too fair a trial
should be caged in a cage with a hyena's smile
or maybe an elephant with an elephant gun
should shoot out his eyes when the verdict is done.   15

There ought to be something, something that's fair
to avenge Mrs. Badger as she waits in her lair
for her husband who lies with his guts spilling out
cause he didn't know what automobiles are about.

Hell on the highway, at the very least   20
          should await the driver
    driving over a beast.

Who kills a man kills a bit of himself
But a cat too is an extension of God.

William Stafford (b. 1914)

Traveling Through the Dark   1962

Traveling through the dark I found a deer
dead on the edge of the Wilson River road.
It is usually best to roll them into the canyon:
that road is narrow; to swerve might make more dead.

By glow of the tail-light I stumbled back of the car   5
and stood by the heap, a doe, a recent killing;
she had stiffened already, almost cold.
I dragged her off; she was large in the belly.

My fingers touching her side brought me the reason —
her side was warm; her fawn lay there waiting,   10
alive, still, never to be born.
Beside that mountain road I hesitated.

The car aimed ahead its lowered parking lights;
under the hood purred the steady engine.
I stood in the glare of the warm exhaust turning red;   15
around our group I could hear the wilderness listen.

I thought hard for us all — my only swerving —
then pushed her over the edge into the river.

1. Compare these poems by Rod McKuen and William Stafford. How are they similar in subject?
2. Explain Stafford's title. Who are all those traveling through the dark?
3. Comment on McKuen's use of language: how consistent is it? Consider especially: *unspeakable, unpardonable crime* (line 3), *kitty cat* (4), *scatter the scampering squirrels* (9), and *cause he didn't know* (19).
4. Compare the meaning of Stafford's last two lines and McKuen's last two. Does either poem have a moral? Can either poem be said to moralize?
5. How just is McKuen's justice? How well does the punishment fit the crime?
6. Which poem might be open to the charge of sentimentality? Why?

Ralph Waldo Emerson (1803–1882)

DAYS   1867

Daughters of Time, the hypocritic Days,
Muffled and dumb like barefoot dervishes,
And marching single in an endless file,
Bring diadems and fagots in their hands.
To each they offer gifts after his will,   5
Bread, kingdom, stars, and sky that holds them all.

I, in my pleachèd garden, watched the pomp°,   *solemn procession*
Forgot my morning wishes, hastily
Took a few herbs and apples, and the Day
Turned and departed silent. I, too late,   10
Under her solemn fillet° saw the scorn.   *headband*

DAYS. 1. *hypocritic:* Our word *hypocrite* comes from Greek: "one who plays a part" (as in a play or a procession). 2. *dervishes:* members of a Moslem religious order, whose vows of poverty obliged them to give away their possessions. 7. *pleachèd:* To pleach is to bend and interweave—a stylized, artificial method of prettifying natural branches.

Philip Larkin (b. 1922)

DAYS   1964

What are days for?
Days are where we live.
They come, they wake us
Time and time over.
They are to be happy in: 5
Where can we live but days?

Ah, solving that question
Brings the priest and the doctor
In their long coats
Running over the fields.   10

O. Emil Rauter (b. 1950)

OUR MINTED DAYS   1978

Each day is a shiny penny
Which Jove drops in our piggy bank's slot.
Spend them wisely, O you humans,
Or they will be gone but not forgot —
　　gone but not forgot —
　　　　And then you'll REALLY be sorry!!!

QUESTIONS

1. What has each poet to say on the subject of days? Sum up the theme of each poem.
2. To which of these three poems does each of the following student-written critical descriptions seem to refer? With which points of the description do you agree, or disagree?
   a. The entire poem sustains one metaphor. The poem goes into vivid detail and has memorable images.
   b. This poem makes one ootsy-cutesy comparison, expressed in stale clichés, unnecessary words, and excess punctuation.
   c. The poem is written in beautifully speakable language and has a beautiful simplicity. It gently kids those who believe in ignoring the simple pleasures that days bring.
   d. This poem is poverty-stricken. Its first six lines have no figures of speech and no imagery. Its language is as dull as dishwater. The poet sort of thumbs his nose at religion and science as if he is better than they are, and thinks them slightly ridiculous.
   e. Starting with a truly beautiful comparison involving the bright copper of the morning sun, this poem ends up speaking in the real everyday language of modern America.

In the collected writings of Abraham Lincoln, the earliest lines are these, which Lincoln as a boy set down in his arithmetic copybook:

Abraham Lincoln
his hand and pen
he will be good but
god knows When

That the lines are original with Lincoln is uncertain, but we do know that, even as a young man embarked on a busy political career, Lincoln now and again entertained a desire to write poetry. Referring to a poem he admired, Lincoln told a friend, "I would give all I am worth, and go in debt, to be able to write so fine a piece as I think that is." (The poem that so impressed him was by one William Knox, whom the world has little noted, nor long remembered.) In 1846 Lincoln sent three versions or partial versions of the following poem to the same friend, who had it printed in Quincy (Illinois) *Whig*, a local newspaper. Lincoln explained how he had come to write it:

In the fall of 1844, thinking I might aid some to carry the State of Indiana for Mr. Clay, I went into the neighborhood in that State in which I was raised, where my mother and only sister were buried, and from which I had been absent about fifteen years. That part of the country is, within itself, as unpoetical as any spot of the earth; but still, seeing it and its objects and inhabitants aroused feelings in me which were certainly poetry; though whether my expression of those feelings is poetry is quite another question.[5]

Abraham Lincoln (1809–1865)

My Childhood-Home I See Again   (1844–1846)

My childhood-home I see again,
   And gladden with the view;
And still as mem'ries crowd my brain,
   There's sadness in it too.

O memory! thou mid-way world   5
   'Twixt Earth and Paradise,
Where things decayed, and loved ones lost
   In dreamy shadows rise.

And freed from all that's gross or vile,
   Seem hallowed, pure, and bright,   10
Like scenes in some enchanted isle,
   All bathed in liquid light.

As distant mountains please the eye,
   When twilight chases day—
As bugle-tones, that, passing by,   15
   In distance die away—

As leaving some grand water-fall
   We ling'ring, list its roar,
So memory will hallow all
   We've known, but know no more.   20

Now twenty years have passed away,
   Since here I bid farewell
To woods, and fields, and scenes of play
   And school-mates loved so well.

Where many were, how few remain   25
   Of old familiar things!
But seeing these to mind again
   The lost and absent brings.

[5] Letter of April 18, 1846, to Andrew Johnston, *The Collected Works of Abraham Lincoln*, ed. Roy P. Basler (New Brunswick, N.J.: Rutgers University Press, 1953), 1:378.

The friends I left that parting day —
  How changed, as time has sped!
Young childhood grown, strong manhood grey,
  And half of all are dead.

I hear the lone survivors tell
  How nought from death could save,
Till every sound appears a knell,
  And every spot a grave.

I range the fields with pensive tread,
  And pace the hollow rooms;
And feel (companions of the dead)
  I'm living in the tombs.

And here's an object more of dread,
  Than aught the grave contains —
A human-form, with reason fled,
  While wretched life remains.

Poor Matthew! Once of genius bright, —
  A fortune-favored child
Now locked for aye, in mental night,
  A haggard mad-man wild.

Poor Matthew! I have ne'er forgot
  When first with maddened will,
Yourself you maimed, your father fought,
  And mother strove to kill;

And terror spread, and neighbors ran,
  Your dang'rous strength to bind;
And soon a howling crazy man,
  Your limbs were fast confined.

How then you writhed and shrieked aloud,
  Your bones and sinews bared;
And fiendish on the gaping crowd,
  With burning eyeballs glared.

And begged, and swore, and wept, and prayed,
  With maniac laughter joined —
How fearful are the signs displayed,
  By pangs that kill the mind!

And when at length, tho' drear and long,
  Time soothed your fiercer woes —
How plaintively your mournful song
  Upon the still night rose.

I've heard it oft, as if I dreamed,
  Far-distant, sweet, and lone;
The funeral dirge it ever seemed
  Of reason dead and gone.

•

To drink its strains, I've stole away,
   All silently and still,
Ere yet the rising god of day   75
   Had streaked the Eastern hill.

Air held his breath; the trees all still
   Seemed sorr'wing angels round.
Their swelling tears in dew-drops fell
   Upon the list'ning ground.   80

But this is past, and naught remains
   That raised you o'er the brute.
Your mad'ning shrieks and soothing strains
   Are like forever mute.

Now fare thee well: more thou the cause   85
   Than subject now of woe.
All mental pangs, but time's kind laws,
   Hast lost the power to know.

And now away to seek some scene
   Less painful than the last—   90
With less of horror mingled in
   The present and the past.

The very spot where grew the bread
   That formed my bones, I see.
How strange, old field, on thee to tread,   95
   And feel I'm part of thee!

My Childhood-Home I See Again. The "mad-man" portrayed in lines 41–88 is Matthew
Gentry; as boys, he and Lincoln had gone to school together. "He was rather a bright lad,"
Lincoln explained to Johnston, "and the son of *the* rich man in our very poor neighborhood. At the age of nineteen he unaccountably became furiously mad, from which
condition he gradually settled down into harmless insanity. When, as I told you . . . I
visited my old home in the fall of 1844, I found him still lingering in this wretched condition" (letter of Sept. 6, 1846).

Questions

1. At one point during the composition of this poem, Lincoln apparently saw
   the first 40 lines as one distinct section and the Matthew portrait (lines 41–88)
   as another. "When I got to writing," he told Johnston, "the change of subjects divided the thing into four little divisions or cantos." But either Lincoln
   did not write the other two cantos or they have not survived. Does the poem
   seem to you complete and self-contained as it stands? How does the Matthew
   portrait follow from the beginning? Do the two parts of the poem go together?
2. After you have formed your own opinion of Lincoln's poem, see which of the
   following statements comes nearest to it:

   This is an amateurish poem of some merit, but it is spoiled by too many
   inept and sentimental things in it.

   This is a flawed poem, but it contains memorable lines, and as a whole it
   succeeds for me.

This is an excellent poem that places Lincoln among the world's noteworthy poets.

This is a bad poem that deserves no charity just because Lincoln wrote it. Support your judgment of the poem by pointing to particulars.

Fred Emerson Brooks (1850–1923)

PAT'S OPINION OF FLAGS   1894

Every man in the world thinks his banner the best,
    And his national song
    Is often too long,
Yet in praising his flag he makes sport of the rest,
Though there's many a truth that is spoken in jest,   5
    Save wid malice prepense
    There should be no offense.

There's the Hawaiian kingdom stuck out in the ocean;
    'Twas made as a site
    For the seabirds to light;   10
There they worship their colors wid colored devotion,
And they never have war, but internal commotion,
    For those islands contain, O,
    Queen Lilli's volcano.

            . . .

There's the flag of the Chinese, as everywan knows,   15
    Cut three-cornered wid care,
    Like they'd no cloth to spare;
Yet they seem to have plenty when makin' their clothes;
Havin' no fashion plate, they've cut big, I suppose;
    Hangin' loose roundabout   20
    So the fleas will drop out.

You can judge of those men by the wardrobe they wear:
    They don't look to get fits
    For a "dollar six bits."
Their flag was made yellow, as people declare,   25
Because they've the smallpox so much over there;
    Be warned, if ye're wise,
    By the dragon it flies.

But one of the prettiest flags that I know
    Is the great oroflam   30
    Of our old Uncle Sam;
Wid the red and white bars all laid out in a row,
And a nice pasture blue for the bright stars to grow;
    Wid the eagle above
    And around it the dove.   35

Of the Star-spangled Banner alone, it is said
        She has earned this renown —
        She was niver pulled down.
With the green on my grave and that flag overhead
I think I'll rest aisy! But wait till I'm dead!   40
        Wid that flag in the sky
        I'm in no haste to die.

Anthony Hecht (b. 1923)

JAPAN   1954

It was a miniature country once
To my imagination; Home of the Short,
And also the academy of stunts
    Where acrobats are taught
  The famous secrets of the trade: 5
  To cycle in the big parade
While spinning plates upon their parasols,
Or somersaults that do not touch the ground,
    Or tossing seven balls
In Most Celestial Order round and round.   10

A child's quick sense of the ingenious stamped
All their invention: toys I used to get
At Christmastime, or the peculiar, cramped
    Look of their alphabet.
  Fragile and easily destroyed,   15
  Those little boats of celluloid
Driven by camphor round the bathroom sink,
And delicate the folded paper prize
    Which, dropped into a drink
Of water, grew up right before your eyes.   20

Now when we reached them it was with a sense
Sharpened for treachery compounding in their brains
Like mating weasels; our Intelligence
    Said: The Black Dragon reigns
  Secretly under yellow skin,   25
  Deeper than dyes of atabrine
And deadlier. The War Department said:
Remember you are Americans; forsake
    The wounded and the dead
At your own cost; remember Pearl and Wake.   30

And yet they bowed us in with ceremony,
Told us what brands of Sake were the best,
Explained their agriculture in a phony
    Dialect of the West,

Meant vaguely to be understood   35
As a shy sign of brotherhood
In the old human bondage to the facts
Of day-to-day existence. And like ants,
    Signaling tiny pacts
With their antennae, they would wave their hands.   40

At last we came to see them not as glib
Walkers of tightropes, worshipers of carp,
Nor yet a species out of Adam's rib
    Meant to preserve its warp
    In Cain's own image. They had learned   45
    That their tough eye-born goddess burned
Adoring fingers. They were very poor.
The holy mountain was not moved to speak.
    Wind at the paper door
Offered them snow out of its hollow peak.   50

Human endeavor clumsily betrays
Humanity. Their excrement served in this;
For, planting rice in water, they would raise
    Schistosomiasis
    Japonica, that enters through   55
    The pores into the avenue
And orbit of the blood, where it may foil
The heart and kill, or settle in the brain.
    This fruit of their nightsoil
Thrives in the skull, where it is called insane.   60

Now the quaint early image of Japan
That was so charming to me as a child
Seems like a bright design upon a fan,
    Of water rushing wild
    On rocks that can be folded up,   65
    A river which the wrist can stop
With a neat flip, revealing merely sticks
And silk of what had been a fan before,
    And like such winning tricks,
It shall be buried in excelsior.   70

JAPAN. 24. *The Black Dragon:* militarist organization that had urged the expansion of the
Japanese empire. 26. *atabrine:* a drug used against malaria. A side effect of it is that it gives
a yellow tinge to the user's skin. 30. *Pearl and Wake:* Pearl Harbor and Wake Island, at-
tacked by the Japanese on December 7, 1941. Wake fell after a prolonged defense by a
small garrison of Marines. 54–55. *Schistosomiasis Japonica:* a disease caused by parasitic
worms in the bloodstream.

QUESTIONS

1. The preceding two poems by Brooks and Hecht have something in common:
   an American speaker's view of foreigners. Who is the speaker in each poem?

2. Pat opens with an apology for what he is about to say. Do you find this apology satisfactory? Why or why not?
3. Consider Pat's attitude toward flags in Brooks's lines 1–7 and his attitude toward Old Glory in the last two stanzas. What contradiction do you notice between these two attitudes?
4. A word worth knowing is *jingoism*, from a patriotic ditty sung in English music halls in 1878, when a British fleet was sent into Turkish waters to resist Russian advances: "We don't want to fight, but by jingo, if we do / We've got the ships, we've got the men, and got the money, too!" For what reasons might Brooks's poem be called jingoistic?
5. In Hecht's poem, what is the speaker's attitude toward the Japanese at the beginning of the poem? At the end? What changes it?
6. What is the effect of Hecht's references to medicine and disease? How does the speaker feel toward victims of Schistosomiasis Japonica? Compare this with Pat's reference to smallpox (line 33).
7. What is the theme of each poem? To what extent does each poet make us see his theme in concrete terms, using imagery and detailed observation?
8. These two poems point toward a larger topic for discussion. What does the quality of a poem have to do with the poet's ability to understand people and to sympathize with them?

15 Knowing Excellence

How can we tell an excellent poem from any other? To give reasons for excellence in poetry is harder than to give reasons for failure in poetry (so often due to familiar, old-hat sorts of imprecision and sentimentality). A bad poem tends to be stereotyped, an excellent poem unique. In judging either, we can have no absolute preexisting specifications. A poem is not a simple mechanism like an electric toaster that an inspector in a factory can test by a check-off list. It has to be judged on the basis of what it evidently is trying to be and how well it succeeds in its effort. Nor is excellence simply due to regularity and symmetry. For the sake of meaning, a competent poet often will depart from a pattern. There is satisfaction, said Robert Frost, in things not mechanically straight: "We enjoy the straight crookedness of a good walking stick."

To judge a poem, we first have to understand it. At least, we need to understand it *almost* all the way; there is, to be sure, a poem such as Hopkins's "The Windhover" (p. 352), which most readers probably would call excellent even though its meaning is still being debated. While it is a good idea to give a poem at least a couple of considerate readings before judging it, sometimes our first encounter with a poem starts turning into an act of evaluation. Moving along into the poem, becoming more deeply involved in it, we may begin forming an opinion. In general, the more a poem contains for us to understand, the more rewarding we are likely to find it. This does not mean that an obscure and highly demanding poem is always to be preferred to a relatively simple one. Difficult poems can be pretentious and incoherent, but there is something to be said for the poem complicated enough to leave us something to discover on our fifteenth reading (unlike most limericks, which yield their all at a single look). Here is such a poem, one not readily fathomed and exhausted.

William Butler Yeats (1865–1939)

SAILING TO BYZANTIUM   1927

That is no country for old men. The young
In one another's arms, birds in the trees

—Those dying generations—at their song,
The salmon-falls, the mackerel-crowded seas,
Fish, flesh, or fowl, commend all summer long   5
Whatever is begotten, born, and dies.
Caught in that sensual music all neglect
Monuments of unaging intellect.

An aged man is but a paltry thing,
A tattered coat upon a stick, unless   10
Soul clap its hands and sing, and louder sing
For every tatter in its mortal dress,
Nor is there singing school but studying
Monuments of its own magnificence;
And therefore I have sailed the seas and come   15
To the holy city of Byzantium.

O sages standing in God's holy fire
As in the gold mosaic of a wall,
Come from the holy fire, perne in a gyre°,   *spin down a spiral*
And be the singing-masters of my soul.   20
Consume my heart away; sick with desire
And fastened to a dying animal
It knows not what it is; and gather me
Into the artifice of eternity.

Once out of nature I shall never take   25
My bodily form from any natural thing,
But such a form as Grecian goldsmiths make
Of hammered gold and gold enameling
To keep a drowsy Emperor awake;
Or set upon a golden bough to sing   30
To lords and ladies of Byzantium
Of what is past, or passing, or to come.

SAILING TO BYZANTIUM. Byzantium was the capital of the Byzantine Empire, the city now
called Istanbul. Yeats means, though, not merely the physical city. Byzantium is also a
name for his conception of paradise.

Though *salmon-falls* (line 4) suggests Yeats's native Ireland, the
poem, as we find out in line 25, is about escaping from the entire natural world. If the poet desires this escape, then probably the *country*
mentioned in the opening line is no political nation but the cycle of
birth and death in which human beings are trapped; and, indeed, the
poet says his heart is "fastened to a dying animal." Imaginary landscapes, it would seem, are merging with the historical Byzantium. Lines
17-18 refer to mosaic images, adornments of the Byzantine cathedral of
St. Sophia, in which the figures of saints are inlaid against backgrounds
of gold. The clockwork bird of the last stanza is also a reference to something actual. Yeats noted: "I have read somewhere that in the Emperor's
palace at Byzantium was a tree made of gold and silver, and artificial
birds that sang." This description of the role the poet would seek—that

of a changeless, immortal singer—directs us back to the earlier references to music and singing. Taken all together, they point toward the central metaphor of the poem: the craft of poetry can be a kind of singing. One kind of everlasting monument is a great poem. To study masterpieces of poetry is the only "singing school"—the only way to learn to write a poem.

We have no more than skimmed through a few of this poem's suggestions, enough to show that, out of allusion and imagery, Yeats has woven at least one elaborate metaphor. Surely one thing the poem achieves is that, far from merely puzzling us, it makes us aware of relationships between what a person can imagine and the physical world. There is the statement that a human heart is bound to the body that perishes, and yet it is possible to see consciousness for a moment independent of flesh, to sing with joy at the very fact that the body is crumbling away. Expressing a similar view of mortality, the Japanese artist Hokusai has shown a withered tree letting go of its few remaining leaves, while under it two graybeards shake with laughter. Like Hokusai's view, that of Yeats is by no means simple. Much of the power of Yeats's poem comes from the physical terms with which he states the ancient quarrel between body and spirit, body being a "tattered coat upon a stick." There is all the difference in the world between the work of the poet like Yeats whose eye is on the living thing and whose mind is awake and passionate, and that of the slovenly poet whose dull eye and sleepy mind focus on nothing more than some book read hastily long ago. The former writes a poem out of compelling need, the latter as if it seems a nice idea to write something.

Yeats's poem has the three qualities essential to beauty, according to the definition of Thomas Aquinas: wholeness, harmony, and radiance. The poem is all one; its parts move in peace with one another; it shines with emotional intensity. There is an orderly progression going on in it: from the speaker's statement of his discontent with the world of "sensual music," to his statement that he is quitting this world, to his prayer that the sages will take him in, and his vision of future immortality. And the images of the poem relate to one another—*dying generations* (line 3), *dying animal* (line 22), and the undying golden bird (lines 27-32) —to mention just one series of related things. "Sailing to Byzantium" is not the kind of poem that has, in Pope's words, "One simile, that solitary shines / In the dry desert of a thousand lines." Rich in figurative language, Yeats's whole poem develops a metaphor, with further metaphors as its tributaries.

"Sailing to Byzantium" has a theme that matters to us. What human being does not long, at times, to shed timid, imperfect flesh, to live in a state of absolute joy, unperishing? Being human, perhaps we too are stirred by Yeats's prayer: "Consume my heart away, sick with desire / And fastened to a dying animal. . . ." If it is true that in poetry (as Ezra Pound declared) "only emotion endures," then Yeats's poem ought to endure. (No reasons to be moved by a poem, however, can be of much use. If you happen not to feel moved by this particular poem, try another—but come back to "Sailing to Byzantium" after a while.)

Most excellent poems, it might be argued, contain significant themes, as does "Sailing to Byzantium." But the presence of such a theme is not enough to render a poem excellent. That classic tear-jerker "The Old Arm-Chair" (p. 238) expresses in its way, too, faith in a kind of immortality. Not theme alone makes an excellent poem, but how well a theme is stated.

Yeats's poem, some would say, is the match of any lyric in our language. Some might call it inferior to an epic (to Milton's *Paradise Lost*, say, or to the *Iliad*), but this is to lead us into a different argument: whether certain genres are innately better than others. Such an argument usually leads to a dead end. Evidently, *Paradise Lost* has greater range, variety, matter, length, and ambitiousness. But any poem— whether an epic or an epigram—may be judged by how well it fulfills the design it undertakes. God, who created both fleas and whales, pronounced all good. Fleas, like epigrams, have no reason to feel inferior.

EXERCISE: *Two Poems to Compare*

Here are two poems with a similar theme. Which contains more qualities of excellent poetry? Decide whether the other is bad or whether it may be praised for achieving something different.

Arthur Guiterman (1871–1943)
ON THE VANITY OF EARTHLY GREATNESS   1936

The tusks that clashed in mighty brawls
Of mastodons, are billiard balls.

The sword of Charlemagne the Just
Is ferric oxide, known as rust.

The grizzly bear whose potent hug
Was feared by all, is now a rug.

Great Caeser's bust is on the shelf,
And I don't feel so well myself.

Percy Bysshe Shelley (1792–1822)
OZYMANDIAS   1818

I met a traveler from an antique land
Who said: Two vast and trunkless legs of stone
Stand in the desert. Near them, on the sand,
Half sunk, a shattered visage lies, whose frown,

And wrinkled lip, and sneer of cold command,   5
Tell that its sculptor well those passions read
Which yet survive, stamped on these lifeless things,
The hand that mocked° them and the heart that fed;   *imitated*
And on the pedestal these words appear:
"My name is Ozymandias, king of kings: 10
Look on my works, ye Mighty, and despair!"
Nothing beside remains. Round the decay
Of that colossal wreck, boundless and bare
The lone and level sands stretch far away.

Some excellent poems of the past will remain sealed to us unless we are willing to sympathize with their conventions. Pastoral poetry, for instance — Marlowe's "Passionate Shepherd" and Milton's "Lycidas" — asks us to accept certain conventions and situations that may seem old-fashioned: idle swains, oaten flutes. We are under no grim duty, of course, to admire poems whose conventions do not appeal to us. But there is no point in blaming a poet for playing a particular game or for observing its rules.

There are, however, inferior poems that appear to be pieced together from conventions: patchwork quilts of old unwanted words.

John Lyly (1554–1606?)
DAPHNE   1590

My Daphne's hair is twisted gold,
Bright stars apiece her eyes do hold;
My Daphne's brow enthrones the graces,
My Daphne's beauty stains all faces;
On Daphne's cheek grow rose and cherry,   5
On Daphne's lip a sweeter berry;
Daphne's snowy hand but touched does melt,
And then no heavenlier warmth is felt;
My Daphne's voice tunes all the spheres,
My Daphne's music charms all ears.   10
Fond° am I thus to sing her praise;   *foolish*
These glories now are turned to bays.

DAPHNE. 12. *bays:* evergreen leaves in crowns traditionally awarded to poets; hence, poetic fame.

Lyly's poem isn't worthless: a woman whose beauty *stains* all other women's faces by comparison may be hard to forget. Still, "Daphne" is a mediocre specimen of a kind of poetry that swept England in the sixteenth century, when the influence of Italian sonnets reached its height.

(See the discussion of the sonnet on page 164.) The result was a surplus of Petrarchan **conceits,** or elaborate comparisons (from the Italian *concetto:* concept, bright idea). Shakespeare, who at times helped himself generously from the Petrarchan stockpile, in the following famous sonnet pokes fun at poets who use such handed-down figures of speech thoughtlessly. Which traits of Lyly's Daphne do you find him kidding here?

William Shakespeare (1564–1616)

MY MISTRESS' EYES ARE NOTHING LIKE THE SUN   1609

My mistress' eyes are nothing like the sun;
Coral is far more red than her lips' red;
If snow be white, why then her breasts are dun;
If hairs be wires, black wires grow on her head.
I have seen roses damasked red and white,   5
But no such roses see I in her cheeks;
And in some perfumes is there more delight
Than in the breath that from my mistress reeks.
I love to hear her speak, yet well I know
That music hath a far more pleasing sound;   10
I grant I never saw a goddess go:
My mistress, when she walks, treads on the ground.
   And yet, by heaven, I think my love as rare
   As any she°, belied with false compare.   *woman*

Contrary to what you might expect, for years after Shakespeare's time, poets continued to write fine poems with the aid of such conventions.

Thomas Campion (1567–1620)

THERE IS A GARDEN IN HER FACE   1617

   There is a garden in her face
Where roses and white lilies grow;
   A heav'nly paradise is that place
Wherein all pleasant fruits do flow.
   There cherries grow which none may buy   5
   Till "Cherry-ripe" themselves do cry.

   Those cherries fairly do enclose
Of orient pearl a double row,
   Which when her lovely laughter shows,
They look like rose-buds filled with snow;   10
   Yet them nor° peer nor prince can buy,   *neither*
   Till "Cherry-ripe" themselves do cry.

Her eyes like angels watch them still;
Her brows like bended bows do stand,
 Threat'ning with piercing frowns to kill   15
All that attempt, with eye or hand
  Those sacred cherries to come nigh
  Till "Cherry-ripe" themselves do cry.

THERE IS A GARDEN IN HER FACE. 6. *"Cherry-ripe"*: cry of fruit-peddlers in London streets.

QUESTIONS

1. What does Campion's song owe to Petrarchan tradition?
2. What in it strikes you as fresh observation of actual life?
3. Comment in particular on the last stanza. Does the comparison of eyebrows to threatening bowmen seem too silly or far-fetched? What sense do you find in it?
4. Try to describe the tone of this poem. What do you understand, from this portrait of a young girl, to be the poet's feelings?

Excellent poetry might be easier to recognize if each poet had a fixed position on the slopes of Mount Parnassus, but from one century to the next, the reputations of some poets have taken humiliating slides, or made impressive clambers. We decide for ourselves which poems to call excellent, but readers of the future may reverse our opinions. Most of us no longer would share this popular view of Walt Whitman by one of his contemporaries:

> Walt Whitman (1819-1892), by some regarded as a great poet; by others, as no poet at all. Most of his so-called poems are mere catalogues of things, without meter or rime, but in a few more regular poems and in lines here and there he is grandly poetical, as in "O Captain! My Captain!"[1]

Walt Whitman (1819–1892)
O CAPTAIN! MY CAPTAIN!   1865

O Captain! my Captain! our fearful trip is done,
The ship has weather'd every rack, the prize we sought is won,
The port is near, the bells I hear, the people all exulting,
While follow eyes the steady keel, the vessel grim and daring;
  But O heart! heart! heart!   5
   O the bleeding drops of red,
    Where on the deck my Captain lies,
    Fallen cold and dead.

O Captain! my Captain! rise up and hear the bells;
Rise up — for you the flag is flung — for you the bugle trills, 10

[1] J. Willis Westlake, A.M., in *Common-school Literature, English and American, with Several Hundred Extracts to be Memorized* (Philadelphia, 1898).

For you bouquets and ribbon'd wreaths — for you the shores a-crowding,
For you they call, the swaying mass, their eager faces turning;
  Here Captain! dear father!
    This arm beneath your head!
      It is some dream that on the deck,   15
        You've fallen cold and dead.

My Captain does not answer, his lips are pale and still,
My father does not feel my arm, he has no pulse nor will,
The ship is anchor'd safe and sound, its voyage closed and done,
From fearful trip the victor ship comes in with object won;   20
  Exult O shores, and ring O bells!
    But I with mournful tread,
      Walk the deck my Captain lies,
        Fallen cold and dead.

O Captain! My Captain! Written soon after the death of Abraham Lincoln, this was, in
Whitman's lifetime, by far the most popular of his poems.

Questions

1. Compare this with other Whitman poems. (See another elegy for Lincoln,
   "When Lilacs Last in the Dooryard Bloom'd," quoted in part on page 171.) In
   what ways is "O Captain! My Captain!" uncharacteristic of his works? Do
   you agree with J. Willis Westlake that this is one of the few occasions on
   which Whitman is "grandly poetical"?
2. Comment on the appropriateness to its subject of the poem's rhythms.
3. Do you find any evidence in this poem than an excellent poet wrote it?

    There is nothing to do but commit ourselves and praise or blame
and, if need be, let time erase our error. In a sense, all readers of poetry
are constantly reexamining the judgments of the past by choosing those
poems they care to go on reading. In the end, we have to admit that the
critical principles set forth in this chapter are all very well for admiring
excellent poetry we already know, but they cannot be carried like a
yardstick in the hand, to go out looking for it. As Ezra Pound said in his
ABC of Reading, "A classic is classic not because it conforms to certain
structural rules, or fits certain definitions (of which its author had quite
probably never heard). It is classic because of a certain eternal and irre-
pressible freshness."
    The best poems, like "Sailing to Byzantium," may offer a kind of
religious experience. In the eighth decade of the twentieth century,
some of us rarely set foot outside an artificial environment. Whizzing
down four-lane superhighways, we observe lakes and trees in the distance. In a way our cities are to us as anthills are to ants, as Frost
reminds us in "Departmental." No less than anthills, they are "natural"
structures. But the "unnatural" world of school or business is, as Wordsworth says, too much with us. Locked in the shells of our ambitions,
our self-esteem, we forget our kinship to earth and sea. We fabricate

self-justifications. But a great poem shocks us into another order of perception. It points beyond language to something still more essential. It ushers us into an experience so moving and true that we feel (to quote King Lear) "cut to the brain." In bad or indifferent poetry, words are all there is.

Matthew Arnold (1822–1888)
BELOW THE SURFACE-STREAM, SHALLOW AND LIGHT　　　　1869

Below the surface-stream, shallow and light,
Of what we *say* we feel—below the stream,
As light, of what we *think* we feel—there flows
With noiseless current strong, obscure and deep,
The central stream of what we feel indeed.

QUESTIONS

1. Speaking of himself and his fellow poets, W. D. Snodgrass has expressed the opinion that:

   our only hope as artists is to continually ask ourselves, "Am I writing what I *really* think? Not what is acceptable; not what my favorite intellectual would think in this situation; not what I wish I felt. Only what I cannot help thinking." ("Finding a Poem," *In Radical Pursuit*, New York, Harper & Row, 1974.)

   Compare Snodgrass's statement and the statement that Arnold makes in his brief poem.
2. Of what value is Arnold's observation to readers of poetry?

Thomas Gray (1716–1771)
ELEGY WRITTEN IN A COUNTRY CHURCHYARD　　　　1753

The curfew tolls the knell of parting day,
　The lowing herd wind slowly o'er the lea,
The plowman homeward plods his weary way,
　And leaves the world to darkness and to me.

Now fades the glimmering landscape on the sight,　　　　　5
　And all the air a solemn stillness holds,
Save where the beetle wheels his droning flight,
　And drowsy tinklings lull the distant folds;

Save that from yonder ivy-mantled tow'r
　The moping owl does to the moon complain　　　　　10
Of such, as wand'ring near her secret bow'r,
　Molest her ancient solitary reign.

Beneath those rugged elms, that yew tree's shade,
  Where heaves the turf in many a mold'ring heap,
Each in his narrow cell forever laid,   15
  The rude forefathers of the hamlet sleep.

The breezy call of incense-breathing morn,
  The swallow twitt'ring from the straw-built shed,
The cock's shrill clarion, or the echoing horn°,   *fox-hunters' horn*
  No more shall rouse them from their lowly bed.   20

For them no more the blazing hearth shall burn,
  Or busy housewife ply her evening care;
No children run to lisp their sire's return,
  Or climb his knees the envied kiss to share.

Oft did the harvest to their sickle yield,   25
  Their furrow oft the stubborn glebe° has broke;   *turf*
How jocund did they drive their team afield!
  How bowed the woods beneath their sturdy stroke!

Let not Ambition mock their useful toil,
  Their homely joys, and destiny obscure;   30
Nor Grandeur hear with a disdainful smile
  The short and simple annals of the poor.

The boast of heraldry, the pomp of pow'r,
  And all that beauty, all that wealth e'er gave,
Awaits alike th' inevitable hour.   35
  The paths of glory lead but to the grave.

Nor you, ye proud, impute to these the fault,
  If Mem'ry o'er their tomb no trophies raise,
Where through the long-drawn aisle and fretted° vault   *decorated*
  The pealing anthem swells the note of praise.   40

Can storied° urn or animated bust   *inscribed*
  Back to its mansion call the fleeting breath?
Can Honor's voice provoke the silent dust,
  Or Flatt'ry soothe the dull cold ear of Death?

Perhaps in this neglected spot is laid   45
  Some heart once pregnant with celestial fire;
Hands that the rod of empire might have swayed,
  Or waked to ecstasy the living lyre.

But knowledge to their eyes her ample page
  Rich with the spoils of time did ne'er unroll;   50
Chill Penury repressed their noble rage,
  And froze the genial current of the soul.

Full many a gem of purest ray serene,
  The dark unfathomed caves of ocean bear:
Full many a flower is born to blush unseen,   55
  And waste its sweetness on the desert air.

Some village Hampden, that with dauntless breast
 The little tyrant of his field withstood;
Some mute inglorious Milton here may rest,
 Some Cromwell guiltless of his country's blood.   60

Th' applause of list'ning senates to command,
 The threats of pain and ruin to despise,
To scatter plenty o'er a smiling land,
 And read their hist'ry in a nation's eyes,

Their lot forbade: nor circumscribed alone   65
 Their growing virtues, but their crimes confined;
Forbade to wade through slaughter to a throne,
 And shut the gates of mercy on mankind,

The struggling pangs of conscious truth to hide,
 To quench the blushes of ingenuous shame,   70
Or heap the shrine of Luxury and Pride
 With incense kindled at the Muse's flame.

Far from the madding° crowd's ignoble strife,   *frenzied*
 Their sober wishes never learned to stray;
Along the cool sequestered vale of life   75
 They kept the noiseless tenor of their way.

Yet ev'n these bones from insult to protect
 Some frail memorial still erected nigh,
With uncouth rhymes and shapeless sculpture decked,
 Implores the passing tribute of a sigh.   80

Their name, their years, spelt by th' unlettered Muse,
 The place of fame and elegy supply:
And many a holy text around she strews,
 That teach the rustic moralist to die.

For who to dumb Forgetfulness a prey,   85
 This pleasing anxious being e'er resigned,
Left the warm precincts of the cheerful day,
 Nor cast one longing ling'ring look behind?

On some fond breast the parting soul relies,
 Some pious drops the closing eye requires;   90
Ev'n from the tomb the voice of Nature cries,
 Ev'n in our ashes live their wonted° fires.   *customary*

For thee, who mindful of th' unhonored dead
 Dost in these lines their artless tale relate;
If chance, by lonely contemplation led,   95
 Some kindred spirit shall inquire thy fate,

Haply some hoary-headed swain° may say,   *shepherd*
 "Oft have we seen him at the peep of dawn
Brushing with hasty steps the dews away
 To meet the sun upon the upland lawn.   100

"There at the foot of yonder nodding beech
  That wreathes its old fantastic roots so high,
His listless length at noontide would he stretch,
  And pore upon the brook that babbles by.

"Hard by yon wood, now smiling as in scorn,   105
  Mutt'ring his wayward fancies he would rove,
Now drooping, woeful wan, like one forlorn,
  Or crazed with care, or crossed in hopeless love.

"One morn I missed him, on the customed hill,
  Along the heath and near his fav'rite tree;   110
Another came; not yet beside the rill,
  Nor up the lawn, nor at the wood was he;

"The next with dirges due in sad array
  Slow though the churchway path we saw him borne.
Approach and read (for thou canst read) the lay,   115
  Graved on the stone beneath yon aged thorn."

The Epitaph

Here rests his head upon the lap of Earth
  A youth to Fortune and to Fame unknown.
Fair Science° frowned not on his humble birth,   Knowledge
  And Melancholy marked him for her own.   120

Large was his bounty, and his soul sincere,
  Heav'n did a recompense as largely send:
He gave to Mis'ry all he had, a tear,
  He gained from Heav'n ('twas all he wished) a friend.

No farther seek his merits to disclose,   125
  Or draw his frailties from their dread abode,
(There they alike in trembling hope repose),
  The bosom of His Father and his God.

ELEGY WRITTEN IN A COUNTRY CHURCHYARD. 57. *Hampden:* John Hampden, who had resisted illegal taxes imposed by Charles I.

QUESTIONS

1. In contrasting the unknown poor buried in this village churchyard and famous men buried in cathedrals (in *fretted vault*, line 39), what is Gray's theme? What do you understand from the line, *The paths of glory lead but to the grave?*

2. Carl J. Weber thinks that Gray's compassion for the village poor anticipates the democratic sympathies of the American Revolution: "Thomas Gray is the pioneer literary spokesman for the Ordinary Man." But another critic, Lyle Glazier, argues that the "Elegy" isn't political at all: that we misread if we think the poet meant "to persuade the poor and obscure that their barren lives are meaningful"; and also misread if we think he meant to assure the privileged classes "in whose ranks Gray was proud to consider himself"

that they need not worry about the poor, "who have already all essential riches." How much truth do you find in either of these views?

3. Cite lines and phrases that show Gray's concern for the musical qualities of words.

4. Who is the *youth* of the closing Epitaph? By *thee* (line 93) does Gray mean himself? Does he mean some fictitious poet supposedly writing the "Elegy" — the first-person speaker (line 4)? Does he mean some village stonecutter, a crude poet whose illiterate Muse (line 81) inspired him to compose tombstone epitaphs? Or could the Epitaph possibly refer to Gray's close friend of school and undergraduate days, the promising poet Richard West, who had died in 1742? Which interpretation seems to you the most reasonable? (Does our lack of absolute certainty negate the value of the poem?)

5. Walter Savage Landor called the Epitaph a tin kettle tied to the tail of a noble dog. Do you agree that the Epitaph is inferior to what has gone before it? What is its function in Gray's poem?

6. Many sources for Gray's phrases and motifs have been found in earlier poets: Virgil, Horace, Dante, Milton, and many more. Even if it could be demonstrated that Gray's poem has not one original line in it, would it be possible to dismiss the "Elegy" as a mere rag-bag of borrowings, like John Lyly's "Daphne"?

7. Gray's poem, a pastoral elegy, is in the same genre as another famous English poem: John Milton's "Lycidas." What conventions are common to both?

8. In the earliest surviving manuscript of Gray's poem, lines 73–76 read:

No more with Reason and thyself at strife;
Give anxious cares and endless wishes room
But through the cool sequester'd vale of Life
Pursue the silent tenor of thy doom.

In what ways does the final version of those lines seem superior?

9. Perhaps the best-known poem in English, Gray's "Elegy" has inspired hundreds of imitations, countless parodies, and translations into eighteen or more languages. (Some of these languages contain dozens of attempts to translate it.) To what do you attribute the poem's fame? What do you suppose has proved so universally appealing in it?

10. Compare Gray's "Elegy" with Shelley's "Ozymandias" and Arthur Guiterman's "On the Vanity of Earthly Greatness." What do the three poems have in common? How would you rank them in order of excellence?

16 Alternatives

THE POET'S REVISIONS

"He / Who casts to write a living line must sweat, / . . . and strike the second heat / Upon the Muse's anvil," wrote Ben Jonson. Indeed, few if any immortal poems can have been perfected with the first blow. The labor of revising seems the usual practice of most bards (other than the Bard of Avon, if we believe the famous rumor that in "whatsoever he penned, he never blotted out line"). As a result, a poet may leave us two or more versions of a poem — perhaps (as Robert Graves has said of his work drafts) "hatched and cross-hatched by puzzling layers of ink."

We need not, of course, rummage the poet's wastebasket in order to assess a poem. If we wish, we can follow a suggestion of the critic Austin Warren: take any fine poem and make changes in it. Then compare the changes with the original. We may then realize why the poem is as it is instead of something else. However, there is a certain undeniable pleasure in watching a poem go through its growth stages. Some readers have claimed that the study of successive versions gives them insight into the process by which poems come to be. More important to a reader whose concern is to read poems with appreciation, we stand to learn something about the rightness of a finished poem from seeing what alternatives occurred to the poet. To a critic who protested two lines in Wordsworth's "The Thorn," a painfully flat description of an infant's grave,

> I've measured it from side to side;
> 'Tis three feet long and two feet wide,

Wordsworth retorted, "They ought to be liked." However, he thought better of them and later made this change:

> Though but of compass small, and bare
> To thirsty suns and parching air.

A novice poet who regards a first draft as inviolable sometimes loses interest in the poem if anyone suggests that more work be done on it. Others have found high excitement in the task. "Months of re-writing! What happiness!" exclaimed William Butler Yeats in a letter to a friend. In fact, Yeats so much enjoyed revision that late in life he kept trying to improve the poems of his youth. The end results seem more youthful and spontaneous than the originals. A merciless self-critic, Yeats discarded lines that a lesser poet would have been grateful for. In some cases his final version was practically a new poem:

William Butler Yeats (1865–1939)

THE OLD PENSIONER   1890

I had a chair at every hearth,
When no one turned to see
With "Look at that old fellow there;
And who may he be?"
And therefore do I wander on,   5
And the fret is on me.

The road-side trees keep murmuring —
Ah, wherefore murmur ye
As in the old days long gone by,
Green oak and poplar tree!   10
The well-known faces are all gone,
And the fret is on me.

THE LAMENTATION OF THE OLD PENSIONER   1939

Although I shelter from the rain
Under a broken tree
My chair was nearest to the fire
In every company
That talked of love or politics,   5
Ere Time transfigured me.

Though lads are making pikes again
For some conspiracy,
And crazy rascals rage their fill
At human tyranny,   10
My contemplations are of Time
That has transfigured me.

There's not a woman turns her face
Upon a broken tree,
And yet the beauties that I loved   15
Are in my memory;
I spit into the face of Time
That has transfigured me.

QUESTIONS

1. "The Old Pensioner" is this poem's first printed version; "Lamentation," its last. From the original, what elements has Yeats in the end retained?

2. What does the final version add to our knowledge of the old man (his character, attitudes, circumstances)?
3. Compare in sound and rhythm the refrain in the "Lamentation" with the original refrain.
4. Why do the statements in the final version seem to follow one another more naturally, and the poem as a whole seem more tightly woven together?

Yeats's practice seems to document the assertion of critic A. F. Scott that "the work of correction is often quite as inspired as the first onrush of words and ideas." Yeats made a revealing comment on his methods of revision:

> In dream poetry, in "Kubla Khan," . . . every line, every word can carry its unanalyzable, rich associations; but if we dramatize some possible singer or speaker we remember that he is moved by one thing at a time, certain words must be dull and numb. Here and there in correcting my early poems I have introduced such numbness and dullness, turned, for instance, the "curd-pale moon" into the "brilliant moon," that all might seem, as it were, remembered with indifference, except some one vivid image. When I began to rehearse a play I had the defects of my early poetry; I insisted upon obvious all-pervading rhythm. Later on I found myself saying that only in those lines or words where the beauty of the passage came to its climax, must rhythm be obvious.[1]

In changing words for "dull and numb" ones, in breaking up and varying rhythms, Yeats evidently is trying for improvement not necessarily in a particular line, but in an entire poem.

Not all revisions are successful. An instance might be the alterations Keats made in "La Belle Dame sans Merci," in which the stanza with the "wild wild eyes" and the exactly counted kisses,

> She took me to her elfin grot,
>   And there she wept and sighed full sore,
> And there I shut her wild wild eyes
>   With kisses four.

was scrapped in favor of:

> She took me to her elfin grot,
>   And there she gazed and sighèd deep,
> And there I shut her wild sad eyes —
>   So kissed to sleep.

When Mark Antony begins his funeral oration, "Friends, Romans, countrymen: lend me your ears," Shakespeare makes him ask something quite different from the modernized version in one high school English textbook: "Friends, Romans, countrymen: listen to me." Strictly speaking, any revised version of a poem is a different poem, even if its only change is a single word.

[1] "Dramatis Personae, 1896–1902," in *The Autobiography of William Butler Yeats* (New York: Macmillan, 1953).

In each of the following pairs, which details of the revised version show an improvement of the earlier one? Exactly what makes the poet's second thoughts seem better (if you agree that they are)? Italics indicate words of one text not found in the other. Notice that in some cases, the poet has also changed word order.

1. Samuel Taylor Coleridge, "The Rime of the Ancient Mariner," from Part III:

   a. One after one, by the hornèd Moon
         (Listen, O Stranger! to me)
      Each turn'd his face with a ghastly pang
         And curs'd me with his *ee.*   *(1799 version)*

   b. One after one, by the *star-dogged* Moon,
      Too quick for groan or sigh,
      Each turned his face with a ghastly pang
         And cursed me with his *eye.*   *(1817 version)*

2. William Blake, last stanza of "London" (complete poem given on page 68):

   a. But most the midnight harlot's curse
      From every *dismal* street I hear,
      Weaves around the marriage hearse
      And blasts the new born infant's tear.   *(first draft, 1793)*

   b. But most *through* midnight streets I hear
      How the *youthful* harlot's curse
      Blasts the new born infant's tear
      And *blights with plagues* the marriage hearse.   *(1794 version)*

3. Edward FitzGerald, *The Rubáiyát of Omar Khayyám,* a quatrain:

   a. *For in and out, above, about, below,*
      'Tis nothing but a Magic Shadow-show,
         Play'd in a Box whose Candle is the Sun,
      Round *which* we *Phantom Figures* come and go.

                                        (first version, 1859 edition)

   b. We *are no other than a moving row*
         Of Magic Shadow-*shapes that* come and go
            Round *with* the Sun-*illumined Lantern held*
         In Midnight by the Master of the Show; . . .

                                        (fifth version, 1889 edition)

Walt Whitman (1819–1892)

A Noiseless Patient Spider

A noiseless patient spider,
I mark'd where on a little promontory it stood isolated,
Mark'd how to explore the vacant vast surrounding,
It launch'd forth filament, filament, filament, out of itself,
Ever unreeling them, ever tirelessly speeding them.   5

And you O my soul where you stand,
Surrounded, detached, in measureless oceans of space,
Ceaselessly musing, venturing, throwing, seeking the spheres to connect
    them,
Till the bridge you will need be form'd, till the ductile anchor hold,
Till the gossamer thread you fling catch somewhere, O my soul.   10

THE SOUL, REACHING, THROWING OUT FOR LOVE

The Soul, reaching, throwing out for love,
As the spider, from some little promontory, throwing out filament after
    filament, tirelessly out of itself, that one at least may catch and form
    a link, a bridge, a connection
O I saw one passing along, saying hardly a word—yet full of love I de-
    tected him, by certain signs
O eyes wishfully turning! O silent eyes!
For then I thought of you o'er the world,
O latent oceans, fathomless oceans of love!
O waiting oceans of love! yearning and fervid! and of you sweet souls
    perhaps in the future, delicious and long:
But Death, unknown on the earth—ungiven, dark here, unspoken, never
    born:
You fathomless latent souls of love—you pent and unknown oceans of
    love!

QUESTIONS

1. One of these two versions of a poem by Whitman is an early draft from the poet's notebook. The other is the final version completed in 1871, about ten years later. Which is the final version?
2. In the final version, what has Whitman done to render his central metaphor (the comparison of soul and spider) more vivid and exact? What proportion of the final version is devoted to this metaphor?
3. In the early draft, what lines seem distracting or nonessential?

Donald Hall (b. 1928)
MY SON, MY EXECUTIONER   1955

My son, my executioner,
    I take you in my arms,
Quiet and small and just astir,
    And whom my body warms.

Sweet death, small son, our instrument   5
    Of immortality,
Your cries and hungers document
    Our bodily decay.

We twenty-five and twenty-two,
  Who seemed to live forever,   10
Observe enduring life in you
  And start to die together.

1. The first line introduces a paradoxical truth, the basic theme of the poem.
   How would you sum up this truth in your own words?
2. Exactly what do these words denote: *instrument* (line 5), *document* (line 7)?
3. When first published, this poem had a fourth stanza:

   I take into my arms the death
     Maturity exacts,
   And name with my imperfect breath
     The mortal paradox.

   Do you think the poet right or wrong to omit this stanza? Explain.

TRANSLATIONS

Poetry, said Robert Frost, is what gets lost in translation. If absolutely true, the comment is bad news for most of us, who have to depend on translations for our only knowledge of great poems in some other languages. However, some translators seem able to save a part of their originals and bring it across the language gap. At times they may even add more poetry of their own, as if to try to compensate for what is lost.

Unlike the writer of an original poem, the translator begins with a meaning that already exists. To convey it, the translator may decide to stick closely to the denotations of the original words or else to depart from them, more or less freely, after something he or she values more. The latter aim is evident in the *Imitations* of Robert Lowell, who said he had been "reckless with literal meaning" and instead had "labored hard to get the tone." Particularly defiant of translation are poems in dialect, uneducated speech, and slang: what can be used for English equivalents? Ezra Pound, in a bold move, translates the song of a Chinese peasant in *The Classic Anthology Defined by Confucius:*

Yaller bird, let my corn alone,
Yaller bird, let my crawps alone,
These folks here won't let me eat,
I wanna go back whaar I can meet
the folks I used to know at home,
            I got a home an' I wanna' git goin'.

Here, it is our purpose to judge a translation not by its fidelity to its original, but by the same standards we apply to any other poem written in English. To do so may be another way to see the difference between appropriate and inappropriate words.

Here are two versions of a famous poem by Callimachus from the Greek (or Palatine) Anthology, a collection of lyrics and epigrams written between 700 B.C. and A.D. 1000. Cory's translation reflects the era of Tennyson; that by Fitts is clearly from the era of Eliot and Pound. What are their differences? Which of these two modes in translation do you prefer? Why? One mode is not intrinsically superior to the other.

William Cory (1832–1892)

HERACLITUS   1858

They told me, Heraclitus, they told me you were dead,
They brought me bitter news to hear and bitter tears to shed.
I wept as I remembered how often you and I
Had tired the sun with talking and sent him down the sky.

And now that thou art lying, my dear Old Carian guest,
A handful of grey ashes, long, long ago at rest,
Still are thy pleasant voices, thy nightingales, awake;
For Death, he taketh all away, but them he cannot take.

Dudley Fitts (1903–1968)

ELEGY ON HERAKLEITOS   1938

One brought me the news of your death, O Herakleitos my friend,
And I wept for you, remembering
How often we had watched the sun set as we talked.

And you are ashes now, old friend from Halikarnassos,
Ashes now:
         but your nightingale songs live on,
And Death, the destroyer of every lovely thing,
Shall not touch them with his blind all-canceling fingers.

Federico García Lorca (1899–1936)

LA GUITARRA   (1921)   GUITAR   1967

Empieza el llanto	Begins the crying
de la guitarra.	of the guitar.
Se rompen las copas	From earliest dawn
de la madrugada.	the strokes are breaking.
Empieza el llanto	Begins the crying 5
de la guitarra.	of the guitar.
Es inútil	It is futile
callarla.	to stop its sound.
Es imposible	It is impossible
callarla.	to stop its sound. 10

Llora monótona	It is crying a monotone
como llora el agua,	like the crying of water,
como llora el viento	like the crying of wind
sobre la nevada.	over fallen snow.
Es imposible	It is impossible 15
callarla.	to stop its sound.
Llora por cosas	It is crying over things
lejanas.	far off.
Arena del Sur caliente	Burning sand of the South
que pide camelias blancas.	which covets white camelias. 20
Llora flecha sin blanco,	It is crying the arrow without aim,
la tarde sin mañana,	the evening without tomorrow,
y el primer pájaro muerto	and the first dead bird on the branch.
sobre la rama.	O guitar!
¡Oh, guitarra!	Heart heavily wounded 25
Corazón malherido	by five sharp swords.
por cinco espadas.	

—Translated by Keith Waldrop

Questions

1. Someone who knows Spanish should read aloud the original and the translation. Although it is impossible for any translation fully to capture the resonance of García Lorca's poem, in what places is the English version most nearly able to approximate it?
2. Another translation renders line 21: "It mourns for the targetless arrow." What is the difference between mourning for something and being the cry of it?
3. Throughout his translation, Waldrop closely follows the line divisions of the original, but in line 23 he combines García Lorca's lines 23 and 24. Can you see any point in his doing so? Would "on the branch" by itself be a strong line of English poetry?

EXERCISE: *Comparing Translations*

Which English translation of each of the following poems is the best poetry? The originals may be of interest to some. For those who do not know the foreign language, the editor's line-by-line prose paraphrases may help indicate what the translator had to work with and how much of the translation is the translator's own idea. In which do you find the diction most felicitous? In which do pattern and structure best move as one? What differences in tone are apparent? It is doubtful that any one translation will surpass the others in every detail.

Horace (65–8 B.C.)
ODES I (38)   (about 20 B.C.)

Persicos odi, puer, apparatus,
Displicent nexae philyra coronae;
Mitte sectari, rosa quo locorum
    Sera moretur.

Simplici myrto nihil allabores
Sedulus curo: neque te ministrum
Dedecet myrtus neque me sub arta
      Vite bibentem.

ODES I (38). Prose translation: (1) Persian pomp, boy, I detest, (2) garlands woven of lin-
den bark displease me; (3–4) give up searching for the place where the late-blooming rose
is. (5–6) Put no laborious trimmings on simple myrtle: (6–7) for myrtle is unbecoming neither to you, a servant, nor to me, under the shade of this (8) vine, drinking.

1. SIMPLICITY   (about 1782)

    Boy, I hate their empty shows,
      Persian garlands I detest,
    Bring me not the late-blown rose
      Lingering after all the rest:
    Plainer myrtle pleases me
      Thus outstretched beneath my vine,
    Myrtle more becoming thee,
      Waiting with thy master's wine.

                             — William Cowper

2. FIE ON EASTERN LUXURY!   (about 1830)

    Nay, nay, my boy — 'tis not for me,
      This studious pomp of Eastern luxury;
    Give me no various garlands — fine
      With linden twine,
    Nor seek, where latest lingering blows,
      The solitary rose.

    Earnest I beg — add not with toilsome pain,
    One far-sought blossom to the myrtle plain,
    For sure, the fragrant myrtle bough
      Looks seemliest on thy brow;
    Nor me mis-seems, while, underneath the vine,
    Close interweaved, I quaff the rosy wine.

                             — Hartley Coleridge

3. THE PREFERENCE DECLARED   1892

    Boy, I detest the Persian pomp;
      I hate those linden-bark devices;
    And as for roses, holy Moses!
      They can't be got at living prices!
    Myrtle is good enough for us, —
      For *you*, as bearer of my flagon;
    For *me*, supine beneath this vine,
      Doing my best to get a jag on!

                             — Eugene Field

Charles Baudelaire (1821–1867)

RECUEILLEMENT   1866

Sois sage, ô ma Douleur, et tiens-toi plus tranquille.
Tu réclamais le Soir; il descend; le voici:
Une atmosphère obscure enveloppe la ville,
Aux uns portant la paix, aux autres le souci.

Pendant que des mortels la multitude vile, 5
Sous le fouet du Plaisir, ce bourreau sans merci,
Va cueillir des remords dans la fête servile,
Ma Douleur, donne-moi la main; viens par ici,

Loin d'eux. Vois se pencher les défuntes Années,
Sur les balcons du ciel, en robes surannées; 10
Surgir du fond des eaux le Regret souriant;

Le Soleil moribond s'endormir sous une arche,
Et, comme un long linceul trainant à l'Orient,
Entends, ma chère, entends la douce Nuit qui marche.

"MEDITATION." Prose translation: (1) Behave yourself [as a mother would say to her child], O my Sorrow, and keep calmer. (2) You called for Evening; it descends; here it is: (3) a dim atmosphere envelops the city, (4) Bringing peace to some; to others anxiety. (5) While the vile multitude of mortals (6) under the whip of Pleasure, that merciless executioner, (7) go to gather remorse in the servile festival, (8) my Sorrow, give me your hand; come this way, (9) far from them. See the dead years lean (10) on the balconies of the sky, in old-fashioned dresses; (11) [see] Regret, smiling, emerge from the depths of the waters; (12) [see] the dying Sun go to sleep under an arch; (13) and like a long shroud trailing in the East, (14) hear, my darling, hear the soft Night who is walking.

1. PEACE, BE AT PEACE, O THOU MY HEAVINESS 1919

Peace, be at peace, O thou my heaviness,
Thou callèdst for the evening, lo! 'tis here,
The City wears a somber atmosphere
That brings repose to some, to some distress.
Now while the heedless throng make haste to press 5
Where pleasure drives them, ruthless charioteer,
To pluck the fruits of sick remorse and fear,
Come thou with me, and leave their fretfulness.
See how they hang from heaven's high balconies,
The old lost years in faded garments dressed,
And see Regret with faintly smiling mouth;
And while the dying sun sinks in the west,
Hear how, far off, Night walks with velvet tread,
And her long robe trails all about the south.

— Lord Alfred Douglas

2. INWARD CONVERSATION 1961

Be reasonable, my pain, and think with more detachment.
You asked to see the dusk; it descends; it is here:
A sheath of dark light robes the city,
To some bringing peace, to some the end of peace.

Now while the rotten herds of mankind, 5
Flogged by pleasure, that lyncher without touch,
Go picking remorse in their filthy holidays,
Let us join hands, my pain; come this way,

Far from them. Look at the dead years that lean on
The balconies of the sky, in their clothes long out of date; 10
The sense of loss that climbs from the deep waters with a smile;

The sun, nearly dead, that drops asleep beneath an arch;
And listen to the night, like a long shroud being dragged
Toward the east, my love, listen, the soft night is moving.

— Robert Bly

Calm down, my Sorrow, we must move with care.
You called for evening; it descends; it's here.
The town is coffined in its atmosphere,
bringing relief to some, to others care.

Now while the common multitude strips bare,   5
feels pleasure's cat o' nine tails on its back,
and fights off anguish at the great bazaar,
give me your hand, my Sorrow. Let's stand back;

back from these people! Look, the dead years dressed
in old clothes crowd the balconies of the sky.   10
Regret emerges smiling from the sea,

the sick sun slumbers underneath an arch,
and like a shroud strung out from east to west,
listen, my Dearest, hear the sweet night march!

—Robert Lowell

PARODY

In a **parody,** one writer imitates — and pokes fun at — another. Skillfully wrought, a parody can be a devastating form of literary criticism. Usually the parodist imitates the characteristic tone, form, language, and other elements of the original model, but sometimes applies them to a ludicrously uncharacteristic subject — as in E. B. White's parody of Walt Whitman, "A Classic Waits for Me" (page 276).

Rather than merely flinging abuse at another poet, the wise parodist imitates with understanding — perhaps with sympathy. The many crude parodies of T. S. Eliot's difficult poem *The Waste Land* show parodists mocking what they cannot fathom, with the result that, instead of illuminating the original, they belittle it (and themselves). Parody can be aimed at poems good or bad; yet there are poems of such splendor and dignity that no parodist seems able to touch them without looking like a small dog defiling a cathedral, and others so illiterate that parody would be squandered on them. In the following original by T. E. Brown, what failings does the parodist, J. A. Lindon, jump upon? (*God wot,* by the way, is an archaism for "God knows.")

T. E. Brown (1830–1897)	**J. A. Lindon** (b. 1914)
My Garden 1887	My Garden 1959
A garden is a lovesome thing,	A garden is a *lovesome* thing?
God wot!	What rot!
Rose plot,	Weed plot,
Fringed pool,	Scum pool,
Ferned grot —	Old pot, 5
The veriest school	Snail-shiny stool

Of peace; and yet the fool
Contends that God is not —
Not God! in gardens! when the eve
   is cool?
Nay, but I have a sign;
'Tis very sure God walks in mine.

In pieces; yet the fool
Contends that snails are not —
Not snails! in gardens! when the
   eve is cool?
Nay, but I see their trails!   10
'Tis very sure *my* garden's full of
   snails!

Hugh Kingsmill
[Hugh Kingsmill Lunn] (1889–1949)
WHAT, STILL ALIVE AT TWENTY-TWO   (about 1920)

What, still alive at twenty-two,
A clean, upstanding chap like you?
Sure, if your throat 'tis hard to slit,
Slit your girl's, and swing for it.

Like enough, you won't be glad   5
When they come to hang you, lad:
But bacon's not the only thing
That's cured by hanging from a string.

So, when the spilt ink of the night
Spreads o'er the blotting-pad of light,   10
Lads whose job is still to do
Shall whet their knives, and think of you.

QUESTIONS

1. A. E. Housman considered this the best of many parodies of his poetry. Read
   his poems in this book, particularly "Terence, this is stupid stuff" and "To an
   Athlete Dying Young" (pp. 353–355). What characteristics of theme, form,
   and language does Hugh Kingsmill's parody convey?
2. What does Kingsmill exaggerate?

Kenneth Koch (b. 1925)
MENDING SUMP   1960

"Hiram, I think the sump is backing up.
The bathroom floor boards for above two weeks
Have seemed soaked through. A little bird, I think,
Has wandered in the pipes, and all's gone wrong."
"Something there is that doesn't hump a sump,"   5
He said; and through his head she saw a cloud
That seemed to twinkle. "Hiram, well," she said,

"Smith is come home! I saw his face just now
While looking through your head. He's come to die
Or else to laugh, for hay is dried-up grass   10
When you're alone." He rose, and sniffed the air.
"We'd better leave him in the sump," he said.

QUESTIONS

1. What poet is the object of this parody? Which of his poems are echoed in it?
2. Koch gains humor by making outrageous statements in the tone and language of his original. Looking at other poems in this book by the poet being
   parodied, how would you describe their tone? Their language?
3. Suppose, instead of casting his parody into blank verse, Koch had written:

   "Hiram, the sump is backing up.
   The bathroom floor boards
   For above two weeks
   Have been soaking through. A little bird,
   I think, has wandered in
   The pipes, and all's gone wrong."

   Why would the biting edge of his parody have been blunted?
4. What, by the way, is a *sump*?

John Frederick Nims (b. 1914)

OLD BETHINKINGS OF A DAY OF "SHOWERS LIKELY"
AT BEANSEY RIDGE   1971

Half twice some ninety-odd and more spans back
    Love oncewhile came.
Sweet Pheena Mente, now seventy years en-graved, 's
    Lesswise the same.

How blithe we picknicked us 'mid showers, throughdrenched   5
    In ditch and field.
Howe'ersowise the sane folk, pointing, snicked
    Our "wig-pates reeled."

How blithe on Beansey Ridge, foam-yodelling scarp,
    We jumped at rope.   10
Old Romans near-entombed-us outgrowled, "They
    Should plotz, we hope."

Alas, 'tis Sooth a drear Hap smote us thwart;
    Gap-grinned to see:
I, old Plutt Hodd, being (year wise-way-like) five;   15
    She, eighty-three.

QUESTIONS

1. Of what poet's work is this a parody? (Beansey Ridge, by the way, is a place-
   name the poet actually employed.)

2. What features of the poet's style is Nims poking fun at? Compare the parody with poems by the poet in this book. Notice especially the poet's choice of words and arrangement of them. (Suggestion: You might find it helpful to translate some of Nims's lines into ordinary conversational English.)
3. What theme or subject matter usual to the poet's work does this parody echo?

E. B. White (b. 1899)
A Classic Waits for Me   1944

(With apologies to Walt Whitman, plus a trial
membership in the Classics Club)

A classic waits for me, it contains all, nothing is lacking,
Yet all were lacking if taste were lacking, or if the endorsement of the right
    man were lacking.
O clublife, and the pleasures of membership,
O volumes for sheer fascination unrivalled.
Into an armchair endlessly rocking,   5
Walter J. Black my president,
I, freely invited, cordially welcomed to membership,
My arm around John Kieran, Pearl S. Buck,
My taste in books guarded by the spirits of William Lyon Phelps, Hendrik
    Willem van Loon,
(From your memories, sad brothers, from the fitful risings and callings I
    heard),   10
I to the classics devoted, brother of rough mechanics, beauty-parlor tech-
    nicians, spot welders, radio-program directors
(It is not necessary to have a higher education to appreciate these books),
I, connoisseur of good reading, friend of connoisseurs of good reading ev-
    erywhere,
I, not obliged to take any specific number of books, free to reject any vol-
    ume, perfectly free to reject Montaigne, Erasmus, Milton,
I, in perfect health except for a slight cold, pressed for time, having only a
    few more years to live,   15
Now celebrate this opportunity.
Come, I will make the club indissoluble,
I will read the most splendid books the sun ever shone upon,
I will start divine magnetic groups,
    With the love of comrades,   20
    With the life-long love of distinguished
      committees.

I strike up for an Old Book.
Long the best-read figure in America, my dues paid, sitter in armchairs
    everywhere, wanderer in populous cities, weeping with Hecuba
    and with the late William Lyon Phelps,
Free to cancel my membership whenever I wish,
Turbulent, fleshy, sensible,   25

Never tiring of clublife,
Always ready to read another masterpiece provided it has the approval of
    my president, Walter J. Black,
Me imperturbe, standing at ease among writers,
Rais'd by a perfect mother and now belonging to a perfect book club,
Bearded, sunburnt, gray-neck'd, astigmatic,   30
Loving the masters and the masters only
(I am mad for them to be in contact with me),
My arm around Pearl S. Buck, only American woman to receive the Nobel
    Prize for Literature,
I celebrate this opportunity.
And I will not read a book nor the least part of a book but has the approval
    of the Committee,   35
For all is useless without that which you may guess at many times and not
    hit, that which they hinted at,
All is useless without readability.
By God! I will accept nothing which all cannot have their counterpart of
    on the same terms (89¢ for the Regular Edition or $1.39 for the De
    Luxe Edition, plus a few cents postage).
I will make inseparable readers with their arms around each other's necks,
    By the love of classics,   40
    By the manly love of classics.

A Classic Waits for Me. Advertisements for the Classics Club used to proclaim that its books were selected by a committee of the popular writers and interpreters of culture named in lines 8–9. 10. *your memories, sad brothers:* Phelps and van Loon had died shortly before White's satire was first printed in 1944. 23. *Hecuba:* in Homer's *Iliad*, the wife of Priam, defeated king of Troy, and mother of Hector, Trojan hero slain by Achilles. 28. *Me imperturbe:* Whitman's poem by this title begins, "Me imperturbe, standing at ease in Nature . . ." (The Latinate phrase could be roughly translated, "I, the unflappable.")

Questions

1. What is E. B. White making fun of, besides Walt Whitman's poetry? How timely does White's satire remain? (Have you noticed any recent book club ads?)
2. Compare White's opening lines with those of Whitman's "A Woman Waits for Me," a celebration of the joys of reproduction:

    A woman waits for me, she contains all, nothing is lacking,
    Yet all were lacking if sex were lacking, or if the
        moisture of the right man were lacking.

    In White's lines, how does the phrase *nothing is lacking* change in meaning? The phrase *the right man?*
3. What traits of Whitman's style does White imitate? (See other poems by Whitman in this book.)
4. The more you read of Whitman, the more you will appreciate White's parody. Look up "A Woman Waits for Me" in Whitman's *Leaves of Grass*. See also "Out of the Cradle Endlessly Rocking" and "Song of Myself." What further echoes of Whitman do you find in White's take-off? How closely does White remind you of Whitman's attitudes toward himself and toward the world?

EXPERIMENT: *Writing an Imitation or a Parody*

Write a poem in the manner of Emily Dickinson, William Carlos Williams, E. E. Cummings, or any other modern poet whose work interests you and which you feel able to imitate. Decide, before you start, whether to write a serious imitation (that could be slipped into the poet's *Collected Poems* without anyone being the wiser), or a humorous parody. Read all the poet's poems included in this book; perhaps you will find it helpful also to consult a larger selection or collection of the poet's work. It might be simplest to choose a particular poem as your model; but, if you like, you may echo any number of poems. Choose a model within the range of your own skill: to imitate a sonnet, for instance, you need to be able to rime and to write in meter. Probably, if your imitation is serious, and not a parody like E. B. White's parody of Whitman, it is a good idea to pick a subject or theme characteristic of the poet. This is a difficult project, but if you can do it even fairly well, you will know a great deal more about poetry and your poet.

17 Writing about Poems

Assignment: a paper about a poem. You can approach it as a grim duty, of course: any activity can so be regarded. For Don Juan, in Spanish legend, even the act of love became a chore. But the act of writing, like the act of love, is much easier if your feelings take part in it. Write about anything you dislike and don't understand, and you not only set yourself the labors of Hercules, but you guarantee your reader discouragingly hard labor, too.

To write about a poem informatively, you need first of all to experience it. It helps to live with the poem for as long as possible: there is little point in trying to encompass the poem in a ten-minute tour of inspection on the night before the paper falls due. However challenging, writing about poetry has immediate rewards, and to mention just one, the poem you spend time with and write about is going to mean much more to you than poems skimmed quickly ever do.

Most of the problems you will meet in writing about a poem will be the same ones you meet in writing about a play or a story: finding a topic, organizing your thoughts, writing, revising. For general advice on writing papers about any kind of literature, see the Appendix at the back of this book. There are, however, a few ways in which a poem requires a different approach. This chapter will deal briefly with some of them, and it will offer a few illustrations of papers that students have written. These papers may not be works of inimitable genius, but they are pretty good papers, the likes of which most students can write with a modest investment of time and care.

Briefer than most stories and most plays, lyric poems *look* easier to write about. They call, however, for your keenest attention. You may find that, before you can discuss a short poem, you will have to read it slowly and painstakingly, with your mind (like your pencil) sharp and ready. Unlike a play or a short story, a lyric poem tends to have very little plot, and perhaps you will find little to say about what happens in it. In order to understand a poem, you'll need to notice elements other than narrative: the connotations or suggestions of its words, surely, and the rhythm of phrases and lines. The subtleties of language, almost apart from story, are so essential to a poem (and so elusive) that Robert

Frost was moved to say, "Poetry is what gets lost in translation." Once in a while, of course, you'll read a story whose prose abounds in sounds, rhythms, figures of speech, imagery, and other elements you expect of poetry. Certain novels of Herman Melville and William Faulkner contain paragraphs that, if extracted, seem in themselves prose-poems—so lively are they in their word-play, so rich in metaphor. But such writing is exceptional, and the main business of most fiction is to get a story told. To take an extreme case of a fiction writer who didn't want his prose to sound poetic, Georges Simenon, best known for his mystery novels, said that whenever he noticed in his manuscript any word or phrase that called attention to itself, he struck it out. That method of writing would never do for a poet, who revels in words and phrases that fix themselves in memory. It is safe to say that, in order to write well about a poem, you have to read it carefully enough to remember at least part of it word for word.

Let's consider three commonly useful approaches to writing about poetry.

EXPLICATION

In an **explication** (literally, "an unfolding") of a poem, a writer explains the entire poem in detail, unraveling any particular complexities to be found in it. This method is a valuable one in approaching a lyric poem, especially if the poem is rich in complexities (or in suggestions worth rendering explicit). Most poems that you'll ever be asked to explicate are short enough to discuss thoroughly within a limited time; fully to explicate a long and involved work, such as John Milton's epic *Paradise Lost*, might require a lifetime. (To explicate a short passage of Milton's long poem would be a more usual course assignment.)

All the details or suggestions in a poem that a sensitive and intelligent reader might consider, the writer of an explication considers and tries to unfold. These might include allusions, the denotations or connotations of words, the possible meanings of symbols, the effects of certain sounds and rhythms and formal elements (rime schemes, for instance), the sense of any statements that contain irony, and other particulars. Not intent on ripping a poem to pieces, the author of a useful explication instead tries to show how each part contributes to the whole.

An explication is easy to organize. You can start with the first line of the poem and keep working straight on through. An explication should not be confused with a paraphrase. A paraphrase simply puts the words of the poem into other words; it is a sort of translation, useful in getting at the plain prose sense and therefore especially helpful in clarifying a poem's main theme. Perhaps in writing an explication you will wish to do some paraphrasing; but an explication (unlike a paraphrase) does not simply restate: it explains a poem, in great detail.

Here, for example, is a famous poem by Robert Frost, followed by a student's concise explication. (The assignment was to explain whatever in "Design" seemed most essential, in not more than 750 words.)

Robert Frost (1874–1963)

Design   1936

I found a dimpled spider, fat and white,
On a white heal-all, holding up a moth
Like a white piece of rigid satin cloth —
Assorted characters of death and blight
Mixed ready to begin the morning right,   5
Like the ingredients of a witches' broth —
A snow-drop spider, a flower like a froth,
And dead wings carried like a paper kite.

What had that flower to do with being white,
The wayside blue and innocent heal-all?   10
What brought the kindred spider to that height,
Then steered the white moth thither in the night?
What but design of darkness to appall? —
If design govern in a thing so small.

An Unfolding of Robert Frost's "Design"

Starting with the title, "Design," any reader of this poem will find it full of meaning. As Webster's New World Dictionary defines design, the word can denote among other things a plan, or "purpose; intention; aim." Some arguments for the existence of God (I remember from Sunday School) are based on the "argument from design": that because the world shows a systematic order, there must be a Designer who made it. But the word design can also mean "a secret or sinister scheme" -- such as we attribute to a "designing person." As we shall see, Frost's poem incorporates all of these meanings. His poem raises the question of whether there is a Designer, or an evil Designer, or no Designer at all.

Like many other sonnets, the poem is divided into two parts. The first eight lines draw a picture centering on the spider, who at first seems almost jolly. It is dimpled and fat like a baby, or Santa Claus. It stands on a wild flower whose name, heal-all, seems an irony: a heal-all is supposed to cure any disease, but it certainly has no power to restore life to the dead moth. (Later, in line ten, we learn that the heal-all used to be blue. Presumably it has died and become bleached-looking.) In this second line we discover, too, that the spider has hold of another creature. Right away we might feel sorry for the moth, were it not for the simile applied to it in line three: "Like a white piece of rigid satin cloth." Suddenly the moth becomes not a creature but a piece of fabric -- lifeless and dead -- and yet satin has connotations also beautiful. For me satin, used in rich ceremonial costumes such as coronation gowns and brides' dresses, has a formality and luxury about it. Besides, there is great accuracy in the word: the smooth and slightly plush surface of satin is like the powdersmooth surface of moths' wings. But this "cloth," rigid and white, could be the lining to Dracula's coffin. Like the spider, with its snow-drop-shaped body, the moth reminds us both of beauty and of grim death. Spider, flower, and moth are indeed "assorted characters."

In the fifth line an invisible hand enters. The characters are "mixed" like ingredients in an evil potion. Some force doing the mixing is behind the scene. The characters in themselves are innocent enough, but when brought together and concocted, their whiteness and look of rigor mortis are overwhelming. There is something diabolical in the spider's feast. The "morning right" echoes the word rite, a ritual -- in this case apparently a Black Mass or a Witches' Sabbath. The simile in line seven ("a flower like a froth") is more ambiguous and harder to describe. A froth is white, foamy, and delicate -- something found on a brook in the woods or on a beach after a wave recedes. However, in the natural world, froth also can be ugly: the foam on a dead dog's mouth. The dualism in nature -- its beauty and its horror -- is there in that one simile.

So far, the poem has portrayed a small, frozen scene, with the dimpled killer holding its victim as innocently as a boy holds a kite. Already, Frost has hinted that Nature may be, as Radcliffe Squires suggests, "nothing but an ash-white plain without love or faith or hope, where ignorant appetites cross by chance."[1] Now, in the last six lines of the sonnet, Frost comes out and directly states his theme. What else could bring these deathly pale, stiff things together "but design of darkness to appall?" The question is clearly rhetorical, meant to be answered, "Why, nothing but that, of course!" I take the next-to-last line to mean, "What except a design so dark and sinister that we're appalled by it." "Appall," by the way, is the second pun in the poem: it sounds like a pall or shroud. Steered carries the suggestion of a steering-wheel or rudder that some pilot had to control. Like the word brought, it implies that some Captain charted the paths of spider, heal-all, and moth, so that they arrived together.

Having suggested that the universe is in the hands of that sinister Captain (Fate? the Devil?), Frost adds a final note of doubt. The Bible tells us that "His eye is on the sparrow," but at the moment the poet doesn't seem sure. Maybe, he hints, when things in the universe drop below a certain size, they pass completely out of the Designer's notice. When creatures are that little, maybe He doesn't bother to govern them, but just lets them run wild. And possibly the same mindless chance is all that governs human lives. Maybe we're not even "sinners in the hands of an angry God,"[2] but are nothing but little dice being slung. And that -- because it is even more senseless -- is the worst suspicion of all.

1 The Major Themes of Robert Frost (Ann Arbor, Mich.: University of Michigan Press, 1963), p. 87.

2 Title of an early American sermon by Jonathan Edwards.

This excellent paper, while finding something worth unfolding in every line in Frost's poem, does so without seeming mechanical. Notice that, although the student proceeds through the poem from the title to the last line, she takes up points when necessary, in any sequence. In paragraph one, the writer looks ahead to the end of the poem and briefly states its main theme. (She does so in order to relate this theme to the poem's title.) In the second paragraph, she deals with the poem's *later* image of the heal-all, relating it to the first image. Along the way, she comments on the form of the poem ("Like many other sonnets"), on its similes and puns, its denotations and connotations.

Incidentally, this paper demonstrates good use of manuscript form. Each word in a quotation is reproduced faithfully. The student is within her rights to give Frost's *steered* a capital letter when beginning her own sentence with it. The critic she quotes (Radcliffe Squires) is identified in the essay and his book is given a footnote. Another footnote proves useful to give Jonathan Edwards credit for a memorable phrase. This paper demonstrates, too, how to make final corrections without retyping. In the last paragraph, notice how the student legibly added a word and neatly changed another word by crossing it out and writing a substitute above it. In her next-to-last sentence, the writer clearly transposes two letters with a handy mark (∩), deletes a word, and strikes out a superfluous letter.

It might seem that to work through a poem line by line is a lockstep task; and yet there can be high excitement in it. Randall Jarrell once wrote an explication of "Design" in which he managed to convey such excitement. In the following passage taken from it, see if you can sense the writer's joy in his work. (Don't, incidentally, feel obliged to compare the quality of your own insights with Jarrell's, nor the quality of your own prose. Be fair to yourself: unlike most students, Jarrell had the advantage of being an excellent poet and a gifted critic; besides, he had read and pondered Frost for years before he wrote his essay, and as a teacher he probably had taught "Design" many times.)

> Frost's details are so diabolically good that it seems criminal to leave some unremarked; but notice how *dimpled, fat,* and *white* (all but one; all but one) come from our regular description of any baby; notice how the *heal-all,* because of its name, is the one flower in all the world picked to be the altar for this Devil's Mass; notice how *holding up* the moth brings something ritual and hieratic, a ghostly, ghastly formality, to this priest and its sacrificial victim; notice how terrible to the fingers, how full of the stilling rigor of death, that *white piece of rigid satin cloth* is. And *assorted characters of death and blight* is, like so many things in this poem, sharply ambiguous: *a mixed bunch of actors* or *diverse representative signs.* The tone of the phrase *assorted characters of death and blight* is beautifully developed in the ironic Breakfast-Club-calisthenics, Radio-Kitchen heartiness of *mixed ready to begin the morning right* (which assures us, so unreassuringly, that this isn't any sort of Strindberg *Spook Sonata,* but hard fact), and con-

cludes in the *ingredients* of the witches' broth, giving the soup a sort of cuddly shimmer that the cauldron in *Macbeth* never had; the *broth*, even, is brought to life — we realize that witches' broth *is* broth, to be supped with a long spoon.[1]

Evidently, Jarrell's cultural interests are broad: ranging from August Strindberg's ground-breaking modern classic down to the Breakfast Club (a once-popular radio program that cheerfully exhorted its listeners to march around their tables). And yet breadth of knowledge, however much it deepens and enriches Jarrell's writing, isn't all that he brings to the reading of poetry. For him, an explication isn't a dull plod, but a voyage of discovery. His prose — full of figures of speech (*diabolically good, cuddly shimmer*) — conveys the apparent delight he takes in showing off his findings. Such a joy, of course, can't be acquired deliberately. But it can grow, the more you read and study poetry.

ANALYSIS

An **analysis** of a poem, like a news commentator's analysis of a crisis in the Middle East or a chemist's analysis of an unknown fluid, separates its subject into elements, as a means to understand that subject — to see what composes it. Usually, the writer of such an essay singles out one of those elements for attention: "Imagery of Light and Darkness in Frost's 'Design' "; "The Character of Satan in *Paradise Lost.*"

Like explication, analysis can be particularly useful in dealing with a short poem. Unlike explication (which inches through a poem line by line), analysis often suits a long poem too, because it allows the writer to discuss just one manageable element in the poem. A good analysis casts intense light upon a poem from one direction. If you care enough about a poem, and about some perspective on it — its theme, say, or its symbolism, or its singability — writing an analysis can enlighten and give pleasure.

In this book you probably have met a few brief analyses: the discussion of connotations in John Masefield's "Cargoes" (page 67), for instance, or the examination of symbols in T. S. Eliot's "The *Boston Evening Transcript*" (page 198). In fact, most of the discussions in this book are analytic. Temporarily, we have separated the whole art of poetry into elements such as tone, irony, literal meaning, suggestions, imagery, figures of speech, sound, rhythm, and so on. No element of a poem, of course, exists apart from all the other elements. Still, by taking a closer look at particular elements, one at a time, we see them more clearly and more easily study them.

---

[1] From *Poetry and the Age* (New York: Alfred A. Knopf, 1953).

Long analyses of metrical feet, rime schemes, and indentations tend to make ponderous reading: such formal and technical elements are perhaps the hardest to discuss engagingly. And yet formal analysis (at least a little of it) can be interesting and illuminating: it can measure the very pulsebeat of lines. If you do care about the technical side of poetry, then write about it, by all means. You will probably find it helpful to learn the terms for the various meters, stanzas, fixed forms, and other devices, so that you can summon them to your aid with confidence. Here is a short formal analysis of "Design" by a student who evidently cares for technicalities yet who manages not to be a bore in talking about them. Concentrating on the sonnet form of Frost's poem, the student actually casts light upon the poem in its entirety.

The Design of "Design"

For "Design," the sonnet form has at least two advantages. First, as in most strict *Italian* sonnets, the argument of the poem falls into two parts. In the octave Frost draws his pale still-life of spider, flower, and moth; then in the sestet he contemplates the meaning of it. The sestet deals with a more general idea: the possible existence of a vindictive deity who causes the spider to catch the moth, and no doubt also causes other suffering. Frost weaves his own little web. The unwary reader is led into the poem by its opening story, and pretty soon is struggling with more than he expected. Even the rime scheme, by the way, has something to do with the poem's meaning. The word white ends the first line of the sestet. The same sound is echoed in the rimes that follow. All in all, half the lines in the poem end in an "ite." It seems as if Frost places great weight on the whiteness of his little scene, for the riming words both introduce the term white and keep reminding us of it.

A sonnet has a familiar design, and that is its second big advantage to this particular poem. In a way, writing "Design" as a sonnet almost seems a foxy joke. (I can just imagine Frost chuckling to himself, wondering if anyone will get it.) A sonnet, being a classical form, is an orderly world with certain laws in it. There is ready-made irony in its containing a meditation on whether there is any order in the universe at large. Obviously there's design in back of the poem, but is there any design to insect life, or human life? Whether or not the poet can answer this question (and it seems he can't), at least he discovers an order *while* writing the poem. Actually, that is just what Frost said a poet achieves: "a momentary stay against confusion."[1]

Although design clearly governs in this poem -- in "this thing so small" -- the design isn't entirely predictable. The poem starts out as an Italian sonnet, with just two riming sounds; then (unlike an Italian sonnet) it keeps the "ite" rimes going. It ends in a couplet, like a Shakespearean sonnet. From these unexpected departures from the pattern of the Italian sonnet announced in the opening lines, I get the impression that Frost's poem is somewhat like the larger universe. It looks perfectly orderly, until you notice the small details in it.

[1]"The Figure a Poem Makes," preface to Complete Poems of Robert Frost (New York: Holt, Rinehart and Winston, 1949), p. vi.

COMPARISON AND CONTRAST

To write a **comparison** of two poems, you place them side by side and point out their likenesses; to write a **contrast,** you point out their differences. If you wish, you can combine the two methods in the same paper. For example, even though you may emphasize similarities you may also call attention to differences, or vice versa.

Such a paper makes most sense if you pair two poems that have much in common. It would be possible to compare Ern Alpaugh and Dewey G. Pell's trivial pop song lyric "Swinging Chick" with Milton's profound "Lycidas," but comparison would be difficult, perhaps futile. Though both poems are in English, the two seem hopelessly remote from each other in diction, in tone, in complexity, and in worth.

Having found, however, a couple of poems that throw light on each other, you then go on in your paper to show further, unsuspected resemblances—not just the ones that are obvious (" 'Design' and 'Wing-Spread' are both about bugs"). The interesting resemblances are ones that take thinking to discover. Similarly, you may want to show noteworthy differences—besides those your reader will see without any help.

In comparing two poems, you may be tempted to discuss one of them and be done with it, then spend the latter half of your paper discussing the other. This simple way of organizing an essay can be dangerous if it leads you to keep the two poems in total isolation from each other. The whole idea of such an assignment, of course, is to get you to do some comparing. There is nothing wrong in discussing all of poem A first, then discussing poem B—*if* in discussing B you keep looking back at A. Another procedure is to keep comparing the two poems all the way through your paper—dealing first, let's say, with their themes; then with their metaphors; and finally, with their respective merits.

More often than not, a comparison is an analysis: a study of a theme common to two poems, for instance; or of two poets' similar fondness for the myth of Eden. But you also can evaluate poems by comparing and contrasting them: placing them side by side in order to decide which poet deserves the brighter laurels. Here, for example, is a paper that considers "Design" and "Wing-Spread," a poem of Abbie Huston Evans (first printed in 1938, two years later than Frost's poem). By comparing and contrasting the two poems for (1) their language and (2) their themes, this student shows us reasons for his evaluation.

"Wing-Spread" Does a Dip

The midge spins out to safety

Through the spider's rope;

But the moth, less lucky,

Has to grope.

Mired in glue-like cable   5

See him foundered swing

By the gap he opened

With his wing,

Dusty web enlacing

All that blue and beryl.   10

In a netted universe

Wing-spread is peril.

-- Abbie Huston Evans

"Wing-Spread," quoted above, is a good poem, but it is not in the same class with "Design." Both poets show us a murderous spider and an unlucky moth, but there are two reasons for Robert Frost's superiority. One is his more suggestive use of language, the other is his more memorable theme.

Let's start with language. "Design" is full of words and phrases rich in suggestions. "Wing-Spread," by comparison, contains few. To take just one example, Frost's "dimpled spider, fat and white" is certainly a more suggestive description. Actually, Evans doesn't describe her spider; she just says, "the spider's rope." (I have to hand Evans the palm for showing us the spider and moth in action. In Frost's view, they are dead and petrified -- but I guess that is the impression he is after.) In "Design," the spider's dimples show that it is like a chubby little kid, who further turns out to be a kite-flier. This seems an odd, almost freaky way to look at a spider. I find it more refreshing than Evans's view (although I like her word cable, suggesting that the spider's web is a kind of suspension bridge). Frost's word-choice -- his harping on white -- paints a more striking scene than Evans's slightly vague "All that blue and beryl." Except for her personification of the moth in her second stanza, Evans doesn't go in for any figures of speech, and even that one isn't a clear personification -- she simply gives the moth a sex by referring to it as "him." Frost's striking metaphors, similes, and even puns (right, appall) show him, as usual, to be a master of figures of speech. He calls the moth's wings "satin cloth" and "a paper kite"; Evans just refers in line 8 to a moth's wing. As far as the language of the two poems goes, you might as well compare a vase ~~full of~~ _brimming_ with flowers and a single flower stuck in a vase. (That is a poor metaphor, since Frost's poem contains only one flower, but I hope you will know what I mean.)

In fairness to Evans, I would say that she picks a pretty good solitary flower. And her poem has powerful sounds: short lines with the riming words coming at us again and again very frequently. In theme, however, "Wing-Spread" seems much more narrow than "Design." The first time I read Evans's poem all I felt was: Ho hum, the moth too was wide and got stuck. The second time I read it, I figured that she is saying something with a universal application. This _message_ comes out in line 11, in "a netted universe." That is the most interesting phrase in her poem, one that you can think about. <u>Netted</u> makes me imagine the universe as being full of nets rigged by someone who is fishing for us. Maybe, like Frost, Evans sees an evil plan operating. She does not, though, investigate it. She says that the midge escapes because it is tiny. On the other hand, things with wide wing-spreads get stuck. Her theme as I read it is, "Be small and inconspicuous if you want to survive," or maybe, "Isn't it too bad that in this world the big beautiful types crack up and die, while the miserable little puny punks keep sailing?" Now, that is a valuable idea. I have often thought that very same thing myself. But Frost's closing note ("If design govern in a thing so small") is really devastating, because it raises a huge uncertainty. "Wing-Spread" leaves us with not much besides a moth stuck in a web, and a moral. In both language and theme, "Design" climbs to a higher altitude.

HOW TO QUOTE A POEM

Preparing to discuss a short poem, it is a good idea to emulate the student who wrote on "Wing-Spread" and to quote the whole text of the poem at the beginning of your paper, with its lines numbered. Then you can refer to it with ease, and your instructor, without having to juggle a book, can follow you.

Quoted to illustrate some point, memorable lines can add interest to your paper, and good commentators on poetry tend to be apt quoters, helping their readers to experience a word, a phrase, a line, or a passage that otherwise might be neglected. However, to quote from poetry is slightly more awkward than to quote from prose. There are lines to think about — important and meaningful units whose shape you will need to preserve. If you are quoting more than a couple of lines, it is good policy to arrange your quotation just as its lines occur in the poem, white space and all:

```
At the outset, the poet tells us of his discovery of

            a dimpled spider, fat and white,
    On a white heal-all, holding up a moth
    Like a white piece of rigid satin cloth --

and implies that the small killer is both childlike and sinister.
```

But if you are quoting less than two lines of verse, it would seem wasteful of paper to write:

```
The color white preoccupies Frost.  The spider is

                    fat and white,
        On a white heal-all

and even the victim moth is pale, too.
```

In such a case, it saves space to transform Frost's line arrangement into prose:

```
The color white preoccupies Frost.  The spider is "fat and white, /

On a white heal-all" -- and even the victim moth is pale, too.
```

Here, a diagonal (/) indicates the writer's respect for where the poet's lines begin and end. Some writers prefer to note line-breaks without diagonals, just by keeping the initial capital letter of a line (if there is any): "fat and white, On a white heal-all. . . ." Incidentally, the ellipsis (. . .) in that last remark indicates that words are omitted from the end of Frost's sentence; the fourth dot is a period. Some writers — meticulous souls — also stick in an ellipsis at the *beginning* of a quotation, if they're leaving out words from the beginning of a sentence in the original:

The color white preoccupies Frost in his description of the spider

" . . .fat and white, / On a white heal-all. . . ."

Surely there's no need for an initial ellipsis, though, if you begin quoting at the beginning of a sentence. No need for a final ellipsis, either, if your quotation goes right to the end of a sentence in the original. If it is obvious that only a phrase is being quoted, no need for an ellipsis in any case:

The speaker says he "found a dimpled spider" and he goes on to

portray it as a kite-flying boy.

If you leave out whole lines, indicate the omission by an ellipsis all by itself on a line:

The midge spins out to safety
Through the spider's rope;
        . . .
In a netted universe
Wing-spread is peril.

BEFORE YOU BEGIN

Ready at last to write, you will have spent considerable time in reading, thinking, and feeling. After having chosen your topic, you probably will have taken a further look at the poem or poems you have picked, letting further thoughts and feelings come to you. The quality of your paper will depend, above all, upon the quality of your readiness to write.

Exploring a poem, a sensitive writer handles it with care and affection as though it were a living animal, and, done with it, leaves it still alive. The unfeeling writer, on the other hand, disassembles the poem in a dull, mechanical way, like someone with a blunt ax filling an order for one horse-skeleton. Again, to write well is a matter of engaging your feelings. Writing to a deadline, on an assigned topic, you easily can sink into a drab, workaday style, especially if you regard the poet as some uninspired builder of chicken-coops who hammers themes and images into place, and then slaps the whole thing with a coat of words. Certain expressions, if you lean on them habitually, may tempt you to think of the poet in that way. Here, for instance, is a discussion — by a plodding writer — of Robert Frost's poem.

The symbols Frost uses in "Design" are very successful. Frost

makes the spider stand for Nature. He wants us to see Nature as

```
blind and cruel.  He also employs good sounds.  He uses a lot of

i's because he is trying to make you think of falling rain.
```

(Underscored words are worth questioning.) What's wrong with that comment? While understandable, the words *uses* and *employs* seem to lead the writer to see Frost only as a conscious tool-manipulator. To be sure, Frost in a sense "uses" symbols, but did he grab hold of them and lay them into his poem? For all we know, perhaps the symbols arrived quite unbidden, and used the poet. To write a good poem, Frost maintained, a poet himself has to be surprised. (How, by the way, can we hope to know what a poet *wants* to do? And there isn't much point in saying that the poet is *trying to* do something. He has already done it, if he has written a good poem.) At least, it is likely that Frost didn't plan to fulfill a certain quota of *i*-sounds. Writing his poem, not by following a blueprint but probably by bringing it slowly to the surface of his mind (like Elizabeth Bishop's hooked fish), Frost no doubt had enough to do without trying to engineer the reactions of his possible audience. Like all true symbols, Frost's spider doesn't *stand for* anything. The writer would be closer to the truth to say that the spider *suggests* or *reminds us* of Nature, or of certain forces in the natural world. (Symbols just hint, they don't indicate.)

After the student discussed the paper in a conference, he rewrote the first two sentences like this:

```
The symbols in Frost's "Design" are highly effective.  The

spider, for instance, suggests the blindness and cruelty of Nature.

Frost's word-sounds, too, are part of the meaning of his poem, for

the i's remind the reader of falling rain.
```

Not every reader of "Design" will hear rain falling, but the student's revision probably comes closer to describing the experience of the poem most of us know.

In writing about poetry, an occasional note of self-doubt can be useful: now and then a *perhaps* or a *possibly*, an *it seems* or a modest *I suppose*. Such expressions may seem timid shilly-shallying, but at least they keep the writer from thinking, "I know all there is to know about this poem."

Facing the showdown with your empty sheaf of paper, however, you can't worry forever about your critical vocabulary. To do so is to risk the fate of the centipede in a bit of comic verse, who was running along efficiently until someone asked, "Pray, which leg comes after which?," whereupon "He lay distracted in a ditch / Considering how to run." It is a safe bet that your instructor is human. Your main task as a writer is to communicate to another human being your sensitive reading of a poem.

TOPICS FOR WRITING

1. Write a concise *explication* of a short poem of your choice, or one suggested by your instructor. In a paper this brief, probably you won't have room to explain everything in the poem; explain what you think most needs explaining. (An illustration of one such explication appears on page 281.)
2. Write an *analysis* of a short poem, first deciding which one of its elements to deal with. (An illustration of such an analysis appears on page 286.) For examples, here are a few specific topics:

   "Language of the Street: What It Contributes to Dylan's 'Subterranean Homesick Blues' "

   "Kinds of Irony in Hardy's 'The Workbox' "

   "The Attitude of the Speaker in Marvell's 'To His Coy Mistress' "

   "Folk Ballad Traits in Randall's 'Ballad of Birmingham' "

   "An Extended Metaphor in Levertov's 'Ways of Conquest' " (Explain the one main comparison that the poem makes and show how the whole poem makes it. Other likely possibilities for a paper on extended metaphor: Rich's "Diving into the Wreck," Dickinson's "Because I could not stop for Death.")

   "What the Skunks Mean in Lowell's 'Skunk Hour' "

   "The Rhythms of Plath's 'Daddy' "

   (To locate any of these poems, see the Index of Authors, Titles, and Quotations at the back of this book.)
3. Select a poem in which the main speaker is a character who for any reason interests you. You might consider, for instance, Betjeman's "In Westminster Abbey," Browning's "My Last Duchess" or "Soliloquy of the Spanish Cloister," Eliot's "Love Song of J. Alfred Prufrock," Frost's "Witch of Coös," or Jarrell's "Woman at the Washington Zoo." Then write a brief profile of this character, drawing only on what the poem tells you (or reveals). What is the character's approximate age? Situation in life? Attitude toward self? Attitude toward others? General personality? Do you find this character admirable?
4. Although each of these poems tells a story, what happens in the poem isn't necessarily obvious: Cummings's "anyone lived in a pretty how town," Eliot's "Love Song of J. Alfred Prufrock," Lawrence's "A Youth Mowing," Stafford's "At the Klamath Berry Festival," Winter's "At the San Francisco Airport," James Wright's "A Blessing." Choose one of these poems and in a paragraph sum up what you think happens in it. Then in a second paragraph ask yourself: what, *besides* the element of story, did you consider in order to understand the poem?
5. Think of someone you know (or someone you can imagine) whose attitude toward poetry in general is dislike. Suggest a particular poem for that person to read—a poem that you personally like—and, addressing your skeptical reader, point out whatever you find to enjoy in it, that you think the skeptic just might enjoy too.

1. Write an explication of a poem short enough for you to work through line by line—for instance, Judith Wright's "Woman to Man" or "Woman to Child," or Williams's "Spring and All," or a sonnet. As though offering the benefit of your reading experience to a friend who hadn't read the poem before, try to point out all the leading difficulties you encountered in your own reading, and set forth in detail your understanding of any lines that contain such difficulties.

2. Write an explication of a longer poem—for instance, Eliot's "Rhapsody on a Windy Night," Frost's "Witch of Coös," Hardy's "Convergence of the Twain," or Rich's "Diving into the Wreck." Although you will not be able to go through every line of the poem, explain what you think most needs explaining.

3. In this book, you will find six to ten poems by each of these poets: Blake, Cummings, Dickinson, Donne, Frost, Hardy, Housman, Keats, Roethke, Shakespeare, Stevens, Whitman, William Carlos Williams, Wordsworth, and Yeats; and multiple selections for many more. (See Index of Authors, Titles, and Quotations.) After you have read a few specimens of the work of a poet who interests you, write an analysis of *more than one* of the poet's poems. To do this, you will need to select just one characteristic theme (or other element) to deal with—something typical of the poet's work, not found only in a single poem. Here are a few specific topics for such an analysis:

   "What Angers William Blake? A Look at Three Poems of Protest"

   "Elements of Song in Lyrics of Emily Dickinson"

   "The Humor of Robert Frost"

   "John Keats's Sensuous Imagery"

   "The Vocabulary of Music in Poems of Wallace Stevens"

   "Non-free Verse: Patterns of Sound in Three Poems of William Carlos Williams"

   "The Moment of Illumination in Elizabeth Bishop's 'Fish,' 'Filling Station,' and 'Five Flights Up' "

   "Yeats as a Poet of Love"

4. Compare and contrast two poems in order to evaluate them: which is more satisfying and effective poetry? To make a meaningful comparison, be sure to choose two poems that genuinely have much in common: perhaps a similar theme or subject. (For an illustration of such a paper, see the one given in this chapter. For suggestions of poems to compare, see the Anthology.)

5. Evaluate by the method of comparison two different versions of a poem: early and late drafts, perhaps, or two translations from another language. For parallel versions to work on, see Chapter Sixteen, "Alternatives."

6. If the previous topic appeals to you, consider this. In 1912, twenty-four years before he printed "Design," Robert Frost sent a correspondent this early version:

   IN WHITE

   A dented spider like a snow drop white
   On a white Heal-all, holding up a moth
   Like a white piece of lifeless satin cloth—
   Saw ever curious eye so strange a sight?—

Portent in little, assorted death and blight   5
Like ingredients of a witches' broth?—
The beady spider, the flower like a froth,
And the moth carried like a paper kite.

What had that flower to do with being white,
The blue prunella every child's delight.   10
What brought the kindred spider to that height?
(Make we no thesis of the miller's plight.)
What but design of darkness and of night?
Design, design! Do I use the word aright?

Compare "In White" with "Design." In what respects is the finished poem superior?

TOPICS FOR LONG PAPERS (1,500 WORDS OR MORE)

1. Write a line-by-line explication of a poem rich in matters to explain, or a longer poem that offers ample difficulty. While relatively short, Donne's "Valediction: Forbidding Mourning" or Hopkins's "The Windhover" are poems that will take a good bit of time to explicate; but even a short, apparently simple poem such as Frost's "Stopping by Woods on a Snowy Evening" can provide more than enough to explicate thoughtfully in a longer paper.
2. Write an analysis of the work of one poet (as suggested above, in the third topic for more extensive papers) in which you go beyond this book to read an entire collection of that poet's work.
3. Write an analysis of a certain theme (or other element) that you find in the work of two or more poets. It is probable that in your conclusion you will want to set the poets' work side by side, comparing or contrasting it, and perhaps making some evaluation. Sample topics:

"The Myth of Eden as Interpreted by James Dickey, Theodore Roethke, and Gary Snyder"

"What It Is to Be a Woman: The Special Knowledge of Sylvia Plath and Judith Wright"

"Language of Science in Some Poems of Eberhart, Merrill, and Ammons"

18 What Is Poetry?

Archibald MacLeish (b. 1892)

ARS POETICA   1926

A poem should be palpable and mute
As a globed fruit,

Dumb
As old medallions to the thumb,

Silent as the sleeve-worn stone   5
Of casement ledges where the moss has grown —

A poem should be wordless
As the flight of birds.

A poem should be motionless in time
As the moon climbs,   10

Leaving, as the moon releases
Twig by twig the night-entangled trees,

Leaving, as the moon behind the winter leaves,
Memory by memory the mind —

A poem should be motionless in time   15
As the moon climbs.

A poem should be equal to:
Not true.

For all the history of grief
An empty doorway and a maple leaf.   20

For love
The leaning grasses and two lights above the sea —

A poem should not mean
But be.

    What is poetry? By now, perhaps, you have formed your own idea, whether or not you feel able to define it. Just in case further efforts at definition can be useful, here are a few memorable ones (including, for a second look, some given earlier):

> the art of uniting pleasure with truth by calling imagination to the help of reason.
>
> —Samuel Johnson

> the imaginative expression of strong feeling, usually rhythmical . . . the spontaneous overflow of powerful feelings recollected in tranquility.
>
> —William Wordsworth

> the best words in the best order.
>
> —Samuel Taylor Coleridge

> musical Thought.
>
> —Thomas Carlyle

> If I read a book and it makes my whole body so cold no fire can ever warm me, I know that it is poetry. If I feel physically as if the top of my head were taken off, I know that it is poetry. Is there any other way?
>
> —Emily Dickinson

> speech framed . . . to be heard for its own sake and interest even over and above its interest of meaning.
>
> —Gerard Manley Hopkins

> a revelation in words by means of the words.
>
> —Wallace Stevens

> not the assertion that something is true, but the making of that truth more fully real to us.
>
> —T. S. Eliot

> the clear expression of mixed feelings.
>
> —W. H. Auden

A poem differs from most prose in several ways. For one, both writer and reader tend to regard it differently. The poet's attitude is something like this: I offer this piece of writing to be read not as prose but as a poem — that is, more perceptively, thoughtfully, and considerately, with more attention to sounds and connotations. This is a great deal to expect, but in return, the reader, too, has a right to certain expectations. Approaching the poem in the anticipation of out-of-the-ordinary knowledge and pleasure, the reader assumes that the poet may use certain enjoyable devices not available to prose: rime, alliteration, meter, and rhythms — definite, various, or emphatic. (The poet may not *always* choose to employ these things.) The reader expects the poet to make greater use, perhaps, of resources of meaning such as figurative language, allusion, symbol, and imagery. As readers of prose we might seek no more than meaning: no more than what could be paraphrased without serious loss. Meeting any figurative language or graceful turns of word order, we think them pleasant extras. But in poetry all these "extras" matter as much as the paraphraseable content, if not more. For, when we finish reading a good poem, we cannot explain precisely to ourselves of what we have experienced — without repeating, word for word, the language of the poem itself.

It is doubtful that anyone can draw an immovable boundary between poetry and prose, nor does such an attempt seem necessary. Certain prose needs only to be arranged in lines to be seen as poetry — especially prose that conveys strong emotion in vivid, physical imagery and in terse, figurative, rhythmical language. Even in translation the words of Chief Joseph of the Nez Percé tribe, at the moment of his surrender to the U.S. Army in 1877, still move us and are memorable:

> Hear me, my warriors, my heart is sick and sad:
> Our chiefs are killed,
> The old men all are dead,
> It is cold and we have no blankets.
>
> The little children freeze to death.
>
> Hear me, my warriors, my heart is sick and sad:
> From where the sun now stands I will fight no more forever.

It may be that a poem can point beyond words to something still more essential. Language has its limits, and probably Edgar Allan Poe was the only poet ever to claim he could always find words for whatever he wished to express. For, of all a human being can experience and imagine, words say only part. "Human speech," said Flaubert, who strove after the best of it, "is like a cracked kettle on which we hammer out tunes to make bears dance, when what we long for is the compassion of the stars."

Like Yeats's chestnut-tree in "Among School Children" (which when asked whether it is leaf, blossom, or bole, has no answer), a poem is to be seen not as a confederation of form, rime, image, metaphor, tone, and theme, but as a whole. We study a poem one element at a time because the intellect best comprehends what it can separate. But only our total attention, involving the participation of our blood and marrow, can see all elements in a poem fused, all dancing together. Yeats knew how to make poems and how to read them:

> God guard me from those thoughts men think
> In the mind alone;
> He that sings a lasting song
> Thinks in a marrow-bone.

Throughout this book, we have been working on the assumption that the patient and conscious explication of poems will sharpen unconscious perceptions. We can only hope that it will; the final test lies in whether you care to go on by yourself, reading other poems, finding in them pleasure and enlightenment. Pedagogy must have a stop; so must the viewing of poems as if their elements fell into chapters. For the total experience of reading a poem surpasses the mind's categories. The wind in the grass, says a proverb, cannot be taken into the house.

Anthology

Sit a while dear son,
Here are biscuits to eat and here is milk to drink,
But as soon as you sleep and renew yourself in sweet clothes,
I kiss you with a good-by kiss and open the gates for your egress hence.

Long enough have you dream'd contemptible dreams,
Now I wash the gum from your eyes,
You must habit yourself to the dazzle of the light and of every moment of
   your life.

Long have you timidly waded holding a plank by the shore,
Now I will you to be a bold swimmer,
To jump off in the midst of the sea, rise again, nod to me, shout, and
   laughingly dash with your hair.

—Walt Whitman, "Song of Myself"

Anonymous (traditional Scottish ballad)

EDWARD

"Why dois your brand° sae° drap wi' bluid,   *sword; so*
    Edward, Edward?
Why dois your brand sae drap wi' bluid?
    And why sae sad gang° yee, O?"   *go*
"O, I hae killed my hauke sae guid,   5
    Mither, mither,
O, I hae killed my hauke sae guid,
    And I had nae mair bot° hee, O."   *but*

"Your haukis bluid was nevir sae reid,
    Edward, Edward,   10
Your haukis bluid was nevir sae reid,
    My deir son I tell thee, O."
"O, I hae killed my reid-roan steid,
    Mither, mither,
O, I hae killed my reid-roan steid,   15
    That erst° was sa fair and frie°, O."   *once; free*

"Your steid was auld, and ye hae gat mair,
    Edward, Edward,
Your steid was auld, and ye hae gat mair,
    Sum other dule° ye drie°, O."   *sorrow; suffer* 20
"O, I hae killed my fadir deir,
    Mither, mither,
O, I hae killed my fadir deir,
    Alas, and wae° is mee, O!"   *woe*

"And whatten penance wul ye drie for that,   25
    Edward, Edward?
And whatten penance will ye drie for that?
    My deir son, now tell me, O."
"Ile set my feit in yonder boat,
    Mither, mither,   30
Ile set my feit in yonder boat,
    And Ile fare ovir the sea, O."

"And what wul ye doe wi' your towirs and your ha'°,   *hall*
    Edward, Edward,
And what wul ye doe wi' your towirs and your ha',   35
    That were sae fair to see, O?"
"Ile let thame stand tul they doun fa',
    Mither, mither,
Ile let thame stand tul they doun fa',
    For here nevir mair maun° I bee, O."   *must* 40

"And what wul ye leive to your bairns° and your wife,   *children*
    Edward, Edward?

And what wul ye leive to your bairns and your wife,
   When ye gang ovir the sea, O?"
"The warldis° room, late° them beg thrae° life,   *world's; let; through*   45
   Mither, mither
The warldis room, late them beg thrae life,
   For thame nevir mair wul I see, O."

"And what wul ye leive to your ain° mither deir,   *own*
   Edward, Edward?   50
And what wul ye leive to your ain mither deir?
   My deir son, now tell me, O."
"The curse of hell frae me sall ye beir,
   Mither, mither,
The curse of hell frae me sall ye beir,   55
   Sic° counseils° ye gave to me, O."   *such; counsel*

Anonymous (traditional Scottish ballad)

Sir Patrick Spence

The king sits in Dumferling toune,
   Drinking the blude-reid wine:
"O whar will I get guid sailor
   To sail this schip of mine?"

Up and spak an eldern knicht,   5
   Sat at the kings richt kne:
"Sir Patrick Spence is the best sailor
   That sails upon the se."

The king has written a braid letter,
   And signed it wi' his hand,   10
And sent it to Sir Patrick Spence,
   Was walking on the sand.

The first line that Sir Patrick red,
   A loud lauch lauchèd he;
The next line that Sir Patrick red,   15
   The teir blinded his ee.

"O wha° is this has don this deid,   *who*
   This ill deid don to me,
To send me out this time o' the yeir,
   To sail upon the se!   20

"Mak haste, mak haste, my mirry men all,
   Our guid schip sails the morne."
"O say na sae°, my master deir,   *so*
   For I feir a deadlie storme.

"Late late yestreen I saw the new moone,   25
    Wi' the auld moone in hir arme,
And I feir, I feir, my deir master,
    That we will cum to harme."

O our Scots nobles wer richt laith°   *loath*
    To weet° their cork-heild schoone°;   *wet; shoes*   30
Bot lang owre° a' the play wer playd,   *before*
    Their hats they swam aboone°.   *above (their heads)*

O lang, lang may their ladies sit,
    Wi' their fans into their hand,
Or ere° they se Sir Patrick Spence   *long before*   35
    Cum sailing to the land.

O lang, lang may the ladies stand,
    Wi' their gold kems° in their hair,   *combs*
Waiting for their ain° deir lords,   *own*
    For they'll se thame na mair.   40

Haf owre°, haf owre to Aberdour,   *halfway over*
    It's fiftie fadom deip,
And thair lies guid Sir Patrick Spence,
    Wi' the Scots lords at his feit.

SIR PATRICK SPENCE. 9. *braid:* Broad, but broad in what sense? Among guesses are *plain-spoken, official,* and *on wide paper.*

Anonymous (traditional English ballad)

THE THREE RAVENS

There were three ravens sat on a tree,
    Down a down, hay down, hay down,
There were three ravens sat on a tree,
    With a down,
There were three ravens sat on a tree,   5
They were as black as they might be.
    With a down derry, derry, derry, down, down.

The one of them said to his mate,
"Where shall we our breakfast take?"

"Down in yonder greene field,   10
There lies a knight slain under his shield.

"His hounds they lie down at his feet,
So well they can their master keep.

"His hawks they fly so eagerly,
There's no fowl dare him come nigh."   15

Down there comes a fallow doe,
As great with young as she might go.

She lift up his bloody head,
And kist his wounds that were so red.

She got him up upon her back,   20
And carried him to earthen lake°.   *the grave*

She buried him before the prime,
She was dead herself ere evensong time.

God send every gentleman
Such hawks, such hounds, and such a leman°.   *lover* 25

THE THREE RAVENS. The lines of refrain are repeated in each stanza. "Perhaps in the folk
mind the doe is the form the soul of a human mistress, now dead, has taken," Albert B.
Friedman has suggested (in *The Viking Book of Folk Ballads*). "Most probably the knight's
beloved was understood to be an enchanted woman who was metamorphosed at certain
times into an animal." 22–23. *prime, evensong:* two of the canonical hours set aside for
prayer and worship. Prime is at dawn, evensong at dusk.

Anonymous (traditional Scottish ballad)

THE TWA CORBIES

As I was walking all alane,
I heard twa corbies° making a mane°;   *ravens; moan*
The tane° unto the t'other say,   *one*
"Where sall we gang° and dine today?"   *go*

"In behint yon auld fail dyke°,   *turf wall* 5
I wot° there lies a new slain knight;   *know*
And naebody kens° that he lies there,   *knows*
But his hawk, his hound, and lady fair.

"His hound is to the hunting gane,
His hawk to fetch the wild-fowl hame,   10
His lady's ta'en another mate,
So we may mak our dinner sweet.

"Ye'll sit on his white hause-bane°,   *neck bone*
And I'll pike out his bonny blue een;
Wi' ae° lock o' his gowden hair   *one* 15
We'll theek° our nest when it grows bare.   *thatch*

"Mony a one for him makes mane,
But nane sall ken where he is gane;
O'er his white banes, when they are bare,
The wind sall blaw for evermair."   20

THE TWA CORBIES. Sir Walter Scott, the first to print this ballad in his *Minstrelsy of the
Scottish Border* (1802–1803), calls it "rather a counterpart than a copy" of "The Three
Ravens." M. J. C. Hodgart and other scholars think he may have written most of it himself.

COMPARE:

"The Three Ravens" and "The Twa Corbies" with "All in green went my love riding" by E. E. Cummings (page 323).

Anonymous (English song)

WESTERN WIND   (about 1500)

Western wind, when wilt thou blow,
The° small rain down can rain?   *(so that) the*
Christ, if my love were in my arms,
And I in my bed again!

James Agee (1909–1955)

SUNDAY: OUTSKIRTS OF KNOXVILLE, TENNESSEE   1937

There, in the earliest and chary spring, the dogwood flowers.

Unharnessed in the friendly sunday air
By the red brambles, on the river bluffs,
Clerks and their choices pair.

Thrive by, not near, masked all away by shrub and juniper,   5
The ford v eight, racing the chevrolet.

They can not trouble her:

Her breasts, helped open from the afforded lace,
Lie like a peaceful lake;
And on his mouth she breaks her gentleness: 10

Oh, wave them awake!

They are not of the birds. Such innocence
Brings us whole to break us only.
Theirs are not happy words.

We that are human cannot hope.   15
Our tenderest joys oblige us most.
No chain so cuts the bone; and sweetest silk most shrewdly strangles.

How this must end, that now please love were ended,
In kitchens, bedfights, silences, women's-pages,
Sickness of heart before goldlettered doors,   20
Stale flesh, hard collars, agony in antiseptic corridors,
Spankings, remonstrances, fishing trips, orange juice,
Policies, incapacities, a chevrolet,

Scorn of their children, kind contempt exchanged,
Recalls, tears, second honeymoons, pity,   25
Shouted corrections of missed syllables,
Hot water bags, gallstones, falls down stairs,
Stammerings, soft foods, confusion of personalities,
Oldfashioned christmases, suspicions of theft,
Arrangements with morticians taken care of by sons in law,   30
Small rooms beneath the gables of brick bungalows,
The tumbler smashed, the glance between daughter and husband,
The empty body in the lonely bed
And, in the empty concrete porch, blown ash
Grandchildren wandering the betraying sun   35

Now, on the winsome crumbling shelves of the horror
God show, God blind these children!

Maya Angelou (b. 1928)

HARLEM HOPSCOTCH   1971

One foot down, then hop! It's hot.
    Good things for the ones that's got.
Another jump, now to the left.
    Everybody for hisself.

In the air, now both feet down.   5
    Since you black, don't stick around.
Food is gone, the rent is due,
    Curse and cry and then jump two.

All the people out of work,
    Hold for three, then twist and jerk.   10
Cross the line, they count you out.
    That's what hopping's all about.

Both feet flat, the game is done.
They think I lost. I think I won.

COMPARE:

"Harlem Hopscotch" with "We Real Cool" by Gwendolyn Brooks (page 141).

Matthew Arnold (1822–1888)

DOVER BEACH   1867

The sea is calm tonight.
The tide is full, the moon lies fair
Upon the straits;—on the French coast the light
Gleams and is gone; the cliffs of England stand,

Glimmering and vast, out in the tranquil bay.   5
Come to the window, sweet is the night-air!
Only, from the long line of spray
Where the sea meets the moon-blanched land,
Listen! you hear the grating roar
Of pebbles which the waves draw back, and fling,   10
At their return, up the high strand,
Begin, and cease, and then again begin,
With tremulous cadence slow, and bring
The eternal note of sadness in.

Sophocles long ago   15
Heard it on the Aegean, and it brought
Into his mind the turbid ebb and flow
Of human misery; we
Find also in the sound a thought,
Hearing it by this distant northern sea.   20

The Sea of Faith
Was once, too, at the full, and round earth's shore
Lay like the folds of a bright girdle furled.
But now I only hear
Its melancholy, long, withdrawing roar,   25
Retreating, to the breath
Of the night-wind, down the vast edges drear
And naked shingles° of the world.   *gravel beaches*

Ah, love, let us be true
To one another! for the world, which seems   30
To lie before us like a land of dreams,
So various, so beautiful, so new,
Hath really neither joy, nor love, nor light,
Nor certitude, nor peace, nor help for pain;
And we are here as on a darkling° plain   *darkened or darkening*   35
Swept with confused alarms of struggle and flight,
Where ignorant armies clash by night.

John Ashbery (b. 1927)

CITY AFTERNOON   1975

A veil of haze protects this
Long-ago afternoon forgotten by everybody
In this photograph, most of them now
Sucked screaming through old age and death.

If one could seize America   5
Or at least a fine forgetfulness
That seeps into our outline
Defining our volumes with a stain
That is fleeting too

But commemorates 10
Because it does define, after all:
Gray garlands, that threesome
Waiting for the light to change,
Air lifting the hair of one
Upside down in the reflecting pool. 15

W. H. Auden (1907–1973)
AS I WALKED OUT ONE EVENING 1940

As I walked out one evening,
  Walking down Bristol Street,
The crowds upon the pavement
  Were fields of harvest wheat.

And down by the brimming river 5
  I heard a lover sing
Under an arch of the railway:
  "Love has no ending.

"I'll love you, dear, I'll love you
  Till China and Africa meet, 10
And the river jumps over the mountain
  And the salmon sing in the street,

"I'll love you till the ocean
  Is folded and hung up to dry
And the seven stars go squawking 15
  Like geese about the sky.

"The years shall run like rabbits,
  For in my arms I hold
The Flower of the Ages,
  And the first love of the world." 20

But all the clocks in the city
  Began to whirr and chime:
"O let not Time deceive you,
  You cannot conquer Time.

"In the burrows of the Nightmare 25
  Where Justice naked is,
Time watches from the shadow
  And coughs when you would kiss.

"In headaches and in worry
  Vaguely life leaks away, 30
And Time will have his fancy
  Tomorrow or today.

"Into many a green valley
  Drifts the appalling snow;

Time breaks the threaded dances 35
    And the diver's brilliant bow.

"O plunge your hands in water,
    Plunge them in up to the wrist;
Stare, stare in the basin
    And wonder what you've missed. 40

"The glacier knocks in the cupboard,
    The desert sighs in the bed,
And the crack in the teacup opens
    A lane to the land of the dead.

"Where the beggars raffle the banknotes 45
    And the Giant is enchanting to Jack,
And the Lily-white Boy is a Roarer,
    And Jill goes down on her back.

"O look, look in the mirror,
    O look in your distress; 50
Life remains a blessing
    Although you cannot bless.

"O stand, stand at the window
    As the tears scald and start;
You shall love your crooked neighbor 55
    With your crooked heart."

It was late, late in the evening,
    The lovers they were gone;
The clocks had ceased their chiming,
    And the deep river ran on. 60

W. H. Auden (1907–1973)
Musée des Beaux Arts   1940

About suffereing they were never wrong,
The Old Masters: how well they understood
Its human position; how it takes place
While someone else is eating or opening a window or just walking dully
        along;
How, when the aged are reverently, passionately waiting 5
For the miraculous birth, there always must be
Children who did not specially want it to happen, skating
On a pond at the edge of the wood:
They never forgot
That even the dreadful martyrdom must run its course 10
Anyhow in a corner, some untidy spot
Where the dogs go on with their doggy life and the torturer's horse
Scratches its innocent behind on a tree.

In Brueghel's *Icarus,* for instance: how everything turns away
Quite leisurely from the disaster; the ploughman may   15
Have heard the splash, the forsaken cry,
But for him it was not an important failure; the sun shone
As it had to on the white legs disappearing into the green
Water; and the expensive delicate ship that must have seen
Something amazing, a boy falling out of the sky,   20
Had somewhere to get to and sailed calmly on.

Elizabeth Bishop (b. 1911–1979)

FILLING STATION   1965

Oh, but it is dirty!
—this little filling station,
oil-soaked, oil-permeated
to a disturbing, over-all
black translucency.   5
Be careful with that match!

Father wears a dirty,
oil-soaked monkey suit
that cuts him under the arms,
and several quick and saucy   10
and greasy sons assist him
(it's a family filling station),
all quite thoroughly dirty.

Do they live in the station?
It has a cement porch   15
behind the pumps, and on it
a set of crushed and grease-
impregnated wickerwork;
on the wicker sofa
a dirty dog, quite comfy.   20

Some comic books provide
the only note of color—
of certain color. They lie
upon a big dim doily
draping a taboret   25
(part of the set), beside
a big hirsute begonia.

Why the extraneous plant?
Why the taboret?
Why, oh why, the doily?   30
(Embroidered in daisy stitch
with marguerites, I think,
and heavy with gray crochet.)

Somebody embroidered the doily.
Somebody waters the plant,   35
or oils it, maybe. Somebody
arranges the rows of cans
so that they softly say:
ESSO—SO—SO—SO
to high-strung automobiles.   40
Somebody loves us all.

Elizabeth Bishop (b. 1911–1979)

FIVE FLIGHTS UP   1976

Still dark.
The unknown bird sits on his usual branch.
The little dog next door barks in his sleep
inquiringly, just once.
Perhaps in his sleep, too, the bird inquires   5
once or twice, quavering.
Questions—if that is what they are—
answered directly, simply,
by day itself.

Enormous morning, ponderous, meticulous;   10
gray light streaking each bare branch,

each single twig, along one side,
making another tree, of glassy veins . . .
The bird still sits there. Now he seems to yawn.

The little black dog runs in his yard.   15
His owner's voice arises, stern,
"You ought to be ashamed!"
What has he done?
He bounces cheerfully up and down;
he rushes in circles in the fallen leaves.   20

Obviously, he has no sense of shame.
He and the bird know everything is answered,
all taken care of,
no need to ask again.
— Yesterday brought to today so lightly!   25
(A yesterday I find almost impossible to lift.)

William Blake (1757–1827)
LONG JOHN BROWN AND LITTLE MARY BELL   (about 1803)

Little Mary Bell had a fairy in a nut,
Long John Brown had the Devil in his gut;
Long John Brown loved Little Mary Bell,
And the fairy drew the Devil into the nut-shell.

Her fairy skipped out and her fairy skipped in;   5
He laughed at the Devil saying "Love is a sin."
The Devil he raged and Devil he was wroth,
And the Devil entered into the young man's broth.

He was soon in the gut of the loving young swain,
For John eat and drank to drive away love's pain;   10
But all he could do he grew thinner and thinner,
Though he eat and drank as much as ten men for his dinner.

Some said he had a wolf in his stomach day and night,
Some said he had the Devil and they guessed right;
The fairy skipped about in his glory, joy and pride,   15
And he laughed at the Devil till poor John Brown died.

Then the fairy skipped out of the old nut-shell,
And woe and alack for pretty Mary Bell!
For the Devil crept in when the fairy skipped out,
And there goes Miss Bell with her fusty old nut.   20

William Blake (1757–1827)

THE SICK ROSE   1794

O Rose, thou art sick!
The invisible worm
That flies in the night,
In the howling storm,

Has found out thy bed
Of crimson joy,
And his dark secret love
Does thy life destroy.

William Blake (1757–1827)

THE TYGER   1794

Tyger! Tyger! burning bright
In the forests of the night,
What immortal hand or eye
Could frame thy fearful symmetry?

In what distant deeps or skies   5
Burnt the fire of thine eyes?
On what wings dare he aspire?
What the hand dare seize the fire?

And what shoulder, and what art,
Could twist the sinews of thy heart?   10
And when thy heart began to beat,
What dread hand? and what dread feet?

What the hammer? what the chain?
In what furnace was thy brain?
What the anvil? what dread grasp   15
Dare its deadly terrors clasp?

When the stars threw down their spears,
And watered heaven with their tears,
Did he smile his work to see?
Did he who made the Lamb make thee?   20

Tyger! Tyger! burning bright
In the forests of the night,
What immortal hand or eye
Dare frame thy fearful symmetry?

Gwendolyn Brooks (b. 1917)

THE BEAN EATERS

1960

They eat beans mostly, this old yellow pair.
Dinner is a casual affair.
Plain chipware on a plain and creaking wood,
Tin flatware.

Two who are Mostly Good.   5
Two who have lived their day,
But keep on putting on their clothes
And putting things away.

And remembering . . .
Remembering, with tinklings and twinges,   10
As they lean over the beans in their rented back room that is full of beads
      and receipts and dolls and cloths, tobacco crumbs, vases and
      fringes.

Robert Browning (1812–1889)

MY LAST DUCHESS

1842

Ferrara

That's my last Duchess painted on the wall,
Looking as if she were alive. I call
That piece a wonder, now; Frà Pandolf's hands
Worked busily a day, and there she stands.
Will 't please you sit and look at her? I said   5
"Frà Pandolf" by design, for never read
Strangers like you that pictured countenance,
The depth and passion of its earnest glance,
But to myself they turned (since none puts by
The curtain I have drawn for you, but I)   10
And seemed as they would ask me, if they durst,
How such a glance came there; so, not the first
Are you to turn and ask thus. Sir, 'twas not
Her husband's presence only, called that spot
Of joy into the Duchess' cheek; perhaps   15
Frà Pandolf chanced to say, "Her mantle laps
Over my lady's wrist too much," or "Paint
Must never hope to reproduce the faint
Half-flush that dies along her throat." Such stuff
Was courtesy, she thought, and cause enough   20
For calling up that spot of joy. She had
A heart—how shall I say?—too soon made glad,
Too easily impressed; she liked whate'er
She looked on, and her looks went everywhere.

Sir, 'twas all one! My favor at her breast,   25
The dropping of the daylight in the West,
The bough of cherries some officious fool
Broke in the orchard for her, the white mule
She rode with round the terrace — all and each
Would draw from her alike the approving speech,   30
Or blush, at least. She thanked men, — good! but thanked
Somehow — I know not how — as if she ranked
My gift of a nine-hundred-years' old name
With anybody's gift. Who'd stoop to blame
This sort of trifling? Even had you skill   35
In speech — which I have not — to make your will
Quite clear to such an one, and say "Just this
Or that in you disgusts me; here you miss,
Or there exceed the mark" — and if she let
Herself be lessoned so, nor plainly set   40
Her wits to yours, forsooth, and made excuse —
E'en then would be some stooping; and I choose
Never to stoop. Oh, sir, she smiled, no doubt,
Whene'er I passed her; but who passed without
Much the same smile? This grew; I gave commands;   45
Then all smiles stopped together. There she stands
As if alive. Will 't please you rise? We'll meet
The company below, then. I repeat,
The Count your master's known munificence
Is ample warrant that no just pretense   50
Of mine for dowry will be disallowed;
Though his fair daughter's self, as I avowed
At starting, is my object. Nay, we'll go
Together down, sir. Notice Neptune, though,
Taming a sea-horse, thought a rarity,   55
Which Claus of Innsbruck cast in bronze for me!

MY LAST DUCHESS. Ferrara, a city in northern Italy, is the scene. Browning may have modeled his speaker after Alonzo, Duke of Ferrara (1533-1598). 3. *Frà Pandolf* and 56. *Claus of
Innsbruck:* fictitious names of artists.

Robert Browning (1812–1889)
SOLILOQUY OF THE SPANISH CLOISTER   1842

Gr-r-r — there go, my heart's abhorrence!
    Water your damned flower-pots, do!
If hate killed men, Brother Lawrence,
    God's blood, would not mine kill you!
What? your myrtle-bush wants trimming?   5
    Oh, that rose has prior claims —
Needs its leaden vase filled brimming?
    Hell dry you up with its flames!

At the meal we sit together;
    Salve tibi!° I must hear   *Hail to thee!*   10
Wise talk of the kind of weather,
    Sort of season, time of year:
Not a plenteous cork-crop: scarcely
    Dare we hope oak-galls, I doubt;
What's the Latin name for "parsley"?   15
    What's the Greek name for "swine's snout"?

Whew! We'll have our platter burnished,
    Laid with care on our own shelf!
With a fire-new spoon we're furnished,
    And a goblet for ourself,   20
Rinsed like something sacrificial
    Ere 'tis fit to touch our chaps—
Marked with L. for our initial!
    (He-he! There his lily snaps!)

Saint, forsooth! While Brown Dolores   25
    Squats outside the Convent bank
With Sanchicha, telling stories,
    Steeping tresses in the tank,
Blue-black, lustrous, thick like horsehairs,
    —Can't I see his dead eye glow,   30
Bright as 'twere a Barbary corsair's?
    (That is, if he'd let it show!)

When he finishes refection,
    Knife and fork he never lays
Cross-wise, to my recollection,   35
    As I do, in Jesu's praise.
I the Trinity illustrate,
    Drinking watered orange-pulp—
In three sips the Arian frustrate;
    While he drains his at one gulp!   40

Oh, those melons! if he's able
    We're to have a feast; so nice!
One goes to the Abbot's table,
    All of us get each a slice.
How go on your flowers? None double?   45
    Not one fruit-sort can you spy?
Strange!—And I, too, at such trouble,
    Keep them close-nipped on the sly!

There's a great text in Galatians,
    Once you trip on it, entails   50
Twenty-nine distinct damnations,
    One sure, if another fails;
If I trip him just a-dying,
    Sure of heaven as sure can be,
Spin him round and send him flying   55
    Off to hell, a Manichee?

Or, my scrofulous French novel
  On grey paper with blunt type!
Simply glance at it, you grovel
  Hand and foot in Belial's gripe;   60
If I double down its pages
  At the woeful sixteenth print,
When he gathers his greengages,
  Ope a sieve and slip it in't?

Or, there's Satan! — one might venture   65
  Pledge one's soul to him, yet leave
Such a flaw in the indenture
  As he'd miss till, past retrieve,
Blasted lay that rose-acacia
  We're so proud of! *Hy, Zy, Hine. . . .*   70
'St, there's Vespers! *Plena gratia*
Ave, Virgo!° Gr-r-r—you swine!   *Hail, Virgin, full of grace!*

SOLILOQUY OF THE SPANISH CLOISTER. 3. *Brother Lawrence:* one of the speaker's fellow monks. 31. *Barbary corsair:* a pirate operating off the Barbary coast of Africa. 39. *Arian:* a follower of Arius, heretic who denied the doctrine of the Trinity. 49. *a great text in Galatians:* a difficult verse in this book of the Bible. Brother Lawrence will be damned as a heretic if he wrongly interprets it. 56. *Manichee:* another kind of heretic, one who (after the Persian philosopher Mani) sees in the world a constant struggle between good and evil, neither able to win. 60. *Belial:* Here, not specifically Satan but (as used in the Old Testament) a name for wickedness. 70. *Hy, Zy, Hine:* Possibly the sound of a bell to announce evening devotions, possibly the beginning of a formula to summon the Devil.

Fred Chappell (b. 1936)

SKIN FLICK   1971

The selfsame surface that billowed once with
The shapes of Trigger and Gene. New faces now
Are in the saddle. Tits and buttocks
Slide rattling down the beam as down
A coal chute; in the splotched light   5
The burning bush strikes dumb.
Different sort of cattle drive:
No water for miles and miles.

In the aisles, new bugs and rats
Though it's the same Old Paint.   10
Audience of lepers, hopeless and homeless,
Or like the buffalo, at home
In the wind only. No
Mushy love stuff for them.

They eye the violent innocence they always knew.   15
Is that the rancher's palomino daughter?
Is this her eastern finishing school?

Same old predicament:
No water for miles and miles,
The horizon breeds no cavalry.   20

Men, draw your wagons in a circle. Be ready.

G. K. Chesterton (1874–1936)

THE DONKEY   1900

When fishes flew and forests walked
    And figs grew upon thorn,
Some moment when the moon was blood
    Then surely I was born;

With monstrous head and sickening cry   5
    And ears like errant wings,
The devil's walking parody
    On all four-footed things.

The tattered outlaw of the earth,
    Of ancient crooked will;   10
Starve, scourge, deride me: I am dumb,
    I keep my secret still.

Fools! For I also had my hour;
    One far fierce hour and sweet:
There was a shout about my ears,   15
    And palms before my feet.

THE DONKEY. For more details of the donkey's hour of triumph see Matthew 21:1–8.

Samuel Taylor Coleridge (1772–1834)

KUBLA KHAN   (1797-1798)

Or, a Vision in a Dream. A Fragment.

In Xanadu did Kubla Khan
A stately pleasure-dome decree:
Where Alph, the sacred river, ran
Through caverns measureless to man
    Down to a sunless sea.   5
So twice five miles of fertile ground
With walls and towers were girdled round;
And there were gardens bright with sinuous rills,
Where blossomed many an incense-bearing tree;
And here were forests ancient as the hills,
Enfolding sunny spots of greenery.   10

But oh! that deep romantic chasm which slanted
Down the green hill athwart a cedarn cover!
A savage place! as holy and enchanted
As e'er beneath a waning moon was haunted   15
By woman wailing for her demon-lover!
And from this chasm, with ceaseless turmoil seething,
As if this earth in fast thick pants were breathing,
A mighty fountain momently was forced:
Amid whose swift half-intermitted burst   20
Huge fragments vaulted like rebounding hail,
Or chaffy grain beneath the thresher's flail:
And 'mid these dancing rocks at once and ever
It flung up momently the sacred river.
Five miles meandering with a mazy motion   25
Through wood and dale the sacred river ran,
Then reached the caverns measureless to man,
And sank in tumult to a lifeless ocean:
And 'mid this tumult Kubla heard from far
Ancestral voices prophesying war!   30

    The shadow of the dome of pleasure
    Floated midway on the waves;
    Where was heard the mingled measure
    From the fountain and the caves.
It was a miracle of rare device,   35
A sunny pleasure-dome with caves of ice!

    A damsel with a dulcimer
    In a vision once I saw:
    It was an Abyssinian maid,
    And on her dulcimer she played,   40
    Singing of Mount Abora.
    Could I revive within me
    Her symphony and song,
    To such a deep delight 'twould win me,
That with music loud and long,   45
I would build that dome in air,
That sunny dome! those caves of ice!
And all who heard should see them there,
And all should cry, Beware! Beware!
His flashing eyes, his floating hair!   50
Weave a circle round him thrice,
And close your eyes with holy dread,
For he on honey-dew hath fed,
And drunk the milk of Paradise.

KUBLA KHAN. There was an actual Kublai Khan, a thirteenth-century Mongol emperor,
and a Chinese city of Xamdu; but Coleridge's dream vision also borrows from travelers'
descriptions of such other exotic places as Abyssinia and America. 51. *circle:* a magic circle
drawn to keep away evil spirits.

Robert Creeley (b. 1926)

NAUGHTY BOY 1959

When he brings home a whale,
she laughs and says, that's not for real.

And if he won the Irish sweepstakes,
she would say, where were you last night?

Where are you now, for that matter? Am   5
I always (she says) to be looking

at you? She says,
if I thought it would get any better I

would shoot you, you
nut, you. Then pats her hair   10

into place, and waits
for Uncle Jim's deep-fired, all-fat, real gone

whale steaks.

Countee Cullen (1903–1946)

SATURDAY'S CHILD 1925

Some are teethed on a silver spoon,
With the stars strung for a rattle;
I cut my teeth as the black racoon —
for implements of battle.

Some are swaddled in silk and down,   5
And heralded by a star;
They swathed my limbs in a sackcloth gown
On a night that was black as tar.

For some, godfather and goddame
The opulent fairies be;   10
Dame Poverty gave me my name,
And Pain godfathered me.

For I was born on Saturday —
"Bad time for planting a seed,"
Was all my father had to say,   15
And, "One mouth more to feed."

Death cut the strings that gave me life,
And handed me to Sorrow,

The only kind of middle wife
My folks could beg or borrow.   20

COMPARE:

"Saturday's Child" with "Dream Deferred" by Langston Hughes (page 355) and
"Ballad of Birmingham" by Dudley Randall (page 382).

E. E. Cummings (1894–1962)

ALL IN GREEN WENT MY LOVE RIDING   1923

All in green went my love riding
on a great horse of gold
into the silver dawn.

four lean hounds crouched low and smiling
the merry deer ran before.   5

Fleeter be they than dappled dreams
the swift sweet deer
the red rare deer.

Four red roebuck at a white water
the cruel bugle sang before.   10

Horn at hip went my love riding
riding the echo down
into the silver dawn.

four lean hounds crouched low and smiling
the level meadows ran before.   15

Softer be they than slippered sleep
the lean lithe deer
the fleet flown deer.

Four fleet does at a gold valley
the famished arrow sang before.   20

Bow at belt went my love riding
riding the mountain down
into the silver dawn.

four lean hounds crouched low and smiling
the sheer peaks ran before.   25

Paler be they than daunting death
the sleek slim deer
the tall tense deer.

Four tall stags at a green mountain
the lucky hunter sang before.   30

All in green went my love riding
on a great horse of gold
into the silver dawn.

four lean hounds crouched low and smiling
my heart fell dead before.   35

COMPARE:

"All in green went my love riding" with the ballads "The Three Ravens" and
"The Twa Corbies" (pages 305–306).

Walter de la Mare (1873–1956)

THE LISTENERS   1912

"Is there anybody there?" said the Traveler,
    Knocking on the moonlit door;
And his horse in the silence champed the grasses
    Of the forest's ferny floor:
And a bird flew up out of the turret,   5
    Above the Traveler's head:
And he smote upon the door again a second time;
    "Is there anybody there?" he said.
But no one descended to the Traveler;
    No head from the leaf-fringed sill   10
Leaned over and looked into his grey eyes,
    Where he stood perplexed and still.
But only a host of phantom listeners
    That dwelt in the lone house then
Stood listening in the quiet of the moonlight   15
    To that voice from the world of men:
Stood thronging the faint moonbeams on the dark stair,
    That goes down to the empty hall,
Hearkening in an air stirred and shaken
    By the lonely Traveler's call.   20
And he felt in his heart their strangeness,
    Their stillness answering his cry,
While his horse moved, cropping the dark turf,
    'Neath the starred and leafy sky;
For he suddenly smote on the door, even   25
    Louder, and lifted his head: —
"Tell them I came, and no one answered,
    That I kept my word," he said.
Never the least stir made the listeners,
    Though every word he spake   30
Fell echoing through the shadowiness of the still house
    From the one man left awake:

Ay, they heard his foot upon the stirrup,
    And the sound of iron on stone,
And how the silence surged softly backward,   35
    When the plunging hoofs were gone.

James Dickey (b. 1923)
CHERRYLOG ROAD   1963

Off Highway 106
At Cherrylog Road I entered
The '34 Ford without wheels,
Smothered in kudzu,
With a seat pulled out to run   5
Corn whiskey down from the hills,

And then from the other side
Crept into an Essex
With a rumble seat of red leather
And then out again, aboard   10
A blue Chevrolet, releasing
The rust from its other color,

Reared up on three building blocks.
None had the same body heat;
I changed with them inward, toward   15
The weedy heart of the junkyard,
For I knew that Doris Holbrook
Would escape from her father at noon

And would come from the farm
To seek parts owned by the sun   20
Among the abandoned chassis,
Sitting in each in turn
As I did, leaning forward
As in a wild stock-car race

In the parking lot of the dead.   25
Time after time, I climbed in
And out the other side, like
An envoy or movie star
Met at the station by crickets.
A radiator cap raised its head,   30

Become a real toad or a kingsnake
As I neared the hub of the yard,
Passing through many states,
Many lives, to reach
Some grandmother's long Pierce-Arrow   35
Sending platters of blindness forth

From its nickel hubcaps
And spilling its tender upholstery
On sleepy roaches,
The glass panel in between   40
Lady and colored driver
Not all the way broken out,

The back-seat phone
Still on its hook.
I got in as though to exclaim,   45
"Let us go to the orphan asylum,
John; I have some old toys
For children who say their prayers."

I popped with sweat as I thought
I heard Doris Holbrook scrape   50
Like a mouse in the southern-state sun
That was eating the paint in blisters
From a hundred car tops and hoods.
She was tapping like code,

Loosening the screws,   55
Carrying off headlights,
Sparkplugs, bumpers,
Cracked mirrors and gear-knobs,
Getting ready, already,
To go back with something to show   60

Other than her lips' new trembling
I would hold to me soon, soon,
Where I sat in the ripped back seat
Talking over the interphone,
Praying for Doris Holbrook   65
To come from her father's farm

And to get back there
With no trace of me on her face
To be seen by her red-haired father
Who would change, in the squalling barn,   70
Her back's pale skin with a strop,
Then lay for me

In a bootlegger's roasting car
With a string-triggered 12-gauge shotgun
To blast the breath from the air.   75
Not cut by the jagged windshields,
Through the acres of wrecks she came
With a wrench in her hand,

Through dust where the blacksnake dies
Of boredom, and the beetle knows   80
The compost has no more life.

Someone outside would have seen
The oldest car's door inexplicably
Close from within:

I held her and held her and held her,   85
Convoyed at terrific speed
By the stalled, dreaming traffic around us,
So the blacksnake, stiff
With inaction, curved back
Into life, and hunted the mouse   90

With deadly overexcitement,
The beetles reclaimed their field
As we clung, glued together,
With the hooks of the seat springs
Working through to catch us red-handed   95
Amidst the gray breathless batting

That burst from the seat at our backs.
We left by separate doors
Into the changed, other bodies
Of cars, she down Cherrylog Road   100
And I to my motorcycle
Parked like the soul of the junkyard

Restored, a bicycle fleshed
With power, and tore off
Up Highway 106, continually   105
Drunk on the wind in my mouth,
Wringing the handlebar for speed,
Wild to be wreckage forever.

Emily Dickinson (1830–1886)

Because I could not stop for Death   (1863)

Because I could not stop for Death–
He kindly stopped for me–
The Carriage held but just Ourselves–
And Immortality.

We slowly drove–He knew no haste   5
And I had put away
My labor and my leisure too,
For His Civility–

We passed the School, where Children strove
At Recess–in the Ring–   10
We passed the Fields of Gazing Grain–
We passed the Setting Sun–

Or rather–He passed Us–
The Dews drew quivering and chill–
For only Gossamer, my Gown–   15
My Tippet°–only Tulle–   *cape*

We paused before a House that seemed
A Swelling of the Ground–
The Roof was scarcely visible–
The Cornice — in the Ground–   20

Since then–'tis Centuries–and yet
Feels shorter than the Day
I first surmised the Horses' Heads
Were toward Eternity–

BECAUSE I COULD NOT STOP FOR DEATH. In the version of this poem printed by Emily
Dickinson's first editors in 1890, stanza four was left out. In line 9 *strove* was replaced by
played; line 10 was made to read "Their lessons scarcely done"; line 20, "The cornice but a
mound"; line 21, "Since then 'tis centuries, but each"; and capitalization and punctuation
were made conventional.

Emily Dickinson (1830–1886)
I STARTED EARLY — TOOK MY DOG   (1862)

I started Early–Took my Dog–
And visited the Sea–
The Mermaids in the Basement
Came out to look at me–

And Frigates–in the Upper Floor   5
Extended Hempen Hands–
Presuming Me to be a Mouse–
Aground–upon the Sands–

But no Man moved Me–till the Tide
Went past my simple Shoe–   10
And past my Apron–and my Belt
And past my Bodice–too–

And made as He would eat me up–
As wholly as a Dew
Upon a Dandelion's Sleeve–   15
And then–I started–too–

And He–He followed–close behind–
I felt His Silver Heel
Upon my Ankle–Then my Shoes
Would overflow with Pearl–   20

Until We met the Solid Town–
No One He seemed to know–
And bowing–with a Mighty look–
At me–The Sea withdrew–

Emily Dickinson (1830–1886)

The Soul selects her own Society

(1862)

The Soul selects her own Society–
Then–shuts the Door–
To her divine Majority–
Present no more–

Unmoved–she notes the Chariots–pausing–   5
At her low Gate–
Unmoved–an Emperor be kneeling
Upon her Mat–

I've known her–from an ample nation–
Choose One–   10
Then–close the Valves of her attention–
Like Stone–

John Donne (1572–1631)

The Bait   1633

Come live with me and be my love,
And we will some new pleasures prove,
Of golden sands and crystal brooks,
With silken lines and silver hooks.

There will the river whispering run,   5
Warmed by thy eyes more than the sun;
And there the enamored fish will stay,
Begging themselves they may betray.

When thou wilt swim in that live bath,
Each fish, which every channel hath,   10
Will amorously to thee swim,
Gladder to catch thee, than thou him.

If thou to be so seen be'st loath,
By sun or moon, thou dark'nest both;
And if myself have leave to see,   15
I need not their light, having thee.

Let others freeze with angling reeds°,   *rods*
And cut their legs with shells and weeds,
Or treacherously poor fish beset
With strangling snare or windowy net.   20

Let coarse bold hands from slimy nest
The bedded fish in banks out-wrest,
Or curious traitors, sleave-silk flies,
Bewitch poor fishes' wand'ring eyes.

For thee, thou need'st no such deceit,   25
For thou thyself art thine own bait;
That fish that is not catched thereby,
Alas, is wiser far than I.

COMPARE:

"The Bait" with "The Passionate Shepherd to His Love" by Christopher
Marlowe (page 370).

John Donne (1572–1631)

THE FLEA   1633

Mark but this flea, and mark in this
How little that which thou deny'st me is;
It sucked me first, and now sucks thee,
And in this flea our two bloods mingled be;
Thou know'st that this cannot be said   5
A sin, nor shame, nor loss of maidenhead,
    Yet this enjoys before it woo,
    And pampered swells with one blood made of two,
    And this, alas, is more than we would do.

Oh stay, three lives in one flea spare,   10
Where we almost, yea more than married are.
This flea is you and I, and this
Our marriage bed, and marriage temple is;
Though parents grudge, and you, we're met
And cloistered in these living walls of jet.   15
    Though use° make you apt to kill me,   custom
    Let not to that, self-murder added be,
    And sacrilege, three sins in killing three.

Cruel and sudden, hast thou since
Purpled thy nail in blood of innocence?   20
Wherein could this flea guilty be,
Except in that drop it sucked from thee?
Yet thou triumph'st, and say'st that thou
Find'st not thyself, nor me, the weaker now;
    'Tis true; then learn how false, fears be;   25
    Just so much honor, when thou yield'st to me,
    Will waste, as this flea's death took life from thee.

COMPARE:

"The Flea" with "The Best Line Yet" by Edward Allen (page 219).

John Donne (1572–1631)

A Valediction: Forbidding Mourning   1633

As virtuous men pass mildly away,
   And whisper to their souls to go,
Whilst some of their sad friends do say
   The breath goes now, and some say no:

So let us melt, and make no noise,   5
   No tear-floods, nor sigh-tempests move;
'Twere profanation of our joys
   To tell the laity our love.

Moving of th' earth° brings harms and fears;   *earthquake*
   Men reckon what it did and meant;   10
But trepidation of the spheres,
   Though greater far, is innocent°.   *harmless*

Dull sublunary lovers' love
   (Whose soul is sense) cannot admit
Absence, because it doth remove   15
   Those things which elemented° it.   *constituted*

But we, by a love so much refined
   That ourselves know not what it is,
Inter-assurèd of the mind,
   Care less, eyes, lips, and hands to miss.   20

Our two souls, therefore, which are one,
   Though I must go, endure not yet
A breach, but an expansiòn,
   Like gold to airy thinness beat.

If they be two, they are two so   25
   As stiff twin compasses are two:
Thy soul, the fixed foot, makes no show
   To move, but doth, if th' other do.

And though it in the center sit,
   Yet when the other far doth roam,   30
It leans and harkens after it,
   And grows erect as that comes home.

Such wilt thou be to me, who must,
   Like th' other foot, obliquely run;
Thy firmness makes my circle just°,   *perfect* 35
   And makes me end where I begun.

A Valediction: Forbidding Mourning. 11. *spheres:* In Ptolemaic astronomy, the concentric spheres surrounding the earth. The trepidation or motion of the ninth sphere was thought to change the date of the equinox.

John Dryden (1631–1700)

TO THE MEMORY OF MR. OLDHAM

1684

Farewell, too little and too lately known,
Whom I began to think and call my own;
For sure our souls were near allied, and thine
Cast in the same poetic mold with mine.
One common note on either lyre did strike,   5
And knaves and fools we both abhorred alike.
To the same goal did both our studies drive:
The last set out the soonest did arrive.
Thus Nissus fell upon the slippery place,
While his young friend performed and won the race.   10
O early ripe! to thy abundant store
What could advancing age have added more?
It might (what Nature never gives the young)
Have taught the numbers° of thy native tongue.   *meters*
But satire needs not those, and wit will shine   15
Through the harsh cadence of a rugged line.
A noble error, and but seldom made,
When poets are by too much force betrayed.
Thy gen'rous fruits, though gathered ere their prime,
Still showed a quickness; and maturing time   20
But mellows what we write to the dull sweets of rhyme.
Once more, hail, and farewell! farewell, thou young
But ah! too short, Marcellus of our tongue!
Thy brows with ivy and with laurels bound;
But fate and gloomy night encompass thee around.   25

TO THE MEMORY OF MR. OLDHAM. John Oldham, poet best remembered for his *Satires upon the Jesuits,* had died at thirty. 9–10. *Nissus; his young friend:* These two close friends, as Virgil tells us in the *Aeneid,* ran a race for the prize of an olive crown. 23. *Marcellus:* Had he not died in his twentieth year, he would have succeeded the Roman emperor Augustus. 25. This line echoes the *Aeneid* (VI, 886), in which Marcellus is seen walking under the black cloud of his impending doom.

COMPARE:

"To the Memory of Mr. Oldham" with "To an Athlete Dying Young" by A. E. Housman (page 354).

Alan Dugan (b. 1923)

LOVE SONG: I AND THOU

1961

Nothing is plumb, level or square:
    the studs are bowed, the joists
are shaky by nature, no piece fits
    any other piece without a gap

or pinch, and bent nails   5
  dance all over the surfacing
like maggots. By Christ
  I am no carpenter, I built
the roof for myself, the walls
  for myself, the floors   10
for myself, and got
  hung up in it myself. I
danced with a purple thumb
  at this house-warming, drunk
with my prime whiskey: rage.   15
  Oh I spat rage's nails
into the frame-up of my work:
  it held. It settled plumb,
level, solid, square and true
  for that great moment. Then   20
it screamed and went on through,
  skewing as wrong the other way.
God damned it. This is hell,
  but I planned it, I sawed it,
I nailed it, and I   25
  will live in it until it kills me.
I can nail my left palm
  to the left-hand cross-piece but
I can't do everything myself.
  I need a hand to nail the right,   30
a help, a love, a you, a wife.

Compare:

"Love Song: I and Thou" with "The Kiss" by Anne Sexton (page 391).

Bob Dylan (b. 1941)
Subterranean Homesick Blues   1965

Johnny's in the basement
Mixing up the medicine
I'm on the pavement
Thinking about the government
The man in the trenchcoat   5
Badge out, laid off
Says he's got a bad cough
Wants to get paid off
Look out kid

Subterranean Homesick Blues by Bob Dylan. Dylan performs this song on *Bringing It All Back Home* (Columbia Records, stereo CS 9128, mono CL 2328), also on *Bob Dylan's Greatest Hits* (Columbia, stereo KCS 9463, mono KCL 2663).

It's something you did   10
God knows when
But you're doin' it again
You better duck down the alley way
Lookin' for a new friend
The man in the coonskin cap   15
By the pig pen
Wants eleven dollar bills
You only got ten.

Maggie comes fleet foot
Face full of black soot   20
Talkin' that the heat put
Plants in the bed but
The phone's tapped anyway
Maggie says that many say
They must bust in early May   25
Orders from the D.A.
Look out kid
Don't matter what you did
Walk on your tip toes
Don't try No-Doz   30
Better stay away from those
That carry around a fire hose
Keep a clean nose
Watch the plain clothes
You don't need a weather man   35
To tell which way the wind blows.

Get sick get well
Hang around an ink well
Ring bell, hard to tell
If anything is goin' to sell   40
Try hard, get barred
Get back, write braille
Get jailed, jump bail
Join the army, if you fail
Look out kid, you're gonna get hit   45
But users, cheaters
Six time losers
Hang around the theatres
Girl by the whirl pool's
Lookin' for a new fool   50
Don't follow leaders
Watch the parkin' meters.

Ah, get born, keep warm
Short pants, romance, learn to dance
Get dressed, get blessed   55
Try to be a success

Please her, please him, buy gifts
Don't steal, don't lift
Twenty years of schoolin'
And they put you on the day shift 60
Look out kid, they keep it all hid
Better jump down a manhole
Light yourself a candle, don't wear sandals
Try to avoid the scandals
Don't wanna be a bum 65
You better chew gum
The pump don't work
'Cause the vandals took the handles.

T. S. Eliot (1888–1965)

JOURNEY OF THE MAGI 1927

"A cold coming we had of it,
Just the worst time of the year
For a journey, and such a long journey:
The ways deep and the weather sharp,
The very dead of winter." 5
And the camels galled, sore-footed, refractory,
Lying down in the melting snow.
There were times we regretted
The summer palaces on slopes, the terraces,
And the silken girls bringing sherbet. 10
Then the camel men cursing and grumbling
And running away, and wanting their liquor and women,
And the night-fires going out, and the lack of shelters,
And the cities hostile and the towns unfriendly
And the villages dirty and charging high prices: 15
A hard time we had of it.
At the end we preferred to travel all night,
Sleeping in snatches,
With the voices singing in our ears, saying
That this was all folly. 20

Then at dawn we came down to a temperate valley,
Wet, below the snow line, smelling of vegetation;
With a running stream and a water-mill beating the darkness,
And three trees on the low sky,
And an old white horse galloped away in the meadow. 25
Then we came to a tavern with vine-leaves over the lintel,
Six hands at an open door dicing for pieces of silver,
And feet kicking the empty wine-skins.
But there was no information, and so we continued
And arrived at evening, not a moment too soon 30
Finding the place; it was (you may say) satisfactory.

All this was a long time ago, I remember,
And I would do it again, but set down
This set down
This: were we led all that way for   35
Birth or Death? There was a Birth, certainly,
We had evidence and no doubt. I had seen birth and death,
But had thought they were different; this Birth was
Hard and bitter agony for us, like Death, our death.
We returned to our places, these Kingdoms,   40
But no longer at ease here, in the old dispensation,
With an alien people clutching their gods.
I should be glad of another death.

JOURNEY OF THE MAGI. The story of the Magi, the three wise men who traveled to Bethlehem to behold the Christ child, is told in Matthew 2:1–12. That the three were kings is a later tradition. 1–5. *A cold coming . . . winter:* Eliot quotes with slight changes from a sermon preached on Christmas day, 1622, by Bishop Lancelot Andrewes. 24. *three times:* foreshadowing the three crosses on Calvary (see Luke 23:32–33). 25. *white horse:* perhaps the steed that carried the conquering Christ in the vision of St. John the Divine (Revelation 19:11–16). 41. *old dispensation:* older, pagan religion about to be displaced by Christianity.

COMPARE:

"Journey of the Magi" with "The Magi" by William Butler Yeats (page 420).

T. S. Eliot (1888–1965)

THE LOVE SONG OF J. ALFRED PRUFROCK   1917

S'io credessi che mia risposta fosse
A persona che mai tornasse al mondo,
Questa fiamma staria senza piu scosse.
Ma perciocche giammai di questo fondo
Non torno vivo alcun, s'i'odo il vero,
Senza tema d'infamia ti rispondo.

Let us go then, you and I,
When the evening is spread out against the sky
Like a patient etherized upon a table;
Let us go, through certain half-deserted streets,
The muttering retreats   5
Of restless nights in one-night cheap hotels
And sawdust restaurants with oyster-shells:
Streets that follow like a tedious argument
Of insidious intent
To lead you to an overwhelming question . . .   10
Oh, do not ask, "What is it?"
Let us go and make our visit.

In the room the women come and go
Talking of Michelangelo.

The yellow fog that rubs its back upon the window-panes,   15
The yellow smoke that rubs its muzzle on the window-panes
Licked its tongue into the corners of the evening,
Lingered upon the pools that stand in drains,
Let fall upon its back the soot that falls from chimneys,
Slipped by the terrace, made a sudden leap,   20
And seeing that it was a soft October night,
Curled once about the house, and fell asleep.

And indeed there will be time
For the yellow smoke that slides along the street,
Rubbing its back upon the window-panes;   25
There will be time, there will be time
To prepare a face to meet the faces that you meet;
There will be time to murder and create,
And time for all the works and days of hands
That lift and drop a question on your plate;   30
Time for you and time for me,
And time yet for a hundred indecisions,
And for a hundred visions and revisions,
Before the taking of a toast and tea.

In the room the women come and go   35
Talking of Michelangelo.

And indeed there will be time
To wonder, "Do I dare?" and, "Do I dare?"
Time to turn back and descend the stair,
With a bald spot in the middle of my hair—   40
[They will say: "How his hair is growing thin!"]
My morning coat, my collar mounting firmly to the chin,
My necktie rich and modest, but asserted by a simple pin—
[They will say: "But how his arms and legs are thin!"]
Do I dare   45
Disturb the universe?
In a minute there is time
For decisions and revisions which a minute will reverse.

For I have known them all already, known them all:—
Have known the evenings, mornings, afternoons,   50
I have measured out my life with coffee spoons;
I know the voices dying with a dying fall
Beneath the music from a farther room.
   So how should I presume?

And I have known the eyes already, known them all—   55
The eyes that fix you in a formulated phrase,
And when I am formulated, sprawling on a pin,
When I am pinned and wriggling on the wall,
Then how should I begin
To spit out all the butt-ends of my days and ways?   60
   And how should I presume?

And I have known the arms already, known them all —
Arms that are braceleted and white and bare
[But in the lamplight, downed with light brown hair!]
Is it perfume from a dress   65
That makes me so digress?
Arms that lie along a table, or wrap about a shawl.
    And should I then presume?
    And how should I begin?

                    .   .   .   .   .

Shall I say, I have gone at dusk through narrow streets   70
And watched the smoke that rises from the pipes
Of lonely men in shirt-sleeves, leaning out of windows? . . .

I should have been a pair of ragged claws
Scuttling across the floors of silent seas.

                    .   .   .   .   .

And the afternoon, the evening, sleeps so peacefully!   75
Smoothed by long fingers,
Asleep . . . tired . . . or it malingers,
Stretched on the floor, here beside you and me.
Should I, after tea and cakes and ices,
Have the strength to force the moment to its crisis?   80
But though I have wept and fasted, wept and prayed,
Though I have seen my head [grown slightly bald] brought in upon a plat-
        ter,
I am no prophet — and here's no great matter;
I have seen the moment of my greatness flicker,
And I have seen the eternal Footman hold my coat, and snicker,   85
And in short, I was afraid.

And would it have been worth it, after all,
After the cups, the marmalade, the tea,
Among the porcelain, among some talk of you and me,
Would it have been worth while,   90
To have bitten off the matter with a smile,
To have squeezed the universe into a ball
To roll it toward some overwhelming question,
To say: "I am Lazarus, come from the dead,
Come back to tell you all, I shall tell you all" —   95
If one, settling a pillow by her head,
    Should say: "That is not what I meant at all.
    That is not it, at all."

And would it have been worth it, after all,
Would it have been worth while,   100
After the sunsets and the dooryards and the sprinkled streets,
After the novels, after the teacups, after the skirts that trail along the
        floor —
And this, and so much more? —
It is impossible to say just what I mean!

But as if a magic lantern threw the nerves in patterns on a screen: 105
Would it have been worth while
If one, settling a pillow or throwing off a shawl,
And turning toward the window, should say:
    "That is not it at all,
    That is not what I meant, at all."   110
                        .   .   .   .   .   .

No! I am not Prince Hamlet, nor was meant to be;
Am an attendant lord, one that will do
To swell a progress, start a scene or two,
Advise the prince; no doubt, an easy tool,
Deferential, glad to be of use,   115
Politic, cautious, and meticulous;
Full of high sentence, but a bit obtuse;
At times, indeed, almost ridiculous —
Almost, at times, the Fool.

I grow old . . . I grow old . . .   120
I shall wear the bottoms of my trousers rolled.

Shall I part my hair behind? Do I dare to eat a peach?
I shall wear white flannel trousers, and walk upon the beach.
I have heard the mermaids singing, each to each.

I do not think that they will sing to me.   125

I have seen them riding seaward on the waves
Combing the white hair of the waves blown back
When the wind blows the water white and black.

We have lingered in the chambers of the sea
By sea-girls wreathed with seaweed red and brown   130
Till human voices wake us, and we drown.

THE LOVE SONG OF J. ALFRED PRUFROCK. The epigraph, from Dante's *Inferno*, is the speech
of one dead and damned, who thinks that his hearer also is going to remain in Hell. Count
Guido da Montefeltro, whose sin has been to give false counsel after a corrupt prelate had
offered him prior absolution and whose punishment is to be wrapped in a constantly
burning flame, offers to tell Dante his story: "If I thought my reply were to someone who
could ever return to the world, this flame would waver no more. But since, I'm told, nobody ever escapes from this pit, I'll tell you without fear of ill fame." 29. *works and days:*
title of a poem by Hesiod (eighth century B.C.), depicting his life as a hard-working Greek
farmer and exhorting his brother to be like him. 82. *head . . . platter:* like that of John the
Baptist, prophet and praiser of chastity, whom King Herod beheaded at the demand of
Herodias, his unlawfully wedded wife (see Mark 6:17–28). 92–93. *squeezed . . . To roll it:* an
echo from Marvell's "To His Coy Mistress," lines 41–42 (see p. 371). 94. *Lazarus:* Probably
the Lazarus whom Christ called forth from the tomb (John 11:1–44), but possibly the
beggar seen in Heaven by the rich man in Hell (Luke 16:19–25).

Robert Frost (1874–1963)

Mending Wall

1914

Something there is that doesn't love a wall,
That sends the frozen-ground-swell under it,
And spills the upper boulders in the sun;
And makes gaps even two can pass abreast.
The work of hunters is another thing: 5
I have come after them and made repair
Where they have left not one stone on a stone,
But they would have the rabbit out of hiding,
To please the yelping dogs. The gaps I mean,
No one has seen them made or heard them made,   10
But at spring-mending time we find them there.
I let my neighbor know beyond the hill;
And on a day we meet to walk the line
And set the wall between us once again.
We keep the wall between us as we go.   15
To each the boulders that have fallen to each.
And some are loaves and some so nearly balls
We have to use a spell to make them balance:
'Stay where you are until our backs are turned!'
We wear our fingers rough with handling them.   20
Oh, just another kind of outdoor game,
One on a side. It comes to little more:
There where it is we do not need the wall:
He is all pine and I am apple orchard.
My apple trees will never get across   25
And eat the cones under his pines, I tell him.
He only says, 'Good fences make good neighbors.'
Spring is the mischief in me, and I wonder
If I could put a notion in his head:
'Why do they make good neighbors? Isn't it   30
Where there are cows? But here there are no cows.
Before I built a wall I'd ask to know
What I was walling in or walling out,
And to whom I was like to give offense.
Something there is that doesn't love a wall,   35
That wants it down.' I could say 'Elves' to him,
But it's not elves exactly, and I'd rather
He said it for himself. I see him there
Bringing a stone grasped firmly by the top
In each hand, like an old-stone savage armed.   40
He moves in darkness as it seems to me,
Not of woods only and the shade of trees.
He will not go behind his father's saying,
And he likes having thought of it so well
He says again, 'Good fences make good neighbors.'   45

COMPARE:

"Mending Wall" with "Mending Sump" by Kenneth Koch (page 274).

Robert Frost (1874–1963)
STOPPING BY WOODS ON A SNOWY EVENING   1923

Whose woods these are I think I know.
His house is in the village though;
He will not see me stopping here
To watch his woods fill up with snow.

My little horse must think it queer   5
To stop without a farmhouse near
Between the woods and frozen lake
The darkest evening of the year.

He gives his harness bells a shake
To ask if there is some mistake.   10
The only other sound's the sweep
Of easy wind and downy flake.

The woods are lovely, dark and deep,
But I have promises to keep,
And miles to go before I sleep,   15
And miles to go before I sleep.

Robert Frost (1874–1963)
THE WITCH OF COÖS   1923

I stayed the night for shelter at a farm
Behind the mountain, with a mother and son,
Two old-believers. They did all the talking.

MOTHER. Folks think a witch who has familiar spirits
She could call up to pass a winter evening,   5
But won't, should be burned at the stake or something.
Summoning spirits isn't 'Button, button,
Who's got the button,' I would have them know.

SON. Mother can make a common table rear
And kick with two legs like an army mule.   10

MOTHER. And when I've done it, what good have I done?
Rather than tip a table for you, let me
Tell you what Ralle the Sioux Control once told me.
He said the dead had souls, but when I asked him
How could that be—I thought the dead were souls,   15
He broke my trance. Don't that make you suspicious
That there's something the dead are keeping back?
Yes, there's something the dead are keeping back.

SON. You wouldn't want to tell him what we have
Up attic, mother?   20

MOTHER. Bones—a skeleton.

SON. But the headboard of mother's bed is pushed
Against the attic door: the door is nailed.
It's harmless. Mother hears it in the night
Halting perplexed behind the barrier   25
Of door and headboard. Where it wants to get
Is back into the cellar where it came from.

MOTHER. We'll never let them, will we, son! We'll never!

SON. It left the cellar forty years ago
And carried itself like a pile of dishes   30
Up one flight from the cellar to the kitchen,
Another from the kitchen to the bedroom,
Another from the bedroom to the attic,
Right past both father and mother, and neither stopped it.
Father had gone upstairs; mother was downstairs.   35
I was a baby: I don't know where I was.

MOTHER. The only fault my husband found with me—
I went to sleep before I went to bed,
Especially in winter when the bed
Might just as well be ice and the clothes snow.   40
The night the bones came up the cellar-stairs
Toffile had gone to bed alone and left me,
But left an open door to cool the room off
So as to sort of turn me out of it.
I was just coming to myself enough   45
To wonder where the cold was coming from,
When I heard Toffile upstairs in the bedroom
And thought I heard him downstairs in the cellar.
The board we had laid down to walk dry-shod on
When there was water in the cellar in spring   50
Struck the hard cellar bottom. And then someone
Began the stairs, two footsteps for each step,
The way a man with one leg and a crutch,
Or a little child, comes up. It wasn't Toffile:
It wasn't anyone who could be there.   55
The bulkhead double-doors were double-locked
And swollen tight and buried under snow.
The cellar windows were banked up with sawdust
And swollen tight and buried under snow.
It was the bones. I knew them—and good reason.   60
My first impulse was to get to the knob
And hold the door. But the bones didn't try
The door; they halted helpless on the landing,
Waiting for things to happen in their favor.
The faintest restless rustling ran all through them.   65

I never could have done the thing I did
If the wish hadn't been too strong in me
To see how they were mounted for this walk.
I had a vision of them put together
Not like a man, but like a chandelier.   70
So suddenly I flung the door wide on him.
A moment he stood balancing with emotion,
And all but lost himself. (A tongue of fire
Flashed out and licked along his upper teeth.
Smoke rolled inside the sockets of his eyes.)   75
Then he came at me with one hand outstretched,
The way he did in life once; but this time
I struck the hand off brittle on the floor,
And fell back from him on the floor myself.
The finger-pieces slid in all directions.   80
(Where did I see one of those pieces lately?
Hand me my button-box—it must be there.)
I sat up on the floor and shouted. "Toffile,
It's coming up to you.' It had its choice
Of the door to the cellar or the hall.   85
It took the hall door for the novelty,
And set off briskly for so slow a thing,
Still going every which way in the joints, though,
So that it looked like lightning or a scribble,
From the slap I had just now given its hand.   90
I listened till it almost climbed the stairs
From the hall to the only finished bedroom,
Before I got up to do anything;
Then ran and shouted, "Shut the bedroom door,
Toffile, for my sake!' 'Company?' he said,   95
'Don't make me get up; I'm too warm in bed.'
So lying forward weakly on the handrail
I pushed myself upstairs, and in the light
(The kitchen had been dark) I had to own
I could see nothing. 'Toffile, I don't see it.   100
It's with us in the room though. It's the bones.'
'What bones?' 'The cellar bones—out of the grave.'
That made him throw his bare legs out of bed
And sit up by me and take hold of me.
I wanted to put out the light and see   105
If I could see it, or else mow the room,
With our arms at the level of our knees,
And bring the chalk-pile down. 'I'll tell you what—
It's looking for another door to try.
The uncommonly deep snow has made him think   110
Of his old song, *The Wild Colonial Boy*,
He always used to sing along the tote road.
He's after an open door to get outdoors.
Let's trap him with an open door up attic.'
Toffile agreed to that, and sure enough,   115

Almost the moment he was given an opening,
The steps began to climb the attic stairs.
I heard them. Toffile didn't seem to hear them.
'Quick!' I slammed to the door and held the knob.
'Toffile, get nails.' I made him nail the door shut   120
And push the headboard of the bed against it.
Then we asked was there anything
Up attic that we'd ever want again.
The attic was less to us than the cellar.
If the bones liked the attic, let them have it.   125
Let them stay in the attic. When they sometimes
Come down the stairs at night and stand perplexed
Behind the door and headboard of the bed,
Brushing their chalky skull with chalky fingers,
With sounds like the dry rattling of a shutter,   130
That's what I sit up in the dark to say —
To no one any more since Toffile died.
Let them stay in the attic since they went there.
I promised Toffile to be cruel to them
For helping them to be cruel once to him.   135

SON. We think they had a grave down in the cellar.

MOTHER. We know they had a grave down in the cellar.

SON. We never could find out whose bones they were.

MOTHER. Yes, we could too, son. Tell the truth for once.
They were a man's his father killed for me.   140
I mean a man he killed instead of me.
The least I could do was to help dig their grave.
We were about it one night in the cellar.
Son knows the story: but 'twas not for him
To tell the truth, suppose the time had come.   145
Son looks surprised to see me end a lie
We'd kept all these years between ourselves
So as to have it ready for outsiders.
But tonight I don't care enough to lie —
I don't remember why I ever cared.   150
Toffile, if he were here, I don't believe
Could tell you why he ever cared himself. . . .

She hadn't found the finger-bone she wanted
Among the buttons poured out in her lap.
I verified the name next morning: Toffile.   155
The rural letter box said Toffile Lajway.

THE WITCH OF COÖS. Coös is the northernmost county in New Hampshire. 13. *Ralle the Sioux Control*: the spirit of a dead Indian. In spiritualism, a control is a spirit who serves as a contact between a medium and other spirits of the departed.

Donald Hall (b. 1928)
THE TOWN OF HILL

1975

Back of the dam, under
a flat pad

of water, church
bells ring

in the ears of lilies, 5
a child's swing

curls in the current
of a yard, horned

pout sleep
in a green 10

mailbox, and
a boy walks

from a screened
porch beneath

the man-shaped 15
leaves of an oak

down the street looking
at the town

of Hill that water
covered forty 20

years ago,
and the screen

door shuts
under dream water.

Thomas Hardy (1840–1928)
CHANNEL FIRING

1914

That night your great guns, unawares,
Shook all our coffins as we lay,
And broke the chancel window-squares,
We thought it was the Judgment-day

And sat upright. While drearisome   5
Arose the howl of wakened hounds:
The mouse let fall the altar-crumb,
The worms drew back into the mounds,

The glebe cow drooled. Till God called, "No;
It's gunnery practice out at sea   10
Just as before you went below;
The world is as it used to be:

"All nations striving strong to make
Red war yet redder. Mad as hatters
They do no more for Christés sake   15
Than you who are helpless in such matters.

"That this is not the judgment-hour
For some of them's a blessed thing,
For if it were they'd have to scour
Hell's floor for so much threatening . . .   20

"Ha, ha. It will be warmer when
I blow the trumpet (if indeed
I ever do; for you are men,
And rest eternal sorely need)."

So down we lay again. "I wonder,   25
Will the world ever saner be,"
Said one, "than when He sent us under
In our indifferent century!"

And many a skeleton shook his head.
"Instead of preaching forty year,"   30
My neighbor Parson Thirdly said,
"I wish I had stuck to pipes and beer."

Again the guns disturbed the hour,
Roaring their readiness to avenge,
As far inland as Stourton Tower,   35
And Camelot, and starlit Stonehenge.

CHANNEL FIRING. 9. *glebe:* land belonging to the church, used for grazing. 35. *Stourton Tower:* a monument to the defeat of the Danes by Alfred the Great in 879 A.D. 36. *Camelot:* where King Arthur held court; *Stonehenge:* circle of huge stones thought to be the ruins of a prehistoric place of worship.

COMPARE:

"Channel Firing" with "The Fury of Aerial Bombardment" by Richard Eberhart (page 50).

Thomas Hardy (1840–1928)

THE CONVERGENCE OF THE TWAIN

1912

Lines on the Loss of the "Titanic"

I

      In a solitude of the sea
      Deep from human vanity,
And the Pride of Life that planned her, stilly couches she.

II

      Steel chambers, late the pyres
      Of her salamandrine fires,
Cold currents thrid°, and turn to rhythmic tidal lyres.

      5   *thread*

III

      Over the mirrors meant
      To glass the opulent
The sea-worm crawls — grotesque, slimed, dumb, indifferent.

IV

      Jewels in joy designed
      To ravish the sensuous mind
Lie lightless, all their sparkles bleared and black and blind.

    10

V

      Dim moon-eyed fishes near
      Gaze at the gilded gear
And query: "What does this vaingloriousness down here?"

    15

VI

      Well: while was fashioning
      This creature of cleaving wing,
The Immanent Will that stirs and urges everything

VII

      Prepared a sinister mate
      For her — so gaily great —
A Shape of Ice, for the time far and dissociate.

    20

VIII

      And as the smart ship grew
      In stature, grace, and hue,
In shadowy silent distance grew the Iceberg too.

IX

      Alien they seemed to be:
      No mortal eye could see
The intimate welding of their later history,

    25

X

   Or sign that they were bent
   By paths coincident
On being anon twin halves of one august event.   30

XI

   Till the Spinner of the Years
   Said "Now!" And each one hears,
And consummation comes, and jars two hemispheres.

THE CONVERGENCE OF THE TWAIN. The luxury liner *Titanic*, supposedly unsinkable, went down in 1912 after striking an iceberg, on its first Atlantic voyage. 5. *salamandrine:* like the salamander, a lizard that supposedly thrives in fires, or like a spirit of the same name that inhabits fire (according to alchemists).

Robert Hayden (1913–1980)
A ROAD IN KENTUCKY   1966

And when that ballad lady went
   to ease the lover whose life she broke,
oh surely this is the real road she took,
   road all hackled through barberry fire,
through cedar and alder and sumac and thorn.   5

Red clay stained her flounces
   and stones cut her shoes
and the road twisted on to his loveless house
   and his cornfield dying
in the scarecrow's arms.   10

And when she had left her lover lying
   so stark and so stark, with the Star-of-Hope
drawn over his eyes, oh this is the road
   that lady walked in the cawing light,
so dark and so dark in the briary light.   15

COMPARE:

"A Road in Kentucky" with the anonymous ballad "Bonny Barbara Allan" (page 516).

Seamus Heaney (b. 1939)
DIGGING   1966

Between my finger and my thumb
The squat pen rests; snug as a gun.

Under my window, a clean rasping sound
When the spade sinks into gravelly ground:
My father, digging. I look down   5

Till his straining rump among the flowerbeds
Bends low, comes up twenty years away
Stooping in rhythm through potato drills
Where he was digging.

The coarse boot nestled on the lug, the shaft   10
Against the inside knee was levered firmly.
He rooted out tall tops, buried the bright edge deep
To scatter new potatoes that we picked
Loving their cool hardness in our hands.

By God, the old man could handle a spade.   15
Just like his old man.

My grandfather cut more turf in a day
Than any other man on Toner's bog.
Once I carried him milk in a bottle
Corked sloppily with paper. He straightened up   20
To drink it, then fell to right away

Nicking and slicing neatly, heaving sods
Over his shoulder, going down and down
For the good turf. Digging.

The cold smell of potato mould, the squelch and slap   25
Of soggy peat, the curt cuts of an edge
Through living roots awaken in my head.
But I've no spade to follow men like them.

Between my finger and my thumb
The squat pen rests.   30
I'll dig with it.

Anthony Hecht (b. 1923)

THE VOW   1967

In the third month, a sudden flow of blood.
The mirth of tabrets ceaseth, and the joy
Also of the harp. The frail image of God
Lay spilled and formless. Neither girl nor boy,
But yet blood of my blood, nearly my child.   5
        All that long day
Her pale face turned to the window's mild
        Featureless grey.

And for some nights she whimpered as she dreamed
The dead thing spoke, saying: "Do not recall   10
Pleasure at my conception. I am redeemed
From pain and sorrow. Mourn rather for all
Who breathlessly issue from the bone gates,
        The gates of horn,
For truly it is best of all the fates   15
        Not to be born.

"Mother, a child lay gasping for bare breath
On Christmas Eve when Santa Claus had set
Death in the stocking, and the lights of death
Flamed in the tree. O, if you can, forget   20
You were the child, turn to my father's lips
        Against the time
When his cold hand puts forth its fingertips
        Of jointed lime."

Doctors of Science, what is man that he   25
Should hope to come to a good end? *The best
Is not to have been born.* And could it be
That Jewish diligence and Irish jest
The consent of flesh and a midwinter storm
        Had reconciled,   30
Was yet too bold a mixture to inform
        A simple child?

Even as gold is tried, Gentile and Jew.
If that ghost was a girl's, I swear to it:
Your mother shall be far more blessed than you.   35
And if a boy's, I swear: The flames are lit
That shall refine us; they shall not destroy
        A living hair.
Your younger brothers shall confirm in joy
        This that I swear.   40

THE VOW. 2. *tabrets:* small drums used to accompany traditional Jewish dances. 14. *gates of horn:* According to Homer and Virgil pleasant, lying dreams emerge from the underworld through gates of ivory; ominous, truth-telling dreams, through gates of horn.

George Herbert (1593–1633)

LOVE   1633

Love bade me welcome; yet my soul drew back,
        Guilty of dust and sin.
But quick-eyed Love, observing me grow slack
        From my first entrance in,
Drew nearer to me, sweetly questioning   5
        If I lacked anything.

"A guest," I answered, "worthy to be here";
        Love said, "You shall be he."
"I, the unkind, ungrateful? Ah, my dear,
        I cannot look on Thee."   10
Love took my hand, and smiling did reply,
        "Who made the eyes but I?"

"Truth, Lord, but I have marred them; let my shame
        Go where it doth deserve."
"And know you not," says Love, "who bore the blame?"   15
        "My dear, then I will serve."
"You must sit down," says Love, "and taste My meat."
        So I did sit and eat.

COMPARE

"Love" with "Batter my heart, three-personed God, for You" by John Donne
(page 36).

Robert Herrick (1591–1674)
DELIGHT IN DISORDER   1633

A sweet disorder in the dress
Kindles in clothes a wantonness.
A lawn° about the shoulders thrown   *linen*
Into a fine distractión;
An erring lace, which here and there   5
Enthralls the crimson stomacher;
A cuff neglectful, and thereby
Ribbons to flow confusedly;
A winning wave, deserving note,
In the tempestuous petticoat;   10
A careless shoestring, in whose tie
I see a wild civility;
Do more bewitch me than when art
Is too precise in every part.

Robert Herrick (1591–1674)
TO THE VIRGINS, TO MAKE MUCH OF TIME   1648

Gather ye rose-buds while ye may,
    Old Time is still a-flying;
And this same flower that smiles today,
    Tomorrow will be dying.

The glorious lamp of heaven, the sun,   5
    The higher he's a-getting,
The sooner will his race be run,
    And nearer he's to setting.

That age is best which is the first,
    When youth and blood are warmer;   10
But being spent, the worse, and worst
    Times still succeed the former.

Then be not coy, but use your time,
    And while ye may, go marry;   15
For having lost but once your prime,
    You may for ever tarry.

COMPARE:

"To the Virgins, to Make Much of Time" with "To His Coy Mistress" by
Andrew Marvell (page 370).

Gerard Manley Hopkins (1844–1889)

THE WINDHOVER   (1877)

To Christ Our Lord

I caught this morning morning's minion, king-
    dom of daylight's dauphin, dapple-dawn-drawn Falcon, in his riding
    Of the rolling level underneath him steady air, and striding
High there, how he rung upon the rein of a wimpling wing
In his ecstasy! then off, off forth on swing,
    As a skate's heel sweeps smooth on a bow-bend: the hurl and gliding
    Rebuffed the big wind. My heart in hiding
Stirred for a bird,—the achieve of, the mastery of the thing!

Brute beauty and valor and act, oh, air, pride, plume, here
    Buckle! and the fire that breaks from thee then, a billion   10
Times told lovelier, more dangerous, O my chevalier!

    No wonder of it: shéer plód makes plow down sillion°   *furrow*
Shine, and blue-bleak embers, ah my dear,
    Fall, gall themselves, and gash gold-vermilion.

THE WINDHOVER. A windhover is a kestrel, or small falcon, so called because it can hover
upon the wind. 4. *rung . . . wing:* A horse is "rung upon the rein" when its trainer holds
the end of a long rein and has the horse circle him. The possible meanings of *wimpling*
include (1) curving; (2) pleated, arranged in many little folds one on top of another; (3)
rippling or undulating like the surface of a flowing stream.

A. E. Housman (1859–1936)

"Terence, this is stupid stuff:
You eat your victuals fast enough;
There can't be much amiss, 'tis clear,
To see the rate you drink your beer.
But oh, good Lord, the verse you make,   5
It gives a chap the belly-ache.
The cow, the old cow, she is dead;
It sleeps well, the horned head:
We poor lads, 'tis our turn now
To hear such tunes as killed the cow.   10
Pretty friendship 'tis to rhyme
Your friends to death before their time
Moping melancholy mad:
Come, pipe a tune to dance to, lad."

Why, if 'tis dancing you would be,   15
There's brisker pipes than poetry.
Say, for what were hop-yards meant,
Or why was Burton built on Trent?
Oh many a peer of England brews
Livelier liquor than the Muse,   20
And malt does more than Milton can
To justify God's ways to man.
Ale, man, ale's the stuff to drink
For fellows whom it hurts to think:
Look into the pewter pot   25
To see the world as the world's not.
And faith, 'tis pleasant till 'tis past:
The mischief is that 'twill not last.
Oh I have been to Ludlow fair
And left my necktie God knows where,   30
And carried half-way home, or near,
Pints and quarts of Ludlow beer:
Then the world seemed none so bad,
And I myself a sterling lad;
And down in lovely muck I've lain,   35
Happy till I woke again.
Then I saw the morning sky:
Heigho, the tale was all a lie;
The world, it was the old world yet,
I was I, my things were wet,   40
And nothing now remained to do
But begin the game anew.

Therefore, since the world has still
Much good, but much less good than ill,

And while the sun and moon endure   45
Luck's a chance, but trouble's sure,
I'd face it as a wise man would,
And train for ill and not for good.
'Tis true, the stuff I bring for sale
Is not so brisk a brew as ale: 50
Out of a stem that scored the hand
I wrung it in a weary land.
But take it: if the smack is sour,
The better for the embittered hour;
It should do good to heart and head   55
When your soul is in my soul's stead;
And I will friend you, if I may,
In the dark and cloudy day.

   There was a king reigned in the East:
There, when kings will sit to feast,   60
They get their fill before they think
With poisoned meat and poisoned drink.
He gathered all that springs to birth
From the many-venomed earth;
First a little, thence to more,   65
He sampled all her killing store;
And easy, smiling, seasoned sound,
Sate the king when healths went round.
They put arsenic in his meat
And stared aghast to watch him eat;   70
They poured strychnine in his cup
And shook to see him drink it up:
They shook, they stared as white's their shirt:
Them it was their poison hurt.
—I tell the tale that I heard told.   75
Mithridates, he died old.

TERENCE, THIS IS STUPID STUFF. 1. *Terence:* As a name for himself, Housman takes that of a
Roman poet, author of satiric comedies. 18. *why was Burton built on Trent?* The answer is:
to use the river's water in the town's brewing industry.

A. E. Housman (1859–1936)
TO AN ATHLETE DYING YOUNG   1896

The time you won your town the race
We chaired you through the market-place;
Man and boy stood cheering by,
And home we brought you shoulder-high.

Today, the road all runners come,   5
Shoulder-high we bring you home,
And set you at your threshold down,
Townsman of a stiller town.

Smart lad, to slip betimes away
From fields where glory does not stay,   10
And early though the laurel grows
It withers quicker than the rose.

Eyes the shady night has shut
Cannot see the record cut,
And silence sounds no worse than cheers   15
After earth has stopped the ears.

Now you will not swell the rout
Of lads that wore their honors out,
Runners whom renown outran
And the name died before the man.   20

So set, before its echoes fade,
The fleet foot on the sill of shade,
And hold to the low lintel up
The still-defended challenge-cup.

And round that early-laureled head   25
Will flock to gaze the strengthless dead,
And find unwithered on its curls
The garland briefer than a girl's.

COMPARE:

"To an Athlete Dying Young" with "To the Memory of Mr. Oldham" by John
Dryden (page 332).

Langston Hughes (1902–1967)
DREAM DEFERRED   1951

What happens to a dream deferred?

    Does it dry up
    like a raisin in the sun?
    Or fester like a sore—
    And then run?   5
    Does it stink like rotten meat?
    Or crust and sugar over—
    like a syrupy sweet?

    Maybe it just sags
    like a heavy load.   10

    Or does it explode?

COMPARE:

"Dream Deferred" with "Black Tambourine" by Hart Crane (page 205), "Saturday's Child" by Countee Cullen (page 322), and "Ballad of Birmingham" by
Dudley Randall (page 382).

Ted Hughes (b. 1930)

EXAMINATION AT THE WOMB-DOOR

Who owns these scrawny little feet? *Death.*
Who owns this bristly scorched-looking face? *Death.*
Who owns these still-working lungs? *Death.*
Who owns this utility coat of muscles? *Death.*
Who owns these unspeakable guts? *Death.*   5
Who owns these questionable brains? *Death.*
All this messy blood? *Death.*
These minimum-efficiency eyes? *Death.*
This wicked little tongue? *Death.*
This occasional wakefulness? *Death.*
                                              10

Given, stolen, or held pending trial?
Held.

Who owns the whole rainy, stony earth? *Death.*
Who owns all of space? *Death.*

Who is stronger than hope? *Death.*   15
Who is stronger than the will? *Death.*
Stronger than love? *Death.*
Stronger than life? *Death.*

But who is stronger than death?
                              Me, evidently.

Pass, Crow.   20

EXAMINATION AT THE WOMB-DOOR. This poem and the following two are from *Crow*, a book-length series of songs and fables whose central character, like some figures in African and American Indian legend, seems part bird, part human being, and part supernatural hero.

CROW'S FIRST LESSON

1972

God tried to teach Crow how to talk.
'Love,' said God. 'Say, Love.'
Crow gaped, and the white shark crashed into the sea
And went rolling downwards, discovering its own depth.

'No, no,' said God, 'Say Love. Now try it. LOVE.'   5
Crow gaped, and a bluefly, a tsetse, a mosquito
Zoomed out and down
To their sundry flesh-pots.

'A final try,' said God. 'Now, LOVE.'
Crow convulsed, gaped, retched and   10

Man's bodiless prodigious head
Bulbed out onto the earth, with swivelling eyes,
Jabbering protest—

And Crow retched again, before God could stop him.
And woman's vulva dropped over man's neck and tightened.   15
The two struggled together on the grass.
God struggled to part them, cursed, wept—

Crow flew guiltily off.

CROW AND STONE   1972

Crow was nimble but had to be careful
Of his eyes, the two dewdrops.
Stone, champion of the globe, lumbered towards him.

No point in detailing a battle
Where stone battered itself featureless   5
While Crow grew perforce nimbler.

The subnormal arena of space, agog,
Cheered these gladiators many aeons.
Still their struggle resounds.

But by now the stone is a dust—flying in vain,   10
And Crow has become a monster—his mere eyeblink
Holding the very globe in terror.

And still he who never has been killed
Croaks helplessly
And is only just born.   15

David Ignatow (b. 1914)
GET THE GASWORKS   1948

Get the gasworks into a poem,
and you've got the smoke and smokestacks,
the mottled red and yellow tenements,
and grimy kids who curse with the pungency
of the odor of gas. You've got America, boy.   5

Sketch in the river and barges,
all dirty and slimy.
How do the seagulls stay so white?
And always cawing like little mad geniuses?
You've got the kind of living   10
that makes the kind of thinking we do:

gaswork smokestack whistle tooting wisecracks.
They don't come because we like it that way,
but because we find it outside our window each morning,
in soot on the furniture,   15
and trucks carrying coal for gas,
the kid hot after the ball under the wheel.
He gets it over the belly, all right.
He dies there.

So the kids keep tossing the ball around   20
after the funeral.
So the cops keep chasing them,
so the mamas keep hollering,
and papa flings his newspaper outward,
in disgust with discipline.   25

Randall Jarrell (1914–1965)
The Death of the Ball Turret Gunner   1945

From my mother's sleep I fell into the State
And I hunched in its belly till my wet fur froze.
Six miles from earth, loosed from its dream of life,
I woke to black flak and the nightmare fighters.
When I died they washed me out of the turret with a hose.

THE DEATH OF THE BALL TURRET GUNNER. Mr. Jarrell has written: "A ball turret was a plex-
iglass sphere set into the belly of a B-17 or B-24, and inhabited by two .50 caliber machine-
guns and one man, a short small man. When this gunner tracked with his machine-guns
a fighter attacking his bomber from below, he revolved with the turret; hunched upside-
down in his little sphere, he looked like the fetus in the womb. The fighters which at-
tacked him were armed with cannon firing explosive shells. The hose was a steam hose."

COMPARE:

"The Death of the Ball Turret Gunner" with "Dulce et Decorum Est" by Wilfred
Owen (page 26).

Randall Jarrell (1914–1965)
The Woman at the Washington Zoo   1960

The saris go by me from the embassies.

Cloth from the moon. Cloth from another planet.
They look back at the leopard like the leopard.

And I. . . .
            this print of mine, that has kept its color
Alive through so many cleanings; this dull null   5

Navy I wear to work, and wear from work, and so
To my bed, so to my grave, with no
Complaints, no comment: neither from my chief,
The Deputy Chief Assistant, nor his chief—
Only I complain. . . . this serviceable   10
Body that no sunlight dyes, no hand suffuses
But, dome-shadowed, withering among columns,
Wavy beneath fountains—small, far-off, shining
In the eyes of animals, these beings trapped
As I am trapped but not, themselves, the trap,   15
Aging, but without knowledge of their age,
Kept safe here, knowing not of death, for death—
Oh, bars of my own body, open, open!

The world goes by my cage and never sees me.
And there come not to me, as come to these,   20
The wild beasts, sparrows pecking the llamas' grain,
Pigeons settling on the bears' bread, buzzards
Tearing the meat the flies have clouded. . . .
                                        Vulture,
When you come for the white rat that the foxes left,
Take off the red helmet of your head, the black   25
Wings that have shadowed me, and step to me as man:
The wild brother at whose feet the white wolves fawn,
To whose hand of power the great lioness
Stalks, purring. . . .
                        You know what I was,
You see what I am: change me, change me!   30

John Keats (1795–1821)

ODE ON A GRECIAN URN   1820

Thou still unravished bride of quietness,
    Thou foster-child of silence and slow time,
Sylvan historian, who canst thus express
    A flowery tale more sweetly than our rhyme:
What leaf-fringed legend haunts about thy shape   5
    Of deities or mortals, or of both,
        In Tempe or the dales of Arcady?
    What men or gods are these? What maidens loth?
What mad pursuit? What struggle to escape?
        What pipes and timbrels? What wild ecstasy?   10

Heard melodies are sweet, but those unheard
    Are sweeter; therefore, ye soft pipes, play on;
Not to the sensual° ear, but, more endeared,   *physical*
    Pipe to the spirit ditties of no tone:

Fair youth, beneath the trees, thou canst not leave 15
   Thy song, nor ever can those trees be bare;
     Bold Lover, never, never canst thou kiss,
Though winning near the goal—yet, do not grieve;
     She cannot fade, though thou hast not thy bliss,
   For ever wilt thou love, and she be fair! 20

Ah, happy, happy boughs! that cannot shed
   Your leaves, nor ever bid the Spring adieu;
And, happy melodist, unwearièd,
   For ever piping songs for ever new;
More happy love! more happy, happy love! 25
   For ever warm and still to be enjoyed,
     For ever panting, and for ever young;
All breathing human passion far above,
   That leaves a heart high-sorrowful and cloyed,
     A burning forehead, and a parching tongue. 30

Who are these coming to the sacrifice?
   To what green altar, O mysterious priest,
Lead'st thou that heifer lowing at the skies,
   And all her silken flanks with garlands drest?
What little town by river or sea shore, 35
   Or mountain-built with peaceful citadel,
     Is emptied of this folk, this pious morn?
And, little town, thy streets for evermore
   Will silent be; and not a soul to tell
     Why thou art desolate, can e'er return. 40

O Attic shape! Fair attitude! with brede°   *design*
   Of marble men and maidens overwrought,
With forest branches and the trodden weed;
   Thou, silent form, dost tease us out of thought
As doth Eternity: Cold Pastoral! 45
   When old age shall this generation waste,
     Thou shalt remain, in midst of other woe
Than ours, a friend to man, to whom thou say'st,
Beauty is truth, truth beauty,—that is all
   Ye know on earth, and all ye need to know. 50

ODE ON A GRECIAN URN. 7. *Tempe, dales of Arcady:* valleys in Greece. 41. *Attic:* Athenian, possessing a classical simplicity and grace. 49–50: If Keats had put the urn's words in quotation marks, critics might have been spared much ink. Does the urn say just "beauty is truth, truth beauty," or does its statement take in the whole of the last two lines?

COMPARE:

"Ode on a Grecian Urn" with "Lapis Lazuli" by William Butler Yeats (page 419) and "Anecdote of the Jar" by Wallace Stevens (page 207).

John Keats (1795–1821)

On First Looking into Chapman's Homer   1816

Much have I traveled in the realms of gold,
  And many goodly states and kingdoms seen;
  Round many western islands have I been
Which bards in fealty to Apollo hold.
Oft of one wide expanse had I been told   5
  That deep-browed Homer ruled as his demesne°,   *domain*
  Yet did I never breathe its pure serene
Till I heard Chapman speak out loud and bold.
Then felt I like some watcher of the skies
  When a new planet swims into his ken;   10
Or like stout Cortez when with eagle eyes
  He stared at the Pacific — and all his men
Looked at each other with a wild surmise —
  Silent, upon a peak in Darien.

On First Looking into Chapman's Homer. When one evening in October 1816 Keats's friend and former teacher Cowden Clarke introduced the young poet to George Chapman's vigorous Elizabethan translations of the *Iliad* and the *Odyssey*, Keats stayed up all night reading and discussing them in high excitement; then went home at dawn to compose this sonnet, which Clarke received at his breakfast table. 4. *fealty:* in feudalism, the loyalty of a vassal to his lord; *Apollo:* classical god of poetic inspiration. 11. *stout Cortez:* the best-known boner in English poetry. (What Spanish explorer *was* the first European to view the Pacific?) 14. *Darien:* old name for the Isthmus of Panama.

John Keats (1795–1821)

To Autumn   1820

I

Season of mists and mellow fruitfulness,
  Close bosom-friend of the maturing sun;
Conspiring with him how to load and bless
  With fruit the vines that round the thatch-eves run;
To bend with apples the mossed cottage-trees,   5
  And fill all fruit with ripeness to the core;
    To swell the gourd, and plump the hazel shells
With a sweet kernel; to set budding more,
  And still more, later flowers for the bees,
  Until they think warm days will never cease,   10
    For Summer has o'er-brimmed their clammy cells.

II

Who hath not seen thee oft amid thy store?
  Sometimes whoever seeks abroad may find
Thee sitting careless on a granary floor,
  Thy hair soft-lifted by the winnowing wind;   15

Or on a half-reaped furrow sound asleep,
   Drowsed with the fume of poppies, while thy hook
     Spares the next swath and all its twinèd flowers:
And sometimes like a gleaner thou dost keep
   Steady thy laden head across a brook;   20
   Or by a cider-press, with patient look,
     Thou watchest the last oozings hours by hours.

III

Where are the songs of Spring? Ay, where are they?
   Think not of them, thou hast thy music too, —
While barrèd clouds bloom the soft-dying day,   25
   And touch the stubble-plains with rosy hue;
Then in a wailful choir the small gnats mourn
   Among the river sallows°, borne aloft   *willows*
     Or sinking as the light wind lives or dies;
And full-grown lambs loud bleat from hilly bourn;   30
   Hedge-crickets sing; and now with treble soft
   The red-breast whistles from a garden-croft°;   *garden plot*
     And gathering swallows twitter in the skies.

COMPARE:

"To Autumn" with "In the Elegy Season" by Richard Wilbur (page 38).

Maxine Kumin (b. 1925)

WOODCHUCKS   1972

Gassing the woodchucks didn't turn out right.
The knockout bomb from the Feed and Grain Exchange
was featured as merciful, quick at the bone
and the case we had against them was airtight,
both exits shoehorned shut with puddingstone,   5
but they had a sub-sub-basement out of range.

Next morning they turned up again, no worse
for the cyanide than we for our cigarettes
and state-store Scotch, all of us up to scratch.
They brought down the marigolds as a matter of course   10
and then took over the vegetable patch
nipping the broccoli shoots, beheading the carrots.

The food from our mouths, I said, righteously thrilling
to the feel of the .22, the bullets' neat noses.
I, a lapsed pacifist fallen from grace   15
puffed with Darwinian pieties for killing,
now drew a bead on the littlest woodchuck's face.
He died down in the everbearing roses.

Ten minutes later I dropped the mother. She
flipflopped in the air and fell, her needle teeth   20
still hooked in a leaf of early Swiss chard.
Another baby next. O one-two-three
the murderer inside me rose up hard,
the hawkeye killer came on stage forthwith.

There's one chuck left. Old wily fellow, he keeps   25
me cocked and ready day after day after day.
All night I hunt his humped-up form. I dream
I sight along the barrel in my sleep.
If only they'd all consented to die unseen
gassed underground the quiet Nazi way.   30

COMPARE:

"Woodchucks" with "The Bull Calf" by Irving Layton (page 365) and "Janet
Waking" by John Crowe Ransom (page 383).

Philip Larkin (b. 1922)

VERS DE SOCIÉTÉ   1974

My wife and I have asked a crowd of craps
To come and waste their time and ours: perhaps
You'd care to join us? In a pig's arse, friend.
Day comes to an end.
The gas fire breathes, the trees are darkly swayed.   5
And so *Dear Warlock-Williams: I'm afraid—*

Funny how hard it is to be alone.
I could spend half my evenings, if I wanted,
Holding a glass of washing sherry, canted
Over to catch the drivel of some bitch   10
Who's read nothing but *Which;*
Just think of all the spare time that has flown

Straight into nothingness by being filled
With forks and faces, rather than repaid
Under a lamp, hearing the noise of wind,   15
And looking out to see the moon thinned
To an air-sharpened blade.
A life, and yet how sternly it's instilled

All solitude is selfish. No one now
Believes the hermit with his gown and dish   20
Talking to God (who's gone too); the big wish
Is to have people nice to you, which means
Doing it back somehow.
Virtue is social. Are, then, these routines

Playing at goodness, like going to church?   25
Something that bores us, something we don't do well
(Asking that ass about his fool research)
But try to feel, because, however crudely,
It shows us what should be?
Too subtle, that. Too decent, too. Oh hell,   30

Only the young can be alone freely.
The time is shorter now for company,
And sitting by a lamp more often brings
Not peace, but other things.
Beyond the light stand failure and remorse   35
Whispering *Dear Warlock-Williams: Why, of course* —

VERS DE SOCIÉTÉ. The title is a French term for light verse, especially that written for social occasions. 9. *washing sherry:* sherry the quality of washing liquid, or dish detergent. 11. *Which:* British equivalent of *Consumer Reports.*

Philip Larkin (b. 1922)

WEDDING-WIND   1955

The wind blew all my wedding-day,
And my wedding-night was the night of the high wind;
And a stable door was banging, again and again,
That he must go and shut it, leaving me
Stupid in candlelight, hearing rain,   5
Seeing my face in the twisted candlestick,
Yet seeing nothing. When he came back
He said the horses were restless, and I was sad
That any man or beast that night should lack
The happiness I had.   10

           Now in the day
All's raveled under the sun by the wind's blowing.
He has gone to look at the floods, and I
Carry a chipped pail to the chicken-run,
Set it down, and stare. All is the wind
Hunting through clouds and forests, thrashing   15
My apron and the hanging cloths on the line.
Can it be borne, this bodying-forth by wind
Of joy my actions turn on, like a thread
Carrying beads? Shall I be let to sleep
Now this perpetual morning shares my bed?   20
Can even death dry up
These new delighted lakes, conclude
Our kneeling as cattle by all-generous waters?

COMPARE:

"Wedding-Wind" with "The River Merchant's Wife: a Letter" by Ezra Pound (page 379).

D. H. Lawrence (1885–1930)

A YOUTH MOWING

1917

There are four men mowing down by the Isar;
I can hear the swish of the scythe-strokes, four
Sharp breaths taken: yea, and I
Am sorry for what's in store.

The first man out of the four that's mowing   5
Is mine, I claim him once and for all;
Though it's sorry I am, on his young feet, knowing
None of the trouble he's led to stall.

As he sees me bringing the dinner, he lifts
His head as proud as a deer that looks   10
Shoulder-deep out of the corn; and wipes
His scythe-blade bright, unhooks

The scythe-stone and over the stubble to me.
Lad, thou hast gotten a child in me,
Laddie, a man thou'lt ha'e to be,   15
Yea, though I'm sorry for thee.

A YOUTH MOWING. 1. *Isar:* river in Austria and Germany that flows into the Danube.

Irving Layton (b. 1912)

THE BULL CALF

1959

The thing could barely stand. Yet taken
from his mother and the barn smells
he still impressed with his pride,
with the promise of sovereignty in the way
his head moved to take us in.   5
The fierce sunlight tugging the maize from the ground
licked at his shapely flanks.
He was too young for all that pride.
I thought of the deposed Richard II.

"No money in bull calves," Freeman had said.   10
The visiting clergyman rubbed the nostrils
now snuffing pathetically at the windless day.
"A pity," he sighed.
My gaze slipped off his hat toward the empty sky
that circled over the black knot of men,   15
over us and the calf waiting for the first blow.

Struck,
the bull calf drew in his thin forelegs
as if gathering strength for a mad rush . . .
tottered . . . raised his darkening eyes to us,   20
and I saw we were at the far end

of his frightened look, growing smaller and smaller
till we were only the ponderous mallet
that flicked his bleeding ear
and pushed him over on his side, stiffly,   25
like a block of wood.

Below the hill's crest
the river snuffled on the improvised beach.
We dug a deep pit and threw the dead calf into it.
It made a wet sound, a sepulchral gurgle,   30
as the warm sides bulged and flattened.
Settled, the bull calf lay as if asleep,
one foreleg over the other,
bereft of pride and so beautiful now,
without movement, perfectly still in the cool pit,   35
I turned away and wept.

COMPARE:

"The Bull Calf" with "Woodchucks" by Maxine Kumin (page 362) and "Janet
Waking" by John Crowe Ransom (page 383).

Denise Levertov (b. 1923)
WAYS OF CONQUEST   1975

You invaded my country by accident,
not knowing you had crossed the border.
Vines that grew there touched you.
                        You ran past them,
shaking raindrops off the leaves—you or the wind.   5
It was toward the hills you ran,
inland—

I invaded your country with all my
'passionate intensity,'
pontoons and parachutes of my blindness.   10
But living now in the suburbs of the capital
incognito,
            my will to take the heart of the city
            has dwindled. I love
its unsuspecting life,   15
its adolescents who come to tell me their dreams in the dusty park
among the rocks and benches,
I the stranger who will listen.
I love
the wild herons who return each year to the marshy outskirts.   20
What I invaded has
invaded me.

WAYS OF CONQUEST. 9. *'passionate intensity'*: For the source of this phrase, see William
Butler Yeats's "The Second Coming," page 215.

Philip Levine (b. 1928)

To a Child Trapped in a Barber Shop   1966

You've gotten in through the transom
    and you can't get out
till Monday morning or, worse,
    till the cops come.

That six-year-old red face   5
    calling for mama
is yours; it won't help you
    because your case

is closed forever, hopeless.
    So don't drink   10
the Lucky Tiger, don't
    fill up on grease

because that makes it a lot worse,
    that makes it a crime
against property and the state   15
    and that costs time.

We've all been here before,
    we took our turn
under the electric storm
    of the vibrator   20

and stiffened our wills to meet
    the close clippers
and heard the true blade mowing
    back and forth

on a strip of dead skin,   25
    and we stopped crying.
You think your life is over?
    It's just begun.

Vachel Lindsay (1879–1931)

Factory Windows Are Always Broken   1914

Factory windows are always broken.
Somebody's always throwing bricks,
Somebody's always heaving cinders,
Playing ugly Yahoo tricks.

Factory windows are always broken.   5
Other windows are let alone.
No one throws through the chapel-window
The bitter, snarling, derisive stone.

Factory windows are always broken.
Something or other is going wrong.   10
Something is rotten—I think, in Denmark.
End of the factory-window song.

FACTORY WINDOWS ARE ALWAYS BROKEN. 4. *Yahoo:* In *Gulliver's Travels* by Jonathan Swift,
yahoos are apelike creatures, vicious and destructive—Swift's caricatures of humankind.
11. *Something . . . Denmark:* "Something is rotten in the state of Denmark."—Marcellus in
Hamlet I, iv, 90.

Robert Lowell (1917–1977)

SKUNK HOUR   1959

For Elizabeth Bishop

Nautilus Island's hermit
heiress still lives through winters in her Spartan cottage;
her sheep still graze above the sea.
Her son's a bishop. Her farmer
is first selectman in our village;   5
she's in her dotage.

Thirsting for
the hierarchic privacy
of Queen Victoria's century,
she buys up all   10
the eyesores facing her shore,
and lets them fall.

The season's ill—
we've lost our summer millionaire,
who seemed to leap from an L. L. Bean   15
catalogue. His nine-knot yawl
was auctioned off to lobstermen.
A red fox stain covers Blue Hill.

And now our fairy
decorator brightens his shop for fall;   20
his fishnet's filled with orange cork,
orange, his cobbler's bench and awl;
there is no money in his work,
he'd rather marry.

One dark night,   25
my Tudor Ford climbed the hill's skull;
I watched for love-cars. Lights turned down,
they lay together, hull to hull,
where the graveyard shelves on the town. . . .
My mind's not right.   30

A car radio bleats,
"Love, O careless Love. . . ." I hear
my ill-spirit sob in each blood cell,
as if my hand were at its throat. . . .
I myself am hell;   35
nobody's here—

only skunks, that search
in the moonlight for a bite to eat.
They march on their soles up Main Street:
white stripes, moonstruck eyes' red fire   40
under the chalk-dry and spar spire
of the Trinitarian Church.

I stand on top
of our back steps and breathe the rich air—
a mother skunk with her column of kittens swills the garbage pail.   45
She jabs her wedge-head in a cup
of sour cream, drops her ostrich tail,
and will not scare.

Archibald MacLeish (b. 1892)

The End of the World   1926

Quite unexpectedly as Vasserot
The armless ambidextrian was lighting
A match between his great and second toe,
And Ralph the lion was engaged in biting
The neck of Madame Sossman while the drum   5
Pointed, and Teeny was about to cough
In waltz-time swinging Jocko by the thumb—
Quite unexpectedly the top blew off:

And there, there overhead, there, there hung over
Those thousands of white faces, those dazed eyes,   10
There in the starless dark the poise, the hover,
There with vast wings across the canceled skies,
There in the sudden blackness the black pall
Of nothing, nothing, nothing—nothing at all.

Compare:

"The End of the World" with "Fire and Ice" by Robert Frost (page 76).

Christopher Marlowe (1564–1593)

The Passionate Shepherd to His Love

1600

Come live with me and be my love,
And we will all the pleasures prove
That valleys, groves, hills, and fields,
Woods, or steepy mountain yields.

And we will sit upon the rocks,   5
Seeing the shepherds feed their flocks
By shallow rivers, to whose falls
Melodious birds sing madrigals.

And I will make thee beds of roses
And a thousand fragrant posies,   10
A cap of flowers and a kirtle°   *skirt*
Embroidered all with leaves of myrtle;

A gown made of the finest wool
Which from our pretty lambs we pull;
Fair-linèd slippers for the cold,   15
With buckles of the purest gold;

A belt of straw and ivy buds,
With coral clasps and amber studs.
And if these pleasures may thee move,
Come live with me and be my love.   20

The shepherds' swains shall dance and sing
For thy delight each May morning.
If these delights thy mind may move,
Then live with me and be my love.

Compare:

"The Passionate Shepherd to His Love" with "The Bait" by John Donne (page 329).

Andrew Marvell (1621–1678)

To His Coy Mistress

1681

Had we but world enough, and time,
This coyness°, lady, were no crime.   *modesty, reluctance*
We would sit down and think which way
To walk, and pass our long love's day.
Thou by the Indian Ganges' side   5
Should'st rubies find; I by the tide
Of Humber would complain°. I would   *sing sad songs*
Love you ten years before the Flood,

And you should, if you please, refuse
Till the conversion of the Jews.   10
My vegetable° love should grow   *vegetative, flourishing*
Vaster than empires, and more slow.
An hundred years should go to praise
Thine eyes, and on thy forehead gaze,
Two hundred to adore each breast,   15
But thirty thousand to the rest.
An age at least to every part,
And the last age should show your heart.
For, lady, you deserve this state,
Nor would I love at lower rate.   20
    But at my back I always hear
Time's wingèd chariot hurrying near;
And yonder all before us lie
Deserts of vast eternity.
Thy beauty shall no more be found,   25
Nor in thy marble vault shall sound
My echoing song; then worms shall try
That long preserved virginity,
And your quaint honor turn to dust,
And into ashes all my lust.   30
The grave's a fine and private place,
But none, I think, do there embrace.
    Now therefore, while the youthful hue
Sits on thy skin like morning glew°   *glow*
And while thy willing soul transpires   35
At every pore with instant° fires,   *eager*
Now let us sport us while we may;
And now, like am'rous birds of prey,
Rather at once our time devour,
Than languish in his slow-chapped power,   40
Let us roll all our strength, and all
Our sweetness, up into one ball;
And tear our pleasures with rough strife
Thorough° the iron gates of life.   *through*
Thus, though we cannot make our sun   45
Stand still, yet we will make him run.

To His Coy Mistress. 7. *Humber:* a river that flows by Marvell's town of Hull (on the side
of the world opposite from the Ganges). 10. *conversion of the Jews:* an event that, according to St. John the Divine, is to take place just before the end of the world.

Compare:

"To His Coy Mistress" with "To the Virgins, to Make Much of Time" by Robert
Herrick (page 351).

James Merrill (b. 1926)

LABORATORY POEM

1958

Charles used to watch Naomi, taking heart
And a steel saw, open up turtles, live.
While she swore they felt nothing, he would gag
At blood, at the blind twitching, even after
The murky dawn of entrails cleared, revealing   5
Contours he knew, egg-yellows like lamps paling.

Well then. She carried off the beating heart
To the kymograph and rigged it there, a rag
In fitful wind, now made to strain, now stopped
By her solutions tonic or malign   10
Alternately in which it would be steeped.
What the heart bore, she noted on a chart,

For work did not stop only with the heart.
He thought of certain human hearts, their climb
Through violence into exquisite disciplines   15
Of which, as it now appeared, they all expired.
Soon she would fetch another and start over,
Easy in the presence of her lover.

LABORATORY POEM. 8. *kymograph:* device to record wavelike motions or pulsations on a piece of paper fastened to a revolving drum.

W. S. Merwin (b. 1927)

FOR THE ANNIVERSARY OF MY DEATH

1967

Every year without knowing it I have passed the day
When the last fires will wave to me
And the silence will set out
Tireless traveller
Like the beam of a lightless star   5

Then I will no longer
Find myself in life as in a strange garment
Surprised at the earth
And the love of one woman
And the shamelessness of men   10
As today writing after three days of rain
Hearing the wren sing and the falling cease
And bowing not knowing to what

John Milton (1608–1674)

WHEN I CONSIDER HOW MY LIGHT IS SPENT (1652?)

When I consider how my light is spent,
  Ere half my days in this dark world and wide,
  And that one talent which is death to hide
  Lodged with me useless, though my soul more bent
To serve therewith my Maker, and present   5
  My true account, lest He returning chide;
  "Doth God exact day-labor, light denied?"
  I fondly° ask. But Patience, to prevent   *foolishly*
That murmur, soon replies, "God doth not need
  Either man's work or His own gifts. Who best   10
  Bear His mild yoke, they serve Him best. His state
Is kingly: thousands at His bidding speed,
  And post o'er land and ocean without rest;
  They also serve who only stand and wait."

WHEN I CONSIDER HOW MY LIGHT IS SPENT. 1–2. *my light is spent / Ere half my days:* Milton
had become blind before he was fifty (when half his life was spent out of a possible
hundred years). 3. *that one talent:* For Christ's parable of the talents (measures of money),
see Matthew 25:14–30.

Marianne Moore (1887–1972)

THE MIND IS AN ENCHANTING THING 1944

is an enchanted thing
  like the glaze on a
katydid-wing
     subdivided by sun
     till the nettings are legion.   5
Like Gieseking playing Scarlatti;

like the apteryx-awl
  as a beak, or the
kiwi's rain-shawl
     of haired feathers, the mind   10
     feeling its way as though blind,
walks along with its eyes on the ground.

It has memory's ear
  that can hear without
having to hear.   15
     Like the gyroscope's fall,
     truly unequivocal
because trued by regnant certainty,

it is a power of
      strong enchantment. It   20
is like the dove-
        neck animated by
        sun; it is memory's eye;
it's conscientious inconsistency.

It tears off the veil; tears   25
      the temptation, the
mist the heart wears,
        from its eyes,— if the heart
        has a face; it takes apart
dejection. It's fire in the dove-neck's   30

iridescence; in the
      inconsistencies
of Scarlatti.
        Unconfusion submits
its confusion to proof; it's   35
not a Herod's oath that cannot change.

THE MIND IS AN ENCHANTING THING. 6. *Gieseking* . . . *Scarlatti:* Walter Gieseking (1895–1956), German pianist, was a celebrated performer of the difficult sonatas of Italian composer Domenico Scarlatti (1685–1757). 7. *apteryx-awl:* awl-shaped beak of the apteryx, one of the kiwi family. (An awl is a pointed tool for piercing wood or leather.) 36. *Herod's oath:* King Herod's order condemning to death all infants in Bethlehem (Matthew 2:1–16). In one medieval English version of the Herod story, a pageant play, the king causes the death of his own child by refusing to withdraw his command.

Sylvia Plath (1932–1963)

DADDY   1965

You do not do, you do not do
Any more, black shoe
In which I have lived like a foot
For thirty years, poor and white,
Barely daring to breathe or Achoo.   5

Daddy, I have had to kill you.
You died before I had time—
Marble-heavy, a bag full of God,
Ghastly statue with one grey toe
Big as a Frisco seal   10

And a head in the freakish Atlantic
Where it pours bean green over blue
In the waters off beautiful Nauset.
I used to pray to recover you.
Ach, du.   15

In the German tongue, in the Polish town
Scraped flat by the roller

Of wars, wars, wars.
But the name of the town is common.
My Polack friend 20

Says there are a dozen or two.
So I never could tell where you
Put your foot, your root,
I never could talk to you.
The tongue stuck in my jaw. 25

It stuck in a barb wire snare.
Ich, ich, ich, ich,
I could hardly speak.
I thought every German was you.
And the language obscene 30

An engine, an engine
Chuffing me off like a Jew.
A Jew to Dachau, Auschwitz, Belsen.
I began to talk like a Jew.
I think I may well be a Jew. 35

The snows of the Tyrol, the clear beer of Vienna
Are not very pure or true.
With my gypsy ancestress and my weird luck
And my Taroc pack and my Taroc pack
I may be a bit of a Jew. 40

I have always been scared of *you*,
With your Luftwaffe, your gobbledygoo.
And your neat moustache
And your Aryan eye, bright blue.
Panzer-man, panzer-man, O You— 45

Not God but a swastika
So black no sky could squeak through.
Every woman adores a Fascist,
The boot in the face, the brute
Brute heart of a brute like you. 50

You stand at the blackboard, daddy,
In the picture I have of you,
A cleft in your chin instead of your foot
But no less a devil for that, no not
Any less the black man who 55

Bit my pretty red heart in two.
I was ten when they buried you.
At twenty I tried to die
And get back, back, back at you.
I thought even the bones will do. 60

But they pulled me out of the sack,
And they stuck me together with glue.

And then I knew what to do.
I made a model of you,
A man in black with a Meinkampf look 65

And a love of the rack and the screw.
And I said I do, I do.
So daddy, I'm finally through.
The black telephone's off at the root,
The voices just can't worm through. 70

If I've killed one man, I've killed two—
The vampire who said he was you
And drank my blood for a year,
Seven years, if you want to know.
Daddy, you can lie back now. 75

There's a stake in your fat black heart
And the villagers never liked you.
They are dancing and stamping on you.
They always *knew* it was you.
Daddy, daddy, you bastard, I'm through. 80

DADDY. Introducing this poem in a reading, Sylvia Plath remarked:

The poem is spoken by a girl with an Electra complex. Her father died while she thought
he was God. Her case is complicated by the fact that her father was also a Nazi and her
mother very possibly part Jewish. In the daughter the two strains marry and paralyze
each other—she has to act out the awful little allegory before she is free of it.

(Quoted by A. Alvarez, *Beyond All This Fiddle*, New York, 1971.) In some details "Daddy"
is autobiography: the poet's father, Otto Plath, a German, had come to the United States
from Grabow, Poland. He had died following amputation of a gangrened foot and leg,
when Sylvia was eight years old. Politically, Otto Plath was a Republican, not a Nazi; but
was apparently a somewhat domineering head of the household. (See the recollections of
the poet's mother, Aurelia Schober Plath, in her edition of *Letters Home* by Sylvia Plath,
New York, 1975.) 15. *Ach, du:* Oh, you. 27. *Ich, ich, ich, ich:* I, I, I, I. 51. *blackboard:* Otto
Plath had been a professor of biology at Boston University. 65. *Meinkampf:* Adolf Hitler
entitled his autobiography *Mein Kampf* ("My Life").

COMPARE:

"Daddy" with "American Primitive" by William Jay Smith (page 398) and
"Confession to Settle a Curse" by Rosmarie Waldrop (page 409).

Sylvia Plath (1932–1963)
MORNING SONG 1965

Love set you going like a fat gold watch.
The midwife slapped your footsoles, and your bald cry
Took its place among the elements.

Our voices echo, magnifying your arrival. New statue.
In a drafty museum, your nakedness 5
Shadows our safety. We stand round blankly as walls.

I'm no more your mother
Than the cloud that distils a mirror to reflect its own slow
Effacement at the wind's hand.

All night your moth-breath   10
Flickers among the flat pink roses. I wake to listen:
A far sea moves in my ear.

One cry, and I stumble from bed, cow-heavy and floral
In my Victorian nightgown.
Your mouth opens clean as a cat's. The window square   15

Whitens and swallows its dull stars. And now you try
Your handful of notes;
The clear vowels rise like balloons.

COMPARE:

"Morning Song" with "My Son, My Executioner" by Donald Hall (page 267)
and "Woman to Child" by Judith Wright (page 417).

Sylvia Plath (1932–1963)
POPPIES IN OCTOBER   1965

Even the sun-clouds this morning cannot manage such skirts.
Nor the woman in the ambulance
Whose red heart blooms through her coat so astoundingly —

A gift, a love gift
Utterly unasked for   5
By a sky

Palely and flamily
Igniting its carbon monoxides, by eyes
Dulled to a halt under bowlers.

O my god, what am I   10
That these late mouths should cry open
In a forest of frost, in a dawn of cornflowers.

COMPARE:

"Poppies in October" with "Bavarian Gentians" by D. H. Lawrence (page 212).

Alexander Pope (1688–1744)

AN ESSAY ON MAN (EPISTLE II, PART 1)   1733

Know then thyself, presume not God to scan°;   *scrutinize*
The proper study of Mankind is Man.
Placed on this isthmus of a middle state,
A being darkly wise, and rudely great:
With too much knowledge for the Sceptic side,   5
With too much weakness for the Stoic's pride,
He hangs between; in doubt to act, or rest;
In doubt to deem himself a god, or beast;
In doubt his mind or body to prefer;
Born but to die, and reasoning but to err;   10
Alike in ignorance, his reason such,
Whether he thinks too little, or too much:
Chaos of thought and passion, all confused;
Still by himself abused, or disabused;
Created half to rise, and half to fall;   15
Great lord of all things, yet a prey to all;
Sole judge of truth, in endless error hurled:
The glory, jest, and riddle of the world!
Go, wondrous creature! mount where Science guides,
Go, measure earth, weigh air, and state the tides;   20
Instruct the planets in what orbs° to run,   *orbits*
Correct old Time, and regulate the sun;
Go, soar with Plato to th' empyreal sphere,
To the first good, first perfect, and first fair;
Or tread the mazy round his followers trod,   25
And quitting sense call imitating God;
As Eastern priests in giddy circles run,
And turn their heads to imitate the sun.
Go, teach Eternal Wisdom how to rule—
Then drop into thyself, and be a fool!   30
Superior beings, when of late they saw
A mortal man unfold all Nature's law,
Admired such wisdom in an earthly shape,
And showed a Newton as we show an ape.
Could he, whose rules the rapid Comet bind,   35
Describe or fix one movement of his mind?
Who saw its fires here rise, and there descend,
Explain his own beginning, or his end?
Alas what wonder! Man's superior part
Unchecked may rise, and climb from art to art;   40
But when his own great work is but begun,
What Reason weaves, by Passion is undone.
Trace Science then, with Modesty thy guide;
First strip off all her equipage of pride;
Deduct what is but vanity, or dress,   45
Or learning's luxury, or idleness;

Or tricks to show the stretch of human brain,
Mere curious pleasure, or ingenious pain;
Expunge the whole, or lop th' excrescent° parts   *superfluous*
Of all, our vices have created arts;   50
Then see how little the remaining sum,
Which served the past, and must the times to come!

AN ESSAY ON MAN (EPISTLE II, PART 1). Pope entitles his second epistle "Of the Nature and
State of Man as an Individual." His summary of the argument of this part: "The business
of Man not to pry into God, but to study himself. His middle nature, his powers, frailties,
and the limits of his capacity." 5–6: *Sceptic . . . Stoic's pride:* In Pope's view, both these ancient Greek philosophical schools were in error: the Sceptics in denying that man can at-
tain any knowledge of reality; the Stoics in affirming that man, by ridding himself of his
passions, can achieve Godlike calm. 23. *empyreal sphere:* the farthest sphere of the universe, the highest Heaven. 25. *his followers:* Plotinus and other followers of Plato were said
to have conversed with the divine while in a state of trance. 34. *as we show an ape:* In
eighteenth century London, apes were sometimes displayed as curiosities, made to perform in human clothes. The point is that Newton is to the gods as an ape is to human beings: inferior, but a remarkable imitation. (For another tribute to Newton, see Pope's
epigram on page 125.)

Ezra Pound (1885–1972)

THE RIVER-MERCHANT'S WIFE: A LETTER   1915

While my hair was still cut straight across my forehead
I played about the front gate, pulling flowers.
You came by on bamboo stilts, playing horse,
You walked about my seat, playing with blue plums.
And we went on living in the village of Chokan: 5
Two small people, without dislike or suspicion.
At fourteen I married My Lord you.
I never laughed, being bashful.
Lowering my head, I looked at the wall.
Called to, a thousand times, I never looked back.   10

At fifteen I stopped scowling,
I desired my dust to be mingled with yours
Forever and forever and forever.
Why should I climb the lookout?

At sixteen you departed,   15
You went into far Ku-to-yen, by the river of swirling eddies,
And you have been gone five months.
The monkeys make sorrowful noise overhead.

You dragged your feet when you went out.
By the gate now, the moss is grown, the different mosses,   20
Too deep to clear them away!
The leaves fall early this autumn, in wind.
The paired butterflies are already yellow with August
Over the grass in the West garden;

They hurt me. I grow older.   25
If you are coming down through the narrows of the river Kiang,
Please let me know beforehand,
And I will come out to meet you
           As far as Cho-fu-sa.

THE RIVER-MERCHANT'S WIFE: A LETTER. A free translation from the Chinese poet Li Po
(eighth century).

COMPARE:

"The River Merchant's Wife: a Letter" with "Wedding-Wind" by Philip Larkin
(page 364).

Ezra Pound (1885–1972)
THE SEAFARER   1912

From the Anglo-Saxon

May I for my own self song's truth reckon,
Journey's jargon, how I in harsh days
Hardship endured oft.
Bitter breast-cares have I abided,
Known on my keel many a care's hold,   5
And dire sea-surge, and there I oft spent
Narrow nightwatch nigh the ship's head
While she tossed close to cliffs. Coldly afflicted,
My feet were by frost benumbed.
Chill its chains are; chafing sighs   10
Hew my heart round and hunger begot
Mere-weary mood. Lest man know not
That he on dry land loveliest liveth,
List how I, care-wretched, on ice-cold sea,
Weathered the winter, wretched outcast   15
Deprived of my kinsmen;
Hung with hard ice-flakes, where hail-scur flew,
There I heard naught save the harsh sea
And ice-cold wave, at whiles the swan cries,
Did for my games the gannet's clamour,   20
Sea-fowls' loudness was for me laughter,
The mews' singing all my mead-drink.
Storms, on the stone-cliffs beaten, fell on the stern
In icy feathers; full oft the eagle screamed
With spray on his pinion.
                          Not any protector   25
May make merry man faring needy.
This he little believes, who aye in winsome life
Abides 'mid burghers some heavy business,

Wealthy and wine-flushed, how I weary oft
Must bide above brine.   30
Neareth nightshade, snoweth from north,
Frost froze the land, hail fell on earth then,
Corn of the coldest. Nathless° there knocketh now   *nevertheless*
The heart's thought that I on high streams
The salt-wavy tumult traverse alone.   35
Moaneth alway my mind's lust
That I fare forth, that I afar hence
Seek out a foreign fastness.
For this there's no mood-lofty man over earth's midst,
Not though he be given his good, but will have in his youth greed;   40
Nor his deed to the daring, nor his king to the faithful
But shall have his sorrow for sea-fare
Whatever his lord will.
He hath not heart for harping, nor in ring-having
Nor winsomeness to wife, nor world's delight   45
Nor any whit else save the wave's slash,
Yet longing comes upon him to fare forth on the water.
Bosque° taketh blossom, cometh beauty of berries,   `bush`
Fields to fairness, land fares brisker,
All this admonisheth man eager of mood,   50
The heart turns to travel so that he then thinks
On flood-ways to be far departing.
Cuckoo calleth with gloomy crying,
He singeth summerward, bodeth sorrow,
The bitter heart's blood. Burgher knows not—   55
He the prosperous man—what some perform
Where wandering them widest draweth.
So that but now my heart burst from my breastlock,
My mood 'mid the mere-flood,
Over the whale's acre, would wander wide.   60
On earth's shelter cometh oft to me,
Eager and ready, the crying lone-flyer,
Whets for the whale-path the heart irresistibly,
O'er tracks of ocean; seeing that anyhow
My lord deems to me this dead life   65
On loan and on land, I believe not
That any earth-weal eternal standeth
Save there be somewhat calamitous
That, ere a man's tide go, turn it to twain.
Disease or oldness or sword-hate   70
Beats out the breath from doom-gripped body.
And for this, every earl whatever, for those speaking after—
Laud of the living, boasteth some last word,
That he will work ere he pass onward,
Frame on the fair earth 'gainst foes his malice,   75
Daring ado, . . .
So that all men shall honour him after
And his laud beyond them remain 'mid the English,

Aye, for ever, a lasting life's-blast,
Delight 'mid the doughty.
                              Days little durable,   80
And all arrogance of earthen riches,
There come now no kings nor Cæsars
Nor gold-giving lords like those gone.
Howe'er in mirth most magnified,
Whoe'er lived in life most lordliest,   85
Drear all this excellence, delights undurable!
Waneth the watch, but the world holdeth.
Tomb hideth trouble. The blade is layed low.
Earthly glory ageth and seareth.
No man at all going the earth's gait,   90
But age fares against him, his face paleth,
Grey-haired he groaneth, knows gone companions,
Lordly men, are to earth o'ergiven,
Nor may he then the flesh-cover, whose life ceaseth,
Nor eat the sweet nor feel the sorry,   95
Nor stir hand nor think in mid heart,
And though he strew the grave with gold,
His born brothers, their buried bodies
Be an unlikely treasure hoard.

COMPARE:

"The Seafarer" with "Junk" by Richard Wilbur (page 410).

Dudley Randall (b. 1914)

BALLAD OF BIRMINGHAM   1966

*(On the Bombing of a Church in
Birmingham, Alabama, 1963)*

"Mother dear, may I go downtown
Instead of out to play,
And march the streets of Birmingham
In a Freedom March today?"

"No, baby, no, you may not go,   5
For the dogs are fierce and wild,
And clubs and hoses, guns and jail
Aren't good for a little child."

"But, mother, I won't be alone.
Other children will go with me,   10
And march the streets of Birmingham
To make our country free."

"No, baby, no, you may not go,
For I fear those guns will fire.

But you may go to church instead   15
And sing in the children's choir."

She has combed and brushed her night-dark hair,
And bathed rose petal sweet,
And drawn white gloves on her small brown hands,
And white shoes on her feet.   20

The mother smiled to know her child
Was in the sacred place,
But that smile was the last smile
To come upon her face.

For when she heard the explosion,   25
Her eyes grew wet and wild.
She raced through the streets of Birmingham
Calling for her child.

She clawed through bits of glass and brick,
Then lifted out a shoe.   30
"O here's the shoe my baby wore,
But, baby, where are you?"

COMPARE:

"Ballad of Birmingham" with the anonymous ballads "Edward" (page 303) and
"The Cruel Mother" (page 101). Compare its theme with the themes of "Satur-
day's Child" by Countee Cullen (page 322) and "Dream Deferred" by Langston
Hughes (page 355).

John Crowe Ransom (1888–1974)

JANET WAKING   1927

Beautifully Janet slept
Till it was deeply morning. She woke then
And thought about her dainty-feathered hen,
To see how it had kept.

One kiss she gave her mother,   5
Only a small one gave she to her daddy
Who would have kissed each curl of his shining baby;
No kiss at all for her brother.

"Old Chucky, Old Chucky!" she cried,
Running on little pink feet upon the grass   10
To Chucky's house, and listening. But alas,
Her Chucky had died.

It was a transmogrifying° bee   *change-working*
Came droning down on Chucky's old bald head
And sat and put the poison. It scarcely bled,   15
But how exceedingly

And purply did the knot
Swell with the venom and communicate
Its rigor! Now the poor comb stood up straight
But Chucky did not.   20

So there was Janet
Kneeling on the wet grass, crying her brown hen
(Translated far beyond the daughters of men)
To rise and walk upon it.

And weeping fast as she had breath   25
Janet implored us, "Wake her from her sleep!"
And would not be instructed in how deep
Was the forgetful kingdom of death.

COMPARE:

"Janet Waking" with "Woodchucks" by Maxine Kumin (page 362) and "The
Bull Calf" by Irving Layton (page 365).

Henry Reed (b. 1914)
NAMING OF PARTS   1946

Today we have naming of parts. Yesterday,
We had daily cleaning. And tomorrow morning,
We shall have what to do after firing. But today,
Today we have naming of parts. Japonica
Glistens like coral in all of the neighboring gardens,   5
          And today we have naming of parts.

This is the lower sling swivel. And this
Is the upper sling swivel, whose use you will see,
When you are given your slings. And this is the piling swivel,
Which in your case you have not got. The branches   10
Hold in the gardens their silent, eloquent gestures,
          Which in our case we have not got.

This is the safety-catch, which is always released
With an easy flick of the thumb. And please do not let me
See anyone using his finger. You can do it quite easy   15
If you have any strength in your thumb. The blossoms
Are fragile and motionless, never letting anyone see
          Any of them using their finger.

And this you can see is the bolt. The purpose of this
Is to open the breech, as you see. We can slide it   20
Rapidly backwards and forwards: we call this
Easing the spring. And rapidly backwards and forwards
The early bees are assaulting and fumbling the flowers:
          They call it easing the Spring.

They call it easing the Spring: it is perfectly easy   25
If you have any strength in your thumb: like the bolt,
And the breech, and the cocking-piece, and the point of balance,
Which in our case we have not got; and the almond-blossom
Silent in all of the gardens and the bees going backwards and forwards,
    For today we have naming of parts.   30

COMPARE:

"Naming of Parts" with "The Fury of Aerial Bombardment" by Richard
Eberhart (page 50).

Adrienne Rich (b. 1929)

DIVING INTO THE WRECK   1973

First having read the book of myths,
and loaded the camera,
and checked the edge of the knife-blade,
I put on
the body-armor of black rubber   5
the absurd flippers
the grave and awkward mask.
I am having to do this
not like Cousteau with his
assiduous team   10
aboard the sun-flooded schooner
but here alone.

There is a ladder.
The ladder is always there
hanging innocently   15
close to the side of the schooner.
We know what it is for,
we who have used it.
Otherwise
it's a piece of maritime floss   20
some sundry equipment.

I go down.
Rung after rung and still
the oxygen immerses me
the blue light   25
the clear atoms
of our human air.
I go down.
My flippers cripple me,
I crawl like an insect down the ladder   30
and there is no one
to tell me when the ocean
will begin.

First the air is blue and then
it is bluer and then green and then   35
black I am blacking out and yet
my mask is powerful
it pumps my blood with power
the sea is another story
the sea is not a question of power   40
I have to learn alone
to turn my body without force
in the deep element.

And now: it is easy to forget
what I came for   45
among so many who have always
lived here
swaying their crenellated fans
between the reefs
and besides   50
you breathe differently down here.

I came to explore the wreck.
The words are purposes.
The words are maps.
I came to see the damage that was done   55
and the treasures that prevail.
I stroke the beam of my lamp
slowly along the flank
of something more permanent
than fish or weed   60

the thing I came for:
the wreck and not the story of the wreck
the thing itself and not the myth
the drowned face always staring
toward the sun   65
the evidence of damage
worn by salt and sway into this threadbare beauty
the ribs of the disaster
curving their assertion
among the tentative haunters.   70

This is the place.
And I am here, the mermaid whose dark hair
streams black, the merman in his armored body
We circle silently
about the wreck   75
we dive into the hold.
I am she: I am he

whose drowned face sleeps with open eyes
whose breasts still bear the stress
whose silver, copper, vermeil cargo lies   80

obscurely inside barrels
half-wedged and left to rot
we are the half-destroyed instruments
that once held to a course
the water-eaten log   85
the fouled compass

We are, I am, you are
by cowardice or courage
the one who find our way
back to this scene   90
carrying a knife, a camera
a book of myths
in which
our names do not appear.

Edwin Arlington Robinson (1869–1935)

Mr. Flood's Party   1921

Old Eben Flood, climbing alone one night
Over the hill between the town below
And the forsaken upland hermitage
That held as much as he should ever know
On earth again of home, paused warily.   5
The road was his with not a native near;
And Eben, having leisure, said aloud,
For no man else in Tilbury Town to hear:

"Well, Mr. Flood, we have the harvest moon
Again, and we may not have many more;   10
The bird is on the wing, the poet says,
And you and I have said it here before.
Drink to the bird." He raised up to the light
The jug that he had gone so far to fill,
And answered huskily: "Well, Mr. Flood,   15
Since you propose it, I believe I will."

Alone, as if enduring to the end
A valiant armor of scarred hopes outworn,
He stood there in the middle of the road
Like Roland's ghost winding° a silent horn.   *blowing*   20
Below him, in the town among the trees,
Where friends of other days had honored him,
A phantom salutation of the dead
Rang thinly till old Eben's eyes were dim.

Then, as a mother lays her sleeping child   25
Down tenderly, fearing it may awake,
He set the jug down slowly at his feet
With trembling care, knowing that most things break;

And only when assured that on firm earth
It stood, as the uncertain lives of men   30
Assuredly did not, he paced away,
And with his hand extended paused again:

"Well, Mr. Flood, we have not met like this
In a long time; and many a change has come
To both of us, I fear, since last it was   35
We had a drop together. Welcome home!"
Convivially returning with himself,
Again he raised the jug up to the light;
And with an acquiescent quaver said:
"Well, Mr. Flood, if you insist, I might.   40

"Only a very little, Mr. Flood —
For auld lang syne. No more, sir; that will do."
So, for the time, apparently it did,
And Eben evidently thought so too;
For soon amid the silver loneliness   45
Of night he lifted up his voice and sang,
Secure, with only two moons listening,
Until the whole harmonious landscape rang —

"For auld lang syne." The weary throat gave out,
The last word wavered; and the song being done,   50
He raised again the jug regretfully
And shook his head, and was again alone.
There was not much that was ahead of him,
And there was nothing in the town below —
Where strangers would have shut the many doors   55
That many friends had opened long ago.

Mr. Flood's Party. 11. *the poet:* Omar Khayyám, Persian poet, a praiser of wine, whose
Rubáiyát, translated by Edward FitzGerald, included the lines:

> Come, fill the Cup, and in the fire of Spring
> Your Winter-garment of Repentance fling:
>   The Bird of Time has but a little way
> To flutter and the Bird is on the Wing.

20. *Roland's ghost . . . horn:* In the battle of Roncesvalles (eighth century), Roland fought to
his death, refusing to sound his horn for help until all hope was gone.

Theodore Roethke (1908–1963)

FRAU BAUMAN, FRAU SCHMIDT, AND
FRAU SCHWARTZE   1953

Gone the three ancient ladies
Who creaked on the greenhouse ladders,
Reaching up white strings
To wind, to wind

The sweet-pea tendrils, the smilax,   5
Nasturtiums, the climbing
Roses, to straighten
Carnations, red
Chrysanthemums; the stiff
Stems, jointed like corn,   10
They tied and tucked,—
These nurses of nobody else.
Quicker than birds, they dipped
Up and sifted the dirt;
They sprinkled and shook;   15
They stood astride pipes,
Their skirts billowing out wide into tents,
Their hands twinkling with wet;
Like witches they flew along rows
Keeping creation at ease;   20
With a tendril for needle
They sewed up the air with a stem;
They teased out the seed that the cold kept asleep,—
All the coils, loops, and whorls.
They trellised the sun; they plotted for more than themselves.   25

I remember how they picked me up, a spindly kid,
Pinching and poking my thin ribs
Till I lay in their laps, laughing,
Weak as a whiffet,
Now, when I'm alone and cold in my bed,   30
They still hover over me,
These ancient leathery crones,
With their bandannas stiffened with sweat,
And their thorn-bitten wrists,
And their snuff-laden breath blowing lightly over me in my first sleep. 35

FRAU BAUMAN, FRAU SCHMIDT, AND FRAU SCHWARTZE. Roethke's father ran a commercial greenhouse in Saginaw, Michigan. 29. *whiffet:* a little puff of air; also, a small dog.

Theodore Roethke (1908–1963)

THE WAKING   1953

I wake to sleep, and take my waking slow.
I feel my fate in what I cannot fear.
I learn by going where I have to go.

We think by feeling. What is there to know?
I hear my being dance from ear to ear.   5
I wake to sleep, and take my waking slow.

Of those so close beside me, which are you?
God bless the Ground! I shall walk softly there,
And learn by going where I have to go.

Light takes the Tree; but who can tell us how?   10
The lowly worm climbs up a winding stair;
I wake to sleep, and take my waking slow.

Great Nature has another thing to do
To you and me; so take the lively air,
And, lovely, learn by going where to go.   15

This shaking keeps me steady. I should know.
What falls away is always. And is near.
I wake to sleep, and take my waking slow.
I learn by going where I have to go.

COMPARE:

"The Waking" with "Do not go gentle into that good night" by Dylan Thomas
(page 169).

Anne Sexton (1928–1975)

THE FURY OF OVERSHOES   1974

They sit in a row
outside the kindergarten,
black, red, brown, all
with those brass buckles.
Remember when you couldn't   5
buckle your own
overshoe
or tie your own
shoe
or cut your own meat   10
and the tears
running down like mud
because you fell off your
tricycle?
Remember, big fish,   15
when you couldn't swim
and simply slipped under
like a stone frog?
The world wasn't
yours.   20
It belonged to
the big people.
Under your bed
sat the wolf
and he made a shadow   25
when cars passed by
at night.

They made you give up
your nightlight
and your teddy 30
and your thumb.
Oh overshoes,
don't you
remember me,
pushing you up and down 35
in the winter snow?
Oh thumb,
I want a drink,
it is dark,
where are the big people, 40
when will I get there,
taking giant steps
all day,
each day
and thinking 45
nothing of it?

Anne Sexton (1928–1975)

The Kiss 1969

My mouth blooms like a cut.
I've been wronged all year, tedious
nights, nothing but rough elbows in them
and delicate boxes of Kleenex calling *crybaby*
crybaby, you fool! 5

Before today my body was useless.
Now it's tearing at its square corners.
It's tearing old Mary's garments off, knot by knot
and see—Now it's shot full of these electric bolts.
Zing! A resurrection! 10

Once it was a boat, quite wooden
and with no business, no salt water under it
and in need of some paint. It was no more
than a group of boards. But you hoisted her, rigged her.
She's been elected. 15

My nerves are turned on. I hear them like
musical instruments. Where there was silence
the drums, the strings are incurably playing. You did this.
Pure genuis at work. Darling, the composer has stepped
into fire. 20

Compare:

"The Kiss" with "Love Song: I and Thou" by Alan Dugan (page 332).

William Shakespeare (1564–1616)

THAT TIME OF YEAR THOU MAYST IN ME BEHOLD

1609

That time of year thou mayst in me behold
When yellow leaves, or none, or few, do hang
Upon those boughs which shake against the cold,
Bare ruined choirs where late the sweet birds sang.
In me thou see'st the twilight of such day   5
As after sunset fadeth in the west,
Which by-and-by black night doth take away,
Death's second self that seals up all in rest.
In me thou see'st the glowing of such fire
That on the ashes of his youth doth lie,   10
As the deathbed whereon it must expire,
Consumed with that which it was nourished by.
  This thou perceiv'st, which makes thy love more strong,
  To love that well which thou must leave ere long.

William Shakespeare (1564–1616)

WHEN, IN DISGRACE WITH FORTUNE AND MEN'S EYES

1609

When, in disgrace with Fortune and men's eyes,
I all alone beweep my outcast state,
And trouble deaf heaven with my bootless° cries,   *futile*
And look upon myself and curse my fate,
Wishing me like to one more rich in hope,   5
Featured like him, like him with friends possessed,
Desiring this man's art, and that man's scope,
With what I most enjoy contented least,
Yet in these thoughts myself almost despising,
Haply° I think on thee, and then my state,   *luckily*   10
Like to the lark at break of day arising
From sullen earth, sings hymns at heaven's gate;
  For thy sweet love rememb'red such wealth brings
  That then I scorn to change my state with kings.

William Shakespeare (1564–1616)

WHEN DAISIES PIED AND VIOLETS BLUE

1598

When daisies pied and violets blue
  And lady-smocks all silver-white
And cuckoo-buds° of yellow hue   *buttercups*
  Do paint the meadows with delight,

The cuckoo then, on every tree,   5
Mocks married men; for thus sings he,
            "Cuckoo,
Cuckoo, cuckoo!" —O word of fear,
Unpleasing to a married ear!

When shepherds pipe on oaten straws,   10
    And merry larks are ploughmen's clocks,
When turtles tread°, and rooks, and daws,   *turtledoves mate*
    And maidens bleach their summer smocks,
The cuckoo then, on every tree,
Mocks married men; for thus sings he,   15
            "Cuckoo,
Cuckoo, cuckoo!" —O word of fear,
Unpleasing to a married ear!

WHEN DAISIES PIED. This song and "When icicles hang by the wall" conclude the play
Love's Labor's Lost. 2. *lady-smocks:* also named cuckoo-flowers. 8. *O word of fear:* because it
sounds like the sound *cuckold.*

William Shakespeare (1564–1616)

WHEN ICICLES HANG BY THE WALL   1598

When icicles hang by the wall,
    And Dick the shepherd blows his nail,
And Tom bears logs into the hall,
    And milk comes frozen home in pail,
When blood is nipped and ways° be foul,   *roads*   5
    Then nightly sings the staring owl:
            "Tu-whit, to-who!"
            A merry note,
While greasy Joan doth keel° the pot.   *cool (as by skimming*
                                                                  or stirring)

When all aloud the wind doth blow,   10
    And coughing drowns the parson's saw°,   *old saw, platitude*
And birds sit brooding in the snow,
    And Marian's nose looks red and raw,
When roasted crabs° hiss in the bowl,   *crab apples*
    Then nightly sings the staring owl:
            "Tu-whit, to-who!"   15
            A merry note,
While greasy Joan doth keel the pot.

Karl Shapiro (b. 1913)

THE DIRTY WORD

1947

The dirty word hops in the cage of the mind like the Pondicherry vulture, stomping with its heavy left claw on the sweet meat of the brain and tearing it with its vicious beak, ripping and chopping the flesh. Terrified, the small boy bears the big bird of the dirty word into the house, and grunting, puffing, carries it up the stairs to his own room in the skull. Bits of black feather cling to his clothes and his hair as he locks the staring creature in the dark closet. 5

All day the small boy returns to the closet to examine and feed the bird, to caress and kick the bird, that now snaps and flaps its wings savagely whenever the door is opened. How the boy trembles and delights at the sight of the white excrement of the bird! How the bird leaps and rushes against the walls of the skull, trying to escape from the zoo of the vocabulary! How wildly snaps the sweet meat of the brain in its rage. 10

And the bird outlives the man, being freed at the man's death-funeral by a word from the rabbi. 15

(But I one morning went upstairs and opened the door and entered the closet and found in the cage of my mind the great bird dead. Softly I wept it and softly removed it and softly buried the body of the bird in the hollyhock garden of the house I lived in twenty years before. And out of the worn black feathers of the wing have I made these pens to write these elegies, for I have outlived the bird, and I have murdered it in my early manhood.) 20

Percy Bysshe Shelley (1792–1822)

ODE TO THE WEST WIND

1820

I

O wild West Wind, thou breath of Autumn's being,
Thou, from whose unseen presence the leaves dead
Are driven, like ghosts from an enchanter fleeing,

Yellow, and black, and pale, and hectic red,
Pestilence-stricken multitudes: O thou, 5
Who chariotest to their dark wintry bed

The wingèd seeds, where they lie cold and low,
Each like a corpse within its grave, until
Thine azure sister of the spring shall blow

Her clarion o'er the dreaming earth, and fill 10
(Driving sweet buds like flocks to feed in air)
With living hues and odors plain and hill:

Wild Spirit, which art moving everywhere;
Destroyer and preserver; hear, O, hear!

II

Thou on whose stream, 'mid the steep sky's commotion,   15
Loose clouds like earth's decaying leaves are shed,
Shook from the tangled boughs of Heaven and Ocean,

Angels of rain and lightning: there are spread
On the blue surface of thine airy surge,
Like the bright hair uplifted from the head   20

Of some fierce Maenad, even from the dim verge
Of the horizon to the zenith's height,
The locks of the approaching storm. Thou dirge

Of the dying year, to which this closing night
Will be the dome of a vast sepulcher,   25
Vaulted with all thy congregated might

Of vapors, from whose solid atmosphere
Black rain, and fire, and hail will burst: O, hear!

III

Thou who didst waken from his summer dreams
The blue Mediterranean, where he lay,   30
Lulled by the coil of his crystalline streams,

Beside a pumice isle in Baiae's bay,
And saw in sleep old palaces and towers
Quivering within the wave's intenser day,

All overgrown with azure moss, and flowers   35
So sweet, the sense faints picturing them! Thou
For whose path the Atlantic's level powers

Cleave themselves into chasms, while far below
The sea-blooms and the oozy woods which wear
The sapless foliage of the ocean, know   40

Thy voice, and suddenly grow gray with fear,
And tremble and despoil themselves: O, hear!

IV

If I were a dead leaf thou mightest bear;
If I were a swift cloud to fly with thee;
A wave to pant beneath thy power, and share   45

The impulse of thy strength, only less free
Than thou, O uncontrolable! If even
I were as in my boyhood, and could be

The comrade of thy wanderings over heaven,
As then, when to outstrip thy skiey speed   50
Scarce seemed a vision; I would ne'er have striven

As thus with thee in prayer in my sore need.
Oh! lift me as a wave, a leaf, a cloud!
I fall upon the thorns of life! I bleed!

A heavy weight of hours has chained and bowed   55
One too like thee: tameless, and swift, and proud.

V

Make me thy lyre, even as the forest is:
What if my leaves are falling like its own!
The tumult of thy mighty harmonies

Will take from both a deep, autumnal tone,   60
Sweet though in sadness. Be thou, spirit fierce,
My spirit! Be thou me, impetuous one!

Drive my dead thoughts over the universe
Like withered leaves, to quicken a new birth!
And, by the incantation of this verse,   65

Scatter, as from an unextinguished hearth
Ashes and sparks, my words among mankind!
Be through my lips to unawakened earth

The trumpet of a prophecy! O wind,
If Winter comes, can Spring be far behind?   70

ODE TO THE WEST WIND. 10. *clarion:* narrow-tubed trumpet once used on the battlefield
because its shrill, clear call could be heard afar. 21. *Maenad:* in ancient Greece, a woman of
the cult of the god Dionysus who would show her devotion by dancing herself into a
frenzy. 32. *pumice isle in Baiae's bay:* an island of solidified lava in the bay of Naples, Italy.
At Baiae are the ruins of villas of the Roman emperors. 57. *lyre:* Shelley is probably thinking of an Aeolian harp, which placed in a window produces deep strumming sounds
when the wind blows over it.

Christopher Smart (1722–1771)

FOR I WILL CONSIDER MY CAT JEOFFRY   (1759–1763)

For I will consider my Cat Jeoffry.
For he is the servant of the Living God, duly and daily serving him.
For at the first glance of the glory of God in the East he worships in his
      way.
For is this done by wreathing his body seven times round with elegant
      quickness.
For then he leaps up to catch the musk°, which is the   *catnip*
      blessing of God upon his prayer.   5

For he rolls upon prank to work it in.

For having done duty and received blessing he begins to consider himself.

For this he performs in ten degrees.

For first he looks upon his fore-paws to see if they are clean.

For secondly he kicks up behind to clear away there.   10

For thirdly he works it upon stretch° with the fore-paws   *he works his*
extended.   *muscles, stretching*

For fourthly he sharpens his paws by wood.

For fifthly he washes himself.

For sixthly he rolls upon wash.

For seventhly he fleas himself, that he may not be interrupted upon the
beat°.   *his patrol*   15

For eighthly he rubs himself against a post.

For ninthly he looks up for his instructions.

For tenthly he goes in quest of food.

For having considered God and himself he will consider his neighbor.

For if he meets another cat he will kiss her in kindness.   20

For when he takes his prey he plays with it to give it a chance.

For one mouse in seven escapes by his dallying.

For when his day's work is done his business more properly begins.

For he keeps the Lord's watch in the night against the Adversary.

For he counteracts the powers of darkness by his electrical skin and glar-
ing eyes.   25

For he counteracts the Devil, who is death, by brisking about the life.

For in his morning orisons he loves the sun and the sun loves him.

For he is of the tribe of Tiger.

For the Cherub Cat is a term of the Angel Tiger.

For he has the subtlety and hissing of a serpent, which in goodness he
suppresses.   30

For he will not do destruction if he is well-fed, neither will he spit without
provocation.

For he purrs in thankfulness when God tells him he's a good Cat.

For he is an instrument for the children to learn benevolence upon.

For every house is incomplete without him, and a blessing is lacking in
the spirit.

For the Lord commanded Moses concerning the cats at the departure of
the Children of Israel from Egypt.   35

For every family had one cat at least in the bag.

For the English cats are the best in Europe.

For he is the cleanest in the use of his fore-paws of any quadruped.

For the dexterity of his defense is an instance of the love of God to him exceedingly.

For he is the quickest to his mark of any creature.   40

For he is tenacious of his point.

For he is a mixture of gravity and waggery.

For he knows that God is his Savior.

For there is nothing sweeter than his peace when at rest.

For there is nothing brisker than his life when in motion. 45
For he is of the Lord's poor, and so indeed is he called by benevolence
  perpetually—Poor Jeoffry! poor Jeoffry! the rat has bit thy throat.
For I bless the name of the Lord Jesus that Jeoffry is better.
For the divine spirit comes about his body to sustain it in complete cat.
For his tongue is exceeding pure so that it has in purity what it wants in
  music.
For he is docile and can learn certain things. 50
For he can sit up with gravity which is patience upon approbation.
For he can fetch and carry, which is patience in employment.
For he can jump over a stick which is patience upon proof positive.
For he can spraggle upon waggle at the word of command.
For he can jump from an eminence into his master's bosom. 55
For he can catch the cork and toss it again.
For he is hated by the hypocrite and miser.
For the former is afraid of detection.
For the latter refuses the charge.
For he camels his back to bear the first notion of business. 60
For he is good to think on, if a man would express himself neatly.
For he made a great figure in Egypt for his signal services.
For he killed the Icneumon-rat, very pernicious by land.
For his ears are so acute that they sting again.
For from this proceeds the passing quickness of his attention. 65
For by stroking of him I have found out electricity.
For I perceived God's light about him both wax and fire.
For the electrical fire is the spiritual substance which God sends from
  heaven to sustain the bodies both of man and beast.
For God has blessed him in the variety of his movements.
For, though he cannot fly, he is an excellent clamberer. 70
For his motions upon the face of the earth are more than any other quad-
  ruped.
For he can tread to all the measures upon the music.
For he can swim for life.
For he can creep.

FOR I WILL CONSIDER MY CAT JEOFFRY. This is a self-contained extract from Smart's long
poem *Jubilate Agno* ("Rejoice in the Lamb"), written during his confinement for insanity.
35. *For the Lord commanded Moses concerning the cats:* No such command is mentioned in
Scripture. 54. *spraggle upon waggle:* W. F. Stead, in his edition of Smart's poem, suggests
that this means Jeoffry will sprawl when his master waggles a finger or a stick. 59. *the
charge:* perhaps the cost of feeding a cat.

William Jay Smith (b. 1918)

AMERICAN PRIMITIVE   1953

Look at him there in his stovepipe hat,
His high-top shoes, and his handsome collar;
Only my Daddy could look like that,
And I love my Daddy like he loves his Dollar.

The screen door bangs, and it sounds so funny—
There he is in a shower of gold;
His pockets are stuffed with folding money,
His lips are blue, and his hands feel cold.

He hangs in the hall by his black cravat,
The ladies faint, and the children holler:
Only my Daddy could look like that,
And I love my Daddy like he loves his Dollar.

COMPARE:

"American Primitive" with "Daddy" by Sylvia Plath (page 374).

W. D. Snodgrass (b. 1926)

THE OPERATION   1959

From stainless steel basins of water
They brought warm cloths and they washed me,
From spun aluminum bowls, cold Zephiran sponges, fuming;
Gripped in the dead yellow glove, a bright straight razor
Inched on my stomach, down my groin,   5
Paring the brown hair off. They left me
White as a child, not frightened. I was not
Ashamed. They clothed me, then,
In the thin, loose, light, white garments,
The delicate sandals of poor Pierrot,   10
A schoolgirl first offering her sacrament.

I was drifting, inexorably, on toward sleep.
In skullcaps, masked, in blue-green gowns, attendants
Towed my cart, afloat in its white cloths,
The body with its tributary poisons borne   15
Down corridors of the diseased, thronging:
The scrofulous faces, contagious grim boys,
The huddled families, weeping, a staring woman
Arched to her gnarled stick,—a child was somewhere
Screaming, screaming—then, blind silence, the elevator rising   20
To the arena, humming, vast with lights; blank hero,
Shackled and spellbound, to enact my deed.

Into flowers, into women, I have awakened.
Too weak to think of strength, I have thought all day,
Or dozed among standing friends. I lie in night, now,   25
A small mound under linen like the drifted snow.
Only by nurses visited, in radiance, saying, Rest.
Opposite, ranked office windows glare; headlamps, below,
Trace out our highways; their cargoes under dark tarpaulins,

Trucks climb, thundering, and sirens may   30
Wail for the fugitive. It is very still. In my brandy bowl
Of sweet peas at the window, the crystal world
Is inverted, slow and gay.

THE OPERATION. 3. *Zephiran:* like Zephirus, Greek personification of the west wind:
gentle, cool and soothing. Also the name of an antiseptic used in hospitals. 10. *Pierrot:*
traditional clown in French pantomime, white-faced, wearing loose pantaloons.

Gary Snyder (b. 1930)

MILTON BY FIRELIGHT   1959

Piute Creek, August 1955

"O hell, what do mine eyes
    with grief behold?"
Working with an old
Singlejack miner, who can sense
The vein and cleavage   5
In the very guts of rock, can
Blast granite, build
Switchbacks that last for years
Under the beat of snow, thaw, mule-hooves.
What use, Milton, a silly story   10
Of our lost general parents,
    eaters of fruit?

The Indian, the chainsaw boy,
And a string of six mules
Came riding down to camp   15
Hungry for tomatoes and green apples.
Sleeping in saddle-blankets
Under a bright night-sky
Han River slantwise by morning.
Jays squall   20
Coffee boils

In ten thousand years the Sierras
Will be dry and dead, home of the scorpion.
Ice-scratched slabs and bent trees.
No paradise, no fall,   25
Only the weathering land
The wheeling sky,
Man, with his Satan
Scouring the chaos of the mind.
Oh Hell!   30

Fire down
Too dark to read, miles from a road
The bell-mare clangs in the meadow

That packed dirt for a fill-in
Scrambling through loose rocks
On an old trail
All of a summer's day.

MILTON BY FIRELIGHT. 1–2. "*O hell, what do mine eyes with grief behold?*" Satan's envious words as he looks upon Adam and Eve in the Garden of Eden (Book IV, line 358 in Milton's *Paradise Lost*).

William Stafford (b. 1914)
AT THE KLAMATH BERRY FESTIVAL   1966

The war chief danced the old way —
the eagle wing he held before his mouth —
and when he turned the boom-boom
stopped. He took two steps. A sociologist
was there; the Scout troop danced.   5
I envied him the places where he had not been.

The boom began again. Outside he heard
the stick game, and the Blackfoot gamblers
arguing at poker under lanterns.
Still-moccasined and bashful, holding   10
the eagle wing before his mouth,
listening and listening, he danced after others stopped.

He took two steps, the boom caught up,
the mountains rose, the still deep river
slid but never broke its quiet.   15
I looked back when I left:
he took two steps, he took two steps,
past the sociologist.

AT THE KLAMATH BERRY FESTIVAL. The Klamath Indians have a reservation at the base of the Cascade Range in southern Oregon.

William Stafford (b. 1914)
WRITTEN ON THE STUB OF THE FIRST PAYCHECK   1966

Gasoline makes game scarce.
In Elko, Nevada, I remember a stuffed wildcat
someone had shot on Bing Crosby's ranch.
I stood in the filling station
breathing fumes and reading the snarl of a map.   5

There were peaks to the left so high
they almost got away in the heat;

Reno and Las Vegas were ahead.
I had promise of the California job,
and three kids with me.   10

It takes a lot of miles to equal one wildcat
today. We moved into a housing tract.
Every dodging animal carries my hope in Nevada.
It has been a long day, Bing.
Wherever I go is your ranch.   15

Wallace Stevens (1879–1955)
PETER QUINCE AT THE CLAVIER   1923

I

Just as my fingers on these keys
Make music, so the selfsame sounds
On my spirit make a music, too.

Music is feeling, then, not sound;
And thus it is that what I feel,   5
Here in this room, desiring you,

Thinking of your blue-shadowed silk,
Is music. It is like the strain
Waked in the elders by Susanna.

Of a green evening, clear and warm,   10
She bathed in her still garden, while
The red-eyed elders watching, felt

The basses of their beings throb
In witching chords, and their thin blood
Pulse pizzicati of Hosanna.   15

II

In the green water, clear and warm,
Susanna lay.
She searched
The touch of springs,
And found   20
Concealed imaginings.
She sighed,
For so much melody.

Upon the bank, she stood
In the cool   25
Of spent emotions.
She felt, among the leaves,
The dew
Of old devotions.

She walked upon the grass, 30
Still quavering.
The winds were like her maids,
On timid feet,
Fetching her woven scarves,
Yet wavering. 35

A breath upon her hand
Muted the night.
She turned —
A cymbal crashed,
And roaring horns. 40

III

Soon, with a noise like tambourines,
Came her attendant Byzantines.

They wondered why Susanna cried
Against the elders by her side;

And as they whispered, the refrain 45
Was like a willow swept by rain.

Anon, their lamps' uplifted flame
Revealed Susanna and her shame.

And then, the simpering Byzantines
Fled, with a noise like tambourines. 50

IV

Beauty is momentary in the mind —
The fitful tracing of a portal;
But in the flesh it is immortal.

The body dies; the body's beauty lives.
So evenings die, in their green going, 55
A wave, interminably flowing.
So gardens die, their meek breath scenting
The cowl of winter, done repenting.
So maidens die, to the auroral
Celebration of a maiden's choral. 60

Susanna's music touched the bawdy strings
Of those white elders; but, escaping,
Left only Death's ironic scraping.
Now, in its immortality, it plays
On the clear viol of her memory, 65
And makes a constant sacrament of praise.

PETER QUINCE AT THE CLAVIER. In Shakespeare's *Midsummer Night's Dream*, Peter Quince is a clownish carpenter who stages a mock-tragic play. In The Book of Susanna in the Apocrypha, two lustful elders who covet Susanna, a virtuous married woman, hide in her garden, spy on her as she bathes, then threaten to make false accusations against her unless she submits to them. When she refuses, they cry out, and her servants come running. All ends well when the prophet Daniel cross-examines the elders and proves them liars. 15. *pizzicati:* thin notes made by plucking a stringed instrument. 42. *Byzantines:* Susanna's maidservants.

Mark Strand (b. 1934),

EATING POETRY   1968

Ink runs from the corners of my mouth.
There is no happiness like mine.
I have been eating poetry.

The librarian does not believe what she sees.
Her eyes are sad   5
and she walks with her hands in her dress.

The poems are gone.
The light is dim.
The dogs are on the basement steps and coming up.

Their eyeballs roll,   10
their blond legs burn like brush.
The poor librarian begins to stamp her feet and weep.

She does not understand.
When I get on my knees and lick her hand,
she screams.   15

I am a new man.
I snarl at her and bark.
I romp with joy in the bookish dark.

James Tate (b. 1943)

FLIGHT   1967

For K.

Like a glum cricket
the refrigerator is singing
and just as I am convinced

that it is the only noise
in the building, a pot falls   5
in 2 B. The neighbors on

both sides of me suddenly
realize that they have not
made love to their wives

since 1947. The racket   10
multiplies. The man downhall
is teaching his dog to fly.

The fish are disgusted
and beat their heads blue
against a cold aquarium. I too   15

lose control and consider
the dust huddled in the corner
a threat to my endurance.

Were you here, we would not
tolerate mongrels in the air,   20
nor the conspiracies of dust.

We would drive all night,
your head tilted on my shoulder.
At dawn, I would nudge you

with my anxious fingers and say,   25
Already we are in Idaho.

Alfred, Lord Tennyson (1809–1892)

DARK HOUSE, BY WHICH ONCE MORE I STAND   1850

Dark house, by which once more I stand
   Here in the long unlovely street,
   Doors, where my heart was used to beat
So quickly, waiting for a hand,

A hand that can be clasped no more—   5
   Behold me, for I cannot sleep,
   And like a guilty thing I creep
At earliest morning to the door.

He is not here; but far away
   The noise of life begins again,   10
   And ghastly through the drizzling rain
On the bald street breaks the blank day.

DARK HOUSE. This poem is one part of the series *In Memoriam*, an elegy for Tennyson's
friend Arthur Henry Hallam.

Alfred, Lord Tennyson (1809–1892)

ULYSSES   (1833)

It little profits that an idle king,
By this still hearth, among these barren crags,
Matched with an agèd wife, I mete and dole
Unequal laws unto a savage race
That hoard, and sleep, and feed, and know not me.   5
I cannot rest from travel; I will drink
Life to the lees. All times I have enjoyed

Greatly, have suffered greatly, both with those
That loved me, and alone; on shore, and when
Through scudding drifts the rainy Hyades   10
Vexed the dim sea. I am become a name;
For always roaming with a hungry heart
Much have I seen and known — cities of men
And manners, climates, councils, governments,
Myself not least, but honored of them all —   15
And drunk delight of battle with my peers,
Far on the ringing plains of windy Troy.
I am a part of all that I have met;
Yet all experience is an arch wherethrough
Gleams that untraveled world whose margin fades   20
Forever and forever when I move.
How dull it is to pause, to make an end,
To rust unburnished, not to shine in use!
As though to breathe were life! Life piled on life
Were all too little, and of one to me   25
Little remains; but every hour is saved
From that eternal silence, something more,
A bringer of new things; and vile it were
For some three suns to store and hoard myself,
And this grey spirit yearning in desire   30
To follow knowledge like a sinking star,
Beyond the utmost bound of human thought.
    This is my son, mine own Telemachus,
To whom I leave the scepter and the isle —
Well-loved of me, discerning to fulfill   35
This labor, by slow prudence to make mild
A rugged people, and through soft degrees
Subdue them to the useful and the good.
Most blameless is he, centered in the sphere
Of common duties, decent not to fail   40
In offices of tenderness, and pay
Meet adoration to my household gods,
When I am gone. He works his work, I mine.
    There lies the port; the vessel puffs her sail;
There gloom the dark, broad seas. My mariners,   45
Souls that have toiled, and wrought, and thought with me —
That ever with a frolic welcome took
The thunder and the sunshine, and opposed
Free hearts, free foreheads — you and I are old;
Old age hath yet his honor and his toil.   50
Death closes all; but something ere the end,
Some work of noble note, may yet be done,
Not unbecoming men that strove with Gods.
The lights begin to twinkle from the rocks;
The long day wanes; the low moon climbs; the deep   55
Moans round with many voices. Come, my friends,
'Tis not too late to seek a newer world.

Push off, and sitting well in order smite
The sounding furrows; for my purpose holds
To sail beyond the sunset, and the baths   60
Of all the western stars, until I die.
It may be that the gulfs will wash us down;
It may be we shall touch the Happy Isles,
And see the great Achilles, whom we knew.
Though much is taken, much abides; and though   65
We are not now that strength which in old days
Moved earth and heaven, that which we are, we are —
One equal temper of heroic hearts,
Made weak by time and fate, but strong in will
To strive, to seek, to find, and not to yield.   70

ULYSSES. 10. *Hyades:* daughters of Atlas, who were transformed into a group of stars. Their rising with the sun was thought to be a sign of rain. 63. *Happy Isles:* Elysium, a paradise believed to be attainable by sailing west.

Dylan Thomas (1914–1953)
FERN HILL   1946

Now as I was young and easy under the apple boughs
About the lilting house and happy as the grass was green,
      The night above the dingle° starry,   *wooded valley*
        Time let me hail and climb
      Golden in the heydays of his eyes,   5
And honored among wagons I was prince of the apple towns
And once below a time I lordly had the trees and leaves
        Trail with daisies and barley
        Down the rivers of the windfall light.

And as I was green and carefree, famous among the barns   10
About the happy yard and singing as the farm was home,
      In the sun that is young once only,
        Time let me play and be
      Golden in the mercy of his means,
And green and golden I was huntsman and herdsman, the calves   15
Sang to my horn, the foxes on the hills barked clear and cold,
        And the sabbath rang slowly
        In the pebbles of the holy streams.

All the sun long it was running, it was lovely, the hay
Fields high as the house, the tunes from the chimneys, it was air 20
      And playing, lovely and watery
        And fire green as grass.
      And nightly under the simple stars
As I rode to sleep the owls were bearing the farm away,
All the moon long I heard, blessed among stables, the nightjars 25
      Flying with the ricks, and the horses
        Flashing into the dark.

And then to awake, and the farm, like a wanderer white
With the dew, come back, the cock on his shoulder: it was all
      Shining, it was Adam and maiden, 30
          The sky gathered again
      And the sun grew round that very day.
So it must have been after the birth of the simple light
In the first, spinning place, the spellbound horses walking warm
      Out of the whinnying green stable 35
          On to the fields of praise.

And honored among foxes and pheasants by the gay house
Under the new made clouds and happy as the heart was long,
      In the sun born over and over,
          I ran my heedless ways, 40
      My wishes raced through the house high hay
And nothing I cared, at my sky blue trades, that time allows
In all his tuneful turning so few and such morning songs
      Before the children green and golden
          Follow him out of grace, 45

Nothing I cared, in the lamb white days, that time would take me
Up to the swallow thronged loft by the shadow of my hand,
      In the moon that is always rising,
          Nor that riding to sleep
      I should hear him fly with the high fields 50
And wake to the farm forever fled from the childless land.
Oh as I was young and easy in the mercy of his means,
          Time held me green and dying
        Though I sang in my chains like the sea.

Dylan Thomas (1914–1953)

TWENTY-FOUR YEARS 1939

Twenty-four years remind the tears of my eyes.
(Bury the dead for fear that they walk to the grave in labor.)
In the groin of the natural doorway I crouched like a tailor
Sewing a shroud for a journey
By the light of the meat-eating sun.
Dressed to die, the sensual strut begun,
With my red veins full of money,
In the final direction of the elementary town
I advance for as long as forever is.

Rosmarie Waldrop (b. 1935)

CONFESSION TO SETTLE A CURSE

1972

You don't
know
who I am
because
you don't know   5
my mother
she's always been an exemplary mother
told me so herself
there were reasons she
had to lock   10
everything that could be locked
there's much can be
locked
in a good German household crowded
with wardrobes dressers sideboards   15
bookcases cupboards chests bureaus
desks trunks caskets coffers all with lock
and key
and locked
it was lots of trouble   20
for her
just carry that enormous key ring
be bothered all the time
I wanted scissors stationery
my winter coat and she had to unlock   25
the drawer get it out and lock
all up again
me she reproached for lacking
confidence not being open
I have a mother I can tell everything   30
she told me so
I've
been bound
made fast
locked   35
by the key witch
but a small
winner
I'm not
in turn locking   40
a child
in my arms.

COMPARE:

"Confession to Settle a Curse" with "Daddy" by Sylvia Plath (page 374).

Walt Whitman (1819–1892)

I SAW IN LOUISIANA A LIVE-OAK GROWING

1867

I saw in Louisiana a live-oak growing,
All alone stood it and the moss hung down from the branches,
Without any companion it grew there uttering joyous leaves of dark
    green,
And its look, rude, unbending, lusty, made me think of myself,
But I wonder'd how it could utter joyous leaves standing alone there
    without its friend near, for I knew I could not,   5
And I broke off a twig with a certain number of leaves upon it, and twined
    around it a little moss,
And brought it away, and I have placed it in sight in my room,
It is not needed to remind me as of my own dear friends,
(For I believe lately I think of little else than of them,)
Yet it remains to me a curious token, it makes me think of manly love;   10
For all that, and though the live-oak glistens there in Louisiana solitary in
    a wide flat space,
Uttering joyous leaves all its life without a friend a lover near,
I know very well I could not.

Walt Whitman (1819–1892)

WHEN I HEARD THE LEARN'D ASTRONOMER

1865

When I heard the learn'd astronomer,
When the proofs, the figures, were ranged in columns before me,
When I was shown the charts and diagrams, to add, divide, and measure
    them
When I sitting heard the astronomer where he lectured with much
    applause in the lecture-room,
How soon unaccountable I became tired and sick,
Till rising and gliding out I wander'd off by myself,
In the mystical moist night-air, and from time to time,
Look'd up in perfect silence at the stars.

Richard Wilbur (b. 1921)

JUNK

1961

Huru Welandes
              worc ne geswiceð
monna ænigum
              ðara ðe Mimming can
heardne gehealdan.
              Waldere

An axe angles
                          from my neighbor's ashcan;
It is hell's handiwork,
                          the wood not hickory,
The flow of the grain
                          not faithfully followed.
The shivered shaft
                          rises from a shellheap
Of plastic playthings,
                          paper plates,   5
And the sheer shards
                          of shattered tumblers
That were not annealed
                          for the time needful.
At the same curbside,
                          a cast-off cabinet
Of wavily-warped
                          unseasoned wood
Waits to be trundled
                          in the trash-man's truck.   10
Haul them off! Hide them!
                          The heart winces
For junk and gimcrack,
                          for jerrybuilt things
And the men who make them
                          for a little money,
Bartering pride
                          like the bought boxer
Who pulls his punches,
                          or the paid-off jockey   15
Who in the home stretch
                          holds in his horse.
Yet the things themselves
                          in thoughtless honor
Have kept composure,
                          like captives who would not
Talk under torture.
                          Tossed from a tailgate
Where the dump displays
                          its random dolmens°,   *prehistoric*   20
Its black barrows   *gravestones*
                          and blazing valleys,
They shall waste in the weather
                          toward what they were.
The sun shall glory
                          in the glitter of glass-chips,
Foreseeing the salvage
                          of the prisoned sand,
And the blistering paint
                          peel off in patches,   25

That the good grain
                      be discovered again.
Then burnt, bulldozed,
                      they shall all be buried
To the depths of diamonds,
                      in the making dark
Where halt Hephaestus
                      keeps his hammer
And Wayland's work
                      is worn away.   30

JUNK. Richard Wilbur notes: "The epigraph, taken from a fragmentary Anglo-Saxon poem, concerns the legendary smith Wayland, and may roughly be translated: 'Truly, Wayland's handiwork — the sword Mimming which he made — will never fail any man who knows how to use it bravely.'" 29. *Hephaestus:* another smith and artisan, the Greek god of fire, said to have forged armor for Achilles.

COMPARE:

"Junk" with "The Seafarer" by Ezra Pound (page 380).

William Carlos Williams (1883–1963)

SPRING AND ALL   1923

By the road to the contagious hospital
under the surge of the blue
mottled clouds driven from the
northeast — a cold wind. Beyond, the
waste of broad, muddy fields   5
brown with dried weeds, standing and fallen

patches of standing water
the scattering of tall trees

All along the road the reddish
purplish, forked, upstanding, twiggy   10
stuff of bushes and small trees
with dead, brown leaves under them
leafless vines —

Lifeless in appearance, sluggish
dazed spring approaches —   15

They enter the new world naked,
cold, uncertain of all
save that they enter. All about them
the cold, familiar wind —

Now the grass, tomorrow   20
the stiff curl of wildcarrot leaf

One by one objects are defined —
It quickens: clarity, outline of leaf

But now the stark dignity of
entrance — Still, the profound change   25
has come upon them: rooted, they
grip down and begin to awaken

COMPARE:

"Spring and All" with "in Just-" by E. E. Cummings (page 184) and "Root
Cellar" by Theodore Roethke (page 57).

William Carlos Williams (1883–1963)
To Waken an Old Lady   1921

Old age is
a flight of small
cheeping birds
skimming
bare trees   5
above a snow glaze.
Gaining and failing
they are buffeted
by a dark wind —
But what?   10
On harsh weedstalks
the flock has rested,
the snow
is covered with broken
seedhusks   15
and the wind tempered
by a shrill
piping of plenty.

COMPARE:

"To Waken an Old Lady" with "Castoff Skin" by Ruth Whitman (page 84).

Yvor Winters (1900–1968)
At the San Francisco Airport   1952

To My Daughter, 1954

This is the terminal: the light
Gives perfect vision, false and hard;
The metal glitters, deep and bright.

Great planes are waiting in the yard —
They are already in the night.   5

And you are here beside me, small,
Contained and fragile, and intent
On things that I but half recall —
Yet going whither you are bent.
I am the past, and that is all.   10

But you and I in part are one:
The frightened brain, the nervous will,
The knowledge of what must be done,
The passion to acquire the skill
To face that which you dare not shun.   15

The rain of matter upon sense
Destroys me momently. The score:
There comes what will come. The expense
Is what one thought, and something more —
One's being and intelligence.   20

This is the terminal, the break.
Beyond this point, on lines of air,
You take the way that you must take;
And I remain in light and stare —
In light, and nothing else, awake.   25

William Wordsworth (1770–1850)

Composed upon Westminster Bridge   1807

Earth has not anything to show more fair:
Dull would he be of soul who could pass by
A sight so touching in its majesty:
This City now doth, like a garment, wear
The beauty of the morning; silent, bare,   5
Ships, towers, domes, theatres, and temples lie
Open unto the fields, and to the sky;
All bright and glittering in the smokeless air.
Never did sun more beautifully steep
In his first splendor, valley, rock, or hill;   10
Ne'er saw I, never felt, a calm so deep!
The river glideth at his own sweet will:
Dear God! the very houses seem asleep;
And all that mighty heart is lying still!

William Wordsworth (1770–1850)

STEPPING WESTWARD   1807

While my Fellow-traveler and I were walking by the side of Lock° Ket-   *Lake*
terine, one fine evening after sunset, in our road to a hut where, in the
course of our tour, we had been hospitably entertained some weeks before,
we met, in one of the loneliest parts of that solitary region, two well-
dressed women, one of whom said to us, by way of greeting, "What, are
you stepping westward?"

"What, are you stepping westward?" — "Yea."
— 'Twould be a *wildish* destiny,
If we, who thus together roam
In a strange land, and far from home,
Were in this place the guests of Chance;   5
Yet who would stop, or fear to advance,
Though home or shelter he had none,
With such a sky to lead him on?

The dewy ground was dark and cold;
Behind, all gloomy to behold;   10
And stepping westward seemed to be
A kind of *heavenly* destiny:
I liked the greeting; 'twas a sound
Of something without place or bound
And seemed to give me spiritual right   15
To travel through that region bright.

The voice was soft, and she who spake
Was walking by her native lake;
The salutation had to me
The very sound of courtesy: 20
Its power was felt; and while my eye
Was fixed upon the glowing sky,
The echo of the voice enwrought
A human sweetness with the thought
Of traveling through the world that lay   25
Before me in my endless way.

STEPPING WESTWARD. Wordsworth's "Fellow-traveler" was his sister Dorothy, with
whom in 1803 he made a tour of the Highlands of Scotland.

James Wright (b. 1927)

A BLESSING   1961

Just off the highway to Rochester, Minnesota,
Twilight bounds softly forth on the grass.
And the eyes of those two Indian ponies
Darken with kindness.

They have come gladly out of the willows   5
To welcome my friend and me.
We step over the barbed wire into the pasture
Where they have been grazing all day, alone.
They ripple tensely, they can hardly contain their happiness
That we have come.   10
They bow shyly as wet swans. They love each other.
There is no loneliness like theirs.
At home once more,
They begin munching the young tufts of spring in the darkness.
I would like to hold the slenderer one in my arms,   15
For she has walked over to me
And nuzzled my left hand.
She is black and white,
Her mane falls wild on her forehead,
And the light breeze moves me to caress her long ear   20
That is delicate as the skin over a girl's wrist.
Suddenly I realize
That if I stepped out of my body I would break
Into blossom.

James Wright (b. 1927)
AUTUMN BEGINS IN MARTINS FERRY, OHIO   1963

In the Shreve High football stadium,
I think of Polacks nursing long beers in Tiltonsville,
And gray faces of Negroes in the blast furnace at Benwood,
And the ruptured night watchman of Wheeling Steel,
Dreaming of heroes.   5

All the proud fathers are ashamed to go home.
Their women cluck like starved pullets,
Dying for love.

Therefore,
Their sons grow suicidally beautiful   10
At the beginning of October,
And gallop terribly against each other's bodies.

Judith Wright (b. 1915)
WOMAN TO MAN   1971

The eyeless laborer in the night,
the selfless, shapeless seed I hold,
builds for its resurrection day —
silent and swift and deep from sight
foresees the unimagined light.   5

This is no child with a child's face;
this has no name to name it by;
yet you and I have known it well.
This is our hunter and our chase,
the third who lay in our embrace.   10

This is the strength that your arm knows,
the arc of flesh that is my breast,
the precise crystals of our eyes.
This is the blood's wild tree that grows
the intricate and folded rose.   15

This is the maker and the made;
this is the question and reply;
the blind head butting at the dark,
the blaze of light along the blade.
Oh hold me, for I am afraid.   20

Judith Wright (b. 1915)
WOMAN TO CHILD   1971

You who were darkness warmed my flesh
where out of darkness rose the seed.
Then all a world I made in me:
all the world you hear and see
hung upon my dreaming blood.   5

There moved the multitudinous stars,
and colored birds and fishes moved.
There swam the sliding continents.
All time lay rolled in me, and sense,
and love that knew not its beloved.   10

O node and focus of the world —
I hold you deep within that well
you shall escape and not escape —
that mirrors still your sleeping shape,
that nurtures still your crescent cell.   15

I wither and you break from me;
yet though you dance in living light,
I am the earth, I am the root,
I am the stem that fed the fruit,
the link that joins you to the night.   20

COMPARE:

"Woman to Child" with "Metaphors" (page 82) and "Morning Song" (page 376) by Sylvia Plath.

William Butler Yeats (1865–1939)

Crazy Jane Talks with the Bishop

1933

I met the Bishop on the road
And much said he and I.
"Those breasts are flat and fallen now,
Those veins must soon be dry;
Live in a heavenly mansion, 5
Not in some foul sty."

"Fair and foul are near of kin,
And fair needs foul," I cried.
"My friends are gone, but that's a truth
Nor° grave nor bed denied, *neither* 10
Learned in bodily lowliness
And in the heart's pride.

"A woman can be proud and stiff
When on love intent;
But Love has pitched his mansion in 15
The place of excrement;
For nothing can be sole or whole
That has not been rent."

William Butler Yeats (1865–1939)

The Lake Isle of Innisfree

1892

I will arise and go now, and go to Innisfree,
And a small cabin build there, of clay and wattles made:
Nine bean-rows will I have there, a hive for the honey-bee,
And live alone in the bee-loud glade.

And I shall have some peace there, for peace comes dropping slow, 5
Dropping from the veils of the morning to where the cricket sings;
There midnight's all a glimmer, and noon a purple glow,
And evening full of the linnet's wings.

I will arise and go now, for always night and day
I hear lake water lapping with low sounds by the shore; 10
While I stand on the roadway, or on the pavements grey,
I hear it in the deep heart's core.

THE LAKE ISLE OF INNISFREE. Yeats refers to an island in Lough (Lake) Gill, in County Sligo in the west of Ireland. 2. *wattles:* frameworks of interwoven sticks or branches, used to make walls and roofs.

COMPARE:

"The Lake Isle of Innisfree" with Yeats's "Sailing to Byzantium" (page 250).

William Butler Yeats (1865–1939)

LAPIS LAZULI   1938

For Harry Clifton

I have heard that hysterical women say
They are sick of the palette and fiddle-bow,
Of poets that are always gay,
For everybody knows or else should know
That if nothing drastic is done   5
Aeroplane and Zeppelin will come out,
Pitch like King Billy bomb-balls in
Until the town lie beaten flat.

All perform their tragic play,
There struts Hamlet, there is Lear,   10
That's Ophelia, that Cordelia;
Yet they, should the last scene be there,
The great stage curtain about to drop,
If worthy their prominent part in the play,
Do not break up their lines to weep.   15
They know that Hamlet and Lear are gay;
Gaiety transfiguring all that dread.
All men have aimed at, found and lost;
Black out; Heaven blazing into the head:
Tragedy wrought to its uttermost.   20
Though Hamlet rambles and Lear rages,
And all the drop-scenes drop at once
Upon a hundred thousand stages,
It cannot grow by an inch or an ounce.

On their own feet they came, or on shipboard,   25
Camel-back, horse-back, ass-back, mule-back,
Old civilizations put to the sword.
Then they and their wisdom went to rack:
No handiwork of Callimachus,
Who handled marble as if it were bronze,   30
Made draperies that seemed to rise
When sea-wind swept the corner, stands;
His long lamp-chimney shaped like the stem
Of a slender palm, stood but a day;
All things fall and are built again,   35
And those that build them again are gay.

Two Chinamen, behind them a third,
Are carved in lapis lazuli,
Over them flies a long-legged bird,
A symbol of longevity;   40
The third, doubtless a serving-man,
Carries a musical instrument.

Every discoloration of the stone,
Every accidental crack or dent,
Seems a water-course or an avalanche,   45
Or lofty slope where it still snows
Though doubtless plum or cherry-branch
Sweetens the little half-way house
Those Chinamen climb towards, and I
Delight to imagine them seated there;   50
There, on the mountain and the sky,
On all the tragic scene they stare.
One asks for mournful melodies;
Accomplished fingers begin to play.
Their eyes mid many wrinkles, their eyes,   55
Their ancient, glittering eyes, are gay.

LAPIS LAZULI. Lapis lazuli is a deep blue semiprecious stone. A friend had given Yeats the carving made from it, which he describes in lines 37-56. 7. *King Billy:* William of Orange, king of England who used cannon against the Irish in the Battle of the Boyne, 1690. Yeats also may have in mind Kaiser Wilhelm II of Germany, who sent zeppelins to bomb London in World War I. 29. *Callimachus:* Athenian sculptor, fifth century B.C.

COMPARE:

"Lapis Lazuli" with "Ode on a Grecian Urn" by John Keats (page 359) and "Anecdote of the Jar" by Wallace Stevens (page 207).

William Butler Yeats (1865–1939)
THE MAGI   1914

Now as at all times I can see in the mind's eye,
In their stiff, painted clothes, the pale unsatisfied ones
Appear and disappear in the blue depth of the sky
With all their ancient faces like rain-beaten stones,
And all their helms of silver hovering side by side,
And all their eyes still fixed, hoping to find once more,
Being by Calvary's turbulence unsatisfied,
The uncontrollable mystery on the bestial floor.

COMPARE:

"The Magi" with "Journey of the Magi" by T. S. Eliot (page 335).

Appendix

Writing about Literature

That masterful poet and critic T. S. Eliot once declared that, in approaching a work of literature to write about it, the only method he knew was to be very intelligent. Eliot wasn't boasting about his I.Q.; he was suggesting that to a critic of literature, a keen sensibility is more valuable than a carefully worked out method, any day. Although none of us may be another Eliot, all of us have some powers of reasoning and perception. And when we come to a story, a poem, or a play, we can do little other than to trust whatever powers we have, like one who enters a shadowy room, clutching a decent candle.

After all, in the study of literature, common sense (as poet Gerard Manley Hopkins said) is never out of place. For most of a class hour, a renowned English professor once rhapsodized about the arrangement of the contents of W. H. Auden's *Collected Poems.* Auden, he claimed, was a master of thematic continuity, who had brilliantly placed the poems in the best possible order, in which (to the ingenious mind) they complemented each other. Near the end of the hour, his theories were punctured—with a great inaudible pop—when a student timidly raising a hand pointed out that Auden had arranged the poems in the book not according to theme but in alphabetical order by title. The professor's jaw dropped: "Why didn't you say that sooner?" The student was apologetic: "I—I was afraid I'd sound too *ordinary.*"

Emerson makes a similar point in his essay "The American Scholar": "Meek young men grow up in libraries, believing it their duty to accept the views which Cicero, which Locke, which Bacon have given; forgetful that Cicero, Locke, and Bacon were only young men in libraries when they wrote these books." Don't be afraid to state a conviction, though it seems obvious. Does it matter that you may be repeating something that, once upon a time or even just the other day, has been said before? There are excellent old ideas as well as new.

SOME APPROACHES TO LITERATURE

Though T. S. Eliot may be right in preferring intelligence to method, there are certain familiar approaches to stories, poems, and plays which most critical essays tend to follow. Underlying each of these four approaches is a certain way of regarding the nature of a work of literature.

1. *The Work by Itself.* This view assumes a story, poem, or play to be an individual entity, existing on its page, that we can read and understand in its own right, without necessarily studying the life of its author, or the age in which it was written, or its possible effect on its readers. This is the approach of most papers written in response to college assignments; to study just the work (and not its backgrounds or its influence) does not require the student to spend prolonged time doing research in a library. The three common ways of writing a paper discussed earlier in this book — explication, analysis, and comparison and contrast — are concerned mainly with the work of literature in itself.

2. *The Work as Imitation of Life.* Aristotle called the art of writing a tragedy *mimesis:* the imitation or re-creation of an action that is serious and complete in itself. From this classic theory in the *Poetics* comes the view that a work of literature in some way imitates the world or the civilization in which it was produced. We can say, for instance, that Ibsen's play *A Doll's House* places before our eyes actors whose life-like speeches and movements represent members of an upper-middle-class society in provincial Norway in the late nineteenth century and that the play reflects their beliefs and attitudes. Not only the subject and theme of a work imitate life in this view: John Ciardi has remarked that the heroic couplet, dominant stanza form in poetry read by educated people in eighteenth-century England, reflects, in its exact form and its use of antitheses, the rhythms of the minuet — another contemporary form, fashionable also among the well-to-do: "now on this hand, now on that." The writer concerned with literature as imitation usually studies the world that the literary work imitates. He or she goes into the ideas underlying the writer's society, showing how the themes, assumptions, and conventions of the writer's work arose out of that time and that place. Obviously, this takes more research than one can do for a weekly paper; it is usually the approach taken for a book or a dissertation, or perhaps an honors thesis or a term paper. (The other two approaches we will mention also take research.) Reasonably short studies of the relation between the work and its world are, however, sometimes possible: "World War II as Seen in Henry Reed's 'Naming of Parts' "; "John A. Williams's 'Son in the Afternoon': A Typical Spokesman for Watts, California?"

3. *The Work as Expression.* In this view, a work of literature expresses the feelings of the person who wrote it; therefore, to study it, one studies the author's life. Typical paper topics: "Young Eugene O'Neill's Loneliness and *The Hairy Ape*"; "Sylvia Plath's Lost Father and Her View of Him in 'Daddy.' " To write any truly deep-reaching biographical criticism takes research, clearly, but one could write a term paper on topics such as these by reading a single biography.

Biographical criticism fell into temporary disrepute around 1920, when T. S. Eliot questioned the assumption that a poem has to be a personal statement of the poet's thoughts and emotions.[1] Eliot and other critics did much to clear the air of speculation that the "Ode on a Grecian Urn" may have been shaped by what Keats had had for breakfast. Evidently, in any search for what went on in an author's mind, and for the influence of life upon work, aboslute certainty is unattainable. Besides, such an approach can be grossly reductive — holding, for example, that Shakespeare was sad when he wrote his tragedies and especially happy when he wrote *A Midsummer Night's Dream*. Still, there are works that gain in meaning from even a slight knowledge of the author's biography. In reading *Moby Dick*, it helps to know that Herman Melville served aboard a whaling vessel.

4. *The Work as Influence*. From this perspective, a literary work is a force that affects people. It stirs certain responses in them, rouses their emotions, perhaps argues for ideas that change their minds. The artist, said Tolstoi in a famous pronouncement (*What Is Art?*), "hands on to others those feelings he himself has felt, that they too may be moved, and experience them." Part of the function of art, Tolstoi continued, is to enlighten and to lead its audience into an acceptance of better moral attitudes (religious faith, or a sense of social justice). The critic who takes this approach is generally concerned with the ideas that a literary work imparts and the reception of those ideas by a particular audience: "Did *Uncle Tom's Cabin* Cause the Civil War?"; "The Early Reception of Allen Ginsberg's *Howl*"; "Ed Bullins's Plays and Their Newly Proud Black Audience." As you can see, this whole approach is closely related to viewing a literary work as an imitation of life. Still another way of discussing a work's influence is to trace its impact upon other writers: "Robert Frost's Debt to Emily Dickinson"; "*Moby Dick* and William Faulkner's *The Bear:* Two Threatened Wildernesses."

FINDING A TOPIC

Offered a choice of literary works to write about, you probably will do best if, instead of choosing what you think will impress your instructor, you choose what appeals to you. And how to find out what appeals? Whether you plan to write a short paper that requires no research beyond the story or poem or play itself, or a long term paper that will take you to the library, the first stage of your project is reading — and note taking. To concentrate your attention, one time-honored method is to read with a pencil, marking (if the book is yours) passages that stand out in importance, jotting brief notes in a margin ("*Key symbol — this foreshadows the ending*"; "*Dramatic irony*"; "*IDIOT!!!*"; or other pos-

---

[1] See Eliot's essay "Tradition and the Individual Talent," in *Selected Essays* (New York: Harcourt Brace, 1932).

sibly useful remarks). In a long story or poem or play, some students asterisk certain passages that cry for comparison: for instance, all the places in which they find the same theme or symbol. Later, at a glance, they can review the highlights of a work and, when writing a paper about it, quickly refer to evidence. This method shoots holes in a book's resale value, but many find the sacrifice worthwhile. Patient souls who dislike butchering a book prefer to take notes on looseleaf notebook paper, holding one sheet beside a page in the book and giving it the book's page-number. Later, in writing a paper, they can place book page and companion note page together again. This method has the advantage of affording a lot of room for note taking; it is a good one for short poems closely packed with complexities.

But by far the most popular method of taking notes (besides writing on the pages of books) is to write on index cards — the 3 x 5 kind, for brief notes and titles; 5 x 8 cards for longer notes. Write on one side only; notes on the back of the card usually get overlooked later. Cards are easy to shuffle and, in organizing your material, to deal.

Now that coin-operated photocopy machines are to be found in many libraries, you no longer need to spend hours copying by hand whole poems and longer passages. If accuracy is essential (surely it is) and if a poem or passage is long enough to be worth the investment of a dime, you can lay photocopied material into place in your paper with transparent tape or rubber cement. The latest copyright law permits students and scholars to reproduce books and periodicals in this fashion; it does not, however, permit making a dozen or more copies for public sale.

Certain literary works, because they offer intriguing difficulties, have attracted professional critics by the score. On library shelves, great phalanxes of critical books now stand at the side of James Joyce's complex novels *Ulysses* and *Finnegans Wake,* and T. S. Eliot's allusive poem *The Waste Land.* The student who undertakes to study such works seriously is well advised to profit from the critics' labors. Chances are, too, that even in discussing a relatively uncomplicated work you will want to seek the aid of the finest critics. If you quote them, quote them exactly, in quotation marks, and give them credit. When employed in any but the most superlative student paper, a brilliant phrase (or even a not so brilliant sentence) from a renowned critic is likely to stand out like a golf ball in a gartersnake's midriff, and most English instructors are likely to recognize it. If you rip off the critic's words, then go ahead and steal the whole essay, for good critics tend to write in seamless unities. Then, when apprehended, you can exclaim — like the student whose term paper was found to be the work of a well-known scholar — "I've been robbed! That paper cost me twenty dollars!" But of course the worst rip-off is the one the student inflicted on himself, having got nothing for his money out of a college course but a little practice in touch-typing.

Taking notes on your readings, you will want to jot down the title of every book you might refer to in your paper, and the page number of any passage you might wish to quote. Even if you summarize a critic's idea in your own words, rather than quote, you have to give credit to your source. Nothing is cheaper to give than proper credit. Certainly it's easier to take notes while you read than to have to run back to the library during the final typing.

Choose a topic appropriate to the assigned length of your paper. How do you know the probable length of your discussion until you write it? When in doubt, you are better off to define your topic narrowly. Your paper will be stronger if you go deeper into your subject than if you choose some gigantic subject and then find yourself able to touch on it only superficially. A thorough explication of a short story is hardly possible in a paper of 250 words. There are, in truth, four-line poems whose surface 250 words might only begin to scratch. A profound topic ("The Character of Shakespeare's Hamlet") might overflow a book; but a topic more narrowly defined ("Hamlet's Views of Acting"; "Hamlet's Puns") might result in a more nearly manageable term paper. You can narrow and focus a large topic while you work your way into it. A general interest in "Hemingway's Heroes," for instance, might lead you, in the process of reading, taking notes, and thinking further, to the narrower topic, "Jake Barnes: Spokesman for Hemingway's Views of War."

Many student writers find it helpful, in defining a topic, to state an emerging idea for a paper in a provisional **thesis sentence:** a summing-up of the one main idea or argument that the paper will embody. (A thesis sentence is for your own use; you don't have to implant it in your paper unless your instructor asks for it.) Complete with subject and verb, a good statement of a thesis is not just a disembodied subject; it comes with both subject and verb. ("The Downfall of Oedipus Rex" is not yet a complete idea for a paper; "What Caused the Downfall of Oedipus Rex" is.) A thesis sentence helps you see for yourself what the author you are studying is *saying about* a subject. Not a full thesis, and not a sentence, "The Isolation of City-dwellers in Edward Albee's *A Zoo Story*" might be a decent title for a paper. But it isn't a useful thesis because it doesn't indicate what one might say about that isolation (nor what Albee is saying about it). While it may be obvious that isolation isn't desirable, a clear and workable thesis sentence might be, "In *A Zoo Story* Albee demonstrates that city-dwellers' isolation from one another prompts one city-dweller to action"; the paper might well go on to demonstrate just what that action is.

ORGANIZING YOUR THINKING

Topic in hand, perhaps in the form of a thesis sentence on paper, you now begin to sort your miscellaneous thoughts and impressions. To outline or not to outline? Unless your topic, by its very nature, suggests some obvious way to organize your paper ("An Explication of a Wordsworth Sonnet" might mean simply working through the poem line by line), then some kind of outline is practically indispensable. In high school or other prehistoric times, you perhaps learned how to construct a beautiful outline, laid out with Roman numerals, capital letters, Arabic numerals, and small letters. It was a thing of beauty and symmetry, and possibly even had something to do with paper writing. But if now you are skeptical of the value of outlining, reflect: not every outline needs to be detailed and elaborate. Some students, of course, find it helpful to outline in detail — particularly if they are planning a long term paper involving several literary works, comparing and contrasting several aspects of them. For a 500-word analysis of a short story's figures of speech, however, all you might need is a simple list of points to make, scribbled down in the order in which you will make them. This order is probably not, of course, the order in which the points first occurred to you. Thoughts, when they first come to mind, tend to be a confused rabble.

While granting the need for order in a piece of writing, the present writer confesses that he is a reluctant outliner. His tendency (or curse) is to want to keep whatever random thoughts occur to him; to polish his prose right then and there; and finally to try to juggle his disconnected paragraphs into something like logical order. The usual result is that he has large blocks of illogical thought left over. This process is wasteful, and if you can learn to live with an outline, then you belong to the legion of the blessed, and will never know the pain of scrapping pages that cost you hours. On the other hand, you will never know the joy of meandering — of bursting into words and setting them down however wildly, to see what you truly want to say. There is value in such wasteful and self-indulgent writing — but not if a deadline is imminent.

An outline is not meant to stand as an achievement in itself. It should — as Ezra Pound said literary criticism ought to do — consume itself and disappear. Here, for instance, is a once-valuable outline not worth keeping — a very informal one that enabled a student to organize the paper comparing "Design" by Robert Frost with "Wing-Spread" by Abbie Huston Evans that appears on page 288. Before he wrote, the student simply jotted down the points he had in mind. Looking over this "mess of garbage" (as he then regarded it), he could see that, among his scattered thoughts, two topics predominated. One was about figures of speech and about connotations, and these ideas he decided to join under the heading LANGUAGE. His other emerging idea had to do with the two poets' quite different themes. Having perceived that his thoughts weren't totally jumbled, he then proceeded to go through his list, numbering with the same numbers any ideas that seemed to go together, and so arranging them in the order he wanted to follow. His outline then looked like this:

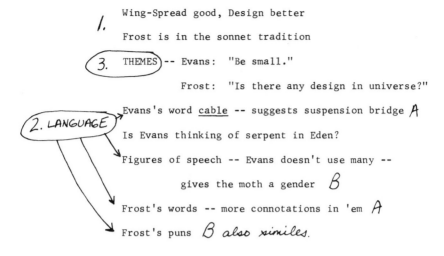

I. Wing-Spread good, Design better

Frost is in the sonnet tradition

3. **THEMES** -- Evans: "Be small."

Frost: "Is there any design in universe?"

Evans's word <u>cable</u> -- suggests suspension bridge *A*

2. LANGUAGE

Is Evans thinking of serpent in Eden?

Figures of speech -- Evans doesn't use many --

gives the moth a gender *B*

Frost's words -- more connotations in 'em *A*

Frost's puns *B* also similes.

Labeling with "A" the two points about words full of connotations, and with "B" the two points about figures of speech, the student indicated to himself that these points were to be taken up together. He found, as you can see in the finished essay, two ideas that didn't seem to relate to his purpose. These were the points about Frost's being in the sonnet tradition and about Evans's possible interest in the Garden of Eden serpent. Reluctantly but wisely, he decided to leave them out. These ideas might have led him to make interesting comments on the individual poems, but would not have got him to *compare* the poems, as the assignment asked. Having made this rough outline, he felt encouraged to return to the two poems; and, on rereading them, noticed some further points, which now fell readily into his plan. One of these points was that Frost's poem also contains similes. He added it to his outline and so remembered it.

WRITING A DRAFT

Seated at last, or striking some other businesslike stance,[2] you prepare to write, only to find yourself besieged with petty distractions. All of a sudden you remember a friend you had promised to call, some dry-cleaning you were supposed to pick up, a neglected Coke (in another room) growing warmer and flatter by the minute. If your paper is to be written, you have one course of action: to collar these thoughts and for the moment banish them.

Other small problems are merely mechanical: for instance, what to call the author whose work you now confront. Decide at the outset. Most critics favor the author's last name alone: "Dickinson implies . . ."

---

[2] R. H. Super of the University of Michigan wrote a definitive biography of Walter Savage Landor while standing up, typing on a machine atop a filing cabinet.

("Miss Dickinson" or "Ms. Dickinson" may sound fussily polite; "Emily," too chummy.) Will you include footnotes in your paper and, if so, do you know how they work? (Some pointers on handling the pesky things will come in a few pages.)

You will want to give credit to any critics who helped you out, and properly to do so is to be painstaking. To paraphrase a critic, you do more than just rearrange the critic's words and phrases; you translate them into language of your own. Say you wish to refer to an insight of Randall Jarrell, who comments on the images of spider, flower, and moth in Robert Frost's poem "Design": "Notice how the *heal-all,* because of its name, is the one flower in all the world picked to be the altar for this Devil's Mass; notice how holding up the moth brings something ritual and hieratic, a ghostly, ghastly formality to this priest and its sacrificial victim. . . ." It would be incorrect to say, without any quotation marks:

```
Frost picks the heal-all as the one flower in all the world to be

the altar for this Devil's Mass.  There is a ghostly, ghastly

formality to the spider holding up the moth, like a priest holding

a sacrificial victim.
```

That rewording, although not exactly in Jarrell's language, manages to steal his memorable phrases without giving him credit. Nor is it sufficient just to list Jarrell's essay in a bibliography at the end of your paper. If you do, you are still a crook; you merely point to the scene of your crime. What is needed, clearly, is to think through Jarrell's words to the point he is making; and if you want to keep any of his striking phrases (and why not?), put them in quotation marks:

```
As Randall Jarrell points out, Frost portrays the spider as a kind

of priest in a Mass, or Black Mass, elevating the moth like an

object for sacrifice, with "a ghostly, ghastly formality."
```

To be scrupulous in your acknowledgment, you could even put a footnote after the phrase in quotation marks, citing the book and the page. But unless your instructor expects you to write such a formal, footnoted paper, the passage as it now stands would make sufficiently clear your source, and your obligation.

One more word of Dutch-uncleish warning. This book has offered you a vocabulary with which to discuss literature: a flurry of terms such as *irony, symbol,* and *image,* printed in **bold face** when first introduced. In your writing, perhaps, you may decide to enlist a few of them. And yet, critical terminology—especially if unfamiliar—can tempt a beginning critic to sling it about. Nothing can be less sophisticated, or more misleading, than a technical term grandly misapplied: "The *myth-symbolism* of this *rime scheme* leaves one aghast." Far better to choose plain words you're already at ease with. Your instructor, no doubt, has met many a critical term and is not likely to be impressed by the mere sight of another one. Knowingly selected and placed, a critical term can help sharpen a thought and make it easier to handle. Clearly it is less cumbersome to refer to the *tone* of a story than to have to say, "the way the author makes you feel that she feels about what she is talking about." But the paper-writer who declares, "The tone of this poem is full of ironic imagery," fries words to a hash—mixed up and indigestible.

REVISING

Is it possible to write with perfect clarity on first try, to drop ideas with a single shot at them? Doubtless there are writers who can do so. Jack Kerouac, a believer in spontaneous prose, used to write entire novels on uncut ribbons of teletype paper, which custom saved him the interruption of stopping at the bottom of each page; and he declared that he rarely felt the need to change a word. His specialty, though, was fiction of ecstasy and hallucination, not essays in explication, or comparison and contrast. D. H. Lawrence also liked to let first drafts stand. If on finishing a story he felt dissatisfied, he sometimes declined to tinker with it but would write the whole thing over from scratch, hoping to do better. This habit accounts for the existence of at least three versions of his novel *Lady Chatterley's Lover*. For most of us, however, good writing is largely a matter of revising—of going back over our first thoughts word by word.

Still, to achieve good writing you have to have the courage to be wild. Aware that no reader need see your rough drafts, you can treat them mercilessly—scissor them apart, rearrange their pieces, reassemble them into a stronger order, using staples or tape or glue. The art of revising calls for a textbook in itself, but here are a few simple rules:

1. When you write your first draft, leave generous space between lines, and enormous margins. You may find later thoughts to add; make room.

2. As you reread your early draft, try to strike out any superfluous words or phrases. Eliminate whole paragraphs if they don't advance your main argument. Watch out, though, for any gaping holes that result. Often, when you eliminate a sizeable passage, you'll need to add a transition to lead your reader on to the next idea.

3. Try reading your first draft aloud. Awkward sound effects may be detected: "An excellent excuse for exercise"; "Doom blooms in the second line . . ."

4. Short, skimpy paragraphs may indicate points that deserve more thought. Can you supply them with any more evidence, more explanation or illustration?

5. A classic method of revision is to lay your manuscript aside for a while, forget about it, and then, after a long interval (the Roman poet Horace recommended nine years), go back to it for a fresh look. If you lack that much time, take a nap, or a walk, or at least a yawn and a stretch before taking yet another look.

If you type your papers, by the way, it is a great help to be a reasonably expert typist—one who uses something other than the Christopher Columbus method (to discover a key and land on it). Then you can revise while you retype. All to what end? "Each clear sentence," according to Robert Russell, "is that much ground stripped clean of the undergrowth of one's own confusion. Sometimes it's thrilling to feel you have written even a single paragraph that makes sense."[3]

THE FORM OF YOUR FINISHED PAPER

Now that you have smoothed your rough draft as fleck-free as you can, your instructor may have specific advice for the form of your finished paper. If none is forthcoming, it is only reasonable

1. to choose standard letter-size (8½ x 11) paper;
2. to give your name at the top of your title page;
3. to leave an inch or more of margin on all four sides of each page, and a few inches of blank paper or an additional sheet after your conclusion, so that your instructor can offer comment;
4. to doublespace, or (if you handwrite) to use paper with widely spaced lines.

And what of titles of works discussed: when to put them in quotation marks, when to underline them? One rule of thumb is that titles of works shorter than book length rate quotation marks (poems, short stories, articles); while titles of books (including book-length poems: *The Odyssey*), plays, and periodicals take underlining. (In a manuscript to be set in type, an underline is a signal to the printer to use *italics*.)

A word about footnotes, if you're using them. A footnote number comes (following any punctuation) after the last word of a quotation or other item of information whose source you wish to credit. So that the number will stand out, roll your typewriter carriage up a click, thus lifting the number slightly above the usual level of your prose. At the bottom of your page, put the footnote itself; like this, for a book:

[8]Sylvan Barnet, A Short Guide to Writing About Literature, 3rd ed. (Boston: Little, Brown, 1975), page 102.

[3] *To Catch an Angel* (New York: Vanguard, 1962), page 301.

Or like this, for a magazine article:

> [9]Paul Ramsey, "The Biding Place: Reflections on Hart Crane,"
> Parnassus: Poetry in Review 5 (Fall/Winter 1976), 187-199.

In that last footnote, the number 5 is the volume number; *187–199* are the pages in it spanned by the article. Of course, you might wish instead to refer to a specific page. Should you return, later in your paper, for another quotation from Ramsey's article, you need not repeat all its information. Just make it

> [10]Ramsey, page 192.

(If your paper quoted two articles by Paul Ramsey, you would have to provide full information for the second article on *its* first mention; and then in further footnote references to either article, would mention its title so that the reader could tell the two apart.)

Footnotes enable your readers to go to the same place you did and read the same material. Most readers, of course, will not take the trouble to do so; but at least you give them a chance, and the process of footnoting keeps you as writer looking carefully at your sources, and so it helps you, as well.

Your readers should not have to interrupt their reading of your essay to glance down at a footnote simply to find out whom you are quoting. It is poor form to write:

> Dylan Thomas's poem "Fern Hill" is a memory of the poet's
> childhood: of his Aunt Ann Jones's farm, where he spent his
> holidays. "Time, which has an art to throw dust on all things,
> broods over the poem."[1] The farm, indeed, is a lost paradise -- a
> personal garden of Eden.

> _____
>
> [1]William York Tindall, A Reader's Guide to Dylan Thomas (New
> York: Noonday Press, 1962), page 268.

That is annoying, because the reader has to stop reading and look at the footnote to find out who made that resonant statement about Time brooding over the poem. A better way:

> "Time," as William York Tindall has observed, "which has an art to
> throw dust on all things, broods over the poem."[1]

> _____
>
> [1]A Reader's Guide to Dylan Thomas (New York: Noonday Press,
> 1962), page 268.

What to do now but hand in your paper? "And good riddance," you may feel, after such an expenditure of thinking, time, and energy. But a good paper is not only worth submitting, it is worth keeping. If you return to it, after a while, you may find to your surprise that it will preserve and even renew what you have learned.

Acknowledgments *(continued)*

Sarah N. Cleghorn. "The Golf Links Lie So Near the Mill" from *Portraits and Protests* by Sarah N. Cleghorn. All rights reserved. Reprinted by permission of Holt, Rinehart and Winston, Publishers.

Cid Corman. "The Tortoise" from *Words for Each Other* by Cid Corman. First appeared in *In Good Time* by Cid Corman. Reprinted by permission of Rapp and Whiting Ltd.

Frances Cornford. "The Watch" from *Collected Poems* by Frances Cornford (Cresset Press). Reprinted by permission of Barrie & Jenkins Ltd.

Hart Crane. "Black Tambourine" from *The Complete Poems and Selected Letters and Prose of Hart Crane*, edited by Brom Weber. Copyright 1933, © 1958, 1966 by Liveright Publishing Corporation. Reprinted by permission of Liveright Publishing Corporation.

Robert Creeley. "Oh No" and "A Naughty Boy" from *For Love* by Robert Creeley. Copyright © 1962 by Robert Creeley. Reprinted by permission of Charles Scribner's Sons.

Countee Cullen. "Saturday's Child" and "For a Lady I Know" from *On These I Stand* by Countee Cullen. Copyright 1925 by Harper & Row, Publishers, Inc.; renewed 1953 by Ida M. Cullen. Reprinted by permission of Harper & Row, Publishers.

E. E. Cummings. These poems from *Complete Poems 1913–1962*: "anyone lived in a pretty how town" (copyright 1940 by E. E. Cummings, copyright © 1968 by Marion Morehouse Cummings); "All in green went my love riding," "Buffalo Bill's," and "in Just-" (all copyright 1923, 1951 by E. E. Cummings); "a politician is an arse upon" (copyright 1944 by E. E. Cummings); and "r-p-o-p-h-e-s-s-a-g-r" (copyright 1935 by E. E. Cummings, copyright © 1963 by Marion Morehouse Cummings). Reprinted by permission of Harcourt Brace Jovanovich, Inc.

J. V. Cunningham. "Friend, on this scaffold . . . ," "Motto for a Sundial," "You serve the best wines . . . ," and "This Humanist whom . . ." from *The Collected Poems and Epigrams of J. V. Cunningham*. Copyright © 1971 by J. V. Cunningham. Reprinted by permission of The Swallow Press, Inc., Chicago.

Peter Davison. "The Last Word" (Part IV of "Four Love Poems") from *Pretending to Be Asleep* by Peter Davison. Copyright © 1970 by Peter Davison. Reprinted by permission of Atheneum Publishers.

Walter de la Mare. "The Listeners," reprinted by permission of the Literary Trustees of Walter de la Mare, and The Society of Authors as their representative.

James Dickey. "Cherrylog Road" from *Poems 1957–1967* by James Dickey. Copyright © 1963 by James Dickey. First appeared in *The New Yorker*. Reprinted by permission of Wesleyan University Press.

Emily Dickinson. "I taste a liquor never brewed," "Because I could not stop for Death," "I heard a Fly buzz–when I died," "I like to see it lap the Miles," "I started early–Took my Dog," "The Lightning is a yellow Fork," "The Soul selects her own Society," "Victory comes late," "It dropped so low–in my regard," and lines from "Hope is the thing with feathers" from *The Poems of Emily Dickinson*, edited by Thomas H. Johnson (Cambridge, Mass.: The Belknap Press of Harvard University Press). Copyright 1951, © 1955 by the President and Fellows of Harvard College. Reprinted by permission of the publishers and the Trustees of Amherst College.

Emanuel diPasquale. "Rain," reprinted by permission of the poet.

Reinhard Döhl. Untitled poem from *Approaches* 2 (1965). Reprinted by permission of Editions André Silvaire.

Alan Dugan. "Love Song: I and Thou" from *Poems* by Alan Dugan. Copyright © 1961 by Alan Dugan. First published by Yale University Press. Reprinted by permission.

Richard Eberhart. "The Fury of Aerial Bombardment" from *Collected Poems 1930–1976* by Richard Eberhart. Copyright © 1976 by Richard Eberhart. Reprinted by permission of Oxford University Press, Inc., and Chatto and Windus Ltd.

T. S. Eliot. "Journey of the Magi," "Rhapsody on a Windy Night," "Virginia" (from "Landscapes"), "The Love Song of J. Alfred Prufrock," and "The Boston Evening Transcript" from *Collected Poems 1909–1962* by T. S. Eliot. Copyright 1936 by Harcourt Brace Jovanovich, Inc., copyright © 1963, 1964 by T. S. Eliot. Reprinted by permission of Harcourt Brace Jovanovich, Inc., and Faber and Faber Ltd.

Abbie Huston Evans. "Wing Spread" from *Collected Poems* by Abbie Huston Evans, © 1970 by Abbie Huston Evans. Reprinted by permission of the University of Pittsburgh Press.

Donald Finkel. "Hands" from *A Joyful Noise* by Donald Finkel. Copyright © 1965, 1966 by Donald Finkel. "Gesture" from *The Garbage Wars* by Donald Finkel. Copyright © 1969, 1970 by Donald Finkel. Reprinted by permission of Atheneum Publishers.

Ian Hamilton Finlay. "The Horizon of Holland. " Reprinted by permission of the poet.

Dudley Fitts. "Elegy on Herakleitos," a translation of the poem by Kollimachos, from *Poems from the Greek Anthology* by Dudley Fitts. Copyright 1938, 1941, © 1956 by New Directions Publishing Corporation. Reprinted by permission of New Directions Publishing Corporation.

Carolyn Forché. Lines from "Dulcimer Maker" from *Gathering the Tribes* by Carolyn Forché. Copyright © 1976 by Carolyn Forché. Reprinted by permission of Yale University Press.

Robert Francis. "Catch" from *The Orb Weaver* by Robert Francis. Copyright 1950 by Robert Francis. Reprinted by permission of Wesleyan University Press.

Robert Frost. "Tree at My Window," "Never Again Would Birds' Song Be the Same," "Stopping by Woods on a Snowy Evening," "Design," "The Secret Sits," "Fire and Ice," "Mending Wall," and "The Witch of Coös" from *The Poetry of Robert Frost*, ed. Edward Connery Latham. Copyright 1923, 1928, © 1969 by Holt, Rinehart and Winston. Copyright 1936, 1942, 1951, © 1956 by Robert Frost. Copyright © 1964, 1970 by Lesley Frost Ballantine. "In White" from *The Dimensions of Robert Frost* by Reginald L. Cook. Copyright © 1958 by Reginald L. Cook. Reprinted by permission of Holt, Rinehart and Winston, Publishers.

Frederico García Lorca. "La guitarra," translated by Keith Waldrop from *Obras Completas* by Frederico Garcia Lorca. Copyright © Aguilar SA de Ediciones 1954. All rights reserved. Permission to publish in original Spanish and in English translation by New Directions Publishing Corporation.

Gary Gildner. "First Practice" from *First Practice* by Gary Gildner, © 1969 by the University of Pittsburgh Press. Reprinted by permission to the University of Pittsburgh Press.

Allen Ginsberg. "Postcard to D----" from *First Blues* by Allen Ginsberg. Reprinted by permission of Full Court Press.

Paul Goodman. Lines from "Hokku" from *Collected Poems* by Paul Goodman. Copyright © 1974 by Paul Goodman. Reprinted by permission of Random House, Inc.

Robert Graves. "Down, Wanton, Down!" from *Collected Poems* by Robert Graves. Copyright 1939, © 1955, 1958, 1961, 1965 by Robert Graves. Reprinted by permission of Curtis Brown, Ltd.

Ronald Gross. "Yield" from *Pop Poems* by Ronald Gross. Copyright © 1967 by Ronald Gross. Reprinted by permission of Simon & Schuster, a Division of Gulf & Western Corporation.

Arthur Guiterman. "On the Vanity of Earthly Greatness" from *Gaily the Troubadour* by Arthur Guiterman. Copyright 1936 by E. P. Dutton & Co., Inc.; renewed 1954 by Mrs. Vida Lindo Guiterman. Reprinted by permission of Louise H. Sclove.

H. D. (Hilda Doolittle). "Heat" from *Selected Poems*. Copyright © 1957 by Norman Holmes Pearson. Reprinted by permission of New Directions Publishing Corporation.

Donald Hall. "The Town of Hill" from *The Town of Hill* by Donald Hall. Copyright © 1975 by Donald Hall. Reprinted by permission of David R. Godine, Publisher. "My Son, My Executioner" from *The Alligator Bride: Poems New and Selected*. Copyright 1954 by Donald Hall. First appeared in *The New Yorker* as "First Child." Reprinted by permission.

Thomas Hardy. "At a Hasty Wedding," "The Oxen," "The Workbox," "Channel Firing," "The Convergence of the Twain," and "Neutral Tones" from *Collected Poems* by Thomas Hardy. Copyright 1925 by Macmillan Publishing Co., Inc. Reprinted by permission of Macmillan Publishing Co., Inc., the Trustees of the Hardy Estate, Macmillan London and Basingstoke, and The Macmillan Company of Canada Limited.

Robert Hayden. "A Road in Kentucky" from *Angle of Ascent, New and Selected Poems* by Robert Hayden. Copyright © 1975, 1972, 1970, 1966 by Robert Hayden. Reprinted by permission of Liveright Publishing Corporation.

Seamus Heaney. "Digging" from *Death of a Naturalist* by Seamus Heaney. Copyright © 1966 by Seamus Heaney. Reprinted by permission of Oxford University Press, Inc., and Faber and Faber Ltd.

John Heath-Stubbs. "A Charm Against the Toothache" fron *Selected Poems* by John Heath-Stubbs (Oxford University Press). Reprinted by permission of David Higham Associates Ltd.

Anthony Hecht. "Japan" and "The Vow" from *The Hard Hours* by Anthony Hecht. Copyright 1954, © 1957, 1967 by Anthony E. Hecht. "Japan" appeared originally in *A Summoning of Stones* by Anthony Hecht. "The Vow" appeared originally in the *Hudson Review*. Reprinted by permission of Atheneum Publishers.

Geoffrey Hill. "Merlin" from *Somewhere is Such a Kingdom* by Geoffrey Hill. Copyright © 1975 by Geoffrey Hill. Reprinted by permission of Houghton Mifflin Company and Andre Deutsch Ltd.

John Hollander. "Skeleton Key" from *Types of Shape* by John Hollander. Copyright © 1969 by John Hollander. Reprinted by permission of Atheneum Publishers.

A. E. Housman. "Loveliest of trees, the cherry now," "To an Athlete Dying Young," "Terence, this is stupid stuff," "With rue my heart is laden," and "When I was one-and-twenty" from *A Shropshire Lad*, authorized edition, from *The Collected Poems of A. E. Housman*. Copyright 1939, 1940, © 1965 by Holt, Rinehart and Winston. Copyright © 1968, 1969 by Robert E. Symons. "From the wash the laundress sends" and "Eight O'Clock" from *The Collected Poems of A. E. Housman*. Copyright 1922 by Holt, Rinehart and Winston. Copyright 1936, 1950 by Barclays Bank Ltd. Copyright © 1964 by Robert E. Symons. Reprinted by permission of Holt, Rinehart and Winston, Publishers; The Society of Authors as literary representative of the Estate of A. E. Housman; and Jonathan Cape Ltd., publishers of A. E. Housman's *Collected Poems*.

Langston Hughes. "Dream Deferred" from *The Panther and the Lash: Poems of Our Times* by Langston Hughes. Copyright 1951 by Langston Hughes. Reprinted by permission of Alfred A. Knopf, Inc.

Ted Hughes. "Secretary" from *The Hawk in the Rain* by Ted Hughes. Copyright © 1957 by Ted Hughes. Reprinted by permission of Harper & Row, Publishers. "Examination at the Womb Door," "Crow's First Lesson," and "Crow and Stone" from *Crow* by Ted Hughes. Copyright © 1971 by Ted Hughes. Reprinted by permission of Harper & Row, Publishers; and Faber and Faber Ltd.

T. E. Hulme. "Image" from *The Life and Opinions of T. E. Hulme* by Alun R. Jones. Copyright © 1960 by Alun R. Jones. Reprinted by permission of Beacon Press.

David Ignatow. "Get the Gasworks" from *Figures of the Human* by David Ignatow. Copyright 1948 by David Ignatow. Reprinted by permission of Wesleyan University Press.

Randall Jarrell. From *The Complete Poems* by Randall Jarrell: "The Death of the Ball Turret Gunner" (Copyright 1945, renewed © 1973 by Mary von Schrader Jarrell) and "A Sick Child" (Copyright 1949 by Randall Jarrell, renewed © 1976 by Mary von Schrader Jarrell). Reprinted by permission of Farrar, Straus & Giroux, Inc. "The Woman at the Washington Zoo" from *The Woman at the Washington Zoo* by Randall Jarrell. Copyright © 1960 by Randall Jarrell. Reprinted by permission of Atheneum Publishers. Excerpt from *Poetry and the Age* by Randall Jarrell. Copyright 1952, 1953 by Randall Jarrell. Reprinted by permission of Alfred A. Knopf, Inc.

Robinson Jeffers. "To the Stone-Cutters" from *The Selected Poetry of Robinson Jeffers*. Copyright 1924 and renewed 1952 by Robinson Jeffers. Reprinted by permission of Random House, Inc.

Elizabeth Jennings. "Delay" from *Collected Poems* by Elizabeth Jennings, 1953, © 1967 by Elizabeth Jennings. Reprinted by permission of Macmillan London and Basingstoke.

James C. Kilgore. "The White Man Pressed the Locks" from *Poets on the Platform*. Copyright © 1970 by James C. Kilgore. Reprinted by permission of the poet.

Hugh Kingsmill. "What, still alive at twenty-two" from *The Best of Hugh Kingsmill*. Reprinted by permission of Victor Gollancz Ltd.

William Knott. "Poem" from *The Naomi Poems: Corpse and Beans* by Saint Geraud. Copyright © 1968 by William Knott. Used by permission of Follett Publishing Company.

Kenneth Koch. "Mending Sump" from *The New American Poetry*, ed. Donald M. Allen. Copyright © 1960 by Kenneth Koch. Reprinted by permission of International Creative Management and the poet.

M. Krishnamurti. "The Spirit's Odyssey" from *Cloth of Gold* by M. Krishnamurti. Reprinted by permission of the publisher, Charles E. Tuttle Co., Inc.

Maxine Kumin. "Woodchucks" from *Up Country* by Maxine Kumin. Copyright © 1971 by Maxine Kumin. Reprinted by permission of Harper & Row, Publishers.

Philip Larkin. "Wedding-Wind" from *The Less Deceived*. Copyright © 1955, 1971 by The Marvell Press. Reprinted by permission of The Marvell Press, England. "Vers de Société" from *High Windows* by Philip Larkin. Copyright © 1974 by Philip Larkin. Reprinted by permission of Farrar, Straus & Giroux, Inc., and Faber and Faber Ltd. "Days" from *The Whitsun Wedding*. Copyright © 1960 by Philip Larkin. Reprinted by permission of Faber and Faber Ltd.

D. H. Lawrence. These poems from *The Complete Poems of D. H. Lawrence*, edited by Vivian de Sola Pinto and F. Warren Roberts: "A Youth Mowing" and "Piano" (Copyright © 1964, 1971 by Angelo Ravagli and C. M. Weekley, Executors of the Estate of Frieda Lawrence Ravagli), "Bavarian Gentians" (Copyright 1933 by Frieda Lawrence. All rights reserved.) Reprinted by permission of The Viking Press.

Irving Layton. "The Bull Calf" from *A Red Carpet for the Sun*. Reprinted by permission of the Canadian publishers, McClelland and Stewart Ltd., Toronto.

Denise Levertov. "Leaving Forever" from *O Taste and See*. Copyright © 1963 by Denise Levertov Goodman. "Sunday Afternoon" and "Six Variations (part iii)" from *The Jacob's Ladder* by Denise Levertov. Copyright © 1958,.1969 by Denise Levertov Goodman. "Ways of Conquest" from *The Freeing of the Dust* by Denise Levertov. Copyright © 1975 by Denise Levertov. "Leaving Forever" and "Six Variations (part iii)" first published in *Poetry*. Reprinted by permission of New Directions Publishing Corporation.

Philip Levine. "To a Child Trapped in a Barber Shop" from *Not This Pig* by Philip Levine. Copyright © 1966 by Philip Levine. Reprinted by permission of Wesleyan University Press.

Abraham Lincoln. "My Childhood-Home I See Again" from *The Collected Works of Abraham Lincoln*. Copyright 1953 by the Abraham Lincoln Association. Reprinted by permission of the Rutgers University Press.

J. A. Lindon. "My Garden," reprinted by permission of the poet.

Vachel Lindsay. "Factory Windows Are Always Broken" from *Collected Poems* by Vachel Lindsay. Copyright 1914 by Macmillan Publishing Co., Inc.; renewed 1942 by Elizabeth C. Lindsay. Reprinted with permission of Macmillan Publishing Co., Inc.

Myra Cohn Livingston. "Driving" from *The Malibu and Other Poems* by Myra Cohn Livingston (A Margaret K. McElderry Book). Copyright © 1972 by Myra Cohn Livingston. Reprinted by permission of Atheneum Publishers.

Robert Lowell. "At the Altar" from *Lord Weary's Castle* by Robert Lowell. Copyright 1946 by Robert Lowell. Reprinted by permission of Harcourt Brace Jovanovich, Inc. "Meditation" from *Imitations* by Robert Lowell. Copyright © 1958, 1959, 1960, 1961 by Robert Lowell. Reprinted by permission of Farrar, Straus & Giroux, Inc. "Skunk Hour" from *Life Studies* by Robert Lowell. Copyright © 1956, 1959 by Robert Lowell. Reprinted by permission of Farrar, Straus & Giroux, Inc.

Mina Loy. "Omen of Victory," reprinted by permission of The Jargon Society, Inc.

Hugh MacDiarmid. "Weesht, Weesht" from *Collected Poems* by Hugh MacDiarmid. Copyright 1948, © 1962 by Christopher Murray Grieve. Reprinted by permission of Macmillan Publishing Co., Inc.

Archibald MacLeish. "Ars Poetica" and "The End of the World" from *Collected Poems, 1917–1952* by Archibald MacLeish. Copyright 1952 by Archibald MacLeish. Reprinted by permission of Houghton Mifflin Company.

John Masefield. "Cargoes" from *Poems* by John Masefield. Copyright 1912 by Macmillan Publishing Co., Inc.; renewed 1940 by John Masefield. Reprinted by permission of Macmillan Publishing Co., Inc.

436 Acknowledgments

Rod McKuen. "Thoughts on Capital Punishment" from *Stanyan Street and Other Sorrows* by Rod McKuen. Copyright 1954, © 1960-1966 by Rod McKuen. Reprinted by permission of Random House, Inc.

James Merrill. "Laboratory Poem" from *The Country of a Thousand Years of Peace* by James Merrill. Copyright © 1958, 1970 by James Merrill. This poem appeared originally in *Poetry*. Reprinted by permission of Atheneum Publishers.

W. S. Merwin. "Dead Hand" from *The Moving Target* by W. S. Merwin. Copyright © 1963 by W. S. Merwin. "For the Anniversary of My Death" from *The Lice* by W. S. Merwin. Copyright © 1967 by W. S. Merwin. Appeared originally in the *Southern Review*. "Song of Man Chipping an Arrowhead" from *Writings to an Unfinished Accompaniment* by W. S. Merwin. Copyright © 1972, 1973 by W. S. Merwin. Reprinted by permission of Atheneum Publishers.

Josephine Miles. "Reason" from *Poems 1930–1960* by Josephine Miles. Reprinted by permission of Indiana University Press.

Edna St. Vincent Millay. "Counting-out Rhyme" from *Collected Poems* by Edna St. Vincent Millay. Copyright 1928, © 1955 by Edna St. Vincent Millay and Norma Millay Ellis. Reprinted by permission of Norma Millay Ellis.

A. A. Milne. Lines from "Disobedience" from *When We Were Very Young* by A. A. Milne. Reprinted by permission of E. P. Dutton & Co., Inc., and the Canadian publishers, McClelland and Stewart Ltd., Toronto.

Marianne Moore. "The Mind is an Enchanting Thing" from *Collected Poems* by Marianne Moore. Copyright 1944, © 1972 by Marianne Moore. Reprinted by permission of Macmillan Publishing Co., Inc.

Edwin Morgan. "Siesta of a Hungarian Snake" from *The Second Life* by Edwin Morgan. Copyright © 1968 by Edwin Morgan and Edinburgh University Press. Reprinted by permission of Edinburgh University Press.

Howard Moss. "Shall I Compare Thee to a Summer's Day?" from *A Swim Off the Rocks* by Howard Moss. Copyright © 1976. This poem appeared originally in *Commentary*. Reprinted by permission of Atheneum Publishers.

Ogden Nash. "Very Like a Whale" from *Verses from 1929 On* by Ogden Nash. Copyright 1934 by Ogden Nash. Reprinted by permission of Little, Brown and Company.

John Frederick Nims. "Perfect Rhyme" from *Of Flesh and Bone* by John Frederick Nims. Copyright © 1967 by Rutgers, the State University. Reprinted by permission of Rutgers University Press. "Odd Bethinkings of a Day of 'Showers Likely' at Beansey Ridge" from *College English* (April 1971). Copyright © 1971 by the National Council of Teachers of English. Reprinted by permission of the publisher.

Alden Nowlan. "The Loneliness of the Long Distance Runner" from *Bread, Wine and Salt* by Alden Nowlan. Copyright © 1967 by Clarke, Irwin & Co. Used by permission.

Charles Olson. "La Chute," copyright by Charles Olson. Reprinted by permission of the Estate of Charles Olson.

Guy Owen. "The White Stallion" from *The White Stallion* by Guy Owen (John F. Blair, Publisher, 1969). Reprinted by permission of the poet.

Wilfred Owen. "Dulce et Decorum Est" from *The Collected Poems of Wilfred Owen*. Copyright 1946, © 1963 by Chatto and Windus Ltd. Reprinted by permission of New Directions Publishing Corporation, the Owen Estate, and Chatto and Windus Ltd.

Dorothy Parker. "Résumé" from *The Portable Dorothy Parker*. Copyright 1926, 1954 by Dorothy Parker. Reprinted by permission of the Viking Press.

Sylvia Plath. "Poppies in October," "Daddy," (all copyright © 1963 by Ted Hughes) and "Morning Song" (Copyright © 1961 by Ted Hughes) from *Ariel* by Sylvia Plath. "Metaphors" from *Crossing the Water* by Sylvia Plath. Copyright © 1960 by Ted Hughes. Reprinted by permission of Harper & Row, Publishers; and Olwyn Hughes, representing the estate of Sylvia Plath.

Ezra Pound. "The Seafarer," "In Station of the Metro," and "The River Merchant's Wife: a Letter" from *Personae* by Ezra Pound. Copyright 1926 by Ezra Pound. Reprinted by permission of New Directions Publishing Corporation. Excerpt beginning "Yaller bird, . . ." from *Shih-ching: The Classic Anthology Defined by Confucius* by Ezra Pound. Copyright© 1954 by the President and Fellows of Harvard College. Reprinted by permission of Harvard University Press.

Dudley Randall. "Ballad of Birmingham" from *Poem Counterpoem* by Margaret Danner and Dudley Randall. Copyright © 1966 by Dudley Randall. Reprinted by permission of the poet.

John Crowe Ransom. "Janet Waking" from *Selected Poems, Third Edition, Revised and Enlarged* by John Crowe Ransom. Copyright 1927 by Alfred A. Knopf, Inc., renewed © 1957 by John Crowe Ransom. Reprinted by permission of the publisher.

Henry Reed. "Naming of Parts" from *A Map of Verona* by Henry Reed (1946). Reprinted by permission of Jonathan Cape Ltd.

Ishmael Reed. ".05" from *Chattanooga* by Ishmael Reed. Copyright © 1973 by Ishmael Reed. Reprinted by permission of Random House, Inc.

Adrienne Rich. "Diving into the Wreck" from *Diving into the Wreck, Poems, 1971–1972* by Adrienne Rich. Copyright © 1973 by W. W. Norton & Company. Reprinted by permission of W. W. Norton & Company, Inc.

Edwin Arlington Robinson. "Mr. Flood's Party" from *Collected Poems* by Edwin Arlington Robinson. Copyright 1921 by Edwin Arlington Robinson, renewed 1949 by Ruth Nivison. Reprinted with permission of Macmillan Publishing Co., Inc. "Richard Cory" from *Children of the Night* (1897). Reprinted by permission of Charles Scribner's Sons.

Theodore Roethke. These poems from *Collected Poems of Theodore Roethke*: "I Knew a Woman" (Copyright 1954 by Theodore Roethke), "The Waking" (Copyright 1953 by Theodore Roethke), "My Papa's Waltz" (Copyright 1942 by Hearst Magazines, Inc.), "Root Cellar" (Copyright 1943 by Modern Poetry Association, Inc.), "Frau Bauman, Frau Schmidt, and Frau Schwartze" (Copyright 1952 by Theodore Roethke), and "Night Crow" (Copyright 1944 by Saturday Review Association, Inc.). All poems reprinted by permission of Doubleday & Company, Inc.

Raymond Roseliep. "Clap" from *Step on the Rain* by Raymond Roseliep (The Rook Press; Derry, Pennsylvania). Copyright © 1977 by Raymond Roseliep. Reprinted by permission of the poet.

Carl Sandburg. "Fog" from *Chicago Poems* by Carl Sandburg. Copyright 1916 by Holt, Rinehart and Winston, Inc., 1944 by Carl Sandburg. Reprinted by permission of Harcourt Brace Jovanovich, Inc.

Aram Saroyan. Lines from "crickets" from *Works* by Aram Saroyan. Copyright © 1966 by Aram Saroyan. Reprinted by permission of the poet.

Anne Sexton. "The Kiss" from *Love Poems* by Anne Sexton. Copyright © 1967, 1968, 1969 by Anne Sexton. "The Fury of the Overshoes" from *The Death Notebooks* by Anne Sexton. Copyright © 1975 by Anne Sexton. Reprinted by permission of Houghton Mifflin Company.

Karl Shapiro. "The Dirty Word" from *Selected Poems* by Karl Shapiro. Copyright 1947 by Karl Shapiro. Reprinted by permission of Random House, Inc.

Frank Sidgwick. "The Aeronaut to His Lady" from *More Verse by "F. S."* (1921). Reprinted by permission of the publishers, Sidgwick & Jackson Ltd.

Charles Simic. "Fork" from *Dismantling the Silence* by Charles Simic. Copyright © 1971 by Charles Simic. Reprinted by permission of the publisher, George Braziller, Inc.

L. E. Sissman. Lines from "In and Out: A Home Away from Home" from *Dying: An Introduction* by L. E. Sissman. Copyright © 1966, 1967, by L. E. Sissman. Reprinted by permission of Little, Brown and Co. in association with The Atlantic Monthly Press.

Knute Skinner. "The Cold Irish Earth" from *A Close Sky over Killaspuglonae* (The Dolman Press, 1968). Reprinted by permission of the poet and the publisher.

Stevie Smith. "I Remember" from *Selected Poems* by Stevie Smith. Copyright © 1962, 1964 by Stevie Smith. Reprinted by permission of New Directions Publishing Corporation.

William Jay Smith. "American Primitive" from *New and Selected Poems* by William Jay Smith. Copyright 1953, © 1970 by William Jay Smith. Reprinted by permission of Delacorte Press/Seymour Lawrence.

W. D. Snodgrass. "The Operation" from *Heart's Needle* by W. D. Snodgrass. Copyright © 1959 by W. D. Snodgrass. Reprinted by permission of Alfred A. Knopf, Inc.

Gary Snyder. "Milton by Firelight," © 1959, 1965 by Gary Snyder. Reprinted by permission of the poet. Poems from "Hitch Haiku" from *The Back Country* by Gary Snyder. Copyright © 1968 by Gary Snyder. Reprinted by permission of New Directions Publishing Corporation.

Richard Snyder. "A Mongoloid Child Handling Shells on the Beach" from *A Keeping in Touch* by Richard Snyder (The Ashland Poetry Press, 1971). Reprinted by permission.

Sir John Squire. Lines from "It did not last," reprinted by permission of Raglan Squire, Executor.

William Stafford. "Written on the Stub of the First Paycheck" and "At the Klamath Berry Festival" from *The Rescued Year* by William Stafford. Copyright© 1960, 1961 by William E. Stafford. "Traveling Through the Dark" from *Traveling Through the Dark* by William Stafford. Copyright © by William Stafford. Reprinted by permission of Harper & Row, Publishers.

James Stephens. These poems from *The Collected Poems of James Stephens:* "The Wind" (Copyright 1915 by Macmillan Publishing Co., Inc., renewed 1943 by James Stephens) and "A Glass of Beer" (Copyright 1918 by Macmillan Publishing Co., Inc., renewed 1946 by James Stephens). Reprinted by permission of Macmillan Publishing Co., Inc., Mrs. Iris Wise, Macmillan London & Basingstoke, and The Macmillan Company of Canada Limited.

Wallace Stevens. These poems from *The Collected Poems of Wallace Stevens:* "The Emperor of Ice Cream," "Disillusionment of Ten O'Clock," "Peter Quince at the Clavier," "Thirteen Ways of Looking at a Blackbird," "Anecdote of the Jar," and lines from "Sunday Morning" and "Bantams in Pine-Woods" (Copyright 1923, renewed 1951 by Wallace Stevens); "Metamorphosis" and "Study of Two Pears" (Copyright 1942 by Wallace Stevens, renewed © 1970 by Holly Stevens). Reprinted by permission of Alfred A. Knopf, Inc.

Mark Strand. "Eating Poetry" from *Reasons for Moving* by Mark Strand. Copyright © 1968 by Mark Strand. Reprinted by permission of Atheneum Publishers.

May Swenson. "Stone Gullets" from *Iconographs* by May Swenson. Copyright © 1970 by May Swenson. Reprinted by permission of the poet.

James Tate. "Flight" from *The Lost Pilot* by James Tate. Copyright © 1967 by Yale University. Reprinted by permission of Yale University Press.

Henry Taylor. "Riding a One-Eyed Horse" from *An Afternoon of Pocket Billiards* by Henry Taylor. Copyright © 1975 by Henry Taylor. Reprinted by permission of the poet and the University of Utah Press.

Cornelius J. Ter Maat. "Etienne de Silouette," reprinted by permission of the poet.

Dylan Thomas. "Twenty-four years," "Fern Hill," and "Do not go gentle into that good night" from *The Poems of Dylan Thomas.* Copyright 1939, 1946 by New Directions Publishing Corporation. Reprinted by permission of New Directions Publishing Corporation, J. M. Dent & Sons Ltd., and the Trustees for the Copyrights of the late Dylan Thomas.

Jean Toomer. "Reapers" from *Cane* by Jean Toomer. Copyright 1923 by Boni & Liveright, renewed 1951 by Jean Toomer. Reprinted by permission of Liveright Publishing Corporation.

John Updike. "Winter Ocean" from *Telephone Poles and Other Poems* by John Updike. Copyright © 1960 by John Updike. Reprinted by permission of Alfred A. Knopf, Inc.

David Wagoner. "Muse" from *Collected Poems 1956–1976* by David Wagoner. Reprinted by permission of the publisher, Indiana University Press.

Keith Waldrop. "On Measure" from *A Windmill Near Calvary* by Keith Waldrop. Copyright © 1968 by The University of Michigan Press. All rights reserved. Reprinted by permission of the publisher.

Rosmarie Waldrop. "Confession to Settle a Curse" from *The Aggressive Ways of the Casual Stranger* by Rosmarie Waldrop. Copyright © 1972 by Rosmarie Waldrop. Reprinted by permission of Random House, Inc.

Wang Wei. "Bird-Singing Stream," translated by Wai-lim Yip. Reprinted by permission of Wai-lim Yip.

E. B. White. "A Classic Waits for Me" from *The Second Tree From the Corner* by E. B. White. Copyright 1944 by E. B. White. Originally appeared in *The New Yorker.* Reprinted by permission of Harper & Row, Publishers, Inc.

Ruth Whitman. "Castoff Skin" from *The Passion of Lizzie Borden* by Ruth Whitman. Copyright © 1973 by Ruth Whitman. Reprinted by permission of October House.

Reed Whittemore. "The Fall of the House of Usher" from *Fifty Poems Fifty* by Reed Whittemore. Reprinted by permission of the University of Minnesota Press.

Richard Wilbur. "In the Elegy Season" and "A Simile for Her Smile" from *Ceremony and Other Poems* by Richard Wilbur. Copyright 1948, 1949, 1950 by Richard Wilbur. "In the Elegy Season" first appeared in *The New Yorker.* "Junk" from *Advice to a Prophet and Other Poems.* Copyright © 1961 by Richard Wilbur. "Sleepless at Crown Point" from *The Mind Reader* by Richard Wilbur. Copyright © 1976 by Richard Wilbur. Reprinted by permission of Harcourt Brace Jovanovich, Inc.

Miller Williams. "On the Symbolic Consideration of Hands and the Significance of Death" from *Halfway from Hoxie: New and Selected Poems* by Miller Williams. Copyright © 1964, 1968, 1971, 1973 by Miller Williams. Reprinted by permission of the publishers, E. P. Dutton.

William Carlos Williams. "The Great Figure," "Spring and All," "Poem," "This Is Just to Say," "The Red Wheelbarrow," "To Waken an Old Lady," "The Descent of Winter (section 10/30)" from *Collected Earlier Poems* by William Carlos Williams. Copyright 1938 by New Directions Publishing Corporation. "The Dance" from *Collected Later Poems* by William Carlos Williams. Copyright 1944 by William Carlos Williams. Reprinted by permission of New Directions Publishing Corporation.

Yvor Winters. "At the San Francisco Airport" from *Collected Poems* by Yvor Winters. Copyright 1952, © 1960 by Yvor Winters. Reprinted by permission of The Swallow Press, Inc., Chicago.

James Wright. "Autumn Begins in Martins Ferry, Ohio" and "A Blessing" from *Collected Poems* by James Wright. Copyright © 1961, 1962 by James Wright. "A Blessing" first appeared in *Poetry.* Reprinted by permission of Wesleyan University Press. "Saying Dante Aloud" from *Moments of the Italian Summer.* Copyright © 1976 by James Wright. Reprinted by permission.

Judith Wright. "Woman to Man" and "Woman to Child" from *Collected Poems 1942–1970* by Judith Wright. Copyright © 1971 by Judith Wright. Reprinted by permission of Angus & Robertson Publishers.

William Butler Yeats. These poems from *The Collected Poems of W. B. Yeats:* "The Lake Isle of Innisfree," "Who Goes with Fergus," "The Lamentation of an Old Pensioner" (Copyright 1906 by Macmillan Publishing Co., Inc.; renewed 1934 by William Bulter Yeats); "The Magi," (Copyright 1916 by Macmillan Publishing Co., Inc.; renewed 1944 by Bertha Georgie Yeats); "Sailing to Byzantium," "Leda and the Swan," and lines from "Among School Children" (Copyright 1928 by Macmillan Publishing Co., Inc.; renewed © 1956 by Georgie Yeats); "Crazy Jane Talks with the Bishop" (Copyright 1933 by Macmillan Publishing Co., Inc.; renewed © 1961 by Bertha Georgie Yeats); "Lapis Lazuli" (Copyright 1940 by Georgie Yeats, renewed © 1968 by Bertha Georgie Yeats, Michael Butler Yeats, and Anne Yeats); lines from "A Prayer for Old Age" (Copyright 1934 by Macmillan Publishing Co., Inc.; renewed © 1962 by Bertha Georgie Yeats); "The Second Coming" (Copyright 1924 by Macmillan Publishing Co., Inc. renewed 1952 by Bertha Georgie Yeats). From *The Variorum Edition of the Poems of W. B. Yeats,* edited by Peter Allt and Russell K. Alspach: "The Old Pensioner." Copyright © 1957 by Macmillan Publishing Co., Inc. Reprinted by permission of Macmillan Publishing Co., Inc., M. B. Yeats, Miss Anne Yeats, and Macmillan London and Basingstoke.

INDEX OF FIRST LINES

About suffering they were never wrong, 311

A classic waits for me, it contains all, nothing is lacking, 276

"A cold coming we had of it, 335

After the doctor checked to see, 177

After the First Communion, 72

After weeks of watching the roof leak, 61

A garden is a lovesome thing, God wot! 273

A garden is a *lovesome* thing? What rot! 273

A great freight truck, 61

Ah, look at all the lonely people! 116

A line in long array where they wind betwixt green islands, 177

All in green went my love riding, 323

All night, this headland, 94

Although I shelter from the rain, 264

Always to want to, 40

Among the rain, 64

Among twenty snowy mountains, 182

An axe angles from my neighbor's ashcan, 411

And when that ballad lady went, 348

A noiseless patient spider, 266

anyone lived in a pretty how town, 49

ApfelApfelApfelApfelA, 193

A piece of green pepper, 61

A poem should be palpable and mute, 297

a politician is an arse upon, 167

As I walked out one evening, 310

As I was laying on the green, 51

As I was walking all alane, 306

A slumber did my spirit seal, 123

As the cat, 206

A sudden blow: the great wings beating still, 130

As virtuous men pass mildly away, 331

A sweet disorder in the dress, 351

A veil of haze protects this, 309

A white horse came to our farm once, 71

Back of the dam, under, 345

Batter my heart, three-personed God, for You, 36

Beat! beat! drums! — blow! bugles! blow! 154

Beautifully Janet slept, 383

Because I could not stop for Death, 327

Begins the crying, 269

Below the surface-stream, shallow and light, 258

Bent double, like old beggars under sacks, 26

Be reasonable, my pain, and think with more detachment, 272

Between my finger and my thumb, 348

Black reapers with the sound of steel on stones, 61

Borgia, thou once wert almost too august, 151

Boy, I detest the Persian pomp, 271

Boy, I hate their empty shows, 271

Bright star! would I were steadfast as thou art, 63

Buffalo Bill's, 174

By the road to the contagious hospital, 412

Cackling, smelling of camphor, crumbs of pink icing, 218

Call the roller of big cigars, 76

Calm down, my Sorrow, we must move with care, 273

Charles used to watch Naomi, taking heart, 372

Christmas Eve, and twelve of the clock, 213

Chugging along in an old open bus, 131

Clap! 61

Come live with me and be my love (Donne), 329

Come live with me and be my love (Marlowe), 370

Crow was nimble but had to be careful, 357

Dark house, by which once more I stand, 405

Daughters of Time, the hypocritic days, 241

Do not go gentle into that good night, 169

Down, wanton, down! Have you no shame, 34

Drink to me only with thine eyes, 100
Driving down the concrete vein, 93
Dylan Thomas, 168

Each day is a shiny penny, 242
Earth has not anything to show more fair, 414
Empieza el llanto, 269
Etienne de Silhouette, 168
Even the sun-clouds this morning cannot manage such skirts, 377
Every man in the world thinks his banner the best, 246
Every year without knowing it I have passed the day, 372

Factory windows are always broken, 367
Fa, mi, fa, re, la, mi, 115
Farewell, too little and too lately known, 332
First having read the book of myths, 385
Flower in the crannied wall, 81
For I will consider my Cat Jeoffry, 396
For the bumps bangs & scratches of, 95
Frankie she was a good woman, Johnny he was her man, 112
Friend, on this scaffold Thomas More lies dead, 40
From a magician's midnight sleeve, 74
From low to high doth dissolution climb, 52
From my mother's sleep I fell into the State, 358
From stainless steel basins of water, 399
From the wash the laundress sends, 94

Gasoline makes game scarce, 401
Gassing the woodchucks didn't turn out right, 362
Gather ye rose-buds while ye may, 351
Get the gasworks into a poem, 357
Glory be to God for dappled things, 62
Go and catch a falling star, 160
God tried to teach Crow how to talk, 356
Gone the three ancient ladies, 388
Green weeds of summer, 61
Gr-r-r—there go, my heart's abhorrence, 317

Had we but world enough, and time, 370
Half twice some ninety-odd and more spans back, 275
Hanging from the beam, 40
Having been tenant long to a rich Lord, 203
Haze, char, and the weather of All Souls', 38
Heat-lightning streak, 60
He clasps the crag with crooked hands, 78
Here she lies, a pretty bud, 176

Her whole life is an epigram: smack smooth, and neatly penned, 167
He says the waves in the ship's wake, 84
He stood, and heard the steeple, 125
He was found by the Bureau of Statistics to be, 20
He would declare and could himself believe, 141
"Hiram, I think the sump is backing up, 274
How did they fume, and stamp, and roar, and chafe! 143

I (Through/Blue/Sky), 179
I am his Highness' dog at Kew, 166
I caught a tremendous fish, 58
I caught this morning morning's minion, king-, 352
I enter the Plaidland Redemption Center, 73
If hours be years the twain are blest, 181
If i had a nickel, 95
If I should touch her she would shriek and weeping, 24
I found a ball of grass among the hay, 41
I found a dimpled spider, fat and white, 281
If you wander far enough, 19
I had a chair at every hearth, 264
I have eaten, 31
I have heard that hysterical women say, 419
I heard a Fly buzz—when I died, 201
I knew a woman, lovely in her bones, 91
I like to see it lap the Miles, 13
I love it, I love it! and who shall dare, 238
I'm a riddle in nine syllables, 82
I met a traveler from an antique land, 253
I met the Bishop on the road, 418
In a soltitude of the sea, 347
In Breughel's great picture, The Kermess, 175
in Just-, 184
Ink runs from the corners of my mouth, 404
In Stamford, at the edge of town, a giant statue stands, 219
In the desert, 176
In the old stone pool, 61
In the Shreve High football stadium, 416
In the third month, a sudden flow of blood, 349
In Xanadu did Kubla Khan, 320
I placed a jar in Tennessee, 207
I saw her first in gleams, 234
I saw in Louisiana a live-oak growing, 410
I shoot the Hippopotamus, 130
I shudder thinking, 33
I sit at a gold table with my girl, 142
I started Early—Took my Dog, 328
I stayed the night for shelter at a farm, 341

"Is there anybody there?" said the Traveler, 324
I taste a liquor never brewed, 6
It did not last: the Devil, howling *Ho!* 125
It dropped so low—in my Regard, 83
I tell you, hopeless grief is passionless, 165
It is a cold and snowy night. The main street is deserted, 64
It little profits that an idle king, 405
It was a big boxy wreck of a house, 49
It was a miniature country once, 247
It was in and about the Martinmas time, 106
It was my bridal night I remember, 180
I wakened on my hot, hard bed, 122
I wake to sleep, and take my waking slow, 389
I wandered lonely as a cloud, 16
I wander through each chartered street, 68
I who by day am function of the light, 43
I will arise and go now, and go to Innisfree, 418
I will consider the outnumbering dead, 75
I woke up this mornin' with the blues all round my bed, 118

James Watt, 168
Jenny kissed me when we met, 179
John Anderson my jo, John, 238
Johnny's in the basement, 333
Julius Caesar, 127
Just as my fingers on these keys, 402
Just off the highway to Rochester, Minnesota, 415

Know then thyself, presume not God to scan, 378

Let me take this other glove off, 21
Let us go then, you and I, 336
Life, friends, is boring. We must not say so, 25
Life, that struck up his cocky tune with *breath*, 128
Life is like a jagged tooth, 233
Like a drummer's brush, 123
Like a glum cricket, 404
Little children you will all go, 96
Little Mary Bell had a fairy in a nut, 314
"London: JOHN LANE, *The Bodley Head*, 146
Long-expected one and twenty, 71
Look at him there in his stovepipe hat, 398
Lord, who createdst man in wealth and store, 187
Love bade me welcome; yet my soul drew back, 350
Loveliest of trees, the cherry now, 3
Love set you going like a fat gold watch, 376

Madam Life's a piece in bloom, 233
Many-maned scud-thumper, tub, 122
Mark but this flea, and mark in this, 330
May I for my own self song's truth reckon, 380
"Mother dear, may I go downtown, 382
Much have I traveled in the realms of gold, 361
My arm sweeps down, 185
My childhood-home I see again, 243
My Daphne's hair is twisted gold, 254
my drum, hollowed out thru the thin slit, 186
My heart leaps up when I behold, 52
My mistress' eyes are nothing like the sun, 255
My mouth blossoms like a cut, 391
My prime of youth is but a frost of cares, 88
My son, my executioner, 267
My wife and I have asked a crowd of craps, 363
My wife bursts into the room, 16
My wife is my shirt, 234

Nature and Nature's laws lay hid in night, 125
Nautilus Island's hermit, 368
Nay, nay, my boy—'tis not for me, 271
Not every man has gentians in his house, 212
Nothing is plumb, level or square, 332
Nothing would sleep in that cellar, dank as a ditch, 57
Not marble nor the gilded monuments, 8
Now as at all times I can see in the mind's eye, 420
Now as I was young and easy under the apple boughs, 407

O Captain! my Captain! our fearful trip is done, 256
Off Highway 106, 325
Oh, but it is dirty! 312
Oh, my love is like a red, red rose, 96
"O hell, what do mine eyes, 400
Old age is, 413
Old Eben Flood, climbing alone one night, 387
Old houses were scaffolding once, 64
O Moon, when I gaze on thy beautiful face, 233
On a flat road runs the well-train'd runner, 64
One brought me the news of your death, O Herakleitos my friend, 269
One foot down, then hop! It's hot, 308
One side of his world is always missing, 33
One thing that literature would be greatly the better for, 96

On the one-ton temple bell, 60
Opusculum paedagogum, 56
O Rose, thou art sick! 315
Out of a fired ship which by no way, 207
Over and over again the papers print, 35
O what can ail thee, knight-at-arms, 222
O wild West Wind, thou breath of Autumn's being, 394
O wind, rend open the heat, 65
O with what key, 189

Paper come out — done strewed de news, 53
Peace, be at peace, O thou my heaviness, 272
Persicos odi, puer, apparatus, 270

Quinquireme of Nineveh from distant Ophir, 67
Quite unexpectedly as Vasserot, 369

Razors pain you, 145
Red river, red river, 134
Rose-cheeked Laura, come, 150
r-p-o-p-h-e-s-s-a-g-r, 190

Said, Pull her up a bit will you, Mac, I want to unload there, 46
Season of mists and mellow fruitfulness, 361
"See, here's the workbox, little wife, 23
Shall I compare thee to a summer's day? 78
She even thinks that up in heaven, 10
She lay in her girlish sleep at ninety-six, 84
She sat down below a thorn, 101
She turns them over in her slow hands, 73
Shlup, shlup, the dog, 170
Silver bark of beech, and sallow, 153
Since there's no help, come let us kiss and part, 164
Sir, say no more, 14
Sir Christopher Wren, 168
Slow, slow, fresh fount, keep time with my salt tears, 142
Smooth it feels, 185
Softly, in the dusk, a woman is singing to me, 239
Sois sage, ô ma Douleur, et tiens-toi plus tranquille, 271
Some are teethed on a silver spoon, 322
Some say the world will end in fire, 76
Something there is that doesn't love a wall, 340
so much depends, 18
Sprayed with strong poison, 61
s sz sz SZ sz SZ sz ZS zs ZS zs zs z, 195
Stella this day is thirty-four, 28
Still dark, 313
Stone-cutters fighting time with marble, you foredefeated, 8
Stone gullets among, 191

Swinging chick, 115

Tell me not, Sweet, I am unkind, 26
Temptations still nest in it like basilisks, 75
"Terence, this is stupid stuff, 353
That is no country for old men. The young, 250
That night your great guns, unawares, 345
That's my last Duchess painted on the wall, 316
That time of year thou mayst in me behold, 392
That which her slender waist confined, 90
The Angel that presided o'er my birth, 128
The apparition of these faces in the crowd, 54
The Assyrian came down like the wolf on the fold, 152
The caryophyllaceae, 51
The crops are all in and the peaches are rotting, 111
The curfew tolls the knell of parting day, 258
The delicate foot of, 167
The dirty word hops in the cage of the mind like the Pondicherry, 394
Thee for my recitative, 12
The eyeless laborer in the night, 416
The fog comes, 63
The fortunes of war, I tell you plain, 94
The golf links lie so near the mill, 23
the horizon of holland, 194
The houses are haunted, 70
The interests of a black man in a cellar, 205
The kingdom of heaven is likened unto a man which sowed good seed in his field, 203
The king sits in Dumferling toune, 304
The lanky hank of a she in the inn over there, 27
The Lightning is a yellow Fork, 199
The midge spins out to safety, 288
The Mind is an Enchanting Thing, 373
The only response, 176
The piercing chill I feel, 54
The poem makes truth a little more disturbing, 7
The postman comes when I am still in bed, 15
The radiance of that star that leans on me, 93
There, in the earliest and chary spring, the dogwood flowers, 307
The readers of the *Boston Evening Transcript*, 198
There are four men mowing down by the Isar, 365
There is a garden in her face, 255
There ought to be capital punishment for cars, 239

There's a crow flying, 117
There was a man of double deed, 83
There was an old man of Pantoum, 168
There were three ravens sat on a tree, 305
The saris go by me from the embassies, 358
The sea is calm tonight, 308
The selfsame surface that billowed once with, 319
The silver swan, who living had no note, 115
The Soul, reaching, throwing out for love, 267
The Soul selects her own Society, 329
The splendor falls on castle walls, 126
The thing could barely stand. Yet taken, 365
The time you won your town the race, 354
The trees they do grow high, and the leaves they do grow green, 109
The tusks that clashed in mighty brawls, 253
The war chief danced the old way, 401
The whiskey on your breath, 9
The wind blew all my wedding-day, 364
The wind stood up and gave a shout, 85
The world is charged with the grandeur of God, 131
The world is too much with us; late and soon, 214
They eat beans mostly, this old yellow pair, 316
They say that Richard Cory owns, 104
They sit in a row, 390
They told me, Heraclitus, they told me you were dead, 269
This *Humanist* whom no beliefs constrained, 167
This is the terminal: the light, 413
This living hand, now warm and capable, 158
This strange thing must have crept, 95
Thou ill-formed offspring of my feeble brain, 11
Thou still unravished bride of quietness, 359
Today we have naming of parts. Yesterday, 384
To freight cars in the air, 154
(To JS/07/M/378, 20
To see a world in a grain of sand, 82
Traveling through the dark I found a deer, 240
Treason doth never prosper; what's the reason? 166
Tree at my window, window tree, 92
True Thomas lay on Huntlie bank, 219
Turning and turning in the widening gyre, 215
'Twas brillig, and the slithy toves, 41
Twelve o'clock, 207

Twenty-four years remind the tears of my eyes, 408
Two boys uncoached are tossing a poem together, 6
Tyger! Tyger! burning bright! 315

Venerable Mother Toothache, 216
Victory comes late, 174

Watch people stop by bodies in funeral homes, 36
We dance round in a ring and suppose, 94
We real cool. We, 141
Western wind, when wilt thou blow, 307
We stood by a pond that winter day, 202
"What, are you stepping westward?" — "Yea," 415
What, still alive at twenty-two, 274
What are days for? 241
What happens to a dream deferred? 355
Wheesht, wheesht, my foolish hert, 47
When, in disgrace with Fortune and men's eyes, 392
When daisies pied and violets blue, 392
Whenever Richard Cory went down town, 104
When fishes flew and forests walked, 320
When God at first made man, 89
When he brings home a whale, 322
When icicles hang by the wall, 393
When I consider how my light is spent, 373
When I heard the learn'd astronomer, 410
When I saw that clumsy crow, 206
When I saw your head bow, I knew I had beaten you, 35
When I was one-and-twenty, 153
When my mother died I was very young, 28
While my hair was still cut straight across my forehead, 379
Who owns these scrawny little feet? *Death*, 356
Who says you're like one of the dog days? 79
Whose woods these are I think I know, 341
Who will go drive with Fergus now, 121
"Why dois your brand sae drap wi' bluid, 303
Wilt Thou forgive that sin where I begun, 90
With rue my heart is laden, 134
With serving still, 144
Women in uniform, 205

Yet once more, O ye laurels, and once more, 223
Yield, 162
Yillow, yillow, yillow, 42
You can feel the muscles and veins rippling . . . , 134

You do not do, you do not do, 374
You don't, 409
You invaded my country by accident, 366
You praise the firm restraint with which
    they write, 162
Your smiling, or the hope, the thought of
    it, 81
Your yen two wol slee me sodenly, 181

You serve the best wines always, my dear
    sir, 166
You that with allegory's curious frame, 204
You've gotten in through the transom, 367
You who were darkness warmed my flesh,
    417
You would think the fury of aerial bom-
    bardment, 50

INDEX OF AUTHORS AND TITLES

(Each page number immediately following a poet's name indicates a line or passage from a poem quoted in the text.)

Aeronaut to His Lady, The, 179
AGEE, JAMES
  Sunday: Outskirts of Knoxville, Tennessee, 307
ALLEN, EDWARD
  Best Line Yet, The, 219
All in green went my love riding, 323
ALPAUGH, ERN, AND DEWEY G. PELL
  Swinging Chick, 115
American Primitive, 398
AMMONS, A. R.
  Auto Mobile, 95
  Spring Coming, 51
Anecdote of the Jar, 207
ANGELOU, MAYA
  Harlem Hopscotch, 308
Angel that presided o'er my birth, The, 128
ANONYMOUS
  As I was laying on the green, 51
  Bonny Barbara Allan, 106
  Cruel Mother, The, 101
  Edward, 303
  Fa, mi, fa, re, la, mi, 115
  fortunes of war, I tell you plain, The, 94
  Frankie and Johnny, 112
  Good Mornin', Blues, 118
  Julius Caesar, 127
  O Moon, when I gaze on thy beautiful face, 233
  Scottsboro, 53
  silver swan, who living had no note, The, 115
  Sir Patrick Spence, 304
  Still Growing, 109
  There was a man of double deed, 83
  Thomas the Rimer, 219
  Three Ravens, The, 305
  Twa Corbies, The, 306
  Western Wind, 307

anyone lived in a pretty how town, 49
ARNOLD, MATTHEW, 231
  Below the surface-stream, shallow and light, 258
  Dover Beach, 308
Ars Poetica, 297
ASHBERY, JOHN
  City Afternoon, 309
As I Walked Out One Evening, 310
As I was laying on the green, 51
At a Hasty Wedding, 181
At the Altar, 142
At the First Avenue Redemption Center, 73
At the Klamath Berry Festival, 401
At the San Francisco Airport, 413
Atticus, 143
AUDEN, W. H., 129
  As I Walked Out One Evening, 310
  James Watt, 168
  Musée des Beaux Arts, 311
  Unknown Citizen, The, 20
Author to Her Book, The, 11
Auto Mobile, 95
Autumn begins in Martins Ferry, Ohio, 416
AXELROD, DAVID B.
  Once in a While a Protest Poem, 35

BAILEY, PHILIP JAMES, 124
Bait, The, 329
Ballad of Birmingham, 382
BASHO, MATSUO
  Green weeds of summer, 61
  Heat-lightning streak, 60
  In the old stone pool, 61
Batter my heart, three-personed God, for You, 36
BAUDELAIRE, CHARLES
  Recueillement, 271
Bavarian Gentians, 212

Bean Eaters, The, 316
Beat! Beat! Drums! 154
Because I could not stop for Death, 327
BEERBOHM, MAX
    On the imprint of the first English edition of "The Works of Max Beerbohm," 146
BELLOC, HILAIRE
    Hippopotamus, The, 130
Below the surface-stream, shallow and light, 258
BENTLEY, EDMUND CLERIHEW
    Sir Christopher Wren, 168
BERRYMAN, JOHN
    Life, friends, is boring. We must not say so, 25
Best Line Yet, The, 219
BETJEMAN, JOHN
    In Westminster Abbey, 21
Bird-Singing Stream, 192
BISHOP, ELIZABETH, 85
    Filling Station, 312
    Fish, The, 58
    Five Flights Up, 313
    Late Air, 74
Black Crow, 117
BLACKMORE, SIR RICHARD, 235
Black Tambourine, 205
BLAKE, WILLIAM, 5, 129, 140, 266
    Angel that presided o'er my birth, 128
    Chimney Sweeper, The, 28
    Her whole life is an epigram, 167
    London, 68
    Long John Brown and Little Mary Bell, 314
    Sick Rose, The, 315
    To see a world in a grain of sand, 82
    Tyger, The, 315
Blessing, A, 415
BLY, ROBERT
    Driving to Town Late to Mail a Letter, 64
    Inward Conversation (translation), 272
Bonny Barbara Allan, 106
Boston Evening Transcript, The, 198
BRADSTREET, ANNE
    Author to Her Book, The, 11
BRAUTIGAN, RICHARD
    Haiku Ambulance, 61
Bright star! would I were steadfast as thou art, 63
BROOKS, FRED EMERSON
    Pat's Opinion of Flags, 246
BROOKS, GWENDOLYN
    Bean Eaters, The, 316
    We Real Cool, 141
BROWN, T. E.
    My Garden, 273
BROWNING, ELIZABETH BARRETT
    Grief, 165

BROWNING, ROBERT, 140, 149
    My Last Duchess, 316
    Soliloquy of the Spanish Cloister, 317
Buffalo Bill's, 174
Bull Calf, The, 365
BURNS, ROBERT, 80, 129
    John Anderson my jo, John, 238
    Oh, my love is like a red, red rose, 96
Burnt Ship, A, 207
BUSON, TANIGUCHI
    On the one-ton temple bell, 60
    piercing chill I feel, The, 54
BUTLER, SAMUEL, 128, 133
BYRON, GEORGE GORDON, LORD, 129
    Destruction of Sennacherib, The, 152

CAMP, JAMES
    At the First Avenue Redemption Center, 73
CAMPBELL, ROY
    On Some South African Novelists, 162
CAMPION, THOMAS
    Rose-cheeked Laura, come, 150
    There is a garden in her face, 255
Cargoes, 67
CARMAN, BLISS, 85
CARROLL, LEWIS
    Jabberwocky, 41
Castoff Skin, 84
Catch, 6
Cavalry Crossing a Ford, 177
Channel Firing, 345
CHAPPELL, FRED
    Skin Flick, 319
CHARLES, DORTHI
    Concrete Cat, 196
Charm Against the Toothache, A, 216
CHAUCER, GEOFFREY
    Your yen two wol slee me sodenly, 181
Cherrylog Road, 325
CHESTERTON, G. K.
    Donkey, The, 320
Chimney Sweeper, The, 28
CHIVERS, THOMAS HOLLEY, 236
City Afternoon, 309
CLARE, JOHN
    Mouse's Nest, 41
Classic Waits for Me, A, 276
CLEGHORN, SARAH N.
    Golf Links, The, 23
CLOSE, JOHN, 237 n
Cold Irish Earth, The, 33
COLERIDGE, HARTLEY
    Fie on Eastern Luxury! (translation), 271
COLERIDGE, SAMUEL TAYLOR, 85, 149–150, 266
    Kubla Khan, 320
COLLINS, WILLIAM, 86
Composed upon Westminster Bridge, 414

Concrete Cat, 196
Confession to Settle a Curse, 409
Convergence of the Twain, The, 347
COOK, ELIZA, 139
    Old Arm-Chair, The, 238
CORMAN, CID
    Tortoise, The, 40
CORNFORD, FRANCES
    Watch, The, 122
CORY, WILLIAM
    Heraclitus, 269
Counting-out Rhyme, 153
COWPER, WILLIAM
    Simplicity (translation), 271
CRABBE, GEORGE, 158
CRANE, HART, 87
    Black Tambourine, 205
CRANE, STEPHEN
    Heart, The, 176
Crazy Jane Talks with the Bishop, 418
CREELEY, ROBERT
    Naughty Boy, 322
    Oh No, 19
Crow and Stone, 357
Crow's First Lesson, 356
Cruel Mother, The, 101
CULLEN, COUNTEE
    For a Lady I Know, 10
    Saturday's Child, 322
CUMMINGS, E. E., 45, 88, 123, 193
    All in green went my love riding, 323
    anyone lived in a pretty how town, 49
    Buffalo Bill's, 174
    in Just-, 184
    politician, a, 167
    r-p-o-p-h-e-s-s-a-g-r, 190
CUNNINGHAM, J. V.
    Friend, on this scaffold Thomas More
        lies dead, 40
    Motto for a Sun Dial, 43
    This *Humanist* whom no beliefs con-
        strained, 167
    You serve the best wines always, my
        dear sir (translation), 166

Daddy, 374
Dance, The, 175
Daphne, 254
Dark house, by which once more I stand,
    405
DAVIDSON, JOHN, 81
DAVISON, PETER
    Last Word, The, 35
Days (Emerson), 241
Days (Larkin), 241
Dead Hand, 75
Death of the Ball Turret Gunner, The, 358
DE LA MARE, WALTER
    Listeners, The, 324

Delay, 93
Delight in Disorder, 351
DENHAM, JOHN, 159
Descent of Winter, The (section 10/30), 154
Design, 281
Destruction of Sennacherib, The, 152
DICKEY, JAMES
    Cherrylog Road, 325
DICKINSON, EMILY, 85, 121, 230
    Because I could not stop for Death, 327
    I heard a Fly buzz–when I died, 201
    I like to see it lap the Miles, 13
    I started Early–Took my Dog, 328
    I taste a liquor never brewed, 6
    It dropped so low–in my Regard, 83
    Lightning is a yellow Fork, The, 199
    Soul selects her own Society, The, 329
    Victory comes late, 174
Digging, 348
DIPASQUALE, EMANUEL
    Rain, 123
Dirty Word, The, 394
Disillusionment of Ten O'Clock, 70
Diving into the Wreck, 385
DODGSON, CHARLES LUTWIDGE. *See* Carroll,
    Lewis
DÖHL, REINHARD
    (untitled concrete poem), 193
Donkey, The, 320
DONNE, JOHN, 138
    Bait, The, 329
    Batter my heart, three-personed God, for
        You, 36
    Burnt Ship, A, 207
    Flea, The, 330
    Hymn to God the Father, A, 90
    Song (Go and catch a falling star), 160
    Valediction: Forbidding Mourning, A,
        331
Do not go gentle into that good night, 169
DOOLITTLE, HILDA. *See* H. D.
DOUGLAS, LORD ALFRED
    Peace, be at peace, O thou my heaviness
        (translation), 272
Dover Beach, 308
Down, Wanton, Down! 34
DRAYTON, MICHAEL
    Since there's no help, come let us kiss
        and part, 164
Dream Deferred, 355
Driving, 185
Driving to Town Late to Mail
    a Letter, 64
DRYDEN, JOHN, 151, 235
    To the Memory of Mr. Oldham, 332
DUGAN, ALAN
    Love Song: I and Thou, 332
Dulce et Decorum Est, 26
DYER, JOHN, 4–5, 87

Dylan, Bob
  Subterranean Homesick Blues, 333

Eagle, The, 78
Easter Wings, 187
Eating Poetry, 404
Eberhart, Richard
  Fury of Aerial Bombardment, The, 50
Edward, 303
Eight O'Clock, 125
Eleanor Rigby, 116
Elegy, Written with His Own Hand in the
  Tower Before His Execution, 88
Elegy on Herakleitos, 269
Elegy Written in a Country Churchyard,
  258
Eliot, T. S., 48, 204
  Boston Evening Transcript, The, 198
  Journey of the Magi, 335
  Love Song of J. Alfred Prufrock, The, 336
  Rhapsody on a Windy Night, 207
  Virginia, 134
Emerson, Ralph Waldo
  Days, 241
Emperor of Ice-Cream, The, 76
End of the World, The, 369
Epigram Engraved on the Collar of a Dog
  Which I Gave to His Royal Highness,
  166
Epitaph, Intended for Sir Isaac Newton in
  Westminster Abbey, 125
Essay on Man, An (Epistle II, part I), 378
Evans, Abbie Huston
  Wing-Spread, 288
Examination at the Womb-door, 356

Fa, mi, fa, re, la, mi, 115
Factory Windows Are Always Broken, 367
Fall of the House of Usher, The, 49
Fern Hill, 407
Field, Eugene
  Preference Declared, The (translation),
  271
Fie on Eastern Luxury! 271
Filling Station, 312
Finkel, Donald
  Gesture, 185
  Hands, 7
Finlay, Ian Hamilton
  Horizon of Holland, The, 194
Fire and Ice, 76
First Practice, 177
Fish, The, 58
Fitts, Dudley
  Elegy on Herakleitos, 269
FitzGerald, Edward, 266, 388 n
.05, 95
Five Flights Up, 313
Flea, The, 330

Flight, 404
Flower in the Crannied Wall, 81
Fog, 63
For a Lady I Know, 10
Forché, Carolyn, 85
For I will consider my Cat Jeoffry, 396
Fork, 95
For the Anniversary of My Death, 372
fortunes of war, I tell you plain, The, 94
Francis, Robert
  Catch, 6
Frankie and Johnny, 112
Frau Bauman, Frau Schmidt, and Frau
  Schwartze, 388
Friend, on this scaffold Thomas More lies
  dead, 40
From the wash the laundress sends, 94
Frost, Robert, 87
  Design, 281
  Fire and Ice, 76
  In White (early version of Design), 295
  Mending Wall, 340
  Never Again Would Birds' Songs Be the
    Same, 141
  Secret Sits, The, 94
  Stopping by Woods on a Snowy Eve-
    ning, 341
  Tree at My Window, 92
  Witch of Coös, The, 341
Fury of Aerial Bombardment, The, 50
Fury of Overshoes, The, 390

García Lorca, Federico
  La guitarra, 269
Gascoigne, George, 37
Gesture, 185
Get the Gasworks, 357
Gildner, Gary
  First Practice, 177
Ginsberg, Allen
  Postcard to D----, 131
Glass of Beer, A, 27
God's Grandeur, 131
Golf Links, The, 23
Goodman, Paul
  Sprayed with strong poison, 61
Good Mornin', Blues, 118
Graves, Robert
  Down, Wanton, Down! 34
Gray, Thomas, 87, 149
  Elegy Written in a Country Churchyard,
  258
Great Figure, The, 64
Grief, 165
Grieve, Christopher Murray. See Mac-
  Diarmid, Hugh
Gross, Ronald
  Yield, 162
Guest, Edgar A., 236

Guitar, 269
GUITERMAN, ARTHUR
  On the Vanity of Earthly Greatness, 253
GUTHRIE, WOODY
  Plane Wreck at Los Gatos (Deportee), 111

H. D.
  Heat, 65
Haiku Ambulance, 61
HALL, DONALD
  My Son, My Executioner, 267
  Town of Hill, The, 345
Hands, 7
HARDY, THOMAS
  At a Hasty Wedding, 181
  Channel Firing, 345
  Convergence of the Twain, The, 347
  Neutral Tones, 202
  Oxen, The, 213
  Workbox, The, 23
Harlem Hopscotch, 308
HARRINGTON, SIR JOHN
  Of Treason, 166
HAYDEN, ROBERT
  Road in Kentucky, A, 348
HEANEY, SEAMUS
  Digging, 348
Heart, The, 176
Heat, 65
HEATH-STUBBS, JOHN
  Charm Against the Toothache, A, 216
HECHT, ANTHONY
  Japan, 247
  Vow, The, 349
HENLEY, WILLIAM ERNEST
  Madam Life's a piece in bloom, 233
Heraclitus, 269
HERBERT, GEORGE
  Easter Wings, 187
  Love, 350
  Pulley, The, 89
  Redemption, 203
HERRICK, ROBERT, 3, 101, 127
  Delight in Disorder, 351
  To the Virgins, to Make Much of Time, 351
  Upon a Child That Died, 176
Her whole life is an epigram, 167
HILL, GEOFFREY
  Merlin, 75
HILMI, ALI S., 236
Hippopotamus, The, 130
HOLLANDER, JOHN
  Skeleton Key, 189
HOOD, THOMAS, 88, 129–130
HOPKINS, GERARD MANLEY, 137–138
  God's Grandeur, 131
  Pied Beauty, 62
  Windhover, The, 352

HORACE
  Odes I (38), 270
Horizon of Holland, The, 194
HOUSMAN, A. E.
  Eight O'Clock, 125
  From the wash the laundress sends, 94
  Loveliest of trees, the cherry now, 3
  Terence, this is stupid stuff, 353
  To an Athlete Dying Young, 354
  When I was one-and-twenty, 153
  With rue my heart is laden, 134
HUGHES, LANGSTON
  Dream Deferred, 355
HUGHES, TED
  Crow and Stone, 357
  Crow's First Lesson, 356
  Examination at the Womb-door, 356
  Secretary, 24
HULME, T. E.
  Image, 64
HUNT, LEIGH
  Rondeau (Jenny kissed me), 179
Hymn to God the Father, A, 90

IGNATOW, DAVID
  Get the Gasworks, 357
I heard a Fly buzz–when I died, 201
I Knew a Woman, 91
I like to see it lap the Miles, 13
Image, 64
In a Station of the Metro, 54
in Just-, 184
In the Elegy Season, 38
Inward Conversation, 272
In Westminster Abbey, 21
In White, 295
I Remember, 180
I Saw in Louisiana a Live-Oak Growing, 410
I started Early–Took my Dog, 328
I taste a liquor never brewed, 6
It did not last, 125
It dropped so low–in my Regard, 83
I Wandered Lonely as a Cloud, 16

Jabberwocky, 41
Janet Waking, 383
Japan, 247
JARRELL, RANDALL
  Death of the Ball Turret Gunner, 358
  Sick Child, A, 15
  Woman at the Washington Zoo, The, 358
JEFFERS, ROBINSON
  To the Stone-Cutters, 8
JENNINGS, ELIZABETH
  Delay, 93
John Anderson my jo, John, 238
JOHNSON, JAMES WELDON, 121

JOHNSON, SAMUEL, 236
Short Song of Congratulation, A, 71
JONES, ERNEST, 110
JONSON, BEN, 263
Slow, slow, fresh fount, keep time with my salt tears, 142
To Celia, 100
Journey of the Magi, 335
Julius Caesar, 127
Junk, 410

KEATS, JOHN, 30, 55, 86, 265
Bright star! would I were steadfast as thou art, 63
La Belle Dame sans Merci, 222
Ode on a Grecian Urn, 359
On First Looking into Chapman's Homer, 361
This living hand, now warm and capable, 158
To Autumn, 361
KILGORE, JAMES C.
White Man Pressed the Locks, The, 93
KING, HENRY, 152
KINGSMILL, HUGH
What, still alive at twenty-two, 274
Kiss, The, 391
KNOTT, BILL. See Saint Geraud
KOCH, KENNETH, 173
Mending Sump, 274
KRISHNAMURTI, M.
Spirit's Odyssey, The, 234
Kubla Khan, 320
KUMIN, MAXINE
Woodchucks, 362

La Belle Dame sans Merci, 222
Laboratory Poem, 372
La Chute, 186
La guitarra, 269
Lake Isle of Innisfree, The, 418
Lamentation of the Old Pensioner, The, 264
LANDOR, WALTER SAVAGE
On Seeing a Hair of Lucretia Borgia, 151
LANGLAND, WILLIAM, 86, 124
Lapis Lazuli, 419
LARKIN, PHILIP
Days, 241
Vers de Société, 363
Wedding-Wind, 364
Last Word, The, 35
Late Air, 74
LAWRENCE, D. H.
Bavarian Gentians, 212
Piano, 239
Youth Mowing, A, 365
LAYTON, IRVING
Bull Calf, The, 365
LEAR, EDWARD, 124

Leaving Forever, 84
Leda and the Swan, 130
LENNON, JOHN, AND PAUL MCCARTNEY
Eleanor Rigby, 116
LEVERTOV, DENISE
Leaving Forever, 84
Six Variations (iii), 170
Sunday Afternoon, 72
Ways of Conquest, 366
LEVINE, PHILIP
To a Child Trapped in a Barber Shop, 367
Life, 233
Life, friends, is boring. We must not say so, 25
Lightning is a yellow Fork, The, 199
LINCOLN, ABRAHAM, 242
My Childhood-Home I See Again, 243
LINDON, J. A.
My Garden, 273
LINDSAY, VACHEL
Factory Windows Are Always Broken, 367
Listeners, The, 324
LIVINGSTON, MYRA COHN
Driving, 185
London, 68
Loneliness of the Long Distance Runner, The, 16
LONGFELLOW, HENRY WADSWORTH, 152
Long John Brown and Little Mary Bell, 314
Love, 350
LOVELACE, RICHARD
To Lucasta, 26
Loveliest of trees, the cherry now, 3
Love Song: I and Thou, 332
Love Song of J. Alfred Prufrock, The, 336
LOWELL, ROBERT, 121
At the Altar, 142
Meditation (translation), 273
Skunk Hour, 368
LOY, MINA
Omen of Victory, 205
LUNN, HUGH KINGSMILL. See Kingsmill, Hugh
Lycidas, 223
LYLY, JOHN
Daphne, 254

MCCARTNEY, PAUL, AND JOHN LENNON
Eleanor Rigby, 116
MACDIARMID, HUGH
Wheesht, Wheesht, 47
MCKUEN, ROD
Thoughts on Capital Punishment, 239
MACLEISH, ARCHIBALD
Ars Poetica, 297
End of the World, The, 369
Madam Life's a piece in bloom, 233
Magi, The, 420

MAGLOW, T. O.
  Dylan Thomas, 168
MARLOWE, CHRISTOPHER, 148
  Passionate Shepherd to His Love, The,
  370
MARTIAL
  You serve the best wines always, my
  dear sir, 166
MARVELL, ANDREW, 86
  To His Coy Mistress, 370
MASEFIELD, JOHN
  Cargoes, 67
Meditation, 273
MELVILLE, HERMAN
  Portent, The, 40
Mending Sump, 274
Mending Wall, 340
Merlin, 75
MERRILL, JAMES
  Laboratory Poem, 372
MERWIN, W. S.
  Dead Hand, 75
  For the Anniversary of My Death, 372
  Song of Man Chipping an Arrowhead, 96
Metamorphosis, 42
Metaphors, 82
MEYNELL, ALICE, 235
MILES, JOSEPHINE
  Reason, 46
MILLAY, EDNA ST. VINCENT
  Counting-out Rhyme, 153
MILLS, HARRY EDWARD, 235
MILNE, A. A., 139
MILTON, JOHN, 5, 47–48, 87, 120, 123, 124
  Lycidas, 223
  When I consider how my light is spent,
  373
Milton by Firelight, 400
Mind is an Enchanting Thing, The, 373
MITCHELL, JONI
  Black Crow, 117
Mongoloid Child Handling Shells on the
  Beach, A, 73
MOORE, MARIANNE, 77
  Mind is an Enchanting Thing, The, 373
MOORE, THOMAS, 132
MORGAN, EDWIN
  Siesta of a Hungarian Snake, 195
Morning Song, 376
MOSS, HOWARD
  Shall I compare thee to a summer's day?
  79
Motto for a Sun Dial, 43
Mouse's Nest, 41
Mr. Flood's Party, 387
Muse, 218
Musée des Beaux Arts, 311
Mutability, 52
My Childhood-Home I See Again, 243

My Garden (Brown), 273
My Garden (Lindon), 273
My heart leaps up when I behold, 52
My Last Duchess, 316
My mistress' eyes are nothing like the sun,
  255
My Papa's Waltz, 9
My Son, My Executioner, 267
My Wife Is My Shirt, 234

Naming of Parts, 384
NASH, OGDEN
  Very Like a Whale, 96
NASHE, THOMAS, 32
Naughty Boy, 322
Neutral Tones, 202
Never Again Would Birds' Song Be the
  Same, 141
NEWTON, JOHN, 108
Night Crow, 206
NIMS, JOHN FREDERICK
  Old Bethinkings of a Day of "Showers
  Likely" at Beansey Ridge, 275
  Perfect Rhyme, 128
Noiseless Patient Spider, A, 266
Not marble nor the gilded monuments, 8
NOWLAN, ALDEN
  Loneliness of the Long Distance Runner,
  The, 16

O Captain! My Captain! 256
Old Bethinkings of a Day of "Showers
  Likely" at Beansey Ridge, 275
Ode on a Grecian Urn, 359
Odes I (38), 270
Ode to the West Wind, 394
Of Treason, 166
Oh, my love is like a red, red rose, 96
Oh No, 19
Old Arm-Chair, The, 238
Old Pensioner, The, 264
OLSON, CHARLES
  La Chute, 186
Omen of Victory, 205
O Moon, when I gaze on thy beautiful face,
  233
On a Girdle, 90
Once in a While a Protest Poem, 35
On First Looking into Chapman's Homer,
  361
On Measure, 167
On Seeing a Hair of Lucretia Borgia, 151
On Some South African Novelists, 162
On Stella's Birthday, 28
On the imprint of the first English edition
  of "The Works of Max Beerbohm,"
  146
On the Symbolic Consideration of Hands
  and the Significance of Death, 36

On the Vanity of Earthly Greatness, 253
Operation, The, 399
Our Minted Days, 242
OWEN, GUY
  White Stallion, The, 71
OWEN, WILFRED
  Dulce et Decorum Est, 26
Oxen, The, 213
Ozymandias, 253

PARKER, DOROTHY
  Résumé, 145
Passionate Shepherd to His Love, The, 370
Pat's Opinion of Flags, 246
Peace, be at peace, O thou my heaviness, 272
PELL, DEWEY, AND ERN ALPAUGH
  Swinging Chick, 115
Perfect Rhyme, 128
Peter Quince at the Clavier, 402
Piano, 239
Pied Beauty, 62
Piercing chill I feel, The, 54
Plane Wreck at Los Gatos (Deportee), 111
PLATH, SYLVIA
  Daddy, 374
  Metaphors, 82
  Morning Song, 376
  Poppies in October, 377
POE, EDGAR ALLAN, 138, 139
Poem (As the cat), 206
Poem (The only response), 176
politician, a, 167
POPE, ALEXANDER, 2, 120, 127–128, 133, 152, 159, 237 n, 252
  Atticus, 143
  Epigram Engraved on the Collar of a Dog . . ., 166
  Epitaph, Intended for Sir Isaac Newton in Westminster Abbey, 125
  Essay on Man, An (Epistle II, part I), 378
Poppies in October, 377
Portent, The, 40
Postcard to D----, 131
POUND, EZRA, 268
  In a Station of the Metro, 54
  River-Merchant's Wife: a Letter, The, 379
  Seafarer, The, 380
Preference Declared, The, 271
Pulley, The, 89

Rain, 123
RANDALL, DUDLEY
  Ballad of Birmingham, 382
RANSOM, JOHN CROWE
  Janet Waking, 383
RAUTER, O. EMIL
  Our Minted Days, 242
Reapers, 61
Reason, 46

Recueillement, 271
Redemption, 203
Red Wheelbarrow, The, 18
REED, HENRY
  Naming of Parts, 384
REED, ISHMAEL
  .05, 95
Résumé, 145
Rhapsody on a Windy Night, 207
RICH, ADRIENNE
  Diving into the Wreck, 385
Richard Cory (Robinson), 104
Richard Cory (Simon), 104
Riding a One-Eyed Horse, 33
River-Merchant's Wife: a Letter, The, 379
Road in Kentucky, A, 348
ROBINSON, EDWIN ARLINGTON
  Mr. Flood's Party, 387
  Richard Cory, 104
ROETHKE, THEODORE, 140
  Frau Bauman, Frau Schmidt, and Frau Schwartze, 388
  I Knew a Woman, 91
  My Papa's Waltz, 9
  Night Crow, 206
  Root Cellar, 57
  Waking, The, 389
Rondeau (Jenny kissed me), 179
Root Cellar, 57
Rose-cheeked Laura, come, 150
ROSELIEP, RAYMOND
  Clap! 61
ROWE, NICHOLAS, 237 n
r-p-o-p-h-e-s-s-a-g-r, 190
Runner, The, 64

Sailing to Byzantium, 250
SAINT GERAUD
  Poem (The only response), 176
SANDBURG, CARL
  Fog, 63
SAROYAN, ARAM, 193, 194
Saturday's Child, 322
Saying Dante Aloud, 134
SCHOLL, J. W., 235
Scottsboro, 53
Seafarer, The, 380
Second Coming, The, 215
Secretary, 24
Secret Sits, The, 94
SERVICE, ROBERT, 138
SEXTON, ANNE, 129
  Fury of Overshoes, The, 390
  Kiss, The, 391
SHAKESPEARE, WILLIAM, 77, 85, 89, 110, 217, 258, 265
  master, the swabber, the boatswain, and I, The, 139
  My mistress' eyes are nothing like the sun, 255

Not marble nor the gilded monuments, 8
Shall I compare thee to a summer's day? 78
That time of year thou mayst in me behold, 392
When, in disgrace with Fortune and men's eyes, 392
When daisies pied and violets blue, 392
When icicles hang by the wall, 393
Shall I compare thee to a summer's day? (Moss), 79
Shall I compare thee to a summer's day? (Shakespeare), 78
SHAPIRO, KARL
Dirty Word, The, 394
SHELLEY, PERCY BYSSHE, 80, 140, 159
Ode to the West Wind, 394
Ozymandias, 253
Short Song of Congratulation, A, 71
Sick Child, A, 15
Sick Rose, The, 315
SIDGWICK, FRANK
Aeronaut to His Lady, The, 179
SIDNEY, SIR PHILIP
You that with allegory's curious frame, 204
Siesta of a Hungarian Snake, 195
silver swan, who living had no note, The, 115
SIMIC, CHARLES
Fork, 95
Simile for Her Smile, A, 81
SIMON, PAUL
Richard Cory, 104
Simplicity, 271
Since there's no help, come let us kiss and part, 164
Sir, say no more, 14
Sir Patrick Spence, 304
SISSMAN, L. E., 40
Six Variations (part iii), 170
Skeleton Key, 189
Skin Flick, 319
SKINNER, KNUTE
Cold Irish Earth, The, 33
Skunk Hour, 368
Sleepless at Crown Point, 94
Slow, slow, fresh fount, keep time with my salt tears, 142
Slumber Did My Spirit Seal, A, 123
SMART, CHRISTOPHER, 123
For I will consider my Cat Jeoffry, 396
SMITH, STEVIE
I Remember, 180
SMITH, WILLIAM JAY
American Primitive, 398
SNODGRASS, W. D.
Operation, The, 399
SNYDER, GARY
After weeks of watching the roof leak, 61

great freight truck, A, 61
Milton by Firelight, 400
SNYDER, RICHARD
Mongoloid Child Handling Shells on the Beach, A, 73
Soliloquy of the Spanish Cloister, 317
Song (Go and catch a falling star), 160
Song of Man Chipping an Arrowhead, 96
Soul, reaching, throwing out for love, The, 267
Soul selects her own Society, The, 329
SOUTHWELL, ROBERT, 158
SPENSER, EDMUND, 125
Spirit's Odyssey, The, 234
splendor falls on castle walls, The, 126
Spring and All, 412
Spring Coming, 51
SQUIRE, J. C.
It did not last, 125
STAFFORD, WILLIAM
At the Klamath Berry Festival, 401
Traveling Through the Dark, 240
Written on the Stub of the First Paycheck, 401
STEPHENS, JAMES
A Glass of Beer, 27
Wind, The, 85
Stepping Westward, 415
STEVENS, WALLACE, 56, 129, 152
Anecdote of the Jar, 207
Disillusionment of Ten O'Clock, 70
Emperor of Ice-Cream, The, 76
Metamorphosis, 42
Peter Quince at the Clavier, 402
Study of Two Pears, 56
Thirteen Ways of Looking at a Blackbird, 182
STICKNEY, TRUMBULL
Sir, say no more, 14
Still Growing, 109
Stone Gullets, 191
Stopping by Woods on a Snowy Evening, 341
STRAND, MARK
Eating Poetry, 404
Study of Two Pears, 56
Subterranean Homesick Blues, 333
Sunday: Outskirts of Knoxville, Tennessee, 307
Sunday Afternoon, 72
SURREY, HENRY HOWARD, EARL OF, 126
SWENSON, MAY
Stone Gullets, 191
SWIFT, JONATHAN
On Stella's Birthday, 28
SWINBURNE, ALGERNON CHARLES, 85, 161
Swinging Chick, 115

TATE, JAMES
Flight, 404

TAYLOR, HENRY
  Riding a One-Eyed Horse, 33
TENNYSON, ALFRED, LORD, 120, 138, 231
  Dark house, by which once more I stand, 405
  Eagle, The, 78
  Flower in the Crannied Wall, 81
  splendor falls on castle walls, The, 126
  Ulysses, 405
Terence, this is stupid stuff, 353
TER MAAT, CORNELIUS J.
  Etienne de Silhouette, 168
That time of year thou mayst in me behold, 392
There is a garden in her face, 255
There was a man of double deed, 83
Thirteen Ways of Looking at a Blackbird, 182
This Humanist whom no beliefs constrained, 167
This Is Just to Say, 31
This living hand, now warm and capable, 158
THOMAS, DYLAN, 161
  Do not go gentle into that good night, 169
  Fern Hill, 407
  Twenty-four years, 408
Thomas the Rimer, 219
Thoughts on Capital Punishment, 239
Three Ravens, The, 305
TICHBORNE, CHIDIOCK
  Elegy, Written with His Own Hand in the Tower Before His Execution, 88
To a Child Trapped in a Barber Shop, 367
To a Locomotive in Winter, 12
To an Athlete Dying Young, 354
To Autumn, 361
To Celia, 100
To His Coy Mistress, 370
To Lucasta, 26
TOOMER, JEAN
  Reapers, 61
Tortoise, The, 40
To see a world in a grain of sand, 82
To the Memory of Mr. Oldham, 332
To the Stone-Cutters, 8
To the Virgins, to Make Much of Time, 351
To Waken an Old Lady, 413
Town of Hill, The, 345
Traveling Through the Dark, 240
TREASONE, GRACE
  Life, 233
Tree at My Window, 92
TROPP, STEPHEN
  My Wife Is My Shirt, 234
Twa Corbies, The, 306
Twenty-four years, 408
Tyger, The, 315

Ulysses, 405
Unknown Citizen, The, 20
UPDIKE, JOHN
  Winter Ocean, 122
Upon a Child That Died, 176

Valediction: Forbidding Mourning, A, 331
Vers de Société, 363
Very Like a Whale, 96
Victory comes late, 174
Virginia, 134
Vow, The, 349

WAGONER, DAVID
  Muse, 218
Waking, The, 389
WALDROP, KEITH
  Guitar (translation), 269
  On Measure, 167
WALDROP, ROSMARIE
  Confession to Settle a Curse, 409
WALLER, EDMUND
  On a Girdle, 90
WANG WEI
  Bird-Singing Stream, 192
Watch, The, 122
Ways of Conquest, 366
Wedding-Wind, 364
We Real Cool, 141
Western Wind, 307
What, still alive at twenty-two, 274
Wheesht, Wheesht, 47
When, in disgrace with Fortune and men's eyes, 392
When daisies pied and violets blue, 392
When icicles hang by the wall, 393
When I consider how my light is spent, 373
When I Heard the Learn'd Astronomer, 410
When I was one-and-twenty, 153
WHITE, E. B.
  Classic Waits for Me, A, 276
White Man Pressed the Locks, The, 93
White Stallion, The, 71
WHITMAN, RUTH
  Castoff Skin, 84
WHITMAN, WALT, 171–172, 301
  Beat! Beat! Drums! 154
  Cavalry Crossing a Ford, 177
  I Saw in Louisiana a Live-Oak Growing, 410
  Noiseless Patient Spider, A, 266
  O Captain! My Captain! 256
  Runner, The, 64
  Soul, reaching, throwing out for love, The, 267
  To a Locomotive in Winter, 12
  When I Heard the Learn'd Astronomer, 410

Whittemore, Reed
  Fall of the House of Usher, The, 49
Who Goes with Fergus? 121
Wilbur, Richard, 150
  In the Elegy Season, 38
  Junk, 410
  Simile for Her Smile, A, 81
  Sleepless at Crown Point, 94
Williams, Miller
  On the Symbolic Consideration of
    Hands and the Significance of Death,
    36
Williams, William Carlos, 190
  Dance, The, 175
  Descent of Winter, The (section 10/30),
    154
  Great Figure, The, 64
  Poem (As the cat), 206
  Red Wheelbarow, The, 18
  Spring and All (By the road to the con-
    tagious hospital), 412
  This Is Just to Say, 31
  To Waken an Old Lady, 413
Wind, The, 85
Windhover, The, 352
Wing-Spread, 288
Winter Ocean, 122
Winters, Yvor
  At the San Francisco Airport, 413
Witch of Coös, The, 341
With rue my heart is laden, 134
With serving still, 144
Woman at the Washington Zoo, The, 358
Woman to Child, 417
Woman to Man, 416
Woodchucks, 362
Woodworth, Samuel, 237
Wordsworth, William, 45, 86, 129, 231,
  263
  Composed upon Westminster Bridge,
    414

I Wandered Lonely as a Cloud, 16
  Mutability, 52
  My heart leaps up when I behold, 52
  Slumber Did My Spirit Seal, A, 123
  Stepping Westward, 415
  World Is Too Much with Us, The, 214
Workbox, The, 23
World Is Too Much with Us, The, 214
Wright, James
  Autumn Begins in Martins Ferry, Ohio,
    416
  Blessing, A, 415
  Saying Dante Aloud, 134
Wright, Judith
  Woman to Child, 417
  Woman to Man, 416
Written on the Stub of the First Paycheck,
  401
Wyatt, Sir Thomas, 126
  With serving still, 144

Yeats, William Butler, 32, 138, 147, 252,
  299
  Crazy Jane Talks with the Bishop, 418
  Lake Isle of Innisfree, The, 418
  Lamentation of the Old Pensioner, The,
    264
  Lapis Lazuli, 419
  Leda and the Swan, 130
  Magi, The, 420
  Old Pensioner, The, 264
  Sailing to Byzantium, 250
  Second Coming, The, 215
  Who Goes with Fergus? 121
Yield, 162
Your yen two wol slee me sodenly, 181
You serve the best wines always, my dear
  sir, 166
You that with allegory's curious frame, 204
Youth Mowing, A 365

To the Student

As publishers, we realize that one way to improve education is to improve textbooks. We also realize that you, the student, largely determine the success or
failure of textbooks. Although the instructor assigns them, the student buys and
uses them. If enough of you don't like a book and make your feelings known,
the chances are your instructor will not assign it again.

Usually only instructors are asked about the quality of a text; their
opinion alone is considered as revisions are planned or as new books are developed. Now, we would like to ask you about X. J. Kennedy's *An Introduction to
Poetry, 4th Edition:* how you liked or disliked it; why it was interesting or dull; if
it taught you anything. Please fill in this form and return it to us at: Little,
Brown and Co., College English, 34 Beacon Street, Boston, Mass. 02106.

School: _____

Instructor's name: _____

Title of course: _____

1. Did you find this book too easy? _____ too difficult? _____

   about right? _____

2. Which chapters did you find the most interesting? _____

   _____

3. Which chapters did you find least interesting? _____

   _____

4. Which poems did you like most? _____

   _____

5. Were there any poems you particularly disliked? _____

   _____

6. Which statement comes closest to expressing your feelings about reading
   and studying literature? (Please check one, or supply your own statement.)

   _____ Love to read literature. It's my favorite subject.

   _____ Usually enjoy reading most literature.

   _____ Can take it or leave it.

_____ Usually find little of interest in most literature.

_____ Literature just is not for me.

Other: _____

7. Did you find this book helped you to enjoy poetry any more than you did?

_____

8. Were the chapters "Writing about Poems" and "Writing about Literature"

very useful? _____ somewhat useful? _____ of no help? _____

9. In the sections about writing papers, do you prefer to see examples of writ-

ing by students? _____ or by professional critics? _____

10. Do you intend to keep this book for your personal library? Yes _____

No _____

11. Any other comments or suggestions: _____

_____

_____

_____

12. May we quote you in our efforts to promote this book? Yes _____

No _____

Date: _____

Signature (optional): _____

Address (optional): _____